DOING WORKING-CLASS HISTORY

Economic and political uncertainty has brought the language of class – especially discussion of the working class – to a broad audience across scholarship and social debate. This introductory volume shows how the history of the working class has, is, and can be researched, written, and represented.

The book is structured in three parts: perspective, context, and application. Each offers an introduction to both classic historiography and new ideas and methodologies. With chapters covering a span of the years c.1750–present, the book focuses on three essential questions: 1. What is working-class history and what should it become? 2. What can a focus on working-class history reveal? 3. What are the possibilities of this research in the university classroom, the heritage world, and beyond?

Doing Working-Class History will appeal to students and scholars of working-class history, whether relative newcomers to the field or veteran researchers interested in new approaches and material. It will also be of interest to local and family historians, museum and heritage professionals, and general readers.

Oliver Betts is Research Lead at the National Railway Museum in York. He specialises in the history of technology and class, exploring how working-class worlds across the Anglophone world were reshaped by technologies. He has published on workers, communities, and industry in history and museums.

Laura Harrison is Associate Professor of Modern History at the University of the West of England. She specialises in histories of youth and youth culture and is the author of *Dangerous Amusements: Leisure, the Young Working Class, and Urban Space in Britain, c.1870–1939* (2022).

Laura Christine Price is a historian, teacher, and writer. Her PhD thesis, completed at the University of York, explored wool textile workers' relationships to trade unionism. She is an independent researcher and teaches at a secondary school in West Yorkshire.

DOING WORKING-CLASS HISTORY

Research, Heritage, and Engagement

Edited by
Oliver Betts, Laura Harrison,
and Laura Christine Price

Routledge
Taylor & Francis Group
LONDON AND NEW YORK

Designed cover image: Women workers working at The Pyjama Factory, Madeley, Britain, 1961. Black Country Images / Alamy Stock Photo.

First published 2025
by Routledge
4 Park Square, Milton Park, Abingdon, Oxon OX14 4RN

and by Routledge
605 Third Avenue, New York, NY 10158

Routledge is an imprint of the Taylor & Francis Group, an informa business

British Library Cataloguing-in-Publication Data
A catalogue record for this book is available from the British Library

Library of Congress Cataloging-in-Publication Data
Names: Betts, Oliver, editor. | Harrison, Laura (Associate professor), editor. | Price, Laura Christine, editor.
Title: Doing working-class history : research, heritage, and engagement / edited by Oliver Betts, Laura Harrison, and Laura Christine Price.
Description: Abingdon, Oxon ; New York, NY : Routledge, 2025. | Includes bibliographical references and index.
Identifiers: LCCN 2024027831 (print) | LCCN 2024027832 (ebook) | ISBN 9780367361341 (hardback) | ISBN 9781032882963 (paperback) | ISBN 9780429344084 (ebook) | ISBN 9781040183892 (adobe pdf) | ISBN 9781040183915 (epub)
Subjects: LCSH: Working class—Study and teaching. | Working class—Historiography. | Working class—Research.
Classification: LCC HD4824 .D64 2025 (print) | LCC HD4824 (ebook) | DDC 305.5/620722—dc23/eng/20240809
LC record available at https://lccn.loc.gov/2024027831
LC ebook record available at https://lccn.loc.gov/2024027832

ISBN: 978-0-367-36134-1 (hbk)
ISBN: 978-1-032-88296-3 (pbk)
ISBN: 978-0-429-34408-4 (ebk)

DOI: 10.4324/9780429344084

Typeset in Sabon
by codeMantra

CONTENTS

FIGURES

CONTRIBUTORS

Shabina Aslam is Artistic Director of Theatre in the Mill on the campus of the University of Bradford. She is a writer, director, and producer specialising in working with marginalised communities to co-create new performance. Shabina was born in Kenya and came to Bradford as a child.

Oliver Betts is Research Lead at the National Railway Museum in York. He specialises in the history of technology and class, exploring how working-class worlds across Anglophone world were reshaped by technologies. He has published numerous articles and chapters on workers, communities, and industry in history and museums.

Ben Curtis is Postdoctoral Research Officer at Swansea University, whose principal research interests are the South Wales coalfield, the British coal industry, industrial disability, and de/industrialisation. He has published extensively on these topics, and his monograph, *The South Wales Miners, 1964–1985*, was published by the University of Wales Press in 2013. He has also appeared on television and radio on numerous occasions, the most high-profile of which being on the BBC television programme 'Who Do You Think You Are?' in August 2017. He is the General Editor for the South Wales Record Society, the Treasurer for Llafur: the Welsh People's History Society, and a Fellow of the Royal Historical Society (FRHistS).

Stephen Etheridge was awarded a PhD from the University of Huddersfield in 2014. His research explored the link between Southern Pennine brass bands and the creation of northern and working-class identity, c. 1840–1914. This has led to several research projects and publications including

'Music Making in Manchester during World War I', a collaboration between the Royal Northern College of Music, and the Henry Watson Music Library, Manchester, and 'Townsounds: A Celebration of Huddersfield's Musical Heritage', funded by Kirklees County Council. Stephen continues to research the links between northernness and working-class identity, most recently Methodism and music-making, c.1900–1940, and the pub bands of the Rossendale Valley in the 1970s.

Erin Geraghty is Postdoctoral Research Associate at the Open University. She is currently working on the Leverhulme-funded project, 'Anti-Catholicism in the UK Since 1945'. The interdisciplinary project unites psychology and history to explore the contrasting experiences of anti-Catholicism in the four nations that make up the UK. She is also working on a book that combines histories of internationalism, feminism, and imperialism, to investigate the participation of left-wing British women in the Irish feminist and labour movements of the early twentieth century.

Daniel J.R. Grey is Reader in Modern History and Programme Leader for the BA (Hons) Sociology at the University of Hertfordshire, UK. He has published a number of articles and essays on the intersection between gender, law, and medicine – especially relating to infanticide – focusing on nineteenth- and twentieth-century England and Wales and on colonial India. He is completing his monograph *Degrees of Guilt: Infanticide in England, 1860–1960* for Liverpool University Press.

Laura Harrison is Associate Professor of Modern History at the University of the West of England, Bristol, and Associate Director of the Regional History Centre. She specialises in histories of youth and youth culture in Britain, exploring the intersections of age, gender, class, and race, and is the author of *Dangerous Amusements: Leisure, the Young Working Class, and Urban Space in Britain, c.1870–1939* (2022). Laura's more recent work examines the intersections of family history, community history, and creative approaches to history and storytelling, working in collaboration with a range of community partners.

Rhian E. Jones is a writer, critic, and broadcaster from South Wales, who writes on history, politics, and popular culture. She is the co-editor of *Red Pepper* and writes for *Tribune* magazine. Her books include *Clampdown: Pop-Cultural Wars on Class and Gender* (Zero, 2013), *Petticoat Heroes: Gender, Culture and Popular Protest* (University of Wales Press, 2015), *Triptych: Three Studies of Manic Street Preachers' The Holy Bible* (Repeater, 2017), the anthology of women's music writing *Under My Thumb: Songs That Hate Women and the Women Who Love Them* (Repeater, 2017), *Paint Your Town Red: How Preston Took Back Control and Your Town Can Too*

(Repeater, 2021), and *Rebecca's Country: A Welsh Story of Riot and Resistance* (University of Wales Press, 2024).

Dan Johnson earned his PhD in History from the University of York in 2019, focusing on ethical implications of interpretations of convict narratives in British Prison Museums. His work has been published in academic and trade publications. Having worked in heritage interpretation for a number of years, Dan is now an independent researcher.

Andrew Kettler is currently serving as Assistant Professor of History at the University of South Carolina-Palmetto College. His work has appeared in *Senses and Society*, *Journal of American Studies*, and *Patterns of Prejudice*. His first monograph, *The Smell of Slavery: Olfactory Racism and the Atlantic World* (Cambridge, 2020), focuses on the development of racist semantics concerning miasma and the contrasting expansion of aromatic consciousness in the making of resistance to racialised olfactory discourses.

Claire Phillips is Tutor in Lifelong Learning at Aberystwyth University and Lecturer in early modern and modern history at The Open University. Her research interests span the fields of childhood and the family, gender, and medicine. She has published widely on the experiences of children in the London Foundling Hospital and is currently working on a project on children in Welsh workhouses, which has been supported by an Early Career Fellowship from the Women's History Network.

Laura Christine Price is a historian, teacher, and writer. Her research explores the wool textile industry and its workers in the twentieth-century West Riding of Yorkshire, especially the relationships wool textile workers had with trade unions. More broadly, she researches the intersections between class, ethnicity, and gender in the twentieth century. She was educated at the University of York and works as a secondary school teacher of history and English in a working-class community in West Yorkshire.

Jennifer Reid is a performer of nineteenth-century Lancashire dialect and Victorian broadside ballads. After volunteering at Chetham's Library and the Working Class Movement Library, Jennifer completed an Advanced Diploma in Local History at Oxford University. Her work has taken her to Venice, Croatia, New York, and lately Bangladesh, and she spoke at the first ethnomusicography conference on the Indian sub-continent about her research into Bangladeshi and Mancunian weaving songs. Jennifer plays the character of Barb in Shane Meadows' period drama *The Gallows Pole*. She has recently supported Pulp and John Cooper Clarke, latterly for Chanel's prestigious Metiers d'Art show.

Brian Shaev is University Lecturer at the Institute for History, Leiden University. He has published articles on socialist parties and the Schuman Plan (*International Review for Social History*, 2016), the Algerian War (*French Historical Studies*, 2018), the Treaties of Rome (*Contemporary European History*, 2018), transnationalism in the 1950s (*History of European Ideas*, 2020), and a co-edited book on social democracy and the history of European competition policy (Routledge, 2024). He was principal investigator for a Swedish research project comparing city policies and responses for migrant reception and integration in post-war Europe. Currently, he is preparing a monograph titled *Transnational Socialism and European Integration: The Socialist Group in the Early European Parliament, 1952–1972.*

Christopher Shoop-Worrall is Senior Lecturer in Media and Journalism at UCFB Manchester, having completed his PhD at the University of Sheffield's Centre for the Study of Journalism and History in 2019. His wider work explores the intersections between politics, the mass press, and mass consumer culture in nineteenth- and twentieth-century Britain.

David Swift's research focuses on how political and cultural identities interacted with class, race, and gender in twentieth-century Britain. His work has appeared in journals including *Modern British History*, the *History Workshop Journal*, and the *Journal of Ethnic and Migration Studies*. He is the author of several books, including *For Class and Country: The Patriotic Left and the First World War*; *A Left for Itself*; and most recently the forthcoming *Scouse Republic: A Personal History of Liverpool*, which will be published by Little, Brown in 2025.

Natasha Synycia received her MA in Art History from the University of Connecticut and her PhD in US History from the University of California, Irvine. She is currently an instructor in Humanities Core at the University of California, Irvine.

Rose Wallis is Associate Professor of British Social History and Director of the Regional History Centre at the University of the West of England, Bristol. Her research focuses on histories of crime, criminal justice, and social protest, and the ways in which the operation of justice shaped and was shaped by social relationships. She also works as a historical consultant and collaborative practitioner, addressing in particular the interpretation of criminal justice histories as heritage and its impact on contemporary understandings of crime, and criminal and social justice. She was part of the interpretation team for Shire Hall courthouse museum 2016–2018, and historical consultant for Creative Youth Network's 'The Courts' redevelopment 2018–2023.

ABBREVIATIONS

DSQ	*Disability Studies Quarterly*
GPO	General Post Office
IDAA	Irish Drapers' Assistants' Union
IRB	Irish Republican Brotherhood
ITUC	Irish Trades Union Congress
ITGWU	Irish Transport and General Workers Union
IWFL	Irish Women's Franchise League
IWWU	Irish Women's Workers' Union
NLI	National Library of Ireland
NSPCC	National Society for the Prevention of Cruelty to Children
NRO	Northumberland Record Office
OED	Oxford English Dictionary
RCA	Royal College of Arts
SPI	Socialist Party of Ireland
TiM	Theatre in the Mill, Bradford
TNA	The National Archives
TUC	Trades Union Congress
TWA	Tyne and Wear Archives
WDYTYA	Who Do You Think You Are?
WSPU	Women's Social and Political Union
YEA	York Explore Archives
YOHP	York Oral History Project

INTRODUCTION

A Time for Working-class Histories

Oliver Betts, Laura Harrison, and Laura Christine Price

Perhaps the most difficult aspect of researching, interpreting, and engaging with working-class history is how broad the terms of reference can be. Rarely a week seems to go by without the working-class, however defined (or undefined), being the subject of debate in the news, in opinion pieces, and online. At a time of rapid technological change, of surging populism in politics, and significant debate about identity and cultural grouping in society at large, the working class, defined or not, seems a significant presence in modern societies around the world. Even as this introduction was being drafted, a letter in the UK's *Guardian* newspaper was published. The letter was a warm reflection on a recent article in the same newspaper, an opinion piece by author Rebecca Smith about how the hidden stories of working-class women needed rescuing in British history.[1] 'Forestry wives, farmer's wives, coalminer's wives' were all the backbone of their respective communities, the byline observed, but had too long been defined by not only the men they married but also the ones who 'write the narratives'. The piece, in part a promotion for Smith's book *Rural: The Lives of the Working Class Countryside*, was warmly received by the letter writer. But it was a heritage that, the letter writer felt, was under threat:

> I can't help worrying that most people who live in the farmhouses and cottages that once homed multiple generations of one family will be far too busy choosing Farrow and Ball paint colours for their spare rooms to sit down and read Smith's book.[2]

It is a sentence laden with references to the place of social class in modern Britain. Selected contrasts abound; the assumed low family-level occupancy

DOI: 10.4324/9780429344084-1

(replete with 'spare rooms') of the present day vs the 'multiple generations of one family' past speaks to not only the ongoing national anxiety about housing stock (with whiffs of the 2010–2015 coalition government's infamous 'Bedroom Tax' of 2012 which levied fees on public housing tenants with 'un-used' spare bedrooms) but also to a more general idea that gentrification (see the reference to the high-price prestige Farrow and Ball paint brand) and property acquisition is quite literally painting over working-class heritage.

This example may seem fleeting – a fractional moment in the pages of a newspaper – but it neatly represents the uneasy position discourse around the working class, both as a current social, cultural, and economic entity (or entities) and as an aspect of history and heritage, occupies in the West.

This book has had a long development process. Partly this is because of the other demands placed on the editors and authors – ranging from unstable working conditions through to a global pandemic. But it is also an indication of the roller-coaster ride it has been as a scholar interested in discourses around the working class in recent years. Economic and political uncertainty has brought the language of class, and especially discussion of the working class, to a broad audience. Authors from across the academic, political, and journalistic spectrum have sought to understand societies in upheaval through the means of class. Joan C. Williams's provocative *White Working Class* (2017) is a key example – an engaging and challenging text that tries to understand a post-Trump America through the lens of class. Americans need to learn more about, and respect, their working-class peers Williams argues, finding it striking that in an era when 'wealthy white Americans have learned to sympathetically imagine the lives of the poor, people of colour, and LGBTQ people' that 'class consciousness has been replaced by class cluelessness – and in some cases, even class callousness'.[3]

Williams is by no means the only one urging contemporaries to look again at the working class. Although noting that, 'more generally, people no longer use class as a way of locating themselves within social space', Cédric Hugrée, Etienne Penissat, and Alexis Spire have argued the increasing intemperate debates about 'insiders' vs 'outsiders' in the media, the Gilet Jaunes protests in France, and the populist debates fuelling Brexit all indicate the need to revisit studies of the working class. 'It is time' they argue 'to ask what the famous Polish plumber has in common with a Romanian senior manager or a Spanish manual worker, and what sets them apart from one another'.[4] Here, as in so much contemporary discourse, the working class are seen as a group at the heart of a fractured, yet dynamic, social, economic, and political scene stretching across borders.

There has, in recent years, been an attempt by sociologists, political scientists, and economists, amongst others, to attempt a redefinition of class. The team of sociologists led by Mike Savage that executed the 2011 Great

British Class Survey, the results of which fed into their *Social Class in the 21st Century* (2015), imagined new class structures based on economic, social, and cultural capital. This balanced, amongst others, a 'traditional working class' with an 'emergent service sector' and a growing 'precariat'.[5] More recently Geoffrey Evans and James Tilley have considered what they see as the 'political exclusion of the British Working Class', feeling that post-millennium sociology has 'forgotten about class'. They have returned to the topic – something they see as increasingly imperative as a growing middle class threatens to swamp the working class.[6] These brief examples are just in a recent British context, and in the last two decades there has been considerable new research across Europe and North America on the subject of class.[7] Across scholarship, commentary, and social debate, the study of the working class seems more vibrant and necessary with every passing day.

For the historian, this outpouring of enthusiasm is both exhilarating and concerning. As in many disciplines, the study of class has been in decline for decades in history, seen (sometimes quite rightly) as a clumsy tool in comparison to new, insightful questions about sexuality, cultural capital, race (particularly in colonial and post-colonial eras), and other ways of understanding identity amongst individuals and groups. That class history, and especially working-class history, is flourishing once again offers exciting opportunities for historians to bring the topic into conversation with these new lines of inquiry, all in front of an increasingly interested public audience. Yet the somewhat 'fast and loose' approach to history that characterises much of this debate must give pause for thought. In her introduction, for instance, Williams cites Archie Bunker, Al Bundy, and Homer Simpson as prime examples of how white working-class men are portrayed as oafish and narrow-minded. Yet each of these fictional men were moments in time – representations of an American working class in flux but also, critically, of changing understandings of what it was to *be* working class in America.[8] Contemporary studies of the working class over the last decade have seen it as both shrinking and growing, intensely politicised and dangerously ostracised, ethnically diverse or strikingly homogenous, and of varying levels of income, culture, and power in society. It is a moment that presents the historian of the working class with a challenge – to build upon this popular interest in, and perceived relevance of, the working class whilst simultaneously maintaining the historian's eye for changing structures and relations in time and space.

The aim of this book is to act as a primer – an introductory text to understanding how the history of the working class has, is, and can be researched, written, and represented. Its imagined audience is newcomers to the subject, just beginning their steps into this field, but also those interested in how this history can be researched, understood, and shared.

Defining Scope

There are many ways, as this introduction has already highlighted, to define the working class. Traditional Marxist definitions have been supplemented over almost two centuries by definitions and classification systems from a myriad of disciplines, perspectives, and languages. We have not been prescriptive in this volume, allowing contributors instead to find their own methodological definitions of working class.

What may be useful, though, is to explain what this volume means by 'working-class history'. Again, to attempt a singular definition of this incredibly broad field would be an exercise in futility, and contributors to this volume have been encouraged to explore their own understandings of the term, and by extension the field, in their work. This reflects, we feel, the sheer scope of the field of working-class history.

Although some scholars were tackling the history of working people as early as to be contemporary with the emergence of an industrial working-class in the modern age, the field really emerged out of the rich milieux of social history in the 1960s and 1970s. Indeed, many of the key innovators of working-class history would, arguably, have more likely described their work in broader terms as social or people's history, or history from below. Certainly, the proliferation of academic journals in this period that sought out and fostered such history is an indication of an emerging, vibrant, field. The American *Labor History* (first published in 1960), the more global *International Labor and Working-Class History* (1972), and the British *History Workshop Journal* (1976) were amongst many showcasing new research into working-class history and community. Some, like *History Workshop Journal,* did not see themselves as purely defined by a quest for working-class history but rather imagined that history as part of a wider story of history from below.

Alongside these journals, or rather surrounding them, was a larger popular surge of interest in working-class or everyday history post-war. The proliferation of folk museums, of preservation movements, and of the steady decline in the West of the traditional heavy industry that was seen by so many as closely connected to the working-class way of life continued and amplified an earlier twentieth-century urge to capture a past that was slipping away. Amplifying this public interest were a number of key volumes of working-class history that slipped the bounds of academic publication into a far wider audience. E.P. Thompson's *The Making of the English Working Class,* first published in 1963, had an electrifying impact on British history and historians.[9] That so many of the British contributors to this volume reference his work, particularly his charge of rescuing working-class voices from 'the enormous condescension of posterity', is but another indication of the work's legacy in British academia. But volumes like Thompson's, and Howard Zinn's controversial but groundbreaking *A People's History of the United States* (1980), show that in many cases working-class history has a profound sphere of influence well beyond academic debate and discussion.[10]

In more recent decades, understanding past societies through relations between social classes has become a less common tool of analysis for historians, supplemented or overtaken by emerging sub-disciplines that offer fresh insight. The decline of Marxist analysis, the cultural turn, and the challenge to traditional histories posed by scholars of women, of race, and of sexuality have all seen the 'history from below' methodology spread amongst historians in many fields and time periods. What remains at the core of working-class history, though, is still that Thompsonian urge to rescue forgotten voices. This is not unique to working-class history, of course, and all historians feel the pull of the archives. But the sheer emotional charge of that rescuing effort seems, as the chapters collected here show across the periods and topics they address, that working-class history remains a deeply held passion and calling for many today. It resounds, like an echo bouncing back and forth, between the traditional Western cities and nations that where working-classes, and working-class history, developed from the nineteenth century onwards and those parts of the Global South where both are continuing to emerge and develop. There has been a strong contention among scholars of the working class, across many disciplines, to understand the working class as a global entity, one bound together by inequalities and struggle. There is certainly no shortage of material that supports this perception as recent studies of the working class on screen by Sarah Attfield and in their own literature by Sonali Perara have ably shown.[11]

Many of the examples in this study are taken from a British, or Anglophone, perspective. This in part reflects the background and experience of the authors themselves, but also is part of a wider debate within working-class studies. Whilst the trend in scholarship towards a global history of the working class is picking up pace, much of the traditional work that still underpins the topic in critical ways remains localised in local, national, or limited multi-national regions. As Hugrée, Penissot, and Spire have noted, for instance, the Gilet Jaunes protests have been defined in the public eye as much by their failure to spread much beyond France as by their dramatic explosion onto the political scene in 2018.[12] Much of the public history of the working class displays a similar trend towards the local, and this too informed our decision, given our desire to explore outlets for working-class history in detail. There is, without a doubt, a companion volume to this book that could, and more importantly *should,* be written about working-class history in thought and practice, especially across the Global South. One that embraces different challenges and contexts that such histories entail but also, importantly, should be directed and defined by scholars working in those traditions and contexts. This volume is intended as a starting point, rather than a last word, on these issues – a guide to research, practice, and understanding of how working-class history and heritage operates in specific contexts.

Structure of This Book

This volume is structured in three parts, each considering the study of working-class history. These three sections, perspective, context, and application, offer an introduction to both classic historiography and new ideas and methodologies.

Part I: Working-class History in Perspective contains seven shorter pieces, all designed to explore key skills or literature that will be of use, the authors and editors hope, to both the newcomers and the hardened veterans of working-class history. The first chapter opens with Ben Curtis offering an important historiographical piece on how new sources, ideas, and methods can enhance our understanding of traditional areas of research. Taking as his example the important, and long recognised, link between industrial work and injury, Curtis shows how new interconnected and international histories of disability can reshape our understandings of working-class communities engaged in heavy, dangerous, industry. In Chapter 2, Andrew Kettler takes a broader approach to the same question. Starting with the new field of sensory history, he quickly moves to a wide-ranging and very well-read perspective on how the sensory world can be read as an example of power and resistance – two key traditional concepts in working-class history. The chapter offers a useful example of how theory and source material can connect in context.

The other five chapters of the first section have been written by the editors themselves. Laura Christine Price uses her first chapter to reflect upon both her personal connection to working-class history and her work as a secondary school teacher. Price's discussion of working-class history as a calling will no doubt resonate with many readers, as it does with other pieces in this volume, but so too will her discussion of the difficult choices faced by many young historians regarding career, health, and income. Reflecting on her experience working with the UK curriculum she reflects on how 'there is much that can be drawn out about working-class people in the teaching of the topics'. In Chapter 4, Laura Harrison considers the multiple decade-long boom of family history and how it connects to the research and practice of working-class history. Family history, she argues, has much to offer the historian both in terms of source material but also as a bond between subject, practitioners, and audience. She also, as Price does, reflects on what a personal journey family history can be for the historian, particularly those with working-class ancestors – an inspiring but emotional process. Chapters 5 and 6 are both by Oliver Betts. In the first he offers an overview of museums and heritage sites as both sources and places of working-class history. Drawing upon visitor feedback on the website

TripAdvisor, he argues that far more could be built upon the vast potential of buildings and material collections to inspire the study of, and engagement with, working-class history. In Chapter 6, he turns to discussing a key skill of historical research – reading source material against the grain. Whilst by no means claiming close textual reading is anything other than a universal tool of the historian, Betts argues that its significance is even more important in a field like working-class history where much of the source material is filtered through the perspective of outsiders in power dynamics explored in greater depth in later chapters. Finally, in Chapter 7, Price offers a detailed bibliography of working-class history. With a primarily, but not exclusively, British slant, she shows how the current field is at a crossroads between a number of classic texts that continue to shape and influence scholars, and the new challenge of emerging fields and new perspectives.

Part II: Working-class History in Context is the longest section of the book. Here nine longer chapters examine working-class history in specific contexts. They range across time and space, although the majority have taken British history of the nineteenth and twentieth centuries as their focus, and each considers an aspect of working-class history that extends far beyond their chosen context. They offer the reader useful examples of how the history of working-class people, communities, and interactions can be drawn out and analysed in numerous different ways.

The first cluster of chapters focuses on tracing class through a variety of political, associational, and literary means. In each case the authors explore how the connections to other classes and groups, and how those groups perceived working-class people and culture, require careful attention. In Chapter 8, Christopher Worrall charts the existence of the *Daily Citizen,* a popular paper designed for working people. It became caught, his chapter shows, between a labour movement attempting to use a popular press it disdained to communicate with working-class readers and the appetite of that very readership for the entertainment of the popular press. In a similar way, Erin Geraghty's chapter considers the gender politics of class in early twentieth-century Ireland. Members of the Irish Women's Franchise League had to navigate divisions of class and gender in their campaign for voting rights, and Geraghty's analysis is an astute insight into how understandings of labour and suffrage shaped (and continue to shape) understandings of class and gender. Chapter 10 shifts the focus to post-war Puerto Rico, as Natasha Synycia examines trade unionism in the garment industry. In the difficult post-war environment of investment, Synycia shows that trade unions, companies, and workers were caught up in complicated negotiations about gender, class, and nationality, all of which defined the experience of the largely female workforce. Complimenting this, despite differences in location and time period, is Chapter 11, where David Swift uses the conflicted loyalties of British workers and trade unionists towards patriotism during the

First World War to explore how working-class men were perceived during a time of crisis.

Following on from this Chapter 12 addresses how working-class people navigated institutions, specifically in Claire Philips's case study of poor men, women, and children in need of medical aid in early nineteenth-century England. Even with groups supposedly engineered to support working people, Philips shows that the working-class was at the mercy of connections, circumstance, and prevailing ideologies. Finally, in Chapter 13 Daniel Grey considers how working-class mothers navigated child-care and child-loss in late nineteenth and early twentieth-century Britain. When decisions or circumstances turned tragic, they were held up as exemplars of everything wrong with working-class motherhood, Grey points out, a critical perspective from wider society that continues to shape attitudes to parents from disadvantaged backgrounds today.

The next cluster of essays in the section moves to consider working-class culture itself. In Chapter 14 Laura Christine Price pushes beyond the established sources of trade unions and other 'official' working-class organisations and instead draws upon rich seams of oral history to explore how textile workers in twentieth-century Bradford felt about class. In Chapter 15 Stephen Etheridge explores brass band culture amongst working-class communities in the late nineteenth and early twentieth-century north of England. What he reveals is, as he puts it, a contest between 'communal holiday revelry' and 'rational recreation' that reveals not only the long-running currents in working-class culture and identity, but also how those were perceived by outsiders and how, in turn, working-class groups navigated (or didn't) those perceptions. Finally, in Chapter 16 Laura Harrison rounds out this trio of chapters on working-class culture in her exploration of street life in British cities between the 1870s and 1960s. Her essay reminds us how important it is to consider the small-scale and the subgroup – beyond the headline-grabbing clashes of youth and authorities in the period, she points out, there was a whole world of small but deeply significant interactions as young working-class people staked a claim to urban space.

A final chapter rounds out this section as Brian Shaev explores the worlds of mine workers and their communities from the end of the nineteenth century through to deindustrialisation in the 1960s–1980s. Shaev offers a useful final note to this section, considering the legacies of mining communities in France and Germany through shifting waves of immigration, war, and industrial change. Even now, he notes there is a power in the memory of these places and their working-class communities, something that leads nicely into the final section of this book.

Finally, Part III: Working-class History in Application presents four longer-form chapters, each offering a different case study of, and reflection upon, working-class history outside of the academy. Together they vividly illustrate how working-class history should not, and arguably cannot, exist as a purely academic subject – it is too steeped in community, meaning, and relevance for too many people for that. Chapter 17 is a study by Dan Johnson and Rose Wallis of criminal justice heritage sites across the UK, and the sites they point out have huge 'potential for collaborative practice: between historians and curators, but also with our audiences and shareholders'. Given current conversations around justice, class inequality before the law, and the historic importance of working-class prisoners and defendants to judicial reform, the authors argue that these are sites not just loaded with working-class history but where the relevance of that history can be profoundly felt and enacted by the public. Chapter 18, still focused on audiences and the power of working-class history, is nonetheless very different. Here Jennifer Reid offers a tour-de-force of ballad history in Greater Manchester and Lancashire. A researcher, performer, and passionate advocate, and consciously working-class herself, Reid offers an invaluable perspective on not just her subject matter but on how passion and expertise lie at the heart of so many different approaches to working-class history. In Chapter 19 creative arts practitioner Shabina Aslam reflects on her work with working-class immigrant students in West Yorkshire in creating an exhibition around the experience of student bussing – an experience which shaped the school experiences of similar students from the 1960s onwards. The chapter not only considers the challenges of representing this difficult aspect of working-class migrant history in northern England but also reflects on the author's own experiences of 'bussing out', once again highlighting the importance of the personal to the writing (and performing) of working-class history. Finally, in Chapter 19 Rhian E. Jones rounds off this volume with a personal and critical look at the past few decades of working-class historiography. A well-read and thoroughly engaging study, it challenges us at the end to adhere to the emerging model of working-class history that 'moves beyond "me" and "they" to "us"' as the key impetus of study.

This volume was never intended as the final word on the topic – it cannot be. The field of working-class history is too broad and the potential it encompasses too great for any one volume to offer a neat overview. Instead, it offers an introduction to working-class history – its ideas, its contexts, its operation, and its application. If it inspires the reader to engage with this history, even if simply to point out what we have missed or neglected, then it will have done its job of thrusting that reader into an ongoing and, we believe, exciting debate that extends far beyond academia into communities past, present, and future.

Notes

1 Rebecca Smith, 'Here's what's missing from the history of rural Britain: the hidden stories of women who shaped it', *The Guardian,* 30 August 2023, (accessed 2 February 2024), https://www.theguardian.com/commentisfree/2023/aug/30/rural-britain-women-forestry-farmer-coalminer-communities#:~:text=They%20

are%20the%20%E2%80%9Cwives%E2%80%9D%20of,the%20women%20made%20everything%20work.

2 Amanda Harvey, 'Rural working-class history is being glossed over – with Farrow and Ball paint', *The Guardian,* 12 September 2023, (accessed 2 February 2024), https://www.theguardian.com/environment/2023/sep/12/rural-working-class-history-is-being-glossed-over-with-farrow-ball-paint#:~:text=But%20I%20can%27t%20help,down%20and%20read%20Smith%27s%20book.

3 Joan C. Williams, *White Working Class: Overcoming Class Cluelessness in America* (Harvard, Harvard Business Review Press: 2017), p. 2.

4 Cédric Hugrée, Étienne Penissat, and Alexis Spire, *Social Class in Europe: New Inequalities in the Old World* (Verso, London: 2020), p. 1.

5 Mike Savage, *Social Class in the 21st Century,* (London, Penguin: 2015), pp. 2–10.

6 Geoffrey Evans and James Tilley, *The New Politics of Class: The Political Exclusion of the British Working Class* (Oxford, Oxford University Press: 2017), pp. 1–6.

7 See, for a very brief starter: Burton J. Bledstein and Robert D. Johnston (eds.), *The Middling Sorts: Explorations in the History of the American Middle Class* (New York, Routledge: 2001); Felix Fuhg, *London's Working Class Youth and the Making of Post-Victorian Britain* (London, Palgrave Macmillan: 2021); Joe William Trotter, *Workers on Arrival: Black Labor in the Making of America* (Oakland, University of California Press, 2019); Blair L.M. Kelley, *Black Folk: The Roots of the Black Working Class* (New York, Liveright, 2023); Selina Todd, *The People: The Rise and Fall of the Working Class* (London, John Murray, 2014).

8 Williams, *White Working Class,* pp. 2–10.

9 E. P. Thompson, *The Making of the English Working Class* (London, Victor Gollancz: 1963)

10 Howard Zinn, *A People's History of the United States* (San Fransisco, Harper and Row: 1980)

11 Sarah Attfield, *Class on Screen: The Global Working Class in Contemporary Cinema* (London, Palgrave Macmillan: 2020); Sonali Perera, *No Country: Working-Class Writing in the Age of Globalization* (New York, Columbia University Press, 2013).

12 Hugrée, Penissat, and Spire, *Social Class in Europe,* p. 4.

PART I

Working-class History in Perspective

1

DISABILITY IN WORKING-CLASS HISTORY[1]

Ben Curtis

In *Men in the Pits*, his important and illuminating study of Britain's coalfield communities published in 1948, Ferdynand Zweig trenchantly observed that 'nowhere else can you see the same relative numbers of disabled men as in a colliery village'.[2] Although coal was a particularly dangerous industry for its workforce, the experience of disability was a central feature of life within working-class communities in general. Disability history *is* working-class history, and vice versa.

Nevertheless, despite industrial work creating widespread physical impairment and workers comprising a significant proportion of total numbers of disabled people, disability history and labour history developed essentially independently from each other. Emerging from the disability rights movement of the 1980s and 1990s, disability history has tended to emphasise certain factors that are reflective of its origins: congenital physical, sensory, and cognitive disabilities; the charitable, institutional, and welfare contexts of disability; and critiques of the state, medical profession, and lay policies which have socially excluded disabled people.[3] Significantly, industrial disability hardly features; therefore, the experiences of disabled workers have been comparatively neglected. Labour history as a field of study first emerged in the 1920s with pioneering work by activist-scholars such as Ness Edwards, and was galvanised and given added impetus by the turn towards 'history from below' in the 1960s; perhaps the most important and influential example of this was the *oeuvre* of E. P. Thompson, particularly his magisterial *The Making of the English Working Class*.[4] Throughout, however, labour historiography has tended to focus overwhelmingly on industrial relations, with disability questions being relatively marginalised.[5]

DOI: 10.4324/9780429344084-3

This is not to say that industrial disability and its associated topics of industrial injury and occupational health were entirely a historiographical *terra incognita*. Kim Howells's 1980 essay, for example, provides an insightful study of victimisation, accidents, and industrial disease in the south Wales coalfield in the 1930s.[6] Published the following year, Carl Gersuny's *Work Hazards and Industrial Conflict* focuses on the labour history of the USA but makes similar points about the relationship between industrial injury and occupational health on the one hand and employer-led workplace imperatives to maximise output and productivity on the other, leading to this subject becoming a key site of industrial tension and dispute.[7] In *Dying for Work*, published a few years later, David Rosner and Gerald Markowitz make a similar point about the importance of occupational health; in 1991, their monograph *Deadly Dust* took a more specific focus on silicosis as an industrial-relations issue.[8] From a different, more theoretical perspective, and drawing upon influential ideas of the 'social model of disability' as articulated by earlier disability-history scholarship, Brendan Gleeson's *Geographies of Disability* is a useful contribution to the industrial disability historiography, persuasively making the case for utilisation of geographical-historical materialism as the basis for an 'embodied materialism' which recognises the material reality of impairment while stressing the specific ways in which this form of embodiment is socialised in different times and places.[9]

Notwithstanding this important early work, a crucial turning point in the historiography of industrial disability history – or working-class disability history – was reached with the publication in 2005 of Sarah F. Rose's highly influential essay '"Crippled" Hands'.[10] In it, she makes some powerful comments on the neglect of disability in labour history, noting the frequency with which 'disability appears in labor and working-class histories – but disabled workers most often do not'.[11] '"Crippled" Hands' concludes with a passionate call for the reformulation of labour history with disability as a central element within its purview:

> Labor history has much to gain by considering disability – and disabled people – as more than a metaphor for poor working conditions or victimized workers. Because so many workers, families, and communities have dealt with (and continue to live with) disabilities, and because disability is also a key issue in labor and industrial policy, incorporating disability into their works will allow labor historians to recover key aspects of work experience and of working-class life. In addition, since disability connects with so many of the field's central themes, a conscious engagement with disability – one attentive to disabled people's agency as well as to changing legal, medical, and cultural definitions of disability – can help us explore familiar topics in startlingly new ways. For instance, disability provides a valuable analytic framework for exploring issues such as the dynamics and

impact of unionization, who is considered to be a worker, and the meanings of work, dependence, and citizenship.[12]

Rose's essay, important though it was in terms of a critique of the treatment of disability within labour, was framed entirely from an American perspective, both in terms of historiography and historical subject matter. In the UK at the same time, meantime, Ronald Johnston and Arthur McIvor had been working on a number of articles which placed the lived experiences of impairment and disability centrally within industrial history, with the emphasis of this being on asbestos work in the shipping and engineering industries of Clydeside.[13] Furthermore, following the publication of '"Crippled" Hands', one of the first full-length studies to address the questions it raised was their monograph *Miners' Lung*.[14] This is an impressively holistic history of the industrial disease pneumoconiosis, which was endemic in the coal industry. Crucially, in addition to the detailed study of the medical history of the aetiology of the disease, the campaigning work by the miners' union to have pneumoconiosis classified as a compensable industrial disease, and the enactment of the subsequent legislation to effect this, there is a detailed study on the lived experiences of this particular disability. Here, extensive use is made of oral history, enabling workers' voices to tell their own stories.

Within the last decade, one of the most important contributions to the study of industrial disability from a UK perspective was the 'Disability and Industrial Society' project. Led initially by the late Anne Borsay and thereafter by David Turner, this examined the sociocultural lived experiences of disability in Britain from 1780 to 1948 via a case-study approach which focused on the important coalfields of north-east England, Scotland, and south Wales.[15] In the project's first monograph, *Disability in the Industrial Revolution: Physical Impairment in British Coalmining, 1780–1880*, Turner and Daniel Blackie examine 'the lives and experiences of [people] … who, until recently, were "never heard of" in histories of industrialisation – the scarred, the mutilated, the "distorted" and the impaired'.[16] They show that coal produced serious injury and illness to its workforce on a literally industrial scale during this period, and then proceed to examine the extent to which impaired miners returned to work wherever possible, assisted by their families and communities, and also the beginnings of a piecemeal network of statutory regulations and welfare programmes. In its second monograph, *Disability in Industrial Britain: A Cultural and Literary History of Impairment in the Coal Industry, 1880–1948*, Kirsti Bohata, Alexandra Jones, Mike Mantin, and Steven Thompson continue this analysis through into the period that saw both the zenith of the coal industry in Britain and also the establishment of systems of compensation for workplace injury and the beginnings of the welfare state; they also reflect critically upon the growth of a significant corpus of coalfield literature in this period, and the various ways in which disability was treated within this.[17] In both of these volumes, as well as the work of the project as a whole, the aim was to use an interdisciplinary approach to examine the lives of disabled mineworkers and their families, as well as to demonstrate the centrality of industrial disability to both industrial history and working-class history. Some specific examples of this include: an examination of the lived experiences of impairment via industrially induced premature ageing, disability and workers' lifecycles, and the conflation of old age and disability through historical usage of such terms as 'aged and infirm'[18]; a study of various systems of mutual provision of prosthetic limbs for its disabled members by a miners' trade union, within which some disabled miners played an important role as lay experts on prostheses[19]; and an article which draws upon a number of sociological models in order to articulate and emphasise the complex social context of disability, and extent to which impaired individuals continued to interact with and be affected by their family, their various local communities and networks, and broader regional and national economic and political developments.[20]

As Blackie and Alexia Moncrieff note, 'the last decade has witnessed a tremendous growth in the practice and visibility of disability history'; they argue that the historiography of this field is characterised by three central features: 'its political impetus; its commitment to a sociocultural approach to disability, and its insistence that disability constitutes a powerful category of historical analysis'.[21] This characterisation holds true for the study of industrial and working-class disability history. One of the best exemplifications of this in recent years is Rose's monograph *No Right to Be Idle*, which is a detailed, multi-faceted study of US working-class disability history.[22] Here, she shows that the nineteenth-century 'shift to an urban, wage-based, and often unsteady industrial economy undermined families' abilities to accommodate relatives with disabilities', arguing that consequently 'the common twentieth-century notion of equating "disability" with unproductivity, poor citizenship, and dependency on public or charitable assistance was, truly, an invention'.[23] Published in the same year, another significant historiographical development was the 2017 special issue of the prominent disability studies journal *Disability Studies Quarterly*.[24] This focused entirely on the presentation of new perspectives on the history of disability and work, with examples including a qualitative study of representations of women's work and disability in UK coalfields literature between 1880 and 1950, and a study of the impact of disability on the lives of young women and men in the Sundsvall region of central Sweden in the nineteenth century via a quantitative analysis of parish-register data.[25] On a related note, it should be emphasised that the study of industrial disability and working-class disability history is an international endeavour; there has been a lot of work published in languages other than English. In terms of French-language scholarship, for instance, the last 20 years have seen the study of an array of related topics, with prominent figures within the francophone historiographical field including Henri-Jacques Stiker, Anne-Sophie Bruno, and Judith Rainhorn.[26] Another example of this is the internationally oriented scholarship that was published in Mandarin in 2019 in a special edition of the Chinese *Journal of the Social History of Medicine and Health*, edited by Yong-an Zhang and McIvor, which focused on the body and health of coal miners.[27]

One of the most important facets of Rose's 2005 critique of traditional labour historiography was its tendency to frame discussion of disability in terms of a powerful rhetorical trope and industrial-relations metaphor, in a way which nevertheless marginalised the actual lived experiences of disabled workers themselves.[28] In subsequent years, then, a key development within the field of industrial disability historiography has been the work which has emphasised the extent of the agency of disabled workers: their ability to shape their own destiny, albeit not in circumstances of their own choosing. One representative example of this, for instance, is Matthias Reiss's *Blind Workers against Charity*: a study of the National League of the Blind, the first nationwide self-represented group of vision-impaired people in the UK.[29] Here, Reiss examines the League's campaign to establish state provision of training, employment, and assistance as a statutory right for vision-impaired people, together with the consequent abolition of all charitable aid for them. Furthermore, in response to the question of the agency of impaired workers within the trade-union movement, an important new contribution to the historiography is the recent work by Turner and Blackie on disability and political activism in the factory reform movement. In this, their findings, echoing Rose's comments in '"Crippled" Hands', emphasise the point that disabled workers were more important as labour activists than labour historians have hitherto tended to appreciate.[30]

Whereas usage of the terms 'industrial disability' and 'working-class disability' on a more-or-less interchangeable basis is understandable when discussing the history of the modern period, it is of course the case that working people's experiences of disability long precede the advent of the Industrial Revolution. Consequently, although the majority of the historiography in this field has tended to deal with the period from the nineteenth century to the present day, in recent years some scholars have begun to reach back further in time and expand the chronological scope of study. The specific subject matter naturally varies quite considerably, and it is worthwhile noting a few examples here: from Sofie De Veirman's comparative study of deaf people in Belgium in the eighteenth and nineteenth centuries, for instance, to Christian Laes's examination of the social and cultural history of disability during the time of the Roman Empire.[31] Angela Schattner's examination of the construction of 'disability' in late medieval and early-modern Germany is particularly useful, in terms of analysing both the functionality of the relationship between impairment and ability to work and also the consequent ways in which disability was a category constructed by societal perceptions of impairment.[32] The newest addition to the historiography is Simon Jarrett's most recent monograph, which discusses the history of disability in England from the medieval period to the present day – and, importantly, is presented in a manner suitable to engage with a wider general readership beyond specialised academia.[33]

Anglophone disability historiography in general has hitherto tended to orientate towards the UK and North America – and, as this survey has demonstrated implicitly, industrial disability has shared this tendency. Within this, too, there has been a tendency towards an intra-national approach both in terms of subject matter and historiography, focusing on developments within a single country – this is particularly so in the case of the USA. Nevertheless, by way of redressing this imbalance, in recent years there have been moves to develop a wider global perspective. An important development a decade or so ago, both in terms of individual countries and the adoption of a more transnational approach, was the collection edited by Michael Rasell and Elena Iarskaia-Smirnova, the geographical focus of which comprised: the history of Soviet Union, some of its post-1991 successor states (the countries of Central Asia, Armenia, Azerbaijan, Georgia, Latvia, and Ukraine), and various other countries in Eastern Europe (Bosnia-Herzegovina, Bulgaria, and Hungary).[34] Even more recently, the edited volume *Disability and Labour in the Twentieth Century* has expanded the historiographical scope of study further, via historical case studies from the Scandinavian countries (mainly Sweden) and Eastern Europe (Bulgaria, Czechoslovakia, Poland, Romania, and the Soviet Union).[35] Moreover, Rada Harald Dinu and Staffan Bengtsson's volume focuses directly on the nexus between labour and disability, via an examination of a range of historical settings and types of workplaces. In so doing, they show that, relative to the mainstream labour force, disabled workers have frequently found themselves operating within a liminal space which incorporates elements of both marginalisation *and* integration. In particular, the Global South has suffered from historiographical neglect – although here, too, the situation has begun to improve. An important scholar here is Aparna Nair, whose ongoing work is representative of a number of key new developments in this respect: prosthetics and rehabilitation of disabled Indian soldiers in the First World War; a study of how disabled colonial subjects experienced colonialism; developing an edited volume on disability histories in the Global South; and a project on labour and disability history in British India.[36]

In the current political and cultural climate of the 'Black Lives Matter' movement and discussions about the *longue durée* legacies of colonialism and empire, the history of enslaved labour is clearly a topic of great significance within disability history historiography. Dea H. Boster's *African American Slavery and Disability* was one of the first volumes to address this hitherto-neglected topic, examining how ideas about race and disability overlapped and reinforced each other's power in a way which served to consolidate power structures in the southern states of the USA in the first half of the nineteenth century.[37] Published in 2020, an important new contribution to this field – which addresses similar themes to some of her earlier work – is Stefanie Hunt-Kennedy's monograph *Between Fitness and Death: Disability and Slavery in the Caribbean*.[38] One of the central arguments which she makes here is:

> that disability categories related to labor predated the Industrial Revolution and [consequently this] sheds new light on the timeline of modern ideas about working bodies and impairment. ... Plantation slavery was a necessary precondition for both industrialization and the emergence of modern concepts and displays of disability.[39]

Hunt-Kennedy's work stands as an exemplar of important trends within the historiography of disability history in general and working-class disability history in particular: the growing emphasis on the significance of intersectional analyses; explorations that look at the topic within an imperial/colonial framework or from a Global South perspective; and examination of periods which predate the twentieth century.

Returning to Rose's 2005 '"Crippled" Hands' critique of labour historiography, it is clear that industrial disability scholarship has come a long way in the years since this essay was published. As this survey has demonstrated, particularly during the past decade, the extent and range of monographs and other published work have expanded significantly, not just with respect to case-study subject matter but also in terms of chronology, geography, and intra-national and international comparative studies. This growth in the historiography of industrial and working-class disability – of the kind alluded to by Zweig in his 1948 study – is unambiguously a very significant and welcome development. By way of a qualification to this, it could be noted that this expansion has been mainly as a specialised subject area rather than a wholesale remaking of labour studies historiography in general; even here, however, there are some signs of progress in this respect as well. Overall, industrial and working-class disability history is currently a vibrant, dynamic, and exciting field of study – and appears very likely to remain so for the foreseeable future.

Notes

1 I am very grateful to David Turner, Daniel Blackie, and Ariane Mak for their comments and suggestions, which were very helpful to me in the writing of this piece.
2 F. Zweig, *Men in the Pits* (London, Victor Gollancz: 1948), p. 6.
3 For example, see Michael Oliver, *The Politics of Disablement* (London, Macmillan Education: 1990); Gary L. Albrecht, Katherine D. Seelman and Michael Bury, eds.,

Handbook of Disability Studies (Thousand Oaks, CA, Sage Publishing: 2001); and Anne Borsay, *Disability and Social Policy in Britain since 1750* (Basingstoke, Palgrave Macmillan: 2005).

4 Ness Edwards, *The Industrial Revolution in South Wales* (London, The Labour Publishing Company: 1924); Ness Edwards, *The History of the South Wales Miners* (London, The Labour Publishing Company: 1926); E. P. Thompson, *The Making of the English Working Class* (London, Victor Gollancz: 1963).

5 For a few British examples of this from various industries, see Philip S. Bagwell, *The Railwaymen: The History of the National Union of Railwaymen* (London, Taylor & Francis: 1963); W. R. Garside, *The Durham Miners, 1919–1960* (London, Allen and Unwin: 1971); John Benson, *British Coalminers in the Nineteenth Century: A Social History* (Dublin, Gill and Macmillan: 1980); Martin Upham, *Tempered – Not Quenched: The History of the ISTC, 1951–1997* (London, Lawrence & Wishart Ltd: 1997); and David Howell, *Respectable Radicals: Studies in the Politics of Railway Trade Unionism* (Ashgate, Aldershot: 1999).

6 Kim Howells, 'Victimisation, Accidents and Disease' in David Smith (ed.), *A People and* a Proletariat: Essays in the History of Wales, 1780–1980 (London, Pluto Press in association with Llafur, the Society for the study of Welsh Labour: 1980), pp. 181–198.

7 Carl Gersuny, *Work Hazards and Industrial Conflict* (Hanover, NH, University Press of New England: 1981).

8 David Rosner and Gerald Markowitz, eds., *Dying for Work: Workers' Safety and Health in Twentieth-Century America* (Bloomington, Indiana University Press: 1986), and David Rosner and Gerald Markowitz, *Deadly Dust: Silicosis and the Politics of Occupational Health in Twentieth Century America* (Princeton, NJ, Princeton University: 1991).

9 Brendan Gleeson, *Geographies of Disability* (London, Taylor & Francis: 1998).

10 Sarah F. Rose, '"Crippled" Hands: Disability in Labor and Working Class History', *Labor: Studies in Working Class History of the Americas* 2.1 (2005), pp. 27–54.

11 Rose, '"Crippled" Hands', p. 29.

12 Rose, '"Crippled" Hands', p. 47.

13 Ronald Johnston and Arthur McIvor, 'Incubating Death: Working with Asbestos in Clydeside Shipping and Engineering, 1945–1990', *Scottish Labour History* 34 (1999), pp. 74–93; Ronald Johnston and Arthur McIvor, 'Dust to Dust: Oral Testimonies of Asbestos-related Disease on Clydeside, c.1930–the Present', *Oral History* 29.2 (2001), pp. 38–62; Ronnie Johnston and Arthur McIvor, 'Dangerous Work, Hard Men and Broken Bodies: Masculinity in the Clydeside Heavy Industries, c.1930–1970s', *Labour History Review* 69.2 (2004), pp. 135–153.

14 Arthur McIvor and Ronald Johnston, *Miners' Lung: A History of Dust Disease in British Coal Mining* (Ashgate, Aldershot: 2007). It perhaps ought to be noted, though, that there is no direct evidence of this monograph having been influenced by Rose's critique of the historiography.

15 All of the academic outputs from this project are available on an Open Access basis, and are accessible via the project's website: www.dis-ind-soc.org.uk.

16 David M. Turner and Daniel Blackie, *Disability in the Industrial Revolution: Physical Impairment in British Coalmining, 1780–1880* (Manchester, Manchester University Press: 2018), p. 2.

17 Kirsti Bohata, Alexandra Jones, Mike Mantin and Steven Thompson, *Disability in Industrial Britain: A Cultural and Literary History of Impairment in the Coal Industry, 1880–1948* (Manchester, Manchester University Press: 2020).

18 Ben Curtis and Steven Thompson, '"This is the country of premature old men": Ageing and Aged Miners in the South Wales Coalfield, c.1880–1947', *Cultural and Social History* 12.4 (2015), pp. 587–606.

19 Ben Curtis and Steven Thompson, '"A plentiful crop of cripples made by all this progress": Disability, Artificial Limbs and Working-Class Mutualism in the South Wales Coalfield, 1890–1948', *Social History of Medicine* 27.4 (2014), pp. 708–727.

20 Ben Curtis and Steven Thompson, 'Disability and the Family in South Wales Coalfield Society, c.1920–1939', *Family and Community History* 20.1 (2017), pp. 25–44.

21 Daniel Blackie and Alexia Moncreiff, 'State of the Field: Disability History', *History* 107.377 (2022), p. 789.

22 Sarah F. Rose, *No Right to be Idle: The Invention of Disability, 1840s–1890s* (Chapel Hill, NC, University of North Carolina Press: 2017).

23 Rose, *No Right to be Idle*, pp. 10–13.

24 *Disability Studies Quarterly* [*DSQ*] 37.4 (2017), Special Issue: 'Disability, Work and Representation: New Perspectives', accessed 8 June 2023, https://doi.org/10.18061/dsq.v37i4.

25 Alexandra Jones, '"Her body [was] like a hard-worked machine": Women's Work and Disability in Coalfields Literature, 1880–1950', *DSQ* 37.4 (2017), accessed 8 June 2023, https://dsq-sds.org/index.php/dsq/article/view/6103, and Lotta Vikström, Erling Häggström Lundevaller and Helena Haage, 'First a Job, and Then a Family? Impacts of Disabilities on Young People's Life Courses in a Nineteenth-century Swedish Region', *DSQ* 37.4 (2017), accessed 8 June 2023, https://dsq-sds.org/index.php/dsq/article/view/6095.

26 André Gueslin and Henri-Jacques Stiker, eds., *Handicaps, pauvreté et exclusion dans la France du XIXe siècle* (Paris, Editions de l'Atelier: 2003); Henri-Jacques Stiker, *Les métamorphoses du handicap de 1970 à nos jours* (Grenoble, Presses universitaires de Grenoble: 2009); Catherine Omnès and Anne-Sophie Bruno, *Les mains inutiles. Inaptitude au travail et emploi en Europe* (Paris, Belin: 2004); Anne-Sophie Bruno, 'Quelques perspectives sur les travaux récents en « santé et travail. Les approches développées dans les revues de sciences sociales (2001–2007)', *Revue française des affaires sociales* 2 (2008), pp. 71–96; Judith Rainhorn, *Santé et travail à la mine, XIXe–XXIe siècles* (Villeneuve d'Ascq, Presses Universitaires du Septentrion: 2014); Judith Rainhorn, *Blanc de plomb. Histoire d'un poison légal* (Paris, Presses de Sciences Po: 2019). For further examples of French scholarship in this field, see: Damien de Blic, 'De la fédération des mutilés du travail à la Fédération nationale des accidentés du travail et des handicapés', *Revue française des affaires sociales* 2–3 (2008), pp. 119–140; François Buton, *L'administration des faveurs. L'état, les sourds et les aveugles (1789–1885)* (Rennes, Presses Universitaires de Rennes: 2009); Gilles Brégain, *Pour une histoire du handicap au XXe siècle. Approches transnationales (Europe et Amériques)* (Rennes, Presses Universitaires de Rennes: 2014); 'Handicap et dépendance. Perspectives historiennes', special issue of *Revue d'histoire de la protection sociale* (2015); Paul-André Rosental, 'Enjeux historiographiques de l'histoire de la santé au travail dans les mines', in Centre Historique Minier, *Santé à la mine. Acteurs et systèmes de soins* (Lewarde, Centre Historique Minier: 2020), pp. 167–172.

27 For an example of one of the contributions to this volume, see Ben Curtis, 不只是工会？———南威尔士地区全国煤矿工人工会和南威尔士　煤矿的因工致残 (1947–1994) ['More Than a Union? The National Union of Mineworkers South Wales Area and Industrial Disability in the South Wales Coalfield, 1947–1994'], in Yong-an Zhang and Arthur McIvor (eds.), 专题　煤矿工人的身体与健康 ['The Body and Health of Coal Miners'], special issue of 医疗社会史研究 [*Journal of the Social History of Medicine and Health*] 4.1 (2019), pp. 33–54.

28 Rose, '"Crippled" Hands', p. 36.

29 Matthias Reiss, *Blind Workers against Charity: The National League of the Blind of Great Britain and Ireland, 1893–1970* (Basingstoke, Palgrave Macmillan: 2015).
30 David M. Turner and Daniel Blackie, 'Disability and Political Activism in Industrialising Britain, c. 1830–1850', *Social History* 47.2 (2022), pp. 117–140.
31 Sofie De Veirman, 'Deaf and Disabled? (Un)employment of Deaf People in Belgium: A Comparison of Eighteenth-century and Nineteenth-century Cohorts', *Disability and Society* 30.3 (2015), pp. 460–474; Christian Laes, *Disabilities and the Disabled in the Roman World: A Social and Cultural History* (Cambridge, Cambridge University Press: 2018).
32 Angela Schattner, 'Disabled to Work? Impairment, the in/ability to Work and Perceptions of Dis/ability in Late Medieval and Early Modern Germany', *DSQ* 37.4 (2017), accessed 8 June 2023, https://dsq-sds.org/article/view/6105/4825.
33 Simon Jarrett, *A History of Disability in England: From the Medieval Period to the Present Day* (Liverpool, Historic England Publishing: 2023).
34 Michael Rasell and Elena Iarskaia-Smirnova, eds., *Disability in Eastern Europe and the Former Soviet Union: History, Policy and Everyday Life* (Abingdon, Routledge: 2013).
35 Rada Harald Dinu and Staffan Bengtsson, eds., *Disability and Labour in the Twentieth Century: Historical and Comparative Perspectives* (Abingdon, Routledge: 2022).
36 Aparna Nair, '"These curly-bearded, olive-skinned warriors": Medicine, Prosthetics, Rehabilitation and the Disabled Sepoy in the First World War, 1914–1920', *Social History of Medicine* 33.3 (2020), pp. 798–818; Aparna Nair, *Fungible Bodies: Disability Histories in British India, 1850–1950* (Urbana, IL; forthcoming); and 'Lives Worth Living: Disability Histories' website, accessed 19 July 2023, https://disabilitystories.com/contact/.
37 Dea H. Boster, *African American Slavery and Disability: Bodies, Property, and Power in the Antebellum South, 1800–1860* (New York, Routledge: 2013).
38 Stefanie Hunt-Kennedy, *Between Fitness and Death: Disability and Slavery in the Caribbean* (Urbana, University of Illinois Press: 2020); see also Stefanie Kennedy, '"Let them be young and stoutly set in limbs": Race, Labor, and Disability in the British Atlantic World', *Social Identities* 21.1 (2015), pp. 37–52.
39 Hunt-Kennedy, *Between Fitness and Death*, pp. 6–7.

2

PARASITES UNITE

Sensory History, the Possibilities of Transgression, and the Perceptual Manifesto of the Proletariat

Andrew Kettler

Bong Joon-ho's *Parasite* (2019) emanates sensory worlds of class, work, and judgement, transforming a black downstairs/upstairs comedy about grifters moving into the home of a naïve rich family into a darkly tragic tale of discrimination, revenge, and odour. The film begins with futile schemes of the lower-class Kim family, making their way in the world through little ploys and persistent work, folding pizza boxes and stealing internet access. Through a bit of luck, the son of the Kim family, Ki-woo, is introduced to the Park household, recently in need of an English tutor for their teenaged daughter. Through both determined manipulation and staged obsequiousness, each of the four members of the Kim family ingratiates themselves into lucrative spaces labouring for their rich patrons.[1]

Personal relationships develop, old labourers return in mysterious ways, violence ensues, and, through all the manoeuvrings of a struggling family attempting to make good through criminal fraudulence, the interlopers remain permanently marked by a working-class identity, both of minds that are unwilling to accept they could ever belong at the revelries of the rich and through bodies emitting the same 'radish' odour that comes from living for decades within South Korea's urban slums, where walls drip with sewage and food and flavour penetrate skin and pore. Tying together media traditions about the working class, from romantic portrayals within *Grapes of Wrath* (1940) and *Let Us Now Praise Famous Men* (1941), through more dystopian images of *Soylent Green* (1973) and *The Matrix* (1999), and into the grifting and eat-the-rich mentality of the UK/US versions of *Shameless* (2004–2013; 2011–), *Parasite* succeeds in describing labouring aromata buried deep within narratives of increasingly hierarchical capitalism that prescribes a revengeful proletariat.[2]

DOI: 10.4324/9780429344084-4

We open with this recent filmic masterpiece relating Marxism and the body to introduce a field of current study ripe with similar tales of destruction and liberation, order and disorder, and rebellious sensation searching for the edges of the Superstructure from deep within the masses. The field of sensory history generally highlights how embodied perceptions are socially constructed within discursive contests. These competitions are consistently informed by the power of capital to assert territorialising discourses about proper body comportment for the streamlining of exchange. Part of that body rationalisation often involves significant learning regarding how the senses should function within understanding of the meanings of labour.[3]

Within the Marxist historiographical tradition of the senses, accounting for many different theoretical variations, the commodity fetish manipulates labour value into abstract value, in turn altering social relations to separate sensory connections between persons who would otherwise use natural community relationships to resist the powers of capital over the means of production. For most scholars who follow critical theory based within Marxist dialectics, capital works to alienate labourers from their natural sensory worlds into more abstract sensory realms where relationships with both objects and other members of the proletariat are disconnected from the worker. As part of the Superstructure, sensory manipulations generally create alienation for the employee; however sensory cultures can also defy disaffection for humans who are able to define inner harmony through self-actualisation of a sensorium apart from the fetish, either grounded within a culture of class consciousness or part of an identarian social setting.[4]

Marx initially noted the importance of sensory control for understanding capitalism when summarising that 'the forming of the five senses is a labour of the entire history of the world down to the present'. In the *Economic and Philosophic Manuscripts* (1844), following economic analysis of cultures from Ludwig Feuerbach, Marx outlined meanings for embodied cognition through the senses that was apart from conscious thought, born as part of the 'social being'.[5] As David Howes has shown, in later works like *Capital* (1867), pressing a more scientific language of finance, Marx was increasingly unable to speak of his more youthful formulations of an abstract, culturally dependent, and socially educated sensorium. Nevertheless, for many scholars of the senses, Marx's sprightly ponderings on sensations represent the ability of capital to degrade the working class and their understandings of possible betterment through aesthetic appreciation of their labour or empathy for other workers.[6]

In different variations on these dialogues of distancing, labour, and the sensorium, debates on meanings of culture are frequently disputed. These rhetorical competitions are important theoretically and in the material world of praxis, as Superstructural forms of culture can be used to oppress as much as forms of class or other cultures of identity can be categorised for resistance. Sensory history, and narratives of sensory experience of workers under the oppression of capitalism, becomes especially important in our current economic moment, as overcoming the acceleration and anxieties of late capitalism, of a worker's body monitored and controlled through the sensory power of the capitalised and collusive state, involves articulating different sensory skills within a lived and embodied praxis that can rise liberated from the chains and charms of the market.[7]

Critical theories in the wake of Marxism and the Frankfurt School frequently offer that recovery, retention, or reimagining of a natural form of sensation, unalienated by the fetish, marks a materialism that appreciates the object in an unabstracted form, as defined by a labour value rather than an immaterial value created through manipulations of sensuousness within the superorganism of the capitalist milieu.[8] Within these dialogues of sensory subjugation, numerous scholars of neoliberalism, algorithmic appropriation, and accelerationism have also defined that the digitisation of labour in late capitalism furthers alienation, marching the worker into the mainframe through a violent process of data gazing and continuing desensitisation.[9]

This sensory chlorination within digital spaces also involves a contested dialectic of great importance for understanding the working class in history, whereby capital has often abused natural forms of human sensation to enchant and exploit malleable labouring bodies that were also categorised into different classes for greater suppression. As Terry Eagleton recently summarised regarding the necessary emancipation of the senses from capitalist hegemony:

> Since material reality constitutes a bond between individuals, to lose touch with that reality is also for them to lose touch with each other. One of the goals of socialism, then, is to return to the body its plundered powers, so that the senses may be allowed to come into their own.[10]

With the accelerating alienations of the contemporary neoliberal world, described often by Steven Shaviro, Paul Virilio, and Benjamin Noys, should academics concerned with liberation speak of the historical sensory worlds of choking miners, groomed prostitutes, poisoned telephone manufacturers, and children without fingers lost to the machine? Or should we not speak of them at all for fear that such a conversation falsely brings history into the activist present?[11] Should historians retreat into protecting the academic space of diachronic impotence, or shall they arm the senses with a history of oppression to critique the continuing epoch of sensory readjustment that further differentiates and subsumes labouring bodies through capitalist percepticide?[12]

Since the rise of capitalism, as many histories have defined, the bourgeoisie generally seeks out a homogenisation, a streamlining of both labouring-class work regimes and aesthetic values within the Superstructure. Methods of capitalist subsumption through the sensorium include both discursive ideas about the inferiority of the lower classes articulated through constructed perceptions and material sensory controls emplaced upon the labouring body.[13] In the former categorisation, the lower classes are told they stink, are loud, are dirty to the sight, lack aesthetic taste, and can take the painful beatings of the working day with greater ease.[14] In this manner, broad ideas about the inferiority of the working class, often puddling in cultural categories of race, gender, and disability, are used to divide labourers into specific categories, unlinking common human empathy from concern over the bodies of others.[15] In the latter sense, capital uses these differentiating discourses to also justify materially deodorised, silent, distant, and gazing spaces where labour is meant to be done without a class consciousness that accesses natural empathy.[16]

Material controls on socially educated perceptions have been studied in many recent works that focus on different forms of the panoptical gaze and legal concepts of nuisance.[17] Important structural works on societies transforming to suppress through technologies of capitalism and ideological apparatuses have been produced on topics such as electricity, sleep regimes, noise control, city lighting, and aesthetics from scholars and theorists including Jonathan Crary, Chris Otter, James Scott, and Emily Thompson.[18] Focusing into analysis of labour and the sensorium highlights how these structural oppressions that are infused with authoritarian tactics of Fordism and Taylorism affect perceptions within the daily lives of labour. For example, nineteenth-century capitalism involved activating the senses through specifically altering the cityscape. Street signs and billboards, especially in New York City, increasingly educated the eye where to move and what to view for disciplined procurement. Through a 'dictatorship of the perpendicular' the height of billboards and street signs portrayed usefulness and power to influence urban behaviours.[19]

New city dwellers of the nineteenth-century Industrial Revolution were also educated how to manoeuvre through metropolises, often to the extent of understanding the touch of different roads beneath their feet. City streets throughout the burgeoning Anglo-Atlantic, as also described by many *flaneurs* analysed by famed theorist Walter Benjamin in the twentieth century and within John Gay's famed *Trivia, or The Art of Walking the Streets of London* (1716), had to be negotiated through the senses, whereby residents came to understand what parts of the city were inhabited by what categories of plutocracy or poverty, and what cacophony, aromatic diets, or unclean odours rang from which class-infused spaces.[20]

Workers throughout history have attempted to overcome these forms of spatial categorisation and economic alienation through attempting to find aesthetic appreciation for their constructions to overcome the separation between worker and the true labour value of their products. The historical phenomenology of labouring life portrays both the plight of many forms of labouring and the ability to build skills to perform well and appreciate the results of work.[21] Within vocational regimes, negotiations constantly occur, whereby labour defines their experiences in different terms, often sensory, that point to survival, improvement, and resistance. Recovering the subjectivity of workers through descriptions of their lives and drudgery marks an important space for understanding the sensory worlds necessary to creatively deconstruct the power of capital that continues alienating the worker from galvanising perceptions of labour value and recognising the plight experienced by other members of the workforce.[22]

Sensory resistance, often portrayed in histories through different sensory skills applied by workers to do their work and possibly come to aesthetic appreciation of labour value for the products they create, as with the female labourers at the Lowell Mills explored in many recent analyses, involves educating an appreciation for sensation apart from the definitions that embourgeoisement emplaces upon the manipulated worker's body.[23] Workers have often found sensory skills to directly resist the confines of capitalism and the conspiring state. When Revolution came to France, as Richard Clay highlighted, labouring classes negotiated their urban landscapes through mediated understandings of the sensory worlds of defiance. Moving beyond visual iconoclasm, citizens increasingly destroyed not only optic texts signifying royal seals through regimes of sight, but became iconoclastic to different sensory regimes of power, as with destruction of sculptures through the senses of touch, the covering of statuaries in re-signifying and foul ordure, and the nonstandard ringing and luddite removal of bells that marked calendric, homogenous, empty, and riverine temporal regimes of the priest, capitalist, and bureaucrat.[24]

Within slave cultures of labour and resistance, sensory skills were also commonly applied to push against the confines of the always capitalised peculiar institution. The enslaved specifically worked often to create aural cultures in urban areas to resist master's desire for quietude that came through outlawing singing and sounding both formally and informally. As masters tried to create sensorially deprived worlds to keep their slaves in labouring lines, coating work with the rhythm of worksong or accepting only silence, enslaved men and women constructed creolised cultures from ethnic pasts to retain traditions they used to resist commodification as both objects and labourers.[25] Those enslaved created soundscapes of both noise and silence, marking secretive rumour as vital within communication networks often connected through familial and fictive kinship webs within the serenity of night. The 'common winds' of slave culture, the movement of knowledge throughout various rumour networks, marks another sensory skill that allowed slaves and free people of colour to resist the alienating forces of capitalism and bondage during the Antebellum Era in the United States and throughout the transnational Atlantic World.[26]

Colonial spaces of labour involved similar attempts at sensory control, manipulation, and embourgeoisement. Whether in the British Empire of southern Africa that fashioned specific clothing regimes by labour and race or within public health campaigns run by American colonialists in the Philippines, colonial endeavours often included creating labouring classes through specific sensory languages.[27] Such attempts at colonisation through sensory control continues within modern cities that frequently also involve similarly struggling negotiations on meanings of 'sensory urbanism' in contested metropolitan spaces.[28] As with debates on smoking as a cultural phenomenon in Singapore, these consultations often involve the room allowed for working-class lifeways to persist in the face of modern desensitisation movements tied to ideals of hygiene, public health, and the continued traditions of marking the worker as a diseased other.[29]

In these more modern senses, urban environs are ripe with workers who produce sensory worlds of difference to mark a carnivalesque return against the tyranny of accelerating capitalist homogeny.[30] Everyday multiculturalism of street markets produces both cultural identities through sensory worlds and generates cross-cultural links to create diverse and empathetic forms of sensory cosmopolitanism. Walking through modern megalopolises often relays these vast multicultural differences in the embodied spaces of urbanity, as with diverse foodways in London markets or the sea-lining aromatic bazaars of Bangladesh.[31]

Through many of these forms of sensory resistance to embourgeoisement, labourers attempt to create a more complex system of work, multiculture, and economic exchange that can involve fresh pathways to greater levels of liberation. In a modern world where universal abundance is possible with a greater distribution of wealth, these new paths are often deeply embodied negotiations within fields of work, gender, and ethnicity that can effort both to discover idiosyncratic places of peace from labour and upset greater trends of the structure through widespread sensory education of skills within a superorganic discourse meant to drive towards revolution. Finding sensory connections between labourers, across the falsely constructed racial and gendered lines of capital, can become an important pathway to use empathy and proximity to compete against sensory alienation.[32]

Scholars often scoff at the binary implications of power and resistance, providing an impotent desire to move beyond an overburdened binary of authority and agency into the fields of inactive deconstruction and post-structural tendencies that frequently neuter more than deploy. Even with these modes of academic wrangling between often bourgeoisie interlocutors, labour rises in resistance with different ideas and material praxis regarding sensation that puddle in fields of everyday opposition and more violent forms of embodied protest. Capital defines working classes as noisy, so the labouring classes use cacophony as part of a resistant and contagious carnivalesque.

Capital asserts that working classes stink, as described memorably by George Orwell, so labouring classes cook stinking food to mark ethnic resistance to homogenisation and McDonaldization.[33] The means of production gaze, and the working class performs beneath the society of the spectacle, resisting through sartorial signals of their struggle and representations of the poverty that capital continues to emplace on the commons.[34]

As histories of working-class sensory worlds portray, only the labourer coming from a conscious space outside of capitalism as a parasite, can unite a proletariat sensorium to seek true liberation from spaces at a distance outside of all that the fetish can commodify, operate, and enchant.[35] Working-class history shows how labourers consistently resisted embourgeoisement of the senses. This historically moulded and embodied revolutionary manifesto of the proletariat seeks to articulate sensory worlds birthed separately from the cultural forces of capital, rather than attempting to negate capital on playing fields where Shell, Toyota, BP, Wal-Mart, the Koch brothers, and Apple construct the rules of the game. The historical working classes have combined a history of sensory oppression and the resistance of sensory skills to show pathways towards perceptual liberation. The working class articulates that attack against the means of production must come from a space of deterritorialisation, from a sensory space that is so uncouth, unrecognisable, and uncommonly mobile to the existing Superstructure that it will avoid the constant subsumption of attempted resistance that is common within hastening neoliberal modernity.[36]

Notes

1 For more on film, the senses, and the working class see Emma Widdis, *Socialist Senses: Film, Feeling, and The Soviet Subject, 1917–1940* (Bloomington, Indiana University Press: 2017); Stefan Jonsson, *Crowds and Democracy: The Idea and Image of the Masses from Revolution to Fascism* (New York, Columbia University Press: 2013). See also, sensory language and phenomenology for understanding resistance through the media within, Ben Tausig, *Bangkok Is Ringing: Sound, Space, and Media at Thailand's Red Shirt Protests* (Oxford, Oxford University Press: 2019), pp. 182–190; Allen Feldman, *Formations of Violence: The Narrative of the Body and Political Terror in Northern Ireland* (Chicago, IL, University of Chicago: 1991), pp. 22–29; Laura Kunreuther, 'Sounds of Democracy: Performance, Protest, and Political Subjectivity', *Cultural Anthropology* 33.1 (2018), pp. 1–31. See also, sound, script, song, and working-class identity within, Yurou Zhong, *Chinese Grammatology: Script Revolution and Literary Modernity, 1916–1958* (Irvington, Columbia University Press: 2019), protest and soundscapes in, Elizabeth Fones-Wolf, *Waves of Opposition: Labor and the Struggle for Democratic Radio* (Urbana, University of Illinois Press: 2006), pp. 13–37, the role of music and folk ballads in eighteenth-century city life within, Peter Borsay, 'Sounding the Town', *Urban History* 29.1 (2002), pp. 92–102, bowery boys asserting a musical culture that defined a conscious working class within, Daniel Cavicchi, *Listening and Longing: Music Lovers in the Age of Barnum* (Middletown, CT, Wesleyan University Press: 2011), pp. 151–152, and the music

of labouring migrants within, Alejandro Madrid, 'Rigo Tovar, Cumbia, and the Transnational Grupero Boom' in Héctor Fernández L'Hoeste and Pablo Vila (eds.), *Cumbia!: Scenes of a Migrant Latin American Music Genre* (Durham, NC, Duke University Press: 2013), pp. 105–118.

2 For introductions to smell and othering see, Kelvin Low, 'Presenting The Self, The Social Body, and The Olfactory: Managing Smells in Everyday Life Experiences', *Sociological Perspectives* 49.4 (2006), pp. 607–631; Keith Thomas, 'Cleanliness and Godliness in Early Modern England' in Patrick Collinson, Anthony Fletcher, and Peter Roberts (eds.), *Religion, Culture, and Society in Early Modern Britain: Essays in Honour of Patrick Collinson* (Cambridge, Cambridge University Press: 1994), pp. 56–83; D. D. Waskul, Phillip Vannini, and Janelle Wilson, 'The Aroma of Recollection: Olfaction, Nostalgia, and the Shaping of the Sensuous Self', *Senses and Society* 4.1 (2009), pp. 5–22; Constance Classen, 'The Odor of the Other: Olfactory Symbolism and Cultural Categories', *Ethos* 20.2 (1992), pp. 133–166; Mark Smith, *How Race Is Made: Slavery, Segregation, and the Senses* (Chapel Hill, University of North Carolina Press: 2006); William Tullett, 'Grease and Sweat: Race and Smell in Eighteenth-Century English Culture', *Cultural and Social History* 13.3 (2016), pp. 307–322; Laura Catherine Frost, *The Problem with Pleasure: Modernism and Its Discontents* (New York, Columbia University Press: 2015), pp. 33–62. See also, olfactory othering through class within Victorian literature in Janice Carlisle, *Common Scents: Comparative Encounters in High-Victorian Fiction* (Oxford, Oxford University Press: 2004); Jonathan Reinarz, 'Uncommon Scents: Smell and Victorian England' in Bronwen Martin and Felizitas Ringham (eds.), *Sense and Scent: An Exploration of Olfactory Meaning* (Dublin, Philomel: 2003), pp. 129–148; Nicholas Daly, 'The Senses in Literature: Industry and Empire' in Constance Classen (ed.), Volume V of *A Cultural History of the Senses* (London, Bloomsbury: 2014), pp. 161–184.

3 Labour historians have often been at odds concerning the meanings of culture; whether materialist readings of culture, wherein culture is used to create common understandings of class consciousness necessary for resistance to capital, can be combined with a belief that culture is dependent on the power of capitalist languages, whereby hegemonic masters within culture create a Superstructure that uses culture for dividing and conquering the masses. As Daniel Bender argues, sensory history allows for a potent recombination of these fields, through showing how human experiences of perception are dependent both on being oppressed into an object through cultures of power and how cultures of resistance can also emerge through patterning of a new habitus based on the human experiences of labouring. Daniel Bender, 'Sensing Labor: The Stinking Working-Class after the Cultural Turn' in Donna Haverty-Stacke and Daniel Walkowitz (eds.), *Rethinking US Labor History: Essays on the Working-Class Experience, 1756–2009* (New York, Continuum: 2010), pp. 243–265. For other introductions to sensory history and the working class see Julia Frankenbach, 'Sensing Disorder: Sensory History and Future Directions for Working-Class and Urban Environmental Scholarship', *Labour / Le Travail* 78 (2016), pp. 281–300; Peter Burke, 'Urban Sensations: Attractive and Repulsive' in Constance Classen and Herman Roodenburg (eds.), Volume III of *A Cultural History of the Senses* (London, Bloomsbury: 2014), pp. 43–60; Constance Classen, 'Introduction: The Transformation of Perception' in Constance Classen (ed.), Volume V of *A Cultural History of the Senses* (London, Bloomsbury: 2014), pp. 1–24; Phillip Vannini, Dennis Waskul, and Simon Gottschalk, *The Senses in Self, Society, and Culture: A Sociology of the Senses* (New York, Routledge: 2014), pp. 126–147. See also, environment and the senses within, Linda Nash, 'Finishing Nature: Harmonizing Bodies and Environments in Late-Nineteenth-Century California', *Environmental History* 8.1 (2003), pp. 25–52; Christopher Sellers, 'Thoreau's Body: Towards an Embodied

Environmental History', *Environmental History* 4.4 (1999), pp. 486–514; Paul Sutter, 'The World with Us: The State of American Environmental History', *JAH* 100.1 (2013), pp. 94–119; Neil Maher, 'Body Counts: Tracking thc Human Body through Environmental History' in Douglas Cazaux Sackman (ed.), *A Companion to American Environmental History* (Chichester, Wiley: 2010), pp. 163–179.

4 For introductions to work on Marx and the senses see defining 'sense' within critical theory in, Martin Jay, 'In the Realm of the Senses', *AHR* 116.2 (2011), pp. 307–315. See also, Orrin Wang, *Romantic Sobriety: Sensation, Revolution, Commodification, History* (Baltimore, Johns Hopkins: 2011). As the work of Michel Serres often prompts, property and propriety come from the same terminology. The ability to own property partly emerged from the idea of controlling enclosed landscape, keeping it proper, and keep those occupying the land in propriety. Michel Serres, *Geometry: The Third Book of Foundations*, trans. Randolph Burks (London, Bloomsbury Academic: 2017). See also, class construction and the senses within, Peter Denney, '"The Sounds of Population Fail": Changing Perceptions of Rural Poverty and Plebian Noise in Eighteenth-Century Britain' in Anne Scott (ed.), *Experiences of Poverty in Late Medieval and Early Modern England and France* (Farnham, Ashgate: 2012), pp. 295–311; Eric Wilson, 'Plagues, Fairs, and Street Cries: Sounding Out Society and Space in Early Modern London', *Modern Language Studies* 25.3 (1995), pp. 1–42; John Crowley, *The Invention of Comfort: Sensibilities & Design in Early Modern Britain & Early America* (Baltimore, MD, Johns Hopkins: 2001), pp. 153–168; Peter Gay, *Education of the Senses* (New York, Norton: 1999); Karen Halttunen, *Confidence Men and Painted Women: A Study of Middle-Class Culture in America, 1830–1870* (New Haven, CT, Yale University Press: 1982), pp. 20–24, 122–124, 154–158; Emily Cockayne, *Hubbub: Filth, Noise & Stench in England 1600–1770* (New Haven, CT, Yale University Press: 2007).

5 Karl Marx, *Economic and Philosophic Manuscripts of 1844*, trans. Martin Milligan (Buffalo, Prometheus Books: 1988), pp. 108–109. See also, the fetish within technologies amongst indigenous groups invaded by capital within, Michael Taussig, *Mimesis and Alterity: A Particular History of the Senses* (New York, Routledge: 1992), issues regarding definitions of working class and inclusiveness within, Kimberly Defazio, *City of the Senses: Urban Culture and Urban Space* (New York, Palgrave Macmillan: 2016), pp. 85–120, and frustrations on worker agency in the post socialist context of existential fear and the altered sensory worlds of capitalism within, David Kideckel, *Getting by in Postsocialist Romania: Labor, the Body, & Working-Class Culture* (Bloomington, Indiana University Press: 2008), pp. 29–63.

6 For more on the senses in Marx's works see roots in Ludwig Feuerbach and Charles Fourier within, David Howes, *Sensual Relations: Engaging the Senses in Culture and Social Theory* (Ann Arbor, The University of Michigan Press: 2003), pp. 204–234. See also critical theories of literature that focus on labour, alienation, and the senses within Susan Stewart, *Poetry and the Fate of the Senses* (Chicago, IL, University of Chicago: 2002), pp. 38–45, defenders of the working class and the senses see, Anne Frances Toews, '"Flesh, Bone, and Blood": Working Class Bodies and the Canadian Communist Press, 1922–1956' in Patrizia Gentile and Jane Nicholas (eds.), *Contesting Bodies and Nation in Canadian History* (Toronto, University of Toronto: 2013), pp. 328–346, and Barbara Foley, *Radical Representations: Politics and Form in U.S. Proletarian Fiction, 1929–41* (Durham, NC, Duke University Press: 1994), pp. 129–139.

7 Anita Sridhar Chari, *A Political Economy of the Senses: Neoliberalism, Reification, Critique* (New York, Columbia University Press: 2016), pp. 111–141, 165–198; Bryan Nelson, 'Politics of the Senses: Karl Marx and Empirical Subjectivity', *Subjectivity* 4.4 (2011), pp. 395–412; Alex Rhys-Taylor, 'Urban

Sensations: A Retrospective of Multisensory Drift' in Constance Classen and David Howes (eds.), Volume VI of *A Cultural History of the Senses* (London, Bloomsbury: 2014), pp. 55–75. For background on sensory skills and 'body techniques', see Nick Crossley, 'Body Techniques, Agency and Intercorporeality: On Goffman's Relations in Public', *Sociology* 29.1 (1995), pp. 133–149; Erving Goffman, *Relations in Public* (Harmondsworth, Penguin: 1972); Marcel Mauss, *Sociologie et Anthropologie* (Paris, Presses Universitaires de France: 1973), pp. 70–88; Tim Ingold, *Being Alive: Essays on Movement, Knowledge and Description* (London, Routledge: 2011), pp. 214–226; Mark Jenner, 'Tasting Lichfield, Touching China: Sir John Floyers' Senses', *The Historical Journal* 53.3 (2010), pp. 647–670; Jonathan Reinarz, 'Learning to Use Their Senses: Visitors to Voluntary Hospitals in Eighteenth-Century England', *Journal for Eighteenth-Century Studies* 35.4 (2012), pp. 505–520; Sarah Maslen, 'Researching the Senses as Knowledge', *Senses and Society* 10.1 (2015), pp. 52–70; Francine Masiello, *The Senses of Democracy: Perception, Politics, and Culture in Latin America* (Austin, University of Texas Press: 2018), pp. 19–70.

8 For alienation of the senses and consumerism see, Serena Dyer, 'Shopping and the Senses: Retail, Browsing and Consumption in 18th-Century England', *History Compass* 12.9 (2014), pp. 694–703; Claire Walsh, 'Shop Design and the Display of Goods in Eighteenth-Century London', *Journal of Design History* 8.3 (1995), pp. 157–176; Evelyn Welch, 'The Senses in the Marketplace: Sensory Knowledge in a Material World' in Constance Classen and Herman Roodenburg (eds.), Volume III of *A Cultural History of the* Senses (London, Bloomsbury: 2014), pp. 61–86; Nancy Cox and Karin Dannehl, *Perceptions of Retailing in Early Modern England* (Aldershot, Ashgate: 2007), pp. 1–8; Spyros Maniatis, 'Scents as Trademarks: Propertisation of Scents and Olfactory Poverty' in Lionel Bently and Leo Flynn (eds.), *Law and the Senses: Sensational Jurisprudence* (London, Pluto Press: 1996), pp. 217–235; Adam Mack, 'The Senses in the Marketplace: Commercial Aesthetics for a Suburban Age' in Constance Classen and David Howes (eds.), Volume VI of *A Cultural History of the* Senses (London, Bloomsbury: 2014), pp. 77–10. See also, navigating realms of consumption through how female shoppers in eighteenth-century England specifically used their sense of touch to ascertain the ceramic workmanship of specific goods, avoiding swindlers who attempted to grift in the fields of profit, within Kate Smith, 'Sensing Design and Workmanship: The Haptic Skills of Shoppers in Eighteenth-Century London', *Journal of Design History* 25.1 (2012), pp. 1–10, and the multiple skills learned to view goods within, Wendy Bellion, *Citizen Spectator: Art, Illusion, and Visual Perception in Early National America* (Chapel Hill, University of North Carolina Press: 2011).

9 Franco Berardi, Jason Smith, Francesca Cadel, and Giuseppina Mecchia, *The Soul at Work: From Alienation to Autonomy* (Los Angeles, CA, Semiotext(e): 2009), pp. 74–96, 133–136. See also, introductions to alterations in the sense of time within, Moishe Postone, *Time, Labor, and Social Domination: A Reinterpretation of Marx's Critical Theory* (Cambridge, Cambridge University Press: 1993), pp. 200–208, 291–297; E. P. Thompson, 'Time, Work-Discipline and Industrial Capitalism', *Past and Present* 38 (1967), pp. 56–97; Antonio Negri, *Time for Revolution* (New York, Continuum: 2004), pp. 122–126; Stavros Tombazos, *Time in Marx: The Categories of Time in Marx's Capital* (Leiden, Brill: 2014), pp. 1–6.

10 Terry Eagleton, *Materialism* (New Haven, CT, Yale University Press: 2017), quote on pp. 79–80; Terry Eagleton, *The Ideology of the Aesthetic* (Malden, Blackwell: 1990), pp. 7–28; Mark Smith, *Sensing the Past: Seeing, Hearing, Smelling, Tasting, and Touching in History* (Berkeley, University of California Press: 2007), pp. 15–28; Elaine Scarry, *Body in Pain* (Oxford, Oxford University Press:

1985); Mario Saenz, 'Living Labor in Marx', *Radical Philosophy Review* 10.1 (2007), pp. 1–31. For more on the body, language, and influences on sensory experience see, Michael Polanyi, *The Tacit Dimension* (Chicago, IL, University of Chicago Press: 1966); George Lakoff and Mark Johnson, *Metaphors We Live By* (Chicago, IL, University of Chicago Press: 2008 [1980]), pp. 57–58; Asifa Majid and Stephen Levinson, 'The Senses in Language and Culture', *Senses and Society* 6 (2011), pp. 5–18; Thomas Sebeok, *Signs: An Introduction to Semiotics* (Toronto, University of Toronto Press: 2001), pp. 11–23, 124–126. See also, a more accessible rendering of Marxism, the senses, and embodiment within, Stuart Walton, *In the Realm of the Senses* (Winchester, Zero Books: 2016).

11 Much of this work on time, resistance, and perception has settled into discussions over 'accelerationism', or whether movements towards worker liberation should accelerate neoliberalism to its fullest extent until a breaking point or directly confront neoliberalism through stalling tactics. For an introduction see, Steven Shaviro, *No Speed Limit Three Essays on Accelerationism* (Minneapolis, University of Minnesota Press: 2016). See also, Paul Virilio, *The Administration of Fear* (Los Angeles, CA, Semiotext(e): 2012); Benjamin Noys, *Malign Velocities: Accelerationism & Capitalism* (Washington, DC, Zero: 2014). For sensory worlds of sex work see the nineteenth-century French prostitutes concerned over contraception, within Alain Corbin, *Time, Desire, and Horror: Towards a History of the Senses* (Cambridge, Polity Press: 1995), pp. 84–110, categories of gender, sex, and labour regarding prostitution in, Kamala Kempadoo, *Sexing the Caribbean: Gender, Race, and Sexual Labor* (New York, Routledge: 2008), and links between class, prostitution, pain, and imprisonment within Michael Meranze, *Laboratories of Virtue: Punishment, Revolution, and Authority in Philadelphia, 1760–1835* (Chapel Hill, University of North Carolina Press: 1996), pp. 253–292.

12 In these discussions of state control and the ability of capital to abuse natural sensory worlds, percepticide involves 'self-blinding' oneself from the politics of torture and pain imposed by the modern state. This is caused by the power of the spectacle and the fear of perceiving the anguish of the other as a threat to the self. Diana Taylor, *Disappearing Acts: Spectacles of Gender and Nationalism in Argentina's "Dirty War"* (Durham, NC, Duke University Press: 1997), pp. 119–182.

13 See telephone workers within, Laura Levine Frader, 'From Muscles to Nerves: Gender, "Race" and the Body at Work in France 1919–1939', *International Review of Social History* 44.7 (1999), pp. 123–147, implications of sensory control on Chicago construction within, Adam Mack, *Sensing Chicago: Noisemakers, Strikebreakers, and Muckrakers* (Urbana, Illinois Press: 2015), pp. 51–70, and spaces of fulfilment away from work within, Lynn Sally, 'Fantasy Lands and Kinesthetic Thrills: Sensorial Consumption, the Shock of Modernity and Spectacle as Total-Body Experience at Coney Island', *Senses and Society* 1.3 (2006), pp. 293–309; Colin Fisher, *Urban Green: Nature, Recreation, and the Working Class in Industrial Chicago* (Chapel Hill, University of North Carolina Press: 2016), pp. 50–56, 124–126.

14 For ability and disability in discussions of work and the senses see, Rosemarie Garland-Thomson, *Extraordinary Bodies: Figuring Physical Disability in American Culture and Literature* (New York, Columbia University Press: 2017), pp. 46–49; Dan Goodley, *Dis/Ability Studies: Theorising Disablism and Ableism* (London, Routledge: 2014), pp. 83–98; Ruth O'Brien, *Crippled Justice: The History of Modern Disability Policy in the Workplace* (Chicago, IL, University of Chicago: 2001), pp. 63–87. See also, Catherine Kudlick, 'Disability History: Why We Need Another "Other"', *AHR* 108.3 (2003), pp. 763–793; D. C. Baynton, 'Disability and the Justification for Inequality in American History' in Paul Longmore

and Lauri Umansky (eds.), *The New Disability History* (New York, New York Universtiy Press: 2001), pp. 33–57. Sarah Rose, '"Crippled" Hands: Disability in Labor and Working-Class History', *Labor: Studies in Working-Class History of the Americas* 2.1 (2005), pp. 27–54. For additional analysis see, deafness and noise abatement within, Hans-Joachim Braun, 'Turning a Deaf Ear? Industrial Noise and Noise Control in Germany since the 1920s' in Trevor Pinch and Karin Bijsterveld (eds.), *The Oxford Handbook of Sound Studies* (New York, Oxford University Press: 2017), pp. 58–78, and analysis of sensory deprivation and deafness within, Allard Dembe, *Occupation and Disease: How Social Factors Affect the Conception of Work-Related Disorders* (New Haven, CT, Yale University Press: 1996), pp. 160–228; Jan Branson and Don Miller, *Damned for Their Difference: The Cultural Construction of Deaf People As "Disabled": a Sociological History* (Washington, DC, Gallaudet: 2002).

15 The pecuniary goals of dividing and categorising labour include vast aspects of sensory othering that include gender, which frequently mark specific bodies into domestic spaces or able to only perform specialised work. Bureaucratic jobs are often tied to reason and rationality deemed masculine whereas affect and empathy positions tie women to specific organisational spaces of education and healthcare. Women stepping outside of these bounds have historically been deemed aggressive. Sound and speech are commonly important in these strictures, as volume and timbre can define women as outside of normal discussion tactics regarding turn-taking and interrupting. Sensory worlds further differentiation of organisational spaces where women are set for greater control from the outlines of patriarchal capital and hegemonic masculinity. Joan Acker, 'Hierarchies, Jobs, Bodies: A Theory of Gendered Organizations', *Gender & Society* 4 (1990), pp. 139–158. See also, earlier separations of domestic spaces at performative fairs within, Catherine Kelly, '"The Consummation of Rural Prosperity and Happiness": New England Agricultural Fairs and the Construction of Class and Gender, 1810–1860', *American Quarterly* 49 (September, 1997), pp. 574–602, domestic work and violations of sexuality and touch within; Laura Gowing, *Common Bodies: Women, Touch, and Power in Seventeenth-Century England* (New Haven, CT, Yale University Press: 2003), pp. 61–77, the obsessive sexual impulses that class inferiority and disability created within, Barry Reay, *Watching Hannah: Sex, Horror and Bodily De-Formation in Victorian England* (London, Reaktion: 2004), the meanings of women's work through the sensory imagination of Margaret Cavendish within, Constance Classen, *The Color of Angels: Cosmology, Gender, and the Aesthetic Imagination* (London, Routledge: 1998), pp. 86–106, and the definitions of the masculine working body and disability in, Edward Steven Slavishak, *Bodies of Work: Civic Display and Labor in Industrial Pittsburgh* (Durham, NC, Duke University Press: 2008).

16 For introduction to senses, modernity, and state power see, David Howes and Constance Classen, *Ways of Sensing: Understanding the Senses in Society* (New York, Routledge: 2014); Lewis Mumford, *Technics and Civilization* (New York, Harcourt Brace: 1934); Norbert Elias, *The Civilizing Process* (Oxford, Blackwell: 2000 [1939]). See also, management of the worker and sensory literature within, Eric Schocket, *Vanishing Moments: Class and American Literature* (Ann Arbor, University of Michigan Press: 2006), pp. 168–180, and embodiment of worker resistance in literature within, William Scott, *Troublemakers: Power, Representation, and the Fiction of the Mass Worker* (New Brunswick, NJ, Rutgers: 2012), pp. 47–61, 101–103.

17 This debate has often been highlighted in discussions of sound and noise control. Jacques Attali, *Noise: The Political Economy of Music* (Minneapolis, University of Minnesota Press: 1985), pp. 69–77; Michael Mopas, 'Howling Winds: Sound,

Sense, and the Politics of Noise Regulation', *Canadian Journal of Law and Society* 34.2 (2019), pp. 307–325; Davina Cooper, 'Far Beyond "The Early Morning Crowing of a Farmyard Cock": Revisiting the Place of Nuisance within Legal and Political Discourse', *Social & Legal Studies* 14.1 (2002), pp. 5–35; David Novak, 'Noise' in Matt Sakakeeny and David Novak (eds.), *Keywords in Sound* (Durham, NC, Duke University Press: 2005), pp. 125–138. Peter Payer, 'The Age of Noise: Early Reactions in Vienna, 1870–1914', *Journal of Urban History* 33.5 (2007), pp. 773–793; Raymond Smilor, 'Cacophony at 34th and 6th: The Noise Problem in America, 1900–1936', *American Studies* 18 (1977), pp. 23–38; Raymond Smilor 'Personal Boundaries in the Urban Environment: The Legal Attack on Noise, 1865–1930', *Environmental Review* 3 (1979), pp. 24–36; John Picker, 'The Soundproof Study: Victorian Professionals, Work Space, and Urban Noise', *Victorian Studies* 42.3 (1999), pp. 427–453; Michael Bass, *Street Music in the Metropolis: Correspondence and Observations on Law, and Proposed Amendments* (London, Murray: 1864); Meredith Ward, *Static in the System: Noise and the Soundscape of American Cinema Culture* (Oakland, University of California Press: 2019); Lawrence Baron, 'Noise and Degeneration: Theodor Lessing's Crusade for Quiet', *Journal of Contemporary History* 17 (1982), pp. 165–178; Karin Bijsterveld, 'The Diabolical Symphony of the Mechanical Age: Technology and Symbolism of Sound in European and North American Noise Abatement Campaigns, 1900–40', *Social Studies of Science* 31.1 (2001), pp. 37–70; Karin Bijsterveld, *Mechanical Sound: Technology, Culture and Public Problems of Noise in the Twentieth Century* (Cambridge, MA, MIT Press: 2008), pp. 167–188. See also, histories of body, machine, and sound control regarding streamlining of modern labour within, Jon Agar, 'Bodies, Machines, and Noise' in Iwan Rhys Morus (ed.), *Bodies/Machines* (Oxford, Berg: 2002), pp. 197–220. Thompson, *Soundscape of Modernity*, pp. 120–148. See also, Peter Coates, 'The Strange Stillness of the Past: Toward an Environmental History of Sound and Noise', *Environmental History* 10 (October, 2005), pp. 636–665; James Mansell, *The Age of Noise in Britain: Hearing Modernity* (Urbana, University of Illinois Press: 2017). Lilian Radovac, 'The "War on Noise": Sound and Space in La Guardia's New York', *American Quarterly* 63.3 (2011), pp. 733–760.

18 Jonathan Crary, *Techniques of the Observer: On Vision and Modernity in the Nineteenth Century* (Cambridge, MA, MIT Press: 1990); Emily Thompson, *The Soundscape of Modernity: Architectural Acoustics and the Culture of Listening in America, 1900–1933* (Cambridge, MA, MIT Press: 2002); Chris Otter, *The Victorian Eye: A Political History of Light and Vision in Britain, 1800–1910* (Chicago, IL, University of Chicago: 2008); James Scott, *Seeing Like a State: How Certain Schemes to Improve the Human Condition Have Failed* (New Haven, CT, Yale University Press: 2008), pp. Christopher Otter, 'Cleansing and Clarifying: Technology and Perception in Nineteenth-Century London', *Journal of British Studies* 43.1 (January, 2004), pp. 40–64; Jonathan Crary, *Suspensions of Perception: Attention, Spectacle, and Modern Culture* (Cambridge, MA, MIT Press: 1999). See also, light and power within, David Nye, *American Illuminations: Urban Lighting, 1800–1920* (Cambridge, MA, MIT Press: 2019), pp. 61–84, constructed sensory categories of visible poverty in English literature within, Ann Jessie van Sant, *Eighteenth-Century Sensibility and the Novel: The Senses in Social Context* (Cambridge, Cambridge University Press: 2004), pp. 17–21, surveillance through the non-visual within, Mark Smith, 'Transcending, Othering, Detecting: Smell, Premodernity, Modernity', *Postmedieval* 3.4 (2012), pp. 380–390, and the reading of sound policies of the SA and streamlining of a stable rhythm of the working class within, Carolyn Birdsall, *Nazi Soundscapes: Sound, Technology and Urban Space in Germany, 1933–1945* (Amsterdam, Amsterdam University Press: 2012), pp. 37–53.

19 David Henkin, *City Reading: Written Words and Public Spaces in Antebellum New York* (New York, Columbia University Press: 1998), quote on p. 64. For more on architecture and sensory influence see, Martino Stierli, *Montage and the Metropolis: Architecture, Modernity, and the Representation of Space* (New Haven, CT, Yale University Press: 2019), pp. 106–124; Juhani Pallasmaa, *The Eyes of the Skin: Architecture and the Senses* (Chichester, Wiley: 2014); Ole Möystad, *Cognition and the Built Environment* (London, Routledge: 2018); Sandy Isenstadt, *Electric Light: An Architectural History* (Cambridge, MA, MIT Press: 2019), pp. 211–231. Mariana Valverde, 'Seeing Like a City: The Dialectic of Modern and Premodern Ways of Seeing in Urban Governance', *Law & Society Review* 45.2 (2011), pp. 277–312. See also, gridding and spatialising the city through the senses within, Clare Brant, 'Urban Sensations: Motion and Commotion in Eighteenth Century Cities' in Constance Classen and Anne Vila (eds.), Volume IV of *A Cultural History of the Senses* (London, Bloomsbury: 2014), pp. 41–64.

20 John Gay, *Trivia, or The Art of Walking the Streets of London* (London, S. Powell for G. Risk: 1716); Penelope Corfield, 'Walking the City Streets', *Journal of Urban History* 16.2 (1990), pp. 132–174; Catharina Löffler, *Walking in the City: Urban Experience and Literary Psychogeography in Eighteenth-Century London* (Metzler, Springer: 2017), pp. 108–113, 150–152. For more on the *flaneur*, walking the city, and sensory skills see, David Howes, 'Hyperesthesia, or, The Sensual Logic of Late Capitalism' in David Howes (ed.), *Empire of the Senses: The Sensual Culture Reader* (London, Bloomsbury: 2005), pp. 281–303; Michael Keith, 'Walter Benjamin, Urban Studies, and the Narratives of City Life' in Gary Bridge and Sophie Watson (eds.), *A Companion to the City* (Oxford, Blackwell: 2003), pp. 410–429; Susan Buck-Morss, *The Dialectics of Seeing: Walter Benjamin and the Arcades Project* (Cambridge, MA, MIT Press: 1991), pp. 304–345; Esther Leslie, 'Ruin and Rubble in the Arcades' in Beatrice Hanssen (ed.), *Walter Benjamin and the Arcades Project* (London, Continuum: 2006), pp. 87–112; Tim Ingold, 'Culture on the Ground: The World Perceived through the Feet', *Journal of Material Culture*, 9 (2004), pp. 315–340. See also phenomenology of the city in, Nicolas Kenny, *The Feel of the City: Experiences of Urban Transformation* (Toronto, University of Toronto Press: 2014), pp. 13–15, 156–166, 203–208, negotiations of sensory deprivation and stimulation in, Deborah Parsons, *Streetwalking the Metropolis: Women, the City, and Modernity* (Oxford, Oxford University Press: 2000), and the literary fears of 'exposure' to an all-seeing city within, Deborah Epstein Nord, *Walking the Victorian Streets: Women, Representation, and the City* (Ithaca, NY, Cornell: 2006), pp. 142–157.

21 For a reading of specific sensory skills see, P. K. Andersson, '"Bustling, Crowding, and Pushing": Pickpockets and the Nineteenth-Century Street Crowd', *Urban History* 41.2 (2014), pp. 291–310. See also, the sensory analysis of labour and touching within, Michael Ondaatje's *Skin of a Lion* (1987) and Tillie Olsen's *Yonnondio* (1975) in, Janet Zandy, *Hands: Physical Labor, Class, and Cultural Work* (New Brunswick, NJ, Rutgers: 2004), pp. 84–93.

22 For background on phenomenology and labour see Simon Charlesworth, *A Phenomenology of Working Class Experience* (Cambridge, Cambridge University Press: 2000); John Hockey and Jacquelyn Allen-Collinson, 'The Sensorium at Work: the Sensory Phenomenology of the Working Body', *The Sociological Review* 57.2 (2009), pp. 217–239; Debra Gimlin, 'What is "Body Work"? A Review of the Literature', *Sociology Compass* 1.1 (2007), pp. 353–370; Kelvin Low and Devorah Kalekin-Fishman, 'Sensory Urbanities: Excursions in the City' in Kelvin Lowmand Devorah Kalekin-Fishman (eds.), *Senses in Cities: Experiences of Urban Settings* (New York, Routledge: 2018), pp. 1–8. See also, the

labouring networks of the Nigerian oil industry within, Robert Sullivan, *The Geography of the Everyday: Toward an Understanding of the Given* (Athens, University of Georgia Press: 2017), and relaying experience as vital for narratives of labour within, Richard Hoggart, *The Uses of Literacy* (London, Routledge: 2017 [1957]), pp. 48–71.

23 Leo Marx, *The Machine in the Garden: Technology and the Pastoral Ideal in America* (New York, Oxford University Press:1973), pp. 367–385. See also, the noise of machine work, altered perceptions, and the sounds of female resistance at the Lowell Mills within, Mark Smith, 'The Garden in the Machine: Listening to Early American Industrialization' in Trevor Pinch and Karin Bijsterveld (eds.), *The Oxford Handbook of Sound Studies* (New York, Oxford University Press: 2017), pp. 39–57. Chad Montrie, '"I Think Less of the Factory Than of My Native Dell": Labor, Nature, and the Lowell Mill Girls', *Environmental History* 9.2 (2004), pp. 275–295. Workers throughout American sweatshops in the Brown Decades wrote often of the sensory worlds of anguish in industrialised America, often from women on the sewing factory floor who faced unwanted touches from managers and co-workers. Daniel Bender, *Sweated Work, Weak Bodies: Anti-Sweatshop Campaigns and Languages of Labor* (New Brunswick, NJ, Rutgers: 2004), pp. 42–60, 113–114.

24 Richard Clay, 'Smells, Bells and Touch: Iconoclasm in Paris during the French Revolution', *Journal for Eighteenth-Century Studies* 35.4 (2012), pp. 521–533. For more on senses, class, and the French Revolution see, Sophia Rosenfeld, 'The Social Life of the Senses: A New Approach to Eighteenth Century Politics and Public Life' in Constance Classen and Anne Vila (eds.), Volume IV of *A Cultural History of the Senses* (London, Bloomsbury: 2014), pp. 21–40. See also, space, protests, and agitation in French theatres of the early nineteenth century within, Corbin, *Time, Desire, and Horror*, pp. 39–61.

25 Take for example, the mandatory whipping allotted to any black sailors who made 'any clamorous noise' or sang any 'indecent songs' outlined in an 1806 law from Charleston, South Carolina. Seth Rockman, *Scraping by: Wage Labor, Slavery, and Survival in Early Baltimore* (Baltimore, MD, Johns Hopkins: 2009), pp. 50–52; Mark Smith, 'Getting in Touch with Slavery and Freedom', *JAH* 95.2 (2008), pp. 381–391. For slave sounds and plantation quietude see, Ronald Radano, 'Black Music Labor and the Animated Properties of Slave Sound', *Boundary 2* 43.1 (2016), pp. 173–208; Mark Smith, *Listening to Nineteenth-Century America* (Chapel Hill, University of North Carolina Press: 2001); Richard Cullen Rath, 'African Music in Seventeenth-Century Jamaica: Cultural Transit and Transition', *WMQ* 50.4 (October, 1993), pp. 700–726.

26 Shane White and Graham White, *The Sounds of Slavery: Discovering African American History through Songs, Sermons, and Speech* (Boston, MA, Beacon: 2005); Katrina Dyonne Thompson, *Ring Shout, Wheel About: The Racial Politics of Music and Dance in North American Slavery* (Urbana, University of Illinois Press: 2014), pp. 13–24. See also, Jennifer Lynn Stoever, *The Sonic Color Line. Race and the Cultural Politics of Listening* (New York, New York University Press: 2016), pp. 29–77; Louis Onuorah Chude-Sokei, *The Sound of Culture: Diaspora and Black Technopoetics* (Middletown, CT, Wesleyan: 2015); Richard Cullen Rath, 'Echo and Narcissus: The Afrocentric Pragmatism of W. E. B. Du Bois', *JAH* 84.2 (September, 1997), pp. 461–495. For more on race, noise, and sound see, Clare Corbould, 'Streets, Sounds and Identity in Interwar Harlem', *Journal of Social History* 40.4 (2007), pp. 859–894; Joel Dinerstein, *Swinging the Machine: Modernity, Technology, and African American Culture between the World Wars* (Amherst, University of Massachusetts Press: 2003), pp. 42–46. Sartorial ideologies also survived the Middle Passage, as slave labourers defined

their subjective identities as resistance through fashioning clothing and hairstyles against masters. Shane White and Graham White, *Stylin': African American Expressive Culture from Its Beginnings to the Zoot Suit* (Ithaca, NY, Cornell: 1998), pp. 56–60; Helen Bradley Foster, *New Raiments of Self: African American Clothing in the Antebellum South* (Oxford, Berg: 1997).

27 For examples, see Jean Comaroff, 'The Empire's Old Clothes: Fashioning the Colonial Subject' in David Howes (ed.), *Cross-Cultural Consumption: Global Markets, Local Realities* (Abingdon, Taylor & Francis: 1996), pp.19–38, Andrew Rotter, 'Empires of the Senses: How Seeing, Hearing, Smelling, Tasting, and Touching Shaped Imperial Encounters', *Diplomatic History* 35.1 (2011), pp. 3–19; Warwick Anderson, 'Excremental Colonialism: Public Health and the Poetics of Pollution', *Critical Inquiry* 21.3 (1995), pp. 640–669; Joseph Childers, 'Foreign Matter: Imperial Filth' in William Cohen and Ryan Johnson (eds.), *Filth: Dirt, Disgust, and Modern Life* (Minneapolis, University of Minnesota Press: 2005), pp. 201–224; David Barnes, 'The Senses in Medicine: Seeing, Hearing and Smelling Disease' in Constance Classen (ed.), *A Cultural History of the Senses in the Age of Empire* (London, Bloomsbury: 2014), pp. 137–160. See also, experiments on sensory acuity regarding race, criminality, and environment from twentieth-century sociologist Frances Kellor within, Khalil Gibran Muhammad, *The Condemnation of Blackness: Race, Crime, and the Making of Modern Urban America* (Cambridge, MA, Harvard University Press: 2011), pp. 89–106, and sensory racism in Paul Gilroy, *Against Race: Imagining Political Culture Beyond the Color Line* (Cambridge, MA, Harvard University Press: 2001), pp. 11–23, 35–48, 155–164.

28 For environmental justice and the senses see, Hsuan Hsu, 'Naturalist Smellscapes and Environmental Justice', *American Literature* 88.4 (2016), pp. 787–814; Laura Pulido, *Environmentalism and Economic Justice: Two Chicano Struggles in the Southwest* (Tucson, University of Arizona Press: 1996); Martin Manalansan IV, 'Immigrant Domesticity and the Politics of Olfaction in the Global City' in Jim Drobnick (ed.), *The Smell Culture Reader* (Oxford, Berg: 2006), pp. 41–52; Claudia Clark, *Radium Girls: Women and Industrial Health Reform, 1910–1935* (Chapel Hill, University of North Carolina Press: 1997); Alan Derickson, 'Industrial Refugees: The Migration of Silicotics from the Mines of North America and South Africa in the Early 20th Century', *Labor History* 29.1 (1988), pp. 66–89; Christine Meisner Rosen, '"Knowing" Industrial Pollution: Nuisance Law and the Power of Tradition in a Time of Rapid Economic Change, 1840–1864', *Environmental History* 8.4 (2003), pp. 565–597. See also, Peter Sloterdijk, *Terror from the Air*, trans. Amy Patton and Steve Corcoran (Los Angeles, CA, Semiotext(e): 2009), the role of portraying pain and toxicity within lawsuits in, Ellen Griffith Spears, *Baptized in PCBs: Race, Pollution, and Justice in an All-American Town* (Chapel Hill, University of North Carolina Press: 2014), pp. 264–290, the pain of colic, arthritis, and encephalopathy felt by painters within, Christopher Sellers, *Hazards of the Job: From Industrial Disease to Environmental Health Science* (Chapel Hill, University of North Carolina Press: 1997), pp. 13–26, the role of women's bodies, the sense of smell, and concerns with ventilation in, Michelle Murphy, *Sick Building Syndrome and the Problem of Uncertainty: Environmental Politics, Technoscience, and Women Workers* (Durham, NC, Duke University Press: 2006), pp. 24–28, and state megaprojects, environmental perception, and altered sensory meanings of the home within, Joy Parr, *Sensing Changes Technologies, Environments and the Everyday, 1953–2003* (Vancouver, University of British Columbia Press: 2014), pp. 1–24.

29 Q. H. Tan, 'Smell in the City: Smoking and Olfactory Politics', *Urban Studies* 50.1 (2013), pp. 55–71; Dipesh Chakrabarty, 'Open Space/Public Place: Garbage, Modernity and India', *South Asia: Journal of South Asian Studies* 14.1 (1991), pp. 15–31; J. D. Esty, 'Excremental Postcolonialism', *Contemporary Literature*

40.1 (1999), pp. 22–59; Stephen Greenblatt, 'Filthy Rites', *Daedalus* 111.3 (1982), pp. 1–16.

30 Much of the debate on senses and the city has focused on historical issues with odor and zoning. Andrew Hurley, 'Busby's Stink Boat and the Regulation of Nuisance Trades, 1865–1918' in Andrew Hurley (ed.), *Common Fields: An Environmental History of St. Louis* (St. Louis, Missouri Historical Society Press: 1997), pp. 145–162; Sarah Buhler, 'Law's Sense of Smell: Odours and Evictions at the Landlord and Tenant Board' in Sheryl Hamilton, Diana Majury, Dawn Moore, Neil Sargent, and Christiane Wilke (eds.), *Sensing Law* (New York, Routledge: 2017), pp. 189–194; Dayna Scott, 'The Smell of Neglect' in Sheryl Hamilton, Diana Majury, Dawn Moore, Neil Sargent, and Christiane Wilke (eds.), *Sensing Law* (New York, Routledge: 2017), pp. 162–178. These zoning issues often centered in racial questions of othering and segregation. C. Y. Chiang, 'Monterey-by-the-Smell: Odors and Social Conflict on the California Coastline', *Pacific Historical Review* 73.2 (2004), pp. 183–214; C. Y. Chiang, 'The Nose Knows: The Sense of Smell in American History', *Journal of American History* 95.2 (2008), pp. 405–416. Carl Zimring, 'Dirty Work: How Hygiene and Xenophobia Marginalized the American Waste Trades, 1870–1930', *Environmental History* 9.1 (2004), pp. 80–101; Ellen Stroud, 'Dead Bodies in Harlem: Environmental History and the Geography of Death' in Andrew Isenberg (ed.), *The Nature of Cities* (Rochester, University of Rochester Press: 2006), pp. 62–76; Julie Sze, *Noxious New York: The Racial Politics of Urban Health and Environmental Justice* (Cambridge, MA, MIT Press: 2007). See also, debates on race, resistance, and targeting of pollution within, Dolores Greenberg, 'Reconstructing Race and Protest: Environmental Justice in New York City', *Environmental History* 5.2 (2000), pp. 223–250, class relations regarding identity and the dead body within, Michael Sappol, *A Traffic of Dead Bodies: Anatomy and Embodied Social Identity in Nineteenth-Century America* (Princeton, NJ, Princeton University Press: 2002), meanings of revolt and dirt within, Ivan Illich, 'The Dirt of Cities, the Aura of Cities, the Smell of the Dead, Utopia in the Odorless City' in Malcolm Miles, Iain Borden, and Tim Hall (eds.), *The Cities Culture Reader* (London, Routledge: 2000), pp. 355–359, and the difficulty of creating linked protest movements within working-class communities in, Janet Ore, 'Mobile Home Syndrome: Engineered Woods and the Making of a New Domestic Ecology in the Post-World War II Era', *Technology and Culture* 52 (2011), pp. 260–286.

31 Alex Rhys-Taylor, 'The Essences of Multiculture: a Sensory Exploration of an Inner-City Street Market', *Identities* 20.4 (2013), pp. 393–406; Alex Rhys-Taylor, 'Urban Sensations: A Retrospective of Multisensory Drift' in Constance Classen and David Howes (eds.), Volume VI *of A Cultural History of the Senses* (London, Bloomsbury: 2014), pp. 55–75; Benjamin Zeitlyn, 'Making Sense of the Smell of Bangladesh', *Childhood* 21.2 (2014), pp. 175–189.

32 For finding common sensory worlds see, Monica Montserrat Degen, *Sensing Cities: Regenerating Public Life in Barcelona and Manchester* (London, Routledge: 2015), pp. 78–83; Richard Schechner, 'Rasaesthetics' in Sally Banes and André Lepecki (eds.), *The Senses in Performance* (New York, Routledge: 2007), pp. 10–28; Alex Rhys-Taylor, *Food and Multiculture: A Sensory Ethnography of East London* (London, Bloomsbury: 2018), pp. 119–136. See also, review of current work on urban sensoriums within, Peter Jackson, 'Urban Ethnography' in Anja Schwanhäußer (ed.), *Sensing the City: A Companion to Urban Anthropology* (Basel, Bauverlag: 2016), pp. 17–40, urban modernity through smell in, Silja Laine, 'Sensory Environments of Poverty Seen through the Writings of Runar Schildt, Toivo Tarvas, and Elvi Sinervo' in Lieven Ameel, Jason Finch, Silja Laine, and Richard Dennis (eds.), *The Materiality of Literary Narratives in Urban History* (New York, Routledge: 2019), pp. 75–92, modern fisherman in Scotland

who use technological apparatuses of the boat to extend their sensoriums deep into the sea within, Penny McCall Howard, *Environment, Labour and Capitalism at Sea: Working the Ground in Scotland* (Manchester, Manchester University Press: 2017), pp. 89–117, sensory skills used at different stages of iron production work in early New England within, Krysta Ryzewski, 'The Production Process as Sensory Experience: Making and Seeing Iron in Colonial New England' in Jo Day (ed.), *Making Senses of the Past: Toward a Sensory Archaeology* (Carbondale, Southern Illinois: 2013), pp. 351–370, and skills of touch used by French seamstresses during the early twentieth century within, Robert Henrey, *The Little Madeleine by Mrs. Robert Henrey* (London, Dent: 1951).

33 George Orwell, *The Road to Wigan Pier* (San Diego, CA, Harcourt Brace: 1958 [1937]), pp. 127–142; Glenn Kuehn, 'The Aesthetics of Smells and Tastes' in Andrew Light and Jonathan Smith (eds.), *The Aesthetics of Everyday Life* (New York, Columbia University Press: 2005), pp. 177–193. For more on degradation of working-class aesthetics see, David Wright, *Understanding Cultural Taste: Sensation, Skill and Sensibility* (London, Palgrave Macmillan: 2015), pp. 36–41. See also, England, Ireland, and the piggishness of domestic cottages in, Joseph Nugent, 'The Human Snout: Pigs, Priests, and Peasants in the Parlor', *Senses and Society* 4.3 (2009), pp. 283–301, the meanings of class, odor, and reform within, Alain Corbin, *The Foul and the Fragrant: Odor and the French Social Imagination* (Cambridge, MA, Harvard University Press: 1986), pp. 111–160, and the hygienic worlds of builders in nineteenth-century Paris in, Corbin, *Time, Desire, and Horror*, pp. 158–171.

34 See, Bender, 'Sensing Labor', pp. 243–265. For some of these original debates regarding culture, class consciousness, and identity see, Lawrence McDonnell, '"You Are Too Sentimental": Problems and Suggestions for a New Labor History', *Journal of Social History* 17 (1983–1984), pp. 629–646; Sean Wilentz, 'Against Exceptionalism: Class Consciousness and the American Labor Movement, 1790–1920', *International Labor and Working Class History* 26 (Fall, 1984), pp. 1–24; Herbert Gutman, 'Work, Culture, and Society in Industrializing America, 1815–1919', *AHR* 78 (June, 1973), pp. 531–588.

35 For parasites, capitalism, and systems see, Shaviro, *No Speed Limit*, pp. 41–60; Michel Serres, *The Parasite*, trans. Lawrence Schehr (Baltimore, MD, Johns Hopkins: 1982).

36 For more on sensory resistance see, Constance Classen, 'Other Ways to Wisdom: Learning through the Senses across Cultures',*International Review of Education* 45.3 (1999), pp. 269–280; Peter Stallybrass and Allon White, *The Politics and Poetics of Transgression* (Ithaca, NY, Cornell: 1986), pp. 27–79; Sami Khatib, '"Sensuous Supra-Sensuous": The Aesthetics of Real Absraction' in Samir Gandesha and Johan Hartle (eds.), *Aesthetic Marx*, *Aesthetic Marx* (London, Bloomsbury: 2018), pp. 49–72; Elizabeth Maddock Dillon, 'Atlantic Aesthesis: Books and *Sensus Communis* in the New World', *Early American Literature* 51.2 (2016), pp. 367–395. See also, ideas of escape, social categorisation of childlike play, and resistance within carnival and fairgrounds in, Alessandro Olsaretti, 'Urban Culture, Curiosity and the Aesthetics of Distance: the Representation of Picturesque Carnivals in Early Victorian Travelogues to the Levant', *Social History* 32.3 (2007), pp. 247–270, and the alternative sensory epistemologies within, Boaventura de Sousa Santos, *The End of the Cognitive Empire: The Coming of Age of Epistemologies of the South* (Durham, NC, Duke University Press: 2018), pp. 166–180.

3

'WHAT ARE THOSE ONES WITH THE HAMMERS?'

Teaching Working-class History in Secondary Schools

Laura Christine Price

> The philosophers have only interpreted the world, in various ways; the point is to change it.[1]
>
> *Karl Marx,* Theses on Feuerbach.

In 2008, I was faced with a choice: having gained places on both a secondary history PGCE programme and a PhD course, I had to decide whether I would pursue teaching – which I felt, as a bright, educated working-class woman, spurred on by Marx's suggestion that we must change the world, was my duty to society – or research, which is what I thought I would ultimately gain more satisfaction from. I opted to take the PhD and tried to ignore the part of my conscience that said I was making a selfish choice. When I failed to gain funding for my PhD, I decided to self-fund and pay for my fees by working part-time in education. After a brief spell as a disability support worker in a local university, I gained employment as a learning mentor at a school near my home in West Yorkshire. Through many changes in government policy following the 2010 election which decimated funding for the project I was working on – to encourage working-class children to go to university – my school kept me on, first as a cover supervisor (an internal supply teacher), then as a higher level teaching assistant, and then as an unqualified teacher of English and history. When I completed my PhD in 2016 I applied for a number of academic jobs, gaining interviews in some, but when offered the chance by my school to train as a teacher, I decided that it was the right thing to do: as someone in poor health, years of precarious contract-based employment seemed daunting, and whilst secondary teaching is an intense, all-consuming profession, I would at least have job stability in a warm, friendly, supportive school in a community that deserves the very best from its teachers. Marx's

DOI: 10.4324/9780429344084-5

grip on me as a graduate student had still not been released, and I knew that secondary teaching was my way to change the world for the better. These reflections, therefore, are based on my experience of being both a historian of working-class history, and a working-class teacher of history (and English) to working-class children. Though I have consulted various texts and documents to structure my thoughts, they remain my own personal philosophy for teaching working-class history, and should not be construed as a rigorously researched roadmap, nor the policy of the school that has, happily, employed me for fourteen years.

This short chapter will consider how working-class history is taught in secondary schools, focusing on Key Stage 3 (Years 7, 8, and 9; students aged 11–14) and Key Stage 4 (Years 10 and 11; students aged 14–16). My teaching experience covers Key Stage 3, Key Stage 4 and undergraduate level, and therefore it would not be appropriate for me to engage with discussions on working-class history at A level.[2] I will also focus on the history curriculum in England, given that my own experience is as a teacher in England.

Heads of history have four key concerns when designing a curriculum: the knowledge and expertise of their staff; the topics that are likely to be enthusiastically received by their students; the National Curriculum at Key Stage 3; and exam specifications at Key Stage 4. Despite the promise of freedom from the National Curriculum offered by the government when it introduced its academisation drive in 2010 (building on work already done by the previous government), schools are obliged to provide a broad and balanced curriculum. Coupled with an increased focus on curriculum design and delivery by Ofsted, this has resulted in many schools reverting to use the history National Curriculum to design their Key Stage 3 curricula. This means that there are many constraints upon heads of department when it comes to devising a curriculum that is stimulating, challenging, engaging, broad, balanced and compliant with both school and governmental policies. Unsurprisingly, a consideration of ensuring the history of working-class people is taught is low on any leader's agenda.

There are, however, plenty of schools who choose to cover topics relating to working-class history. As well as at my own school, and the school I attended in the 1990s, the pages of *Teaching History* show that working-class history is still alive in secondary schools, albeit possibly with a weak pulse. Robert Poole's article on 'Reinterpreting Peterloo' sets out his ideas on how Peterloo should be taught, giving secondary teachers much food for thought on the real role of working-class people at the meeting.[3] More recently, Jacob Olivey presents a thoughtful and thorough approach to designing historical enquiries on Chartism for Year 8 pupils in an article that describes an ambitious and engaging way of teaching a topic that is a regular feature of the Key Stage 3 curriculum in many schools.[4] What was apparent to me as I scanned the last twenty years' worth of articles for *Teaching History*, though, is that working-class history is now very seldom commented upon in its pages. Although this could indicate that the facts of and discourse around working-class history, according to its contributors, are now settled – as unlikely as that sounds – it seems more probable that academic trends, and the increasingly reduced interest in working-class history amongst scholars, are reflected in what is taught in English secondary schools. There is a growing emphasis on the use of historical scholarship in the design of school curricula, and though many historians continue to produce excellent work in our field, we cannot blame teachers for reflecting what they find – for example in the pages of *Teaching History*, which offers both pedagogical and historical articles – in the curricula they design.

Recent publications give us clues about the changing relationship historians, and teachers of history, have to working-class history. A newly published handbook for history teachers, *What is History Teaching, Now?*, edited by Alex Fairlamb and Rachel Ball, refers to working-class history only obliquely, for example in Sasha Smith's chapter on designing a diverse curriculum, which denotes the varied 'voices' that her school's history curriculum includes.[5] There is a great deal of space given in the volume to representing diverse voices and lesser-known histories, and creating both 'windows' (where students can 'see' identities different to theirs) and 'mirrors' (where students have their own identity reflected back to them through curriculum choice).[6] While Smith clearly includes working-class people in her own school's history curriculum, we cannot be sure that this is common practice given working-class history's decline in prominence. Twenty years ago, in David Cannadine's response to E. H. Carr's classic *What is History?*, several historians – including Susan Pedersen and Alice Kessler-Harris – stated that class as a category of historical study and analysis was now 'no longer fashionable'.[7] Fast forward to more recent times and we see that Helen Carr and Suzannah Lipscomb's *What is History, Now?* contains very little reference to working-class history at all, instead focusing on other marginalised histories, such as disability history and the history of indigenous peoples.[8] This is both necessary and deeply significant, and does not mean that working-class history has to be edged out: there is room for all stories in our research and teaching of history, and there are many potential intersections we can investigate between 'unfashionable' working-class history and, for example, the decolonisation of our curricula, which, as Carr and Lipscomb point out, has become part of public discourse – and some degree of moral panic.[9]

Both the National Curriculum and the exam boards give English students the option to study working-class history, but it is rarely given prominence. For example, the National Curriculum for history at Key Stage 3 suggests schools teach topics such as the extension of the franchise, women's suffrage and the development of the welfare state.[10] Whilst the National Curriculum has to be followed by local authority schools and is followed by many multi-academy trusts, it only insists on certain categories of study – for example, the development of church, state and society in medieval Britain, 1066–1509. School leaders can choose which topics within this category to study. This means there is no concrete way of knowing what schools choose to teach, and how much working-class history is on the curriculum nationally. Similarly, the exam boards offer topics that include working-class history in their specifications. A thematic study of medicine through time is a popular GCSE choice in many schools, and is included in all major exam boards' list of options. On Edexcel's history GCSE, which my own school teaches, this topic includes the study of how Germ Theory, vaccinations and the Public Health Act 1875 were developed as they related to conditions in industrial cities populated with workers.[11] Whilst there is little to choose from that is explicitly and primarily concerned with working-class history on the GCSE syllabus, there is much that can be drawn out about working-class people in the teaching of the topics.

My role at school is as a teacher of history and English, rather than a subject leader, and as such my influence on the curriculum is limited. Happily, the history curriculum at my school offers various opportunities to teach working-class history, both explicitly and through drawing out my own interest in other schemes of learning. Unsurprisingly, the biggest opportunity to teach traditional working-class history is in a Year 8 (ages 12 and 13) topic on the Industrial Revolution, in which we investigate the impact of the Industrial Revolution on our local area in West Yorkshire. Through this, we teach students about changes in work in Britain and the shift towards industrialised labour, working conditions in mines and factories, living conditions in industrial towns and cities, and the local and national role of protest movements such as Luddism (which prompted one of my students to ask the question in the title of this piece, when instructing students to recall prior learning) and Chartism. In assessing the consequences of the Industrial Revolution on our town and our region, my students can see the significance of working-class history to their own lives and family histories, for example when we learn about the disaster at the colliery in our village in 1893. Students can link this learning with the thematic study of migration that they took in Year 7 (ages 11 and 12), which tracks migration to Britain over time and includes migration from the Indian subcontinent to Britain, when we learn about why so many people from India, Pakistan and Bangladesh came to northern working-class towns following the Second World War (which also links to our study of the British Empire in Year 8). As a school with a significant population of British Indian and British Pakistani students, this bringing of history to life – of making it relevant to my students' own lives – is one of the key factors in history being a popular GCSE option choice.

Emily Folorushno argues that a powerful way of teaching Black history to secondary school children is by 'weaving, blending, and integrating' it into as many schemes of learning as possible.[12] This approach can also be taken with working-class history. When teaching the history of the First World War, as so many secondary school history teachers do, we can look at the role of the working-class conscript or the working-class nurse; when teaching the Holocaust, as the National Curriculum insists we must, we can investigate the lives of working-class Jews prior to Hitler's rise to power, and at working-class resistance to the Final Solution.[13] This is the way that my school teaches – to draw out the strands of our teaching material that we know will engage our students most, which includes 'mirrors' of their own working-class lives. At a time when history is often in the news as a source of moral outrage, as outlined by Charlotte Lydia Riley,[14] we as historians – researchers and teachers alike – must do what we can to ensure that young people continue to engage with history. We can and should welcome developments on decolonising the curriculum and the rise of teaching and learning ethnically diverse histories, and we can and should weave, blend, and integrate this with other marginalised histories, including the history of working-class people. For those of us who teach working-class students – and Black students, Asian students, disabled students, gay students, and any number of other marginalised identities – it is incumbent upon us to impart the histories of their own people alongside wider histories that broaden their horizons. There is never an either/or needed here: schools are willing and able to provide mirrors and windows in many of the subjects they teach, and teachers know that it is our duty to do so. For history teachers, it is also our duty to ensure that working-class history in schools does not die and that our working-class students continue to learn about the people that E. P. Thompson – a great favourite among many school teachers, myself included – insisted that we 'rescue' from 'the enormous condescension of posterity'.[15]

Notes

1 Karl Marx, *Theses on Feuerbach*, 1845, accessed 10 June 2023, https://www.marxists.org/archive/marx/works/1845/theses/theses.htm.

2 For more information on A level history, see Emily Folorunsho and Jo Brunskill, 'Teaching A Level History' in Alex Fairlamb and Rachel Ball (eds.), *What Is History Teaching, Now?* (Woodbridge, John Catt: 2023), pp. 193–207.

3 Robert Poole, 'Polychronicon: Reinterpreting Peterloo', *Teaching History* 129 (December, 2007), pp. 20–21.

4 Jacob Olivey, 'What Did "class" Mean to a Chartist?' *Teaching History* 176 (September, 2019), pp. 60–71.

5 Sasha Smith, 'Constructing a Diverse and Representative Curriculum' in Alex Fairlamb and Rachel Ball (eds.), *What Is History Teaching, Now?* (Woodbridge, John Catt: 2023), p. 374.

6 Smith, 'Constructing a Diverse and Representative Curriculum', p. 371.

7 Alice Kessler-Harris, 'What Is Gender History Now?' in David Cannadine (ed.), *What Is History Now?* (London, Palgrave Macmillan: 2002), p. 102; Susan

Pedersen, 'What Is Political History Now?' in David Cannadine (ed.), *What Is History Now?* (London, Palgrave Macmillan: 2002), p. 40. See also Richard J. Evans' introduction to the reissued *What Is History?* for information on the growth of working-class history. Richard J. Evans, 'Introduction' in E. H. Carr (ed.), *What Is History* (London, Penguin: 2018), p. xxxvii.

8 Helen Carr and Suzannah Lipscomb, eds., *What Is History, Now?* (London, Weidenfeld and Nicolson: 2021).

9 Helen Carr and Suzannah Lipscomb, 'Prologue: Ways in' in Helen Carr and Suzannah Lipscomb (eds.), *What Is History, Now?* (London, Weidenfeld and Nicolson: 2021), p. 5.

10 Department for Education, *History Programmes of Study: Key Stage 3. National Curriculum in England*, 2013, p. 4, accessed 16 June 2023, https://assets.publishing.service.gov.uk/government/uploads/system/uploads/attachment_data/file/239075/SECONDARY_national_curriculum_-_History.pdf.

11 Pearson Edexcel, *GCSE 9-1 History* specification, p. 16, accessed 16 June 2023, https://qualifications.pearson.com/content/dam/pdf/GCSE/History/2016/specification-and-sample-assessments/gcse-9-1-history-specification.pdf.

12 Emily Folorushno, 'Teaching Black British History' in Alex Fairlamb and Rachel Ball (eds.), *What Is History Teaching, Now?* (Woodbridge, John Catt: 2023), p. 404.

13 Department for Education, *History Programmes of Study: Key Stage 3. National Curriculum in England*, 2013, p. 4, accessed June 16, 2023, https://assets.publishing.service.gov.uk/government/uploads/system/uploads/attachment_data/file/239075/SECONDARY_national_curriculum_-_History.pdf.

14 Charlotte Lydia Riley, 'Why History Should Always Be Rewritten' in Helen Carr and Suzannah Lipscomb (eds.), *What Is History, Now?* (London, Weidenfeld and Nicolson: 2021), p. 283.

15 E. P. Thompson, *The Making of the English Working Class* (London, Penguin: 1991), p. 12.

4

'EVERYONE HAS A TALE TO TELL'

Family History, Family Historians, and Working-class Histories

Laura Harrison

Family history is one of the most widely practised forms of public history today, involving millions in historical research, with family historians tracing their ancestors across the globe. Digitisation, the increasing accessibility of archival sources, and genetic genealogy kits have all made family history research one of the most popular online activities in Britain, falling only behind pornography and online shopping.[1] Following the first broadcast of *Who Do You Think You Are?* (*WDYTYA*) in the UK in 2004, there has been an explosion in the numbers of people researching and recording their family history. The BBC television franchise follows a celebrity tracing his or her family history and has produced over 170 UK episodes, several international spin offs, a monthly magazine publication, and a popular website providing tools and guidance to family history researchers.[2] The programme makers describe how 'lost connections and unfamiliar histories are revealed as celebrities trace their family trees; discover stories of courage, joy, sacrifice and resilience – everyone has a tale to tell'.[3] Each episode allows the viewer to follow the unfolding family story as the celebrity protagonist travels in the footsteps of their ancestors through the means of photographs, memories and archival research, with conveniently placed historians and old family acquaintances, an orderly narrative arc and compelling final conclusion.[4]

Family history research is rarely as neat as the on-screen journey of self-discovery depicted in programmes like *WDYTYA*, with its precisely packaged stories and editing suite. Yet, the programme's central premise, that 'everyone has a tale to tell', can be a useful point of convergence for family historians and historians of the working class. The show itself explores a range of historical experiences, but regularly includes working-class histories and stories, with an approach that seeks to include, and even celebrate, accounts of

DOI: 10.4324/9780429344084-6

forbears who may have been a source of social stigma or shame to previous generations – ancestors sent to the workhouse, criminals, unmarried mothers, illegitimate children. As both journalists and historians have noted, part of the appeal of *WDYTYA* is that the family history of the celebrity can stand in place of that of many of the viewers, and the programme publicity regularly emphasises the focus on how 'ordinary' people experienced the past, and the importance of a personalised, 'bottom-up view' of history.[5]

Family history research, and the work of family historians, is a rich and important site for the field of working-class histories. Delving into personal stories, local contexts and everyday experiences can humanise and individualise the past, and bridge the gap between the past and the present. As Malcolm Chase has reminded us, at the heart of social and labour history is a conviction that labouring lives matter.[6] Family history as a practice, as well as the extensive research conducted by family historians, can help us with the retrieval of these lives. Working-class history and family history share many of the same tools, methods and objectives, looking at the gaps in the historical record, uncovering details about lives 'on the margins' and bringing under-represented voices and experiences to the fore. Family history research can also provide new ways of 'doing' history, and of engaging the public with historical research. It is both personal and political, raising important questions about established historical narratives and who does the telling of those histories.

'Everyone does family history nowadays': Family History Research

Family history and genealogy is a thriving business, in both the public and private sectors, and the family history 'boom' and popularity of *WDYTYA* and other similar genealogy programmes shows no signs of abating.[7] As Alison Light has argued:

> Everyone does family history nowadays. Genealogy used to belong only to the wealthy; once upon a time only they owned the past and laid claim to a history based on land and property. Now everyone who can use a computer or go to a local records office has a stake in the past.[8]

However, family history practitioners have long been labelled as 'sentimental amateurs', as 'misty-eyed and syrupy'; ridiculed for a nostalgic approach to history and dismissed by academic historians for producing naval-gazing work of no consequence or interest beyond their own families, their findings deemed 'irrelevant' to the wider historical community.[9] In recent years, these rather simplistic dismissals have been challenged. Writing about her book, *Common People: The History of An English Family* in the *Guardian* in 2014, Alison Light mounts a 'defence of family history', and a rich, varied, and interdisciplinary field of scholarship has emerged around family history research and the practice of family historians. Light's own work outlines a history of the English poor through the lens of her own family history, offering both a compelling history from below, and a history from the inside.[10] Historians have long utilised, but have now begun to explicitly recognise, the value of genealogical methods, have acknowledged the huge amounts of historical data generated by 'amateur' family historians, published work informed by family history and memoir, increasingly discussed the uses of their own family histories in their historical work, and have collaborated with family history researchers on a range of projects.

While family history research has often been considered conservative, (both big and small 'c') with its focus on patrilineal relationships and patriarchal models, its necessary connections to the records and institutions of the state, and a focus on elite, white, patriarchal sources, when practised critically, family history also has, as Tanya Evans has outlined, 'radical potential':

> The construction of a family tree, the discovery of manifold secrets and lies, throw into question the solidity not only of the history of the family, class relationships and the power relations between men and women but also of the history of nation and empire. Each newly discovered document encourages the historian to add to or question the narrative so far.[11]

Far from only being interested in themselves and their ancestors, family historians and family history can ask bigger questions about the social, economic and political forces in the past. Genealogical research can offer a significant lens through which to examine the intersections of identities within the working class, scrutinising the realm of the intimate and the personal, and uncovering queer, migrant, poor, and indigenous stories and experiences. Justin Bengry has discussed the potential of family history research to open up new ways of thinking about queer lives in the past, filling in details and complexities about individual lives. The methodology and sources of family history can be especially significant when examining queer working-class lives, where surviving sources are often based on violent interactions with the law, the church, and the state.[12]

Family history is also increasingly recognised as significant for those who have, in various ways, been disconnected from their ancestry, and where families have been deliberately broken. In Australia, the *Bringing Them Home* report, drawn from the Inquiry into the forcible separation of Aboriginal and Torres Strait Islander children from their families, published in 1997, suggests one of the lasting traumas of this and similar policies is the difficulties in establishing a continuous line of descent and kinship connections. The *Report* produced 535 survivor submissions, and emphasised the importance of family history research to Indigenous families and communities.[13] Other family history work has revealed the limitations of the colonial archive, and the importance of family history, memories, and survivor testimony. In Canada, survivors of the Sixties Scoop have often contested the way organisational files rendered their experiences, and the experiences of their families, either invisible, or unrecognisable.[14] C. Elizabeth Best has written about the structural barriers for Scoop survivors to tell their own histories, drawing on her own experience of being apprehended by Saskatchewan's child welfare system in 1992, where she was separated from her brother and sister and adopted by a non-Indigenous family. Her own case file was so heavily redacted that there were entire pages of blocked out text, and this redacted case file was only sent 39 months after her original request to view the documents.[15]

Family history research enables historians to explore the interplay between personal stories, local dynamics, and global forces, tracing families across borders and along routes of slavery, sugar and settlement. In *Sugar in the Blood: A Family's Story of Slavery and Empire,* Andrea Stuart uses her own family history, from her earliest traceable maternal ancestor, George Ashby, who travelled from England to Barbados in the late 1630s, to uncover narratives of settlement, slavery, and the making of the Americas.[16] Hazel V. Carby's *Imperial Intimacies: A Tale of Two Islands,* blends family history, autobiography and the history of imperial Britain to offer an intimate history of empire. Retracing the steps of her ancestors, the book features a detailed excavation of the genealogies of Carby's white Welsh mother, Iris, and her Black Jamaican father, Carl.[17] In Australia, the increasing popularity of family history research since the 1970s has been connected to changing perceptions of convict ancestry, once seen as a source of shame but gradually becoming a source of pride, and family historians have examined the transnational journeys of settlers and convicts.[18]

Family history research also touches on significant questions around historical research, sources, and ethics, questions that are particularly relevant to historians of the working class. What obligations do we have to the dead? What responsibilities do we have when we tell the stories of our own, and other, families in the past? In writing histories 'from below', we often name individuals as an intentional act of recovery and visibility. What are the ethical issues with naming and sharing these stories and lives?[19] Ashley Barnwell's work on family secrets touches on the obligation some family history researchers feel to protect the feelings of other family members when considering how to write and share their family stories. Using interviews with family history researchers in Australia, she notes how descendants can develop 'complex emotional relationships with their ancestors, based on feelings of both affinity and resistance'.[20] What are we doing when we pull individuals out of the past, and should we be focused on 'rescuing' individuals from the 'condescension of posterity'? What about those individuals who might prefer to remain in the margins? Family history research confirms the often 'difficult' nature of our historical sources and ethical questions about the recovery of lives and experiences in the past.

Scholars in history, geography and sociology have increasingly located the enthusiasm for family history, and the search for roots and identity, within a broader democratisation of social history.[21] As historians of the working class, we *should* push for and champion a more democratic history, and write material that will be read outside of the academy. The field of family history provides an unrivalled opportunity for scholars, students, and the public to work together to do 'history from below' in various contexts, and historians and other academics have collaborated on various social history projects, and explored the possibilities of collaboration with family and community historians. For example, the 'Living with Dying' project at the University of Leeds saw historians Laura King and Jessica Hammett work with a group of family historians to explore the meanings of family history across generations, and consider how families 'keep alive' memories of those who have died.[22] In the summer of 2021, Julia Laite organised a series of Family History Workshops in partnership with Historians Collaborate and the Raphael Samuel History Centre, exploring topics including the ethics of family history, criminal ancestors, and the collective project of family history research.[23] A recent workshop I organised in Bristol on the importance of local, family and community history saw academics, creative writers, teachers, family historians and community groups come together to explore ideas and practice in family and community history, and consider the multiple ways collaborative and creative approaches to history can be empowering and inclusive. University of the West of England, Bristol final-year History student Ayshah Sahril discussed how for her dissertation project she used her own family history as a way to explore the cultural identity and heritage of the Baba Nyonya of Melaka, demonstrating how family history methodology can support research into a culture that has started to disappear.[24] It is clear, then, that academic history and family history are increasingly engaged in a (long overdue), mutually beneficial conversation.

Telling Stories about Our Own Families

Family history, like any history we write, is drawn from the assortment of ancestors and many stories we have at our disposal. Nowhere is this clearer than in programmes like *WDYTYA,* where producers decide what stories to feature, which ancestors to uncover, and precisely how the narrative will unfold. More subjects are researched than can ever be broadcast, and some prominent celebrities have discussed their disappointment and anger at their family stories not being '"sexy" enough for TV'.[25] Family historians similarly make choices about which family stories to narrate, and which to forget, choices that are made in the context of the present. Like an increasing number of academic historians, I have recently started to research my own family history, using online genealogical databases and newspaper archives, and looking through the unofficial archive of my family; the boxes of unordered photographs, the seemingly random newspaper clippings, the letters and postcards that have survived, as well as talking to family members about the myths, memories and objects that are central to our family story.[26] I have increasingly found myself drawn towards the stories, and searching for the documents, of my gran, Hilda's, early life. Born in 1934, she grew up in a two-up, two-down terraced house in Colne, Lancashire, with her parents, William (Billy) Flanagan, a railway labourer and Nellie, a cotton mill worker, her grandparents, Alma and Jane Lee, and her uncle, Fred, born just nine years before her. Her childhood and the rest of her life was irrevocably marked by the death of her father, Billy, in 1943, while he was a prisoner of war in Thailand.

Family history research enables us to tell the stories of our families, stories that were previously kept private, and were otherwise ignored or neglected by the sweeping narrative of history. Perhaps my increasing interest in finding out more about Hilda and her childhood was spurred on by her ailing health in recent years. She was my last surviving grandparent, though sadly passed away in June 2023. She had been suffering for a number of years with dementia, which meant she spoke frequently about the past, often in ways that were more unfiltered than ever before. Her declining health also gave me a far more immediate sense that so many stories and memories of our family were about to be lost. The relationship between grief and family history is something explored by artist and writer Simon Moreton who has used a blend of writing, illustration, photos, and archival research to produce a series of creative non-fiction works that utilise family history and stories. His 2021 memoir, *WHERE?* is partly a response to his father's death in 2017, and considers the question: 'where are you from?'. His more recent book, *Now is the Time to Know Everything* touches on the grief of miscarriage and reflections on the past, present and future, described as 'a love letter to a person that never quite came to be'.[27] Jessica Meyer has more recently written about how her own grief (and anger) surrounding her mother's death has shaped her thinking about family history, and the boundaries between subjectivity and objectivity that the process of doing family history as an academic historian demands, concluding that there is 'a story to tell in *not* doing family history as well'.[28]

Conclusion

Family history research, and the work of family historians, can offer valuable and potentially transformative perspectives for historians of the working class. The individuals uncovered in family history research may not have changed history, but they can change which histories we believe to be important. Uncovering details about individual lives, family experiences and local contexts allows us to consider how working-class lives in the past were situated in particular social, national and international structures. Family history can both humanise and individualise the past, bring marginalised voices to the forefront, and enrich the historical narrative.

Notes

1 Alison Light, 'In Defence of Family History', *Guardian*, 11 October 2014, and Alison Light, *Common People: The History of an English Family* (London, Penguin: 2015), p. xxi.
2 Dan Waddell, *Who Do You Think You Are? The Essential Guide to Tracing Your Family History* (London, BBC: 2004) and 'Who Do You Think You Are Magazine', accessed 21 August 2023, https://www.whodoyouthinkyouaremagazine.com.
3 'Who Do You Think You Are?', *BBC Online,* accessed 21 August 2023, https://www.bbc.co.uk/programmes/b007t575.
4 For scholarly work on *WDYTYA* see: Amy Holdsworth, *Television, Memory and Nostalgia* (Basingstoke, Palgrave Macmillan: 2011), pp. 65–95; Anne-Marie Kramer, 'Mediatizing Memory: History, Affect and Identity in *Who Do You Think You Are?*', *European Journal of Cultural Studies* 14.4 (2011), pp. 428–445 and Claire Lynch, 'Who Do You Think You Are? Intimate Pasts Made Public', *Biography* 34.1 (2011), pp. 108–118.
5 Jerome de Groot, *Consuming History: Historians and Heritage in Contemporary Popular Culture* (New York, Routledge: 2016), pp. 71–86; 'It Wasn't Just Family History, It Was World History', *Who Do You Think You Are? Magazine*, 12 (2008), p. 16 and 'Who Are We? Researching Family History', *Daily Telegraph*, 12 April 2008, accessed 21 August 2023, https://www.telegraph.co.uk/news/1435139/Who-are-we-Researching-family-history.html.
6 Malcolm Chase, 'Labour History's Biographical Turn', *History Workshop Journal* 92 (2021), pp. 194–207.
7 *WDYTYA* is often credited by genealogists and archivists as a key reason for the current surge of interest in family history in the UK, along with Alex Haley's 1976 book, *Roots* and the hugely popular television adaptation, which is credited with stimulating interest in African-American genealogy and African-American history in the US. Alex Haley, *Roots: The Saga of an American Family* (Hutchinson, Doubleday: 1977).
8 Light, *Common People*, p. xxi.
9 Light, 'In Defence of Family History' and Tanya Evans, 'Secrets and Lies: The Radical Potential of Family History', *History Workshop Journal* 71 (2011), pp. 49–51.
10 Light, *Common People* and Light, 'In Defence of Family History'.
11 Evans, 'Secrets and Lies', p. 51.
12 Justin Bengry, 'Queer Family History & It's Ethical Quandaries & Possibilities' (paper presented at the 2021 Ethics of Family History Workshop, June 2021), https://historianscollaborate.com/family-history-workshops/. See also, Justin Bengry, ' The Case of the Sultry Mountie: Doing Family History Queerly', *Notches,* 2015, accessed 21 August 2023, http://notchesblog.com/2015/05/26/the-case-of-the-sultry-mountie-or-we-need-to-talk-about-cecil/.

13 Human Rights and Equal Opportunity Commission, *Bringing Them Home: Report of the National Inquiry into the Separation of Aboriginal and Torres Strait Islander Children from Their Families* (Sydney, HREOC: 1997).
14 Cody Groat, 'Accessing the Story of My Family: The Sixties Scoop and the Children's Aid Society of London and Middlesex' (paper presented at the 2023 Society for the History of Childhood and Youth Conference, Guelph, Canada, 8 June 2023).
15 C. Elizabeth Best, 'Identity, Memory, and Documents: How Structural Barriers Impact Scoop Survivor Histories 1955–2022' (paper presented at the 2023 Society for the History of Childhood and Youth Conference, Guelph, Canada, 8 June 2023) and 'C. Elizabeth Best: Blog', accessed 21 August 2023, https://www.celizabethbest.com/blog.
16 Andrea Stuart, *Sugar in the Blood: A Family's Story of Slavery and Empire* (London, Portobello Books: 2013).
17 Hazel V. Carby, *Imperial Intimacies: A Tale of Two Islands* (London, Verso: 2021).
18 Ronald D. Lambert, 'Reclaiming the Ancestral Past: Narrative, Rhetoric and the "convict stain"', *Journal of Sociology* 38.2 (2002), pp. 111–127 and Ashley Barnwell, 'Convict Shame to Convict Chic: Intergenerational Memory and Family Histories', *Memory Studies* 12.4 (2019), pp. 398–411.
19 This was a point of discussion at the 2023 Radical History School at the Tolpuddle Festival in Tolpuddle, Dorset.
20 Ashley Barnwell, '"Given it is all so remote from us": Family Secrets, Ancestral Shames and the Proximities of Emotion', *Emotions and Society* 1.1 (2019), p. 96.
21 For example, Annette Kuhn, *Family Secrets: Acts of Memory and Imagination* (London, Verso: 1995); Graeme Davison, *The Use and Abuse of Australian History* (St Leonards, Allen & Unwin: 2000), pp. 80–109; Maria Louise Nugent, 'Aboriginal Family History: Some Reflections', *Australian Cultural History* 23 (2003), pp. 143–154; Catherine Nash, *Of Irish Descent: Origin Stories, Genealogy and the Politics of Belonging* (Syracuse, NY, Syracuse University Press: 2008); Evans, 'Secrets and Lies', pp. 49–73; Wendy Bottero, 'Practising Family History: "Identity" as a Category of Social Practice', *The British Journal of Sociology* 66.3 (2015), pp. 534–556; de Groot, *Consuming History*, pp. 71–86; Ashley Barnwell, 'Hidden Heirlooms: Keeping Family Secrets across Generations', *Journal of Sociology* 54.3 (2018), pp. 446–460; Matthew Stallard and Jerome de Groot, '"Things Are Coming out That Are Questionable, We Never Knew about": DNA and the New Family History', *Journal of Family History* 45.3 (2020), pp. 274–294; and Tanya Evans, 'How Do Family Historians Work with Memory', *Journal of Family History* 46.1 (2021), pp. 92–106.
22 'Living with Dying: Death, Remembrance and Family History in Britain', accessed 21 August 2023, https://livingwithdying.leeds.ac.uk/. See also the AHRC-funded network 'Inheriting the Family', accessed 21 August 2023, https://inheritingthefamily.org/.
23 'Family History Workshops', June 2021, accessed 21 August 2023, https://historianscollaborate.com/family-history-workshops/.
24 Ayshah Sahril, 'Baba and Nyonya of Melaka: Untold Perspectives and Challenging Perceptions' (paper presented at the 'Telling Our Stories: Bristol Family and Community History Workshop', 28 July 2023, Watershed, Bristol).
25 'Christopher Eccleston: My "Who Do You Think You Are?" episode was dropped because working class roots were "not sexy enough"', *Telegraph*, 29 September 2019.
26 For example, a recent panel at the 2023 Social History Society Annual Conference at the University of Essex saw Julia Laite, Cath Feely, Laura King and Lucinda

Matthews-Jones discuss various ways they have used family history in their own work. See also Joe Moran, 'The Scattering: A Family History for a Floating World', *History Workshop Journal* 92 (2021), pp. 5–28.

27 Simon Moreton, *Where? Life and Death in the Shropshire Hills* (Little Toller Books, Beaminster: 2021) and *Now Is the Time to Know Everything* (2023), accessed 21 August 2023, https://www.simon-moreton.co.uk/.

28 Jessica Meyer, 'Not Doing Family History', accessed 21 August 2023, https://armsandthemedicalman.com/2023/07/12/not-doing-family-history/.

5

MUSEUMS AND HERITAGE SITES AS SOURCES FOR WORKING-CLASS HISTORY

Oliver Betts

There is an enormous energy trapped in museums. Ask any Curator or Registrar and they will tell you what is on display, carefully conserved and curated before the public, is a mere fraction of total holdings. Museum collections, and associated heritage locations such as preserved or recreated buildings, factories, and streets, hold far greater potential for telling new and engaging stories about the working-class past than they currently do. This section explores museums and other heritage sites as places of repository, discovery, and reflection that historians seeking insight into working-class history would do well to avail themselves of.

Collections

Museums have come a long way since the post-war challenge of the new museology movement. Defined briefly this movement, emerging in the 1980s and 1990s, challenged the traditional top-down thinking that dominated museums. Its proponents argued for a sea-change in all things, from how (and which) objects were collected, how they were categorised and displayed, and how the stories and access that most inspired audiences should be placed at the heart of museum decision-making. It was a direct challenge to what was seen as the old-fashioned and outdated model of museum display that sought to edify and instruct its audience with little regard for whether the audience could properly engage with that method of display.[1]

During this period considerable thought and effort was put into understanding the lived experiences of past generations, both elite and (increasingly) plebian. In line with the social history boom of the period, and still often referred to as social history in a museum context whilst encompassing

DOI: 10.4324/9780429344084-7

more of a blend of social, cultural, and economic history in a strictly academic sense, this refocusing of attention led to broader social collecting around the worlds of everyday experience.

For those interested in the work of the working-class local and industrial museums hold great collections to be explored. Some of these are tools and other work equipment largely absent from the textual record. José Manuel Vázquez Lijó discusses the context of 'Rastro' – small fishing tools used by Galician coastal communities scouring shellfish from the seashore, specifically a small hoe called a 'sacho'. That one exists in the permanent galleries of the Museo Marea in Porto do Son, Galicia, Spain, is particularly important given that these were rarely made industrially as they 'could easily be acquired in the abundant number of market fairs held all over Galicia'.[2] Tools of trade, like with household items, are often a double-edged sword in terms of survival – mass produced (formally or informally) and in major use, but regularly too damaged to survive long term and frequently disposed of before their value to posterity could be realised.

Museums relating to industries, places, communities, or particular activities (such as organised sports) have always been sites of deposit for people with objects and stories they wish to share, and in a bid to open up access to these collections more and more museums are turning to online platforms. A whole host of collections online websites now exist, often featuring high-quality photography and descriptions of the objects, and these are the best way to access collections.

Intentions

There is a danger of course, as museum staff know well, that just having the objects is not enough. To put it bluntly, as Adele Chynoweth does in the introduction to her very useful edited collection on *Museums and the Working Class*, how relevant are the fraying trade union banners and collections of out-dated household objects of working-class social history displays to ordinary working-class people with their own complex twenty-first-century perspectives?[3] Chynoweth here is not dismissing these objects as inherently irrelevant in themselves, but is instead asking a critically important question about how museums speak (or fail to speak) to working-class visitors.

Many museums are working through new challenges to their displays and collections as they come to grips with an increasingly diverse and informed visitor base. In many cases, too, this exists against a rapidly dwindling stream of funding, leaving many museums trying to do more things, and, critically *new things,* with less. In recent years museums have grappled with issues surrounding colonialism and repatriation of objects, the growing call for LGBTQ+ stories to be drawn out of collections, and for generally a more diverse and inclusive outlook (in terms of not just race but accessibility, neuro-diversity, and education level) to encompass not only in-house displays but also their collaborative activities outside of the museum's physical parameters. In an era of heightened awareness, can heritage institutions continue to 'accept public funds...to which workers have contributed through their hard-earned taxes, and yet refuse to pay meaningful attention to their living history' as Cynoweth argues they currently do?[4]

Going into this context, historians should be aware of not just the potential of museum collections to enhance their research, but for their own research and enthusiasm to in return help the museum. Museums are, increasingly, centres of research in their own right, with passionate and engaged staff members looking through collections. Where many most benefit from academic collaboration is in broadening out that research, in understanding new developments in the field and the wider contexts in which their objects operated. As historians attuned to the needs of supporting working-class history beyond the academy, then museums and heritage institutions are a good place to start in sharing our expertise as well as tapping into their resources and knowledge. There are few academic studies of working-class material culture out there, despite the recent turn towards the objects-as-sources, which seems especially significant given both that museums hold so many objects relating to working-class life *and* that working-class history faces such patchy survival of written source material.

Reflections

There is one other way in which museums and heritage sites can be useful to the historian engaged in studying working-class history, and that is as a source in studying the public history of working-class history. It is generally accepted that visitors look for some connection to the human stories told in museums, be that a directly identifiable connection to an ancestor or pseudo-ancestor ('that could have been me two centuries ago!') or a more universal emotive connection to a story of triumph, struggle, or experience. Indeed, much of the New Museology scholarship and subsequent activity has been heavily focused on understanding that what visitors bring with them to an exhibition or gallery is just as important as what they experience when there.

For the public historian interested in how working-class history is understood by audiences, or how working-class visitors interact with their heritage, the physical and online landscapes surrounding heritage sites are a rich area of research. Just the reviews pages of a website such as Tripadvisor can be a fantastic starting point.

Comparing the reviews left behind by visitors who had experienced two sites relating to working-class history, the Finnish Labour Museum Werstas in Tampere and the Tenement Museum in New York, USA, suggests a number of interesting themes shared between visitors.

Both User A. (from the UK) and User B (Finland) found the display of authentic machinery captivating at the Finnish Labour Museum:

User A

There were photographs, clothing as well as machinery etc.

We learned a lot whilst enjoying the atmosphere.[5]

User B

The exhibition ended with life size replicas of a bank, a grocery store and printing press. Those gave an insight into lives of people in old times.

And last but not the least, the steam engine room. There is an actual steam engine used to produce power. Sheer size of it was exciting.[6]

Visitor User C (UK) felt the same about the Tenement Museum, was concerned that recent renovation work somewhat spoiled the atmosphere:

User C

What for me was a little disappointing was not seeing more of the living conditions. We saw a 70s bed in a room and some 19th-century furniture in a revised location due to building works.[7]

They compared it to a recent trip to the Glasgow Tenement Museum, which they felt offered a similar set-up:

I'm more familiar with the Tenement House in Glasgow which has a 4 room tenement apartment set up much as it was when one family lived there from 1911 to 1965 which you can wander round at your leisure.[8]

Comparison, obviously by the nature of the site a key feature of reviews, indicates that many visitors already had one or more working-class heritage sites in mind when visiting these places. Others, particularly for the Tenement Museum given its location within a vibrant city-wide heritage landscape, were on particular journeys.

User D (USA)

We took our 13 year old granddaughter to Ellis Island the previous day and wanted the "Meet Victoria Confino" tour to be an extension of the immigrant experience. The tour guide was not the greatest, but adequate. She gave us a preview of this family. However, when we entered Victoria's apartment, we were not met by a 14 year old girl but an adult in costume. My expectation was that this "costum ed Interpreter" would talk about her family's experience crossing the Atlantic, how they came upon their apartment and what obstacles they had to overcome as immigrants. It was very awkward. Those of us on tour had to ask questions – there was no information freely offered.[9]

Visitors are, always, sensitive to changes in a museum's operation, and the introduction of guided tours and visitor experiences (by both regular staff and costumed actors playing the roles of previous inhabitants of the tenement at different points in time) seems to have met with mixed reviews. What is interesting here, though, is that Waves27982 and their family were on a journey of discovery, extending their research into migrant life following their prior visit to Ellis Island (a visitor centre on the site of the former immigration processing point for the city) but at the same time did not feel confident in their knowledge to know what they wanted to ask the costumed interpreter playing a recently arrived teenage migrant when they came face-to-face with her. In this instance the experience on offer did not seem to have matched up with these visitors' expectations.

For many, though, the value of both sites lay in the human stories they held. UK-based user User E found the Tenement Museum 'absolutely fascinating':

User E

We took the 1949 to present tour Our guide was extremely knowledgeable on every aspect of the families that lived in these apartments and the traumas they went through to ensure their families wouldn't live the same lives they had to go through. To think a couple could ensure years of torture in death camps to become parents and live "normal" lives is credit to who they were.

The level of detail in each of the rooms, curated by the actual families who lived there and experts in purchasing antiques from the time really set the tone.[10]

Here the re-creation of environments with historical items acquired from outside, similar to many re-creation museums that follow the model of Skansen in Sweden of bringing together material collections (often plebian) from around the country to render 'historic' environments in one place, actually enhanced the visitor's sense of being shown an authentic slice of social history.

Key to many such visits, to museums and heritage sites around the world, is a sense for visitors of capturing a working-class life lost to history. Visitors frequently connected the sites to the experiences of their ancestors:

User F (USA)

My grandparents immigrated from Sicily in the early 1900s, so I was anxious to visit this shrine to the melting pot that was NYC in that era.[11]

User G (USA)

Some fixtures & spaces took me back to my grandparents railroad flat in Queens when I was little.[12]

But it was not just American visitors that found a human connection to the Tenement Museum:

User H (Ireland)

As Irish people on holiday in NYC we decided to do the Irish outsiders tour just to get an idea what it would have been like for the Irish in NYC. Jacob was our guide and he was very knowledgeable and interactive. We were able to tell him that pretty much everything on display was similar to what we would have seen in our grandparents' homes a few decades ago.[13]

For each visitor objects and stories intermingled to create a window into the working-class past.

Conclusions

This brief study has attempted to show what sources exist out there for the intrepid working-class historian interested in reaching into the heritage sector. Material collections abound, many yet to be seriously drawn in to the academic study of industrial or agricultural life, but so to do knowledgeable and interested staff and visitors. There is far more work left to do at the promising intersections between academic study and heritage collections, work that, as the final section of this study has shown, has the potential for really engaging the wider public in working-class stories.

Notes

1 For an introduction to this see Peter Virgo, ed., *The New Museology* (London, Reaktion: 1989).
2 José Manuel Vázquez Lijó, 'Women's Work in Coastal Galicia: Shining a Light on the Unseen at the Medea Museum' in Adele Chynoweth (ed.), *Museums and the Working Class* (London, Routledge: 2021), pp. 104–105.
3 Adele Chynoweth, 'Introduction' in Adele Chynoweth (ed.), *Museums and the Working Class* (London, Routledge: 2021), pp. 3–12.
4 Chynoweth, 'Introduction', p. 12.
5 'Excellent and Free', review on Tripadvisor website, accessed online 1 February 2024, https://www.tripadvisor.co.uk/Attraction_Review-g189948-d4273235-Reviews-The_Finnish_Labour_Museum_Werstas-Tampere_Pirkanmaa.html.
6 'Very Informative and Interesting', review on Tripadvisor website, accessed online 1 February 2024, https://www.tripadvisor.co.uk/Attraction_Review-g189948-d4273235-Reviews-The_Finnish_Labour_Museum_Werstas-Tampere_Pirkanmaa.html.
7 'Interesting', review on the Tripadvisor website, accessed online 3 February 2024, https://www.tripadvisor.com/Attraction_Review-g60763-d104369-Reviews-Tenement_Museum-New_York_City_New_York.html.
8 'Interesting', 3 February 2024.
9 'Not What I Expected', review on the Tripadvisor website, accessed online 3 February 2024, https://www.tripadvisor.com/Attraction_Review-g60763-d104369-Reviews-Tenement_Museum-New_York_City_New_York.html.

10 'Brilliant Museum', review on the Tripadvisor website, accessed online 3 February 2024, https://www.tripadvisor.com/Attraction_Review-g60763-d104369-Reviews-Tenement_Museum-New_York_City_New_York.html.

11 'A Walk through Recent History', review on the Tripadvisor website, accessed online 3 February 2024, https://www.tripadvisor.com/Attraction_Review-g60763-d104369-Reviews-Tenement_Museum-New_York_City_New_York.html.

12 'More Than I Expected', review on the Tripadvisor website, accessed online 3 February 2024, https://www.tripadvisor.com/Attraction_Review-g60763-d104369-Reviews-Tenement_Museum-New_York_City_New_York.html.

13 'Irish Outsiders Tour – Very Authentic', review on the Tripadvisor website, accessed online 3 February 2024, https://www.tripadvisor.com/Attraction_Review-g60763-d104369-Reviews-Tenement_Museum-New_York_City_New_York.html.

6

READING AGAINST THE GRAIN

Non-plebian Sources in Working-class History

Oliver Betts

In 1911, J.L. and Barbara Hammond co-authored *The Village Labourer 1760–1832*. It was, as a reviewer noted, one of many attempts to rectify the neglect of the non-elites in British history that were being published at the time. To modern academic eyes the Hammond's methodology seem very old-fashioned. Aiming to capture the transformation of labouring life in rural England as Enclosure Acts and new technologies changed farming, almost all of the Hammond's analysis came through a narrow selection of sources. Government reports, well-to-do travellers, almanacs, and agricultural treaties, all were combed through to provide insight. But almost no working-class voices themselves appear in *The Village Labourer.*[1]

Of course, such a comparison to the present day state of the field is unfair. The Hammonds were working before the great bloom of social, economic, and cultural histories that reshaped modern academic study. It would be another fifty years in British historiography before E.P. Thompson set out to rescue 'the poor stockinger, the Luddite cropper, the "obsolete" hand-loom weaver' and many others from 'the enormous condescension of posterity' and a further thirty years after that before Anna Clark and others would take Thompson rightly to task for his exclusion of women from that narrative.[2]

Since the Hammonds historians have been awash with new forms of working-class primary sources, diligently preserved by archivists and librarians, cared for within museum collections, collated in oral history projects by academics and community researchers alike, and gathered together in published (and now increasingly online) compendiums. New lines of inquiry and methodologies of research have also brought previously 'elite' sources into working-class spheres – in a British context Jonathan Rose has explored how working-class readers engaged with all manner of literature and Alison

DOI: 10.4324/9780429344084-8

Light's *Common People: The History of an English Family* has explored the interplay between family history and social history even with the predictable working-class absence of 'ego-documents' (letters, diaries, memoirs, etc) within her own family history.[3]

Future historians will be awash with sources with which to document the working-class past. Sonali Perera's excellent recent monograph shows just what is possible with a collection of global working-class literature – weaving anti-colonialism of the 1930s, feminist recovery projects of 1970s, post- and anti-colonial fictions of the 1960s together.[4] Both the availability and types of sources are in flux. That 'extreme heterglossia' that marked out the language of nineteenth-century Stockholm, particularly amongst its workers that has been painstakingly collated by Allan Pred for example, now exists within a digital age and Jack Linchuan Qui's accounts of trying to understand 'an emerging working class of the "information have-less"' in a rapidly changing twenty-first-century China can seem very much like the new frontier of working-class history.[5]

Then why start with the Hammonds at all? Simply because, however the historian frames their methodology, time period, or questions, writing working-class history is an exercise in seeing your subject through a collage of mis-matched sources. Power structures and cultural forms both exclude working-class participants *and* at the same time capture the details of their lives. As the Hammonds found, even without working-class voices in the archive those sources authored by non-plebian actors can still offer up critical information if read against the grain. As Robert Darnton has argued 'the archives of the Old Regime are exceptionally rich, and one can always put new questions to old material' in ways its original authors could not have contemplated.[6] Counter-reading sources in this way is a vital skill of any historian, but has always been as core to working-class history as recovering authentic plebian voices. The two form part of a whole, a compelling methodology for working-class history and are well-worth learning as an aspiring historian.

These two examples, a century apart, are useful to illustrate the importance of reading sources against the grain for working-class history. Both show the potential insights to be gained from sources not authored by working-class men or women themselves despite their differences in age, format, style, and purpose. They also, as the suggested analytical notes below show, ask of the reader the same critical matter of interpretation – are these insights into working-class life or how that life *was perceived by outsiders*?

Source One

Source One is an extract from a very significant piece of fin-de-siecle social investigation. *The Pittsburgh Survey,* conducted in 1907–1908, saw some seventy researchers descend on the steel-working hub of Pittsburgh, Pennsylvania, USA. A classic of the US Progressive Era, the survey has long been studied as a snapshot of an industrial city and populace at a moment of social, cultural, and economic upheaval in the early twentieth century.

Like many social studies and investigations, *The Pittsburgh Survey* featured interviews with all manner of residents and experts, from plant managers and community leaders down to workers on the blast-furnace floor. These were used both critically and uncritically by authors in such social investigations, depending on their political or cultural slant as a writer, and have long been a mainstay of primary source compendiums offering insight into the conditions of late nineteenth- and early twentieth-century cities and peoples.

One of these, John Griswold, was described as a 'Scotch-Irish furnace boss' who had arrived in America decades before and who agreed to an interview in the 'sitting room in his four-room cottage one evening'.

Mighty few men have stood what I have, I can tell you. I've been twenty years at the furnaces and been workin' a twelvehour day all that time, seven days in the week. We go to work at seven in the mornin' and we get through at night at six. We work that way for two weeks and then we work the long turn and change to the night shift of thirteen hours. The long turn is when we go on at seven Sunday mornin' and work through the whole twenty-four hours up to Monday mornin'. That puts us onto the night turn for the next two weeks, and the other crew onto the day. The next time they get the long turn and we get twenty-four hours off, but it don't do us much good. I get home at about half past seven Sunday mornin' and go to bed as soon as I've had breakfast. I get up about noon so as to get a bit o' Sunday to enjoy, but I'm tired and sleepy all the afternoon. Now, if we had eight hours it would be different. I'd start to work, say, at six and I'd be done at two and I'd come home, and after dinner me and the missus could go to the park if we wanted to, or I could take the childer to the country where there ain't any saloons. That's the danger, the childer runnin' on the streets and me with no time to take them any place else. That's what's driven the Irish out of the industry. It ain't the Hunkies, they couldn't do it, but the Irish don't have to work this way. There was fifty of them here with me sixteen years ago and now where are they? I meet 'em sometimes around the city, ridin' in carriages and all of them wearin' white shirts, and here I am with these Hunkies. They don't seem like men to me hardly. They can't talk United States. You tell them something and they just look and say 'Me no fustay, me no fustay,' that's all you can get out of 'em. And I'm here with them all the time, twelve hours a day and every day and I'm all alone, not a mother's son of 'em that I can talk to. Everybody says I'm a fool to stay here, I dunno, mebbe I am. It don't make so much difference though. I'm gettin' along, but I don't want the kids ever to work this way. I'm goin' to educate them so they won't have to work twelve hours.[7]

There is, for the working-class historian, a veritable treasure trove of information to be taken from Griswold's statement. His pride in hard work for long hours, the demands of the gruelling shift system employed at the steel mills, and how the rhythm of the work dominated his free time too is all evident here. Griswold can be read in many ways – a frustrated, older, left-behind worker former colleague who have moved on; a concerned father driven to push his children to 'better' work; a prejudiced man unhappy with a workplace becoming more multi-cultural with each passing year. The critical condemnation of the 'Hunkies' (an idiom for Hungarians but used interchangeably for any Southern and Eastern European migrants appearing in Pittsburgh at the time) complete with its amusingly brusque 'they can't talk United States' offers useful insight into how racial divides between successive waves of immigrants cut through working-class life in this period and context.

But it also requires careful handling. Working-class voices included in sources such as these were always heavily mediated, selected by the authors to be indicative of the wider themes explored in the survey. Authors of *The Pittsburgh Survey* were fascinated by the complex interplay of different ethnic groups amongst the city's migrant population, and Griswold's comments were, for them, proof of ongoing social divisions at the works. Clearly, the source can indeed be read in that way, but historians should be wary of its isolated and selective framing.

The passage is rich in cultural details – for instance, Griswold's contemplation of the problems of being a working-class father with little access to safe play space in the industrial city could be the beginning of a research project all of its own. Likewise Griswold's descriptions of frustrated attempts to communicate can be read as an indication of both the social and physical importance of workplace talk (in the hot confines of the steel mill should 'fustay' be understood as 'thirsty'?). Simply because his account is framed as one reflective of social disharmony at the works, does not mean that it can only be read in that way.

Source Two

Source Two jumps forwards over 100 years and across an ocean. The UK Government's *Universal Credit and You* guide, last updated 10 April 2023, is available online as a resource for those seeking to access Britain's welfare state support. Due to the length of the source, it will only be quoted here in sections.[8]

The website offers a guide to claiming Universal Credit, introduced in 2013–2014 in place of six individual benefit systems, and talks through how the applicant should manage the system and what to expect during the application process. Subsections, entitled 'Working', 'Children', 'Housing', and 'Health and Disability', are marked out to guide applicants towards the most frequent areas of concern, and throughout the website aims at a straightforward, matter-of-fact style in both layout and language. For example the section on work allowances reads:

In some cases, you may be eligible for a work allowance. A work allowance is the amount that you can earn before your Universal Credit payment is affected.

You will be eligible for a work allowance if you (and/or your partner) either have:

- responsibility for a child
- limited capability for work

The monthly work allowances are set at:

- £379 – if your Universal Credit includes housing support
- £631 – if you do not receive housing support

If you have earnings but you (or your partner) are not responsible for a child or do not have limited capability for work you will not be eligible for a work allowance.

Reading Government documents though, as any aspiring historian knows well, is an exercise in partial information receipt. The bigger picture of Universal Credit is that the system has been subject to sustained and often very justified criticism from across politics, welfare organisations, and broader society.

Our interest here, though, is not in the efficacy or not of Universal Credit, but whether this guide can serve as an unintended insight into working-class history in 2023. Certainly, it can quickly be read as evidence of a digitally adept working class. The default assumption is that this document, which in previous decades would certainly have been a printed leaflet, will be accessed online. The text is studded with hyperlinks to take the applicant to other sites, for example, with even the landline phone number for the helpline hidden behind a weblink. It is also very clearly a document that suggests those working-class men, women, and children in need of benefit support in 2023 were well aware of the specifics of income and want they were experiencing. There is no 'feckless poor' here in this document – indeed, applicants are imagined to be well-versed in their financial situation upon applying.

Imagined here, of course, is key. Critics of Universal Credit have pointed out that whilst it was intended to simplify and streamline social security, it has instead been marked by delays, administrative errors, and an unwieldy system that users struggle to engage with.[9] Although the aim may have been to simplify payments, the process imagines a financially literate and digitally equipped applicant who must also have the time and skill to navigate the errors and inconsistencies in the system, something at odds with parts of the working-class population of Britain in the 2020s. Context is key to understanding such a document, especially when the recent global financial crisis is taken into account as both the number of people reading the guide and their economic circumstances were increasingly in flux.

Reading documents against the grain carries with it one vital caveat for the working-class historian – do these documents offer a glimpse of working-class lives past, or simply how institutions and organisations imagined those lives? Exploring this question has been at the very heart of working-class history since its inception, and speaks directly to the power imbalances that shape both working-class lives and the collection of their history for posterity. How the individual researcher answers that question, of course, depends on them.

Notes

1 J. L. Hammond and Barbara Hammond, *The Village Labourer 1760–1832* (London, Longmans: 1911).
2 E. P. Thompson, *The Making of the English Working Class* (London, Penguin: 1963), p. 12; Anna Clark, *The Struggle for the Breeches: Gender and the Making of the British Working Class* (Berkeley, University of California Press: 1995).
3 Jonathan Rose, *The Intellectual Life of the British Working Classes* (New Haven, CT, Yale University Press: 2011); Alison Light, *Common People: The History of an English Family* (London, Fig Tree: 2014).
4 Sonali Perera, *No Country: Working-Class Writing in the Age of Globalization* (New York, Columbia University Press: 2014).
5 Allan Pred, *Lost Words and Lost Worlds: Modernity and the Language of Everyday Life in Late Nineteenth-century Stockholm* (Cambridge, Cambridge University Press: 1990); Jack Linchuan Qiu, *Working-class Network Society: Communication Technology and the Information Have-less in Urban China* (Cambridge, MA, MIT Press: 2009).
6 Robert Darnton, *The Great Cat Massacre and Other Episodes in French Cultural History* (New York, Basic Books: 1985), p. 12.
7 John A. Fitch, *The Steel Workers,* Volume III of *The Pittsburgh Survey* (New York, Charities Committee Publication: 1910), pp. 11–12.
8 Universal Credit and You guide, accessed online on 6 February 2024, https://www.gov.uk/government/publications/universal-credit-and-you/draft-uc-and-you.
9 See for instance Anna Hughes, 'Five Things You Should Know about Universal Credit', *Trussell Trust website,* accessed online 3 March 2024, https://www.trusselltrust.org/2022/04/05/5-things-you-should-know-about-universal-credit/.

7
ACCESSIBLE BIBLIOGRAPHY

Laura Christine Price

The purpose of this accessible bibliography is to introduce the reader to some significant texts in working-class history. This should not be considered an exhaustive reading list, but rather a guide to texts that are both important to the study of working-class history and easily accessible to readers. Not everyone who is interested in working-class history has access to university libraries and subscriptions; therefore, this annotated, accessible bibliography aims to give those new to the field an introduction to the field's foundational texts, classics, and new and significant readings that are easy to find in bookshops and online, as well as some accessible archival sources. It may also serve as a refresher to scholars who are revisiting the study of the working classes after some time away. The focus of this bibliography is on British studies of the working classes, in line with the editors' own expertise. We acknowledge that there are plentiful studies of working-class histories of other countries and, indeed, of the international working classes, but we wished to provide a more coherent list of texts that informed our own understanding of our field. The bibliography gives the author's name, title of their book, and the first date of publication, for the sake of consistency, and are listed in chronological order. In several cases, more recent versions of the text are available.

Foundational Texts

C. L. R. James, The Black Jacobins *(1938)*

James's study of the Haitian Revolution, led by Toussaint L'Ouverture, is a fine-grained analysis of the complexity of economy and society in San Domingo and places the slave-led Haitian Revolution in a comparative

DOI: 10.4324/9780429344084-9

historical context alongside the French Revolution. An essential text for understanding the operation of class consciousness in a slave society, *The Black Jacobins* focuses on the leadership of Toussaint L'Ouverture and highlights the necessity of examining revolutionary movements outside Europe in order to understand the history of the international working classes.

Michael Young and Peter Wilmott, Family and Kinship in East London *(1957)*

A sociological study, this text has much to tell us about working-class life and community in East London in the immediate post-war era. It examines how post-war governments' social housing policies affected the inhabitants of different communities in East London. Given the importance of the concept of community for historians of the working classes, *Family and Kinship in East London* is significant not only in its own field but also to the historian seeking to understand the importance of community in working-class life.

Eric Hobsbawm, Primitive Rebels: Studies in Archaic Forms of Social Movement in the 19th and 20th Centuries *(1959)*

No bibliography of working-class history would be complete without a book by Hobsbawm. Many of his works are available from mainstream publishing houses and his output is wide, including expansive survey works of European and world history as well as more focused studies of popular movements. *Primitive Rebels* examines nineteenth- and twentieth-century social movements at the margins: not the organised labour movement, but the 'social bandits' that were regarded within their own societies as heroes and lacked the legitimacy of organised groups.

E. P. Thompson, The Making of the English Working Class *(1963)*

Thompson's much-lauded text sought to 'rescue' the history of the early English industrial working class from 'the enormous condescension of posterity'. Though it has inspired a great deal of debate and criticism, including authors responding to Thompson's work through their own books (see the bibliography's entries on Anna Clark and Ron Ramdin, below), anyone new to the study of working-class history is advised to dip into this lengthy text given its significant influence on the direction of the study of working-class history. Thompson's focus on the growth of class consciousness, and his insistence on considering the agency of working-class people, resulted in a work that combines detailed analysis of popular working-class movements and an attempt to recreate the lives of working-class people. Perhaps one of the most apposite criticisms of the text is that it focuses on artisan workers and labour aristocrats, at the expense of less skilled, less organised workers.

This is a significant issue in scholarship on the historical working classes. Elsewhere in this volume, Oliver Betts details some of the methods scholars of working-class history can use to 'read against the grain' and learn about those who leave behind few sources.

Raphael Samuel (editor), Village Life and Labour *(1975)*

This volume, under Samuel's editorship, redresses the balance of much labour history of the time by placing the focus on rural workers, including chapters on work, gender, rural identities and oral history methodology. That Samuel – the founder of the History Workshop movement, focusing on 'history from below' – should have presided over such a collection is unsurprising. The movement's *History Workshop Journal* is also highly recommended as a source of continued high-quality historical scholarship.

Classic Texts

Jill Liddington and Jill Norris, One Hand Tied Behind Us: The Rise of the Women's Suffrage Movement *(1978)*

Liddington and Norris's classic examines the role of working-class women's suffragists in nineteenth- and twentieth-century Lancashire. Moving the spotlight away from the more notorious – and sometimes more middle class – suffragettes, the authors focus on the actions of working-class women in agitating for the vote. Two more of Jill Liddington's books may be of interest to the scholar of working-class suffragists: *The Life and Times of a Respectable Rebel: Selina Cooper 1864–1946* (1984) and *Rebel Girls: Their fight for the vote* (2006).

Stuart Macintyre, Little Moscows: Communism and Working Class Militancy in Inter-War Britain *(1980)*

Macintyre's book is a study of three communities – one in Wales, two in Scotland – that turned to communism in the interwar period. As well as considering the political make-up of these communities, Macintyre analyses the dominant industries of Little Moscows (coal mining and textile dyeing in his examples) and the textures of working-class life in these areas. The result is a compelling case study of the limited flourishing of communism in Britain.

David Howell, British Workers and the Independent Labour Party, 1888–1906 *(1983)*

Howell examines the significance of the Independent Labour Party through focus on both the leadership of the ILP and the myriad occupational groups that populated its ranks. A detailed and thorough history of the forerunner of the Labour Party, this text is essential in understanding the interactions between the ILP and the working-class people it served.

Dorothy Thompson, The Chartists *(1984)*

Thompson is the author of several books on Chartism and women's history. *The Chartists* does not solely focus on working-class members of the movement, but, along with her earlier work *The Early Chartists* (1971), it brings to life the world of the Chartist movement and exposes areas of the campaign that were hitherto lesser known, including women's involvement.

Ron Ramdin, The Making of the Black Working Class in Britain *(1987)*

A response to *The Making of the English Working Class,* Ramdin's text is part polemic, part historical examination of the Black working-class presence in Britain from the sixteenth century to the 1980s. Ramdin seeks to uncover the history of a significant British population and the racism that Black Britons have long experienced, including at the hands of the organised white labour movement.

Anna Clark, The Struggle for the Breeches: Gender and the Making of the British Working Class *(1995)*

Clark's book is a direct feminist response to Thompson's *The Making of the English Working Class*, and examines the role of gender in the formation of class consciousness. It analyses the experiences of, among others, cotton textile workers, an occupational group notable for its composition of both men and women. Clark focuses on roughly the same period as Thompson, and makes for an essential companion to the more famous work.

New and Significant Texts

Joanna Bourke, Working Class Culture in Britain, 1890–1960: Gender, Class and Ethnicity *(1994)*

Bourke's text examines the intersections of class with gender and ethnic identities and focuses on class identity as socially and culturally based. Not only useful for its approach of considering key aspects of identity alongside each other, this book also introduces the reader to how historians analyse change and provides a list of further reading.

Jim Phillip, Collieries, Communities and the Miners' Strike in Scotland, 1984–1985 *(2012)*

Phillips' examination of the 1984–1985 Miners' Strike in Scotland is available affordably through second-hand book websites and therefore is included on this list when several similar texts were omitted due to their poor accessibility. This is fortuitous, because *Collieries, Communities and the Miners' Strike in Scotland* examines a significant moment in recent working-class history with reference to community and industrial changes in the coalfield in the decades preceding the strike.

Anandi Ramamurthy, Black Star: Britain's Asian Youth Movements *(2013)*

Among Ramamurthy's diverse scholarly work is this excellent study of working-class Asian youth organisations of the 1970s and 1980s. It features key events in British Asian history such as the Grunwick strike and the trial and acquittal of the Bradford 12, a group who successfully defended their community against the National Front. Alongside this text sits the online archive Ramamurthy curates, Tandana (www.tandana.org), which includes oral history testimonies, educational packs and reading lists on the Asian Youth Movements.

Selina Todd, The People: The Rise and Fall of the Working Class, 1910–2010 *(2014)*

The People uses working-class testimony to form a history of an extended twentieth century, resulting in a social history that is as accessible to lay people as it is useful to the historian seeking to learn more about working-class lives in the last hundred years. Born of Todd's desire to see the history of people like her family on bookshelves, this text is an excellent starting point for people at the very beginning of their study of the working classes.

Laura Beers, Red Ellen: The Life of Ellen Wilkinson, Socialist, Feminist, Internationalist *(2016)*

Beers' biography of a key figure in twentieth-century working-class history gives us not only a portrait of the multi-layered life of Ellen Wilkinson but also an insight into the British left in the twentieth century. Wilkinson is an excellent topic for a biography given her involvement in various working-class movements, including the Jarrow Crusade, and her position as a Labour Cabinet minister.

Archival, Heritage, and Digital Resources

Dictionary of Labour Biography

https://sslh.org.uk/publications/dlb-list-of-names/

Now in its fifteenth volume, this valuable resource is currently edited by Keith Gildart and David Howell and includes John Saville, Joyce M Bellamy and Neville Kirk among its previous editors. It includes entries on over a thousand labour movement figures from the last two hundred years. Although it lacks its own website, the Society for the Study of Labour History provides a useful list of labour movement figures who are included in the *DLB*, cited above. Copies of the *DLB* are readily available to purchase from online book shops.

Marx Memorial Library

https://www.marx-memorial-library.org.uk/collections/digital-resources

The Marx Memorial Library is in London and includes a wealth of material on Marxism, socialism and working-class history. Its website contains a selection of digital resources including plentiful photographs and documents on the International Brigades and the Spanish Civil War, British communist newspapers and a poster gallery based on the Library's extensive poster collection.

Modern Records Centre (MRC), University of Warwick

https://warwick.ac.uk/services/library/mrc/archives_online/digital/

The Modern Records Centre holds a great deal of trade union archive material, including archives of the Trade Union Congress as well as significant British unions such as the Transport and General Workers Union, and radical groups and individuals on the British left. The MRC's website includes a helpful list of guides to the archives for those wishing to explore the extent of the collection. There are also several digitised collections that are freely accessible, including collections on sweated trades, the Spanish Civil War and Britain, Empire and migration.

People's History Museum, Manchester, and Labour History Archive and Study Centre

https://phm.org.uk/learn/learning-resources/

The People's History Museum is dedicated to the history of working people, with a particular focus on activism and campaigns. Although lacking a significant collection of digitised material (at time of publication), the PHM website's learning section provides an accessible introduction to various topics and figures, including the Peterloo Massacre, Mary Wollstonecraft and the Communist Party of Great Britain.

Society for the Study of Labour History (SSLH) Website

https://sslh.org.uk/archives-2/

The SSLH's website offers a range of material for scholars interested in the labour movement. As well as publishing the journal *Labour History Review*, the website provides a helpful section which directs historians to archives containing significant amounts of material on working-class history. In addition, the website contains information on events related to labour history, blog posts, and information on the SSLH's publications, grants and bursaries.

Trade Union Congress Library at London Metropolitan University

https://student.londonmet.ac.uk/library/using-the-library/special-collections/trades-union-congress-library-collections/

This website contains information about the TUC Library collection based at London Metropolitan University, and contains a small number of digitised collections on trade union and working-class history. It includes material on women's campaigns for equal pay at work, TUC reports, and oral histories and documents on changes at work in the post-war twentieth century.

Working Class Movement Library, Salford

https://www.wcml.org.uk/

The physical library in Salford is based on Eddie and Ruth Frow's collection of books and documents, and the WCML's website is also a useful source of material on British working-class history. As well as a catalogue for the Library itself, it includes information on a range of working-class organisations, movements, and people, such as Black and Asian struggles, the Peterloo Massacre, and Margaret Bondfield, a trade unionist and the first female cabinet secretary.

PART II

Working-class History in Context

8

THE DAILY CITIZEN

Class v Consumerism in the Early Labour Press

Christopher Shoop-Worrall

In October 1912, a new newspaper was launched in Britain. This newspaper, to be printed and sold daily at halfpenny an issue and eight pages in length, was specifically created to appeal to the sorts of news-reading audiences that had been buying the hugely successful *Daily Mail* (launched in 1896) and *Daily Express* (launched in 1900) throughout early years of the twentieth century. The intended reader of this new newspaper was identified by both its staff and its backers as the 'man on the street': the archetypal everyday member of the working and lower-middle classes that had become an increasingly central part of British life throughout the long Edwardian era.[1] Alfred Harmsworth, founder of both the *Daily Mail* and the *Daily Mirror,* believed that his newspapers needed to speak to the mass, everyday public, providing them what they wanted.[2] Lord Salisbury, the Conservative Prime Minister at the beginning of the twentieth century, astutely noted that these newspapers were designed by and for 'office-boys', thus noting their appeal to ordinary, lower-class members of British society.[3] This everyman was being better catered for by British society than any previous generation of lower-class citizen. From the growth of association football to the increasing emphasis on worker-orientated political policy, the wants and interests of the mass working public were increasingly at the heart of much of British life.[4]

This newfound emphasis on the everyman was particularly apparent across the British newspaper industry, and best represented by the birth and rapid rise of a new, popular daily press. These new media were heavily influenced by the New Journalism: a late-Victorian 'Americanization' of newspaper style, language and content.[5] Its content skewed heavily towards matters of 'human interest' such as crime reports, household tips, serialised fiction and sports coverage.[6] Newspapers such as the *Mail* and the *Express* were

DOI: 10.4324/9780429344084-11

the commercial peak of this news revolution, with the former becoming the first British daily to sell a million copies a day.[7] It was this success – a cheap, popular daily striving to appeal to its readers interests and beliefs[8] – that this new newspaper wished to emulate. It was not the first, and certainly would not be last, to try and copy the success reaped by Britain's earliest tabloids.

This particular newspaper, however, was unique. The new newspaper – the *Daily Citizen* – was created, financed and run by the recently founded Labour Party. Labour launched the *Citizen* to try and communicate with the mass audiences that were regularly buying the new popular press. Its launch, part of a near decade-long struggle within the wider Labour movement, was intended to spread the cause of socialism to the mass, working-class British public. In reality, the *Daily Citizen* only survived for a little over two years, during which time it hit a peak daily circulation of approximately a quarter-of-a-million copies. Its brief existence has been previously discussed by historians in very brief detail[9] and in reference to a small part of its content,[10] and the paper's eventual demise has long been dismissed as a simple lack of revenue and the crippling costs of the daily newspaper business.[11]

What this chapter will explore is a long overdue discussion of the significance of the *Daily Citizen*. While it failed in its mission, its existence offers a unique insight into the early Labour movement and its complex relationship with both the popular newspaper industry and the mass, working-class public that it claimed to naturally represent. Across the pages of the *Citizen* – and complimented by writings from across the early left press – can be seen an ideological struggle at the heart of the early British left. By trying to speak to the readers of the new dailies, Labour found itself at odds with much of the traditional British left's understanding of the nature of journalism, the purpose of the party, and the lives of the workers they wanted to politically represent. Far from being a forgotten, fleeting experiment, the *Daily Citizen* can and should be seen as a key case study of the British left and its long-standing and often problematic relationships with popular media and the mainstream public.

A Yellow Daily

As Kenneth Brown outlined in his history of the early Labour party, there was considerable effort during the first decade of the party's existence – led particularly by the party's secretary Ramsay MacDonald – to set up a newspaper through which the party could disseminate its political message to a wider audience.[12] Having initially favoured the creation of a Labour weekly, the party finally aligned with the demands of the TUC and pursued the foundation of a daily. After several botched efforts, including an ill-judged effort to purchase George Cadbury's *Daily News*, the *Daily Citizen* was launched. Due to its aim to speak to the 'man on the street', much of its content mirrored that seen in the popular new dailies of the same period. This attention to the 'human interest' and the news genres explored so effectively by early New Journalism innovators such as George Newnes and Alfred Harmsworth[13] resulted in the *Daily Citizen* behaving across significant sections of each edition as a 'yellow' daily: a populist newspaper that prioritised sensation, scandal and entertainment in its coverage of news.[14] The 'yellow' press had its roots in the American newspapers of Joseph Pulitzer and William Randolph Hearst and the coverage of the Spanish-American War.[15] These newspapers set a standard of sensational, emotionally evocative news content that was wildly successful with the mass public. These American dailies had a direct influence on the British popular dailies, with Hearst having a particular personal influence on Alfred Harmsworth.[16] It was this recent Anglo-American context of eye-catching, populist news content that the *Citizen* drew significant influence from.

One of the most prominent ways in which the *Citizen* seemed to try behaving like a popular, 'yellow' daily was how it reported on crime (in particular violent crimes) and summaries from trial proceedings. Salacious coverage of violent or shocking crime was one of the bedrocks of the British New Journalism, most notoriously seen in William Thomas Stead's running articles in the *Pall Mall Gazette* entitled 'The Maiden Tribute of Modern Babylon', which resulted in him serving jail time for his investigative work into child prostitution in London's East End.[17] While nothing on the pages of the *Citizen* reached those levels of controversy, they were similar in their evocative and dramatically headlined reports of horrible crimes.

One crime topic that the *Citizen* showed particular interest in was the issue of 'white slavery': British citizens, often women, who were running the risk of being coerced or forced into a life of morally repugnant servitude. This topic was explored in several different ways, but with a consistent emphasis on the unsavoury intentions of those working in the slave trade. One such article, dated from 1 January 1913, focused on the danger faced by two young girls leaving their homes in Salford to live alone in London. Headlined '*Young Girls in Peril: Narrow Escape from White Slavery*', it explored the risks of running away from home due to the 'dangers of the streets' that faced innocent youths on the streets of the capital. Specifically, it told of a network of people, including a woman offering free taxi rides and 'two foreigners' who tried to ensnare the two girls before the arrival of police, and astute interventions from alert, caring members of the public, scared them into running away.[18] The decision to describe two of the involved by their non-British identity is particularly interesting as an additional link between the *Daily Citizen* and the new dailies, whose jingoistic attitudes to nation and the Empire had become one of their defining features in the aftermath of their reporting on the Second Boer War.[19]

Another white slavery article, published in the same week, outlined guidelines for other young girls who the newspaper saw as running the risk of falling for the '*White Slave Traps*' that had been attempted on the girls from Salford. Readers, and specifically young girls, were warned that they:

> should never speak to strangers... should never ask the way of any but officials on duty, such as policemen... should never loiter or stand about alone in the street... should never stay to help a woman who apparently faints at their feet in the street, and should immediately call a policeman to her aid.[20]

Later that same month, another white slavery article was published in the *Citizen*, this time detailing the '*Attempted Drugging of a Girl*'. The 'traffickers... these pests to society' tried to drug and kidnap a woman 'employed at a well-known Oxford Street drapery establishment' before escaping the attentions of nearby police. This account was made especially shocking both due to the nature of the intended victim – a woman of established society, not a young runaway – and its reporting as 'a bare-faced attempt to drug her in the street (using) an open jar, from which pungent and acrid fumes arose'.[21] This time, the threat was not the shady backstreets, but broad daylight on one of London's most historic and prestigious streets. These dramatic reconstructions of 'white slavery crimes' are a particularly strong case study of the *Citizen's* attempted emulation of new daily crime reporting. Not only was it reported on similarly salacious crimes, but it was evoking the same kinds of emotional emphases: helpless young women, predatory (and non-British) agents and frightful warnings of the risks and ruin facing the unprepared on an everyday street. Such evocative representations of crime was a key part of the *Citizen,* and of the popular press that then, as it does today, featured it as a staple genre of content.

The *Daily Citizen's* sensationalised representations of crime were part of a wider focus on 'human interest' news content: stories that focused on emotive language of matters relating to events and situations that everyday readers of popular papers could better relate to. These human interests were varied in topic, but shared a sensationalist approach to the headlining and construction of the story, where the primary intention of the article was to provoke an instant, emotional response. One such manifestation of human-interest sensation was reporting of high-society scandal. One such example reported on a road accident involving the wife of Winston Churchill, which was described as a 'motor smash' that injured her with 'broken glass'.[22] The fact that the report under this dramatic headline stated her wounds were very minor (a 'slight cut') further underlines how the principle aim of the piece, considering the initial conclusions that are implied from its outlandish headline, was to generate an instinctive, rather than a considered, reader response. In another, a front-page piece from June 1913 concerning the fate of Captain Scott and his Antarctic exploration team refers to the 'Tent of Death' as the scene of their deaths, and advertises how the tent will be on show at an exhibition in Earl's Court later that year.[23] Again, the coverage of high society drama is constructed in very dramatic terms, with headlines that seem to deliberately invite shocked, emotional reactions.

Coverage of high society drama was complemented with reports of drama of the 'everyday'; stories more closely connected to the lives of the people that Labour wanted to be reading their popular daily newspaper. One of the most striking examples of this everyday drama was reports of sudden deaths. Much as with its coverage of high society scandal, the *Citizen's* handling of domestic, everyday tragedies was primarily framed around scenarios designed to provoke primarily emotional responses. The types of intended emotional responses to these stories could vary considerably.

Stories such as one concerning a housewife 'worked to death' seemed principally to wish to provoke heartbreak. Such stories detailed the good nature of the victim, such as this particular woman's 'devoted and cheerful' attitude to her 'exceptionally hard life', which comprised having to run a house of four young children and care for (and work in the place of) her consumption-afflicted husband. This idealistic vision of caring, traditional household woman is then dramatically contrasted with the events that caused death:

> Up to Saturday last she had attended to her frames in the cotton factory with unwavering and unfailing regularity from six o'clock in the morning until 5.30 in the evening... Returning, she put her children to bed and soon afterwards her husband had a sudden seizure.
>
> She was hurrying to the bedroom when she was heard to exclaim, "Oh, my head". Collapsing entirely, she fell across her husband on the bed and passed away.[24]

This extract, indicative of similar reports throughout other editions of the *Citizen,* constructs the everyday tragedy of a woman who died (according the report) due to 'heart failure brought on by overwork' into a short story. By focusing on the emotive qualities of the deceased – caring, devoted, self-sacrificing – and then depicting her death as a dramatic climax (complete with last words), the news report takes on qualities that could easily be attributed to a piece of fiction, or a line from a play. The focus was deliberately and overwhelmingly on the emotive elements of the story – its empathy and its shock reveal – and constructed news less as a recounting of facts, and more as a theatrical reconstruction.

This emphasis on the dramatisation of everyday news was also used to explore or heighten the less serious or even openly comedic aspects of domestic tragedy. One such example, headlined 'Death Bed Mishap' and concerning a dying widow in Florence, stated:

> The woman was dying, and a priest was administering the last sacrament to her in the presence of about 80 relatives and friends, as is the custom in the district. The bedroom, which was on the first floor of the house, was packed to overflowing.
>
> While those assembled were praying the floor gave way, and all the people, including the dying woman, were precipitated to the floor below.[25]

Again, a story of household death is constructed in the *Citizen* as a dramatic story. In his case however, as in others, the story is made to be light-hearted, from the 'mishap' headline to the suddenness of the collapse. The relative absence of detail post-collapse (such as details of specific numbers killed or injured) further emphasises how everyday tragedy in the *Daily Citizen,* whether told dramatically or comically, served a primary role of entertaining, as much as informing, the reader.

This interest in reader entertainment is also very apparent in one of the *Daily Citizen*'s most deliberate attempts to capture a new daily readership, its sports coverage. Coverage of sports, in particular football, had become a defining aspect of the new dailies and the New Journalism as a whole by the beginning of the twentieth century.[26] The particular dedication to football across large sections of the British press spoke considerably of the sport's increasingly prominent place in British mass culture during the by the early twentieth century.[27] Particular newspapers, specifically elements of the daily evening press, prioritised football and sports coverage more generally as a key selling point to large audiences of lower-class readers.[28] Even traditional newspapers such as *The Times,* albeit uncertainly, had begun to include sports coverage by the beginning of the long-Edwardian era due to its undeniable mass popularity.[29] The *Citizen* seemed to fully appreciate the mass appeal of sports reports, and dedicated significant sections of every pre-war addition (often on its own page entitled 'Special Page of Sporting News') to cover news from cricket, horse racing, rugby and, most of all, football.

The most common sports articles in the *Citizen* were football match reports, which detailed the events of matches from across the country. It would often introduce its sports pages published during the football season was a 'League Review' or 'Football in Review', which would provide brief round-ups of games across the top two divisions. Headlines and sub-headings in the football reports seemed to pay particular attention to certain teams such as the London clubs Arsenal and Chelsea, the two Manchester clubs and other successful teams of the era such as Newcastle, Sunderland and Everton. The emphasis of reports on the time's most successful and highest-profile football clubs strongly suggests the paper's eagerness to speak to the largest football-loving audience, by focusing its coverage on the teams that were likely to be the best-supported and most-discussed.

This attention by the *Citizen* on football's most popular elements was especially apparent in how it covered the FA Cup. The tournament, especially its latter stages, made news around the world, and both its prestige and mass appeal resulted in the *Citizen* giving the cup additional coverage outside of its sports section. While the early rounds of the cup would occasionally receive special attention, such as one sports page being retitled entirely to focus on 'Today's Cup Ties', the 1913 FA Cup Final was a standout example of the *Citizen's* attention to popular sports coverage.

The game, played between the First Division's top two teams Aston Villa and Sunderland, received multiple pages of dedicated coverage on both the day of, and the days after, the game. Full page profiles were provided of both teams, with photographs and illustrations of every member of the two squads with a brief description of their position on the field and their personal beginnings.[30] The game itself received a two-page spread in the first edition after the final was played, complete with a full-page cartoon which depicted the events of the game and accompanying speech bubbles speculating on what players and fans were saying at key points during the match.[31] In keeping with the *Citizen's* broader interest in the everyman, there was also attention paid to those who went to watch the game at London's Crystal Palace. Of particular prominence was a photograph taken of people sat watching the final in a tree overlooking the ground, the headline of which approved their 'Tree Top Enthusiasm'.[32]

The coverage of the 1913 FA Cup Final, with its attention to dramatic reconstruction, eye-grabbing headlines and visuals, and the everyman presence in the story, acts as an excellent microcosm of the broader ways in which the *Daily Citizen* strove to be a popular halfpenny daily. It presented news in ways as entertaining as they were informative, using language and visual elements that highlighted the dramatic and narrative elements of the news being presented. It was a concise and content-diverse newspaper that encapsulated many of the popular New Journalism innovations that had helped publications such as the *Mail* become such huge successes.

The problem that faced the *Citizen*, and a hugely significant reason why this Labour daily failed, was that this populist, 'yellow' journalism was not its whole identity. While the dailies it was clearly trying to emulate were consistent in their popular, New Journalism approach, the *Citizen* was not just a popular 'yellow' daily. It was also a 'red' daily: a socialist newspaper that, consistent with other left-wing publications of the period, was opposed to the very kind of press that it was so clearly trying to imitate.

A Red Daily

As well as behaving like a popular new daily, the *Daily Citizen* strongly identified as a traditional socialist newspaper in the style of party-affiliated publications such as the *Labour Leader* and the *Clarion*. With the banner under every front-page reading 'Owned and Controlled by the Labour Movement', it was a daily reminder to readers that this was, above all else, a party-political newspaper. For all the attention to diverse New Journalism content, this was principally a political organ for the party to talk to a larger audience, and had been founded with this as its sole real objective. In this context, the 'yellow' content sits uncomfortably alongside the more traditional socialist newspaper content that was also published in the *Daily Citizen*.

Understandably for a Labour newspaper, considerable space was set aside for matters concerning Labour politics. Page three of most pre-war editions of the citizen was set aside for 'Labour' news, with large sections entitled 'Labour at Home', 'Labour's Vision', and 'Labour Abroad'. These sections were comprised of articles, sometimes written by prominent member or associates of the party such as MPs and trade union leaders, detailing a proposed new Labour policy, or the party's stance on a new piece of government legislation. They would also provide sympathetic summaries of labourer disputes, outlining the reasons for the industrial action and providing readers with updates on ongoing struggles. One high-profile example of these kinds of reports was the paper's running coverage of striking London taxi drivers. The latter struggles of the 'taxi-cab war' received particular attention, and it and other notable strikes would occasionally make the front page.[33] Such occasions included a large miners' strike in early May 1913,[34] and a mass walkout in Belgium which was the first item of front-page news on the same as the before-mentioned 1913 FA Cup Final.[35] The latter front-page story, coupled with the regular inclusion of the news section 'Labour Abroad' showed that the *Citizen* intended readers to have a global understanding of labour struggles, rather than just matters close to home. There was an assumption, or expectation, that its readers would want, or should want, to know about socialism as part of an internationalist understanding of working-class struggle, in addition to the messages included in the paper from domestic leaders of the labour movement.

This content differed considerably from much of the 'yellow' news contained in the *Citizen* as it was considerably more fact-driven, and less dependent on emotional language. For example, the large miner's strike on the front page of 3 May 1913 is reported as matter-of-fact, focusing on the numbers gathering to protest against non-unionist employees:

> In the Rhondda Valley...the strikers number over 11,000. This total includes nearly 7,000 men at the Tylerstown and Ferndale pits. There are

> nearly 12,000 men on strike in the Aberdale Valley, and of these 5,000 are at the Powell Duffryn and 5,000 at Nixon's Navigation.[36]

The story's more traditional and educationalist approach to journalism – a provision of factual details – is a sharp contrast to the popular content that is explored elsewhere in the paper. The different tone of this and other similarly 'red' articles is often made even more striking by being placed alongside sensationalist 'yellow' news. In the case of the mining strike, the story directly next to it showcases the other side to the *Citizen's* content:

> REVOLVER DUEL IN TRAIN
> Bandit's Encounter with Millionaire
> A telegram from Kansas City gives particulars of one of the most daring and melodramatic hold-ups in American railway history.[37]

The most significant aspect of the *Citizen's* inclusion of both sensationalist and educationalist news material was not the diversity of subject matter, as one of the most successful aspects of popular newspapers was the breadth of content that they provided to readers.[38] Rather, it was that the two types of news were approached and represented in fundamentally different ways, using language and sometimes even formatting that spoke of two different newspaper traditions: that of a popular newspaper, and that of a traditional socialist newspaper.

This contrast of newspaper styles and approaches was thrown into even sharper contrast when different articles were discussing the same subject matter. This most noticeably occurred in the *Citizen*'s reporting on sports. Interspersed between the match reports, the photographs and the cartoons, articles would appear that offered an often self-labelled 'socialist' angle into the sport under discussion, most usually football. These included reports on the work of the London Playing Fields Society, who worked to provide sports pitches for Londoners,[39] as well as pieces educating readers on the 'joy of exercise' and why they (workers) should be trying to play more sport in their free time due to sport's real 'significance'.[40] One article also attacks the 'sordid commercialism' that it sees as part of the modern game, in response to a player moving to Blackburn Rovers for a transfer fee of £2,000, bemoaning how no man's skill at football should command such an investment.[41]

These types of articles sat uncomfortably next to the newspaper's more sensationalist sports coverage because they spoke of the *Daily Citizen's* ideological similarity with the more traditional left-wing publications of its time. These titles, such as the *Labour Leader*, gave little-to-no attention to sport in their weekly content, and any inclusion of sport would focus on a negative aspect of that particular sport. Football was spoken of particularly negatively, due to its (according to one long read in an edition of the *Cooperative*

News) negative influence on the moral character of the masses who watched it, as well as the sport's close ties to both gambling and the consumption of alcohol.[42] Therefore, throughout the multitudes of enthusiastic reports into popular sports, the *Daily Citizen* espoused a traditional, left-wing scepticism of popular sport, questioning the real moral and political value of one of its most discussed and, if wanting to be a popular daily, essential genres of news content.

This uncomfortable combination of populist enthusiasm and traditionalist scepticism was present in other sections of most editions of the *Daily Citizen*. For instance, attempts to mirror the women's sections of newspapers such as the *Daily Mail* contained long, moralising articles on certain aspects of popular culture. Most notably, a full-page spread was dedicated to the question 'Is Modern Dancing Decadent?' and strongly argued for:

> A revival of the good, old-fashioned British dances…
>
> (and) I have no hesitation in denouncing in no uncertain terms the freak dances of to-day. Such dances as the Chicken Crawl and the Liverpool Lurch ought not to be tolerated anywhere. The danger is that once made popular in our music halls they find their way to the dancing hall.[43]

Articles such as these, seen both within the context of the newspaper's broader duality of content and the attitudes espoused by its similarly left-wing contemporaries, indicate a broader ideological problem that hampered the *Daily Citizen* throughout much of its time in circulation. However, it included popular content on sensation and sport to try to behave like a popular daily, thus attracting similar numbers of readers as other popular new dailies. However, it never truly became a popular daily due to its persistent inclusion of traditional socialist understandings of what news content should be. The paper's backers seemed to understand that topics like sport, serialised crime and popular culture were genres of news that mass audiences wanted to read. However, it never seemed comfortable just speaking to these readers on their terms. To the leaders of the early Labour movement, a newspaper passed on appropriate knowledge; its job was to inform, not to entertain. It appreciated certain news genres were popular, which is why they were included. However, as was showcased in the criticisms of sport, the sudden switches between types of news language and the above-cited derision of popular sensations such as music-hall dances, it did not understand or appreciate their value to the people reading them.

The *Daily Citizen* therefore had a profound problem of identity – a struggle between trying to be a light-hearted daily, and wanting to be a serious, educationalist Labour paper. Its inclusion of popular content showcased many of the linguistic, narrative and visual innovations popularised so successfully by the new dailies, and demonstrated the party's determination to want to make a newspaper that spoke to a large audience of lower-class British citizens. However, it could not fully embrace this 'yellow' identity to deeply held beliefs across much of the early Labour movement concerning the journalistic merit of the types of news content and popular topics that were so regularly discussed in other popular dailies. This problematic duality in the *Citizen's* content and purpose was further compounded by how the paper represented other popular newspapers, the very press that it was trying to behave like. The attitudes towards the press printed in the *Citizen* – attitudes that were shared by many across the early left – suggest that the problems that faced Labour's daily newspaper were also ones facing the movement as a whole: how to understand and appreciate the wants and interests of the mass, working public.

Embracing an Enemy

The rise of a daily national popular press in Britain at the end of the nineteenth had sparked two simultaneous responses across much of the emerging British left. However, there was an appreciation of its potential use as a political tool. It was this thinking that had driven the party's near decade-long efforts to launch their own newspapers prior to the *Citizen,* and it was one publicly espoused by newspapers affiliated to the Labour party. The *Labour Leader* for instance noted how successful socialist dailies in countries like Germany were evidence enough that a similar enterprise should be launched in Britain, specifically because of such a paper's ability to speak to the 'man in the street'. For all the potential political worth of a daily however, this same article showcased the other side to the early left's response to the new popular press:

> There is no Socialist paper to appeal every morning to the man in the street, and to counteract daily the insidious attacks of the capitalist Press.[44]

The 'capitalist' press was a term used in writings across the early left to refer to the new popular press, in particular the *Daily Mail* and the *Daily Express.* Occasionally, these two newspapers would be referred to by name when being criticised, such as in an article accusing the former of printing advertisements for car companies disguised as news content.[45] More usually however, these newspapers were referred to using one of three common derogatory terms: 'capitalist' (as shown above), 'halfpenny', and 'yellow'. While the first of these terms – through its reference to traditional socialist sentiments of 'capital' versus 'labour' – had the potential to be used on any newspaper that Labour saw as resistant to their cause, the latter two had a particular resonance when used against the popular press.

First, by specifically criticising newspapers that were 'halfpenny', the early labour movement demonstrated a particular problem with newspapers that were cheap to purchase. These newspapers were of specific concern to the movement because of their affordability; these were the newspapers that were readily available to the lower classes of British society. This concern is also apparent in the derogatory term 'yellow': a reference to a newspaper's cheap nature, both in terms of its choice of print paper and its content, which had also been used against the output of Pulitzer and Hearst. Again, key to this labour critique of the popular press is its inexpensive nature, and by extension its potential appeals to the British working classes. More than that however, the use of the term 'yellow' gets to the heart of the discord that existed between Labour, the popular dailies and the mass working public.

By labelling them 'yellow', the popular press was represented as dishonest, a press that relief on lies for much of its content. This conclusion from an article in the *Labour Leader*, while representative of sentiments seen across the leftist press of this period, evokes this critique particularly strongly:

> The publishing of scandalous reports as statements of fact is at all times an abominable practice, and ought to be put a stop to; but if the yellow press in this country were punished every time it published scurrilous unverified rumours, well, where would it be?.[46]

This understanding of the popular press as dishonest, coupled with the understanding of its capitalist and cheap nature, is what made newspapers like the *Daily Mail* such an enemy to many in the early Labour movement. Not only were these newspapers seen to be naturally pro-capital, and were specifically priced for the attention of the everyman, but they were feeding the everyman news that Labour saw as dishonest. Labour understood the role of a newspaper as something that informed a reader of what they needed, or should, know. In the case of the newspaper aiming for a working-class audience, this meant news content detailing labour struggles both home and abroad. It meant providing educationalist approaches to popular topics, so that a reader would know the 'true', socialist worth of a given popular craze. It also meant raising the worker's awareness of what the movement saw as enemies of their quest for self-betterment. The popular press, with its attention to scandalous stories, sensationalist language and entertainment-focused reporting of sports and other parts of mass popular culture, was one of these perceived enemies. More than that, these newspapers were direct rivals to the movement's attempts to educate the British lower classes.

This powerful anti-daily sentiment, the belief in the popular press as an enemy of the labour struggle, was not only present across the traditional Labour press. It was, consistently, present in the pages of the daily-imitating *Daily Citizen*. It would run critical articles of the same popular dailies named and criticised in papers like the *Labour Leader.* For example, an article would criticise the 'illusion' that the daily press was representative of public opinion, instead claiming they were 'reflections of the personal idiosyncrasies and political associations of a man (the newspaper's proprietor) who may or may not have sagacity'.[47] Another would champion the *Citizen* at the expensive of its 'capitalist' rivals, saying 'how could they expect papers depending largely on railway advertisements' to support workers, and that the *Citizen* was 'one of the most important educational influences in the land'.[48] The sentiments shown in articles like these – sentiments that constructed the popular press as anti-labour papers powered by the interests of rich owners and advertisers – were very much a part of wider leftist sentiments towards the early popular press.

The *Daily Citizen* did not just publish occasional anti-press articles, however. Instead, it would dedicate a section at the bottom of page two of every pre-war edition to a section titled 'Their Views and Ours'. This section would be comprised of snippets taken from other newspapers, including frequent reference to the *Mail* and the *Express*, accompanied by a response from the *Citizen* mocking that paper's content:

> "It is still possible to be a worker and a lady", says the Daily Sketch. Perish this foolish delusion![49]
>
> "Take the Tube home", says the Daily Mail. To use as a garden hose, or what?[50]
>
> "Have you ever felt a desperate longing to get away from everything?", asks the Daily Mail. Often, but the ubiquity of our contemporary makes the longing futile.[51]
>
> "In politics we have working-class measures", says Reynold's. The Liberal imagination running riot.[52]

These critiques, aimed mostly at popular national publications of both Liberal and Conservative allegiance, served as a daily reminder of the Labour movement's low opinion of the popular press. It was a reminder that the movement as a whole understood popular newspapers as dishonest, poor-quality publications that fed workers the wrong kind of journalistic diet. It was also a daily statement of the party's perceived superiority over the popular press, as they knew what workers really needed to read about in their daily newspaper. Workers should not be reading unintelligent newspapers such as the *Daily Mail* or *Reynold's*; they should be reading the higher-quality, informed *Daily Citizen.*

This daily stance taken in the *Citizen* exposed two fundamental flaws in the mind-set of the early labour movement. First, these regular reminders of the supposed unscrupulous or unintelligent nature of popular newspapers were being printed in their own take on a popular newspaper. By regularly mocking the entity they were demonstrably using as the *Citizen's* influence, they further enhanced the uncomfortable duality of the Labour daily's content, which was equally enthusiastic about, and entirely dismissive of, popular news content.

More than that however, 'Their Views and Ours' spoke considerably of Labour's attitude towards the British mass public with whom they wished to engage. By launching a cheap, eight-page daily, and including sensationalist and popular news content, they showed an awareness of popular news' appeal to the masses, and wished, to some extent, to give the people what they wanted. However, this provision of content never matured into an understanding of exactly why mass audiences particularly engaged with popular forms of journalism. Labour's expectations of working-class lives – and their needs and demands – fundamentally clashed with the lived realities of working-class experience in long Edwardian Britain. The result was a 'red' and 'yellow' daily: a popular newspaper that consistently showed disdain towards popular journalism; an everyman's daily that struggled to understand the everyman; a Labour party struggling to appreciate the real lives of the workers they assumed to naturally represent.

Conclusion

By the end of the First World War, Labour had begun to understand the importance of speaking to mass, working-class audiences through popular mediums, and the formation of their first ever government was helped considerably by their increasingly intelligent use of popular media to speak to potential voters.[53] As this chapter has demonstrated, Labour was aware of the political potential of popular media since soon after their formation in 1900. The issue that faced pre-war Labour was not whether it understood the potential of popular media. Its problem was due to its traditional socialist understanding of both popular news and the lived realities of daily-reading working-class audiences.

The *Daily Citizen* serves as a fascinating insight into an emergent political movement caught between its ideological understanding of the working-class and the realities of those workers' lives. By choosing to launch and maintain an eight-page halfpenny daily, Labour demonstrated that they knew the appeal of popular news, and that it was a form of journalism particularly liked by the working-class masses they were so keen to speak to. However, their traditional understandings of both journalism's purpose and everyday working reality hindered the paper's chance at truly connecting with a working audience. The *Citizen's* demise, traditionally blamed on poor advertising and high running costs, should instead be understood in the context of the early Labour movement's struggle to reconcile its class ideology with the lives of working-class people.

Notes

1 The 'Long Edwardian' era is used in this chapter to refer to the period from the mid-1890s to the onset of war in 1914.
2 Martin Conboy, *The Language of Newspapers: Socio-historical Perspectives* (London, Bloomsbury: 2010), pp. 115–118.
3 See Adrian Bingham, 'Monitoring the Popular Press: An Historical Perspective', *History & Policy* (June, 2005), accessed at https://www.historyandpolicy.org/policy-papers/papers/monitoring-the-popular-press-an-historical-perspective on 26 October 2023.
4 See Christopher Shoop-Worrall, 'Left Wing', *The Blizzard* 25 (June, 2017), pp. 100–105.
5 Joel H. Wiener, *The Americanization of the British Press, 1830s–1914* (Basingstoke, Palgrave Macmillan: 2011).
6 See Joel H. Wiener, ed., *Papers for the Millions: The New Journalism in Britain 1850–1914* (New York, Greenwood Press: 1988); Martin Conboy, *The Press and Popular Culture* (London, SAGE Publications: 2002), pp. 87–112; Alan J. Lee, *The Origins of the Popular Press in England, 1855–1945* (London, Rowman and Littlefield: 1976); Matthew Engel, *Tickle the Public: One Hundred Years of the Popular Press* (London, Phoenix: 1996).
7 Adrian Bingham and Martin Conboy, *Tabloid Century: The Popular Press in Britain, 1896 to the Present* (Oxford, Peter Lang: 2015), p. 8.
8 By the beginning of the twentieth century, more and more newspapers were moving towards a journalistic approach that wished to reflect reader interests, rather than simply inform. See Mark Hampton, *Visions of the Press in Britain, 1850–1950* (Urbana, University of Illinois Press: 2004).
9 D. Hopkins, "The socialist press in Britain, 1890–1910" in James Curran, George Boyce and Pauline Wingate, eds., *Newspaper History from the Seventeenth Century to the Present Day* (London, Constable: 1978), pp. 265–280.
10 Carolyn Malone, 'Campaigning Journalism: The Clarion, the Daily Citizen, and the Protection of Women Workers, 1898–1912', *Labour History Review* 67.3 (December, 2002), pp. 281–297.
11 Stanley Harrison, *Poor Men's Guardians: A Survey of the Struggles for a Democratic Newspaper Press, 1763–1973* (London, Lawrence and Wishart: 1974).
12 K. D. Brown, ed., *The First Labour Party, 1906–1914* (Dover, Routledge: 1985).
13 Lee, *The Origins of the Popular Press.*
14 For the origins of 'yellow' journalism see W. Joseph Campbell, *Yellow Journalism: Puncturing the Myths, Defining the Legacies* (Westport, Praeger: 2001).
15 Richard L. Kaplan, 'Yellow Journalism' in Wolfgang Donsbach (ed.), *The International Encyclopaedia of Communication* (New York, John Wiley and Sons: 2008), pp. 5369–5271.
16 Joel H. Wiener, *The Americanization of the British Press, 1830s–1914* (Basingstoke, Palgrave Macmillan: 2011), pp. 183–210.
17 See Raymond L. Schults, *Crusader in Babylon: W. T. Stead and the Pall Mall Gazette* (Lincoln, University of Nebraska Press: 1972).
18 'Young Girls in Peril', *Daily Citizen,* 1 January 1913, p. 3.
19 See Gavin Wilkinson, '"The Blessings of War": The Depiction of Military Force in Edwardian Newspaper', *Journal of Contemporary History* 33.1 (1998), pp. 97–115.
20 'White Slave Traps', *Daily Citizen,* 4 January 1913, p. 8.
21 'White Slavers at Work', *Daily Citizen,* 18 January 1913, p. 1.
22 'Mrs Churchill in Motor Smash', *Daily Citizen,* 20 January 1913, p. 3.
23 *Daily Citizen,* 27 June 1913, p. 1.
24 'Woman Worked to Death', *Daily Citizen,* 1 January 1913, p. 1.

25 *Daily Citizen,* 23 May 1913, p. 1.
26 Raymond Boyle and Richard Haynes, *Power Play: Sport, the Media and Popular Culture* (Edinburgh, Edinburgh University Press: 2009), pp. 19–42.
27 Richard Holt, *Sport and the British* (Oxford, Oxford University Press: 1992), pp. 306–307.
28 Lucy Brown, *Victorian News and Newspapers* (Oxford, Oxford University Press: 1985), pp. 271–272, quoted in S. Tate, 'James Catton, 'Tityrus' of The Athletic News (1860 to 1936): A Biographical Study', *Sport in History,* 25.1 (2005), pp. 98–11.
29 J. Chovanec, '"...but there were no broken legs": The Emerging Genre of Football Match Reports in *The Times* in the 1860s', *Journal of Historical Pragmatics* 15.2 (2014), pp. 228–254.
30 *Daily Citizen,* 19 April 1913.
31 'A Thrilling Cup Final', *Daily Citizen*, 21 April 1913, p. 8.
32 'A Thrilling Cup Final', *Daily Citizen*, 21 April 1913, p. 3.
33 *Daily Citizen*, 2 January 1913.
34 *Daily Citizen*, 3 May 1913.
35 *Daily Citizen*, 19 April 1913.
36 *Daily Citizen*, 3 May 1913.
37 *Daily Citizen*, 3 May 1913.
38 Bingham and Conboy, *Tabloid Century,* p. 6.
39 *Daily Citizen,* 10 January 1913, p. 6.
40 *Daily Citizen*, 21 January 1913, p. 6.
41 *Daily Citizen*, 7 January 1913, p. 4.
42 'Should Football Be Stopped?', *Cooperative News*, 21 November 1914.
43 *Daily Citizen*, 20 January 1913, p. 7.
44 'The Need of a Daily', *Labour Leader*, 27 September 1907.
45 'Daily Mail Dodge', *Labour Leader.*
46 'Daily Mail Dodge', 7 February 1907.
47 'The Day's Illusion', *Daily Citizen*, 11 January 1913, p. 2.
48 *Daily Citizen*, 20 June 1913.
49 'Their Views and Ours', *Daily Citizen*, 9 June 1913, p. 2.
50 *Daily Citizen*, 27 June 1913.
51 *Daily Citizen*, 1 July 1913.
52 *Daily Citizen*, 3 May 1913.
53 See Laura Beers, *Your Britain: Media and the Making of the Labour Party* (Cambridge, MA, Harvard University Press: 2010).

9

GENDER POLITICS OF CLASS

Exploring the Connections and Collaboration between the Irish Labour Movement and the Irish Women's Franchise League in Dublin, 1908–1916

Erin Geraghty

Ireland during the years 1908–1914 was a melting pot of political ideologies, agendas, and movements. Both the suffrage and labour movements during this period were competing for political prominence with the Irish nationalist movement. Cooperation took place and alliances were formed between the militant suffrage group, the Irish Women's Franchise League (IWFL) and the labour movement in Dublin.[1] Support was revealed through public declarations, as well as through practical demonstrations of solidarity.

In the first decades of the twentieth century, the labour movement in Ireland underwent a significant transformation. The Irish Trades Union Congress (ITUC) had been formed in 1894 and was an important body in transforming, organising, and uniting unions all over Ireland. Furthermore, emerging male leaders such as James Connolly, James Larkin, and William O'Brien established new unions and new political parties in Dublin, including the Irish Transport and General Workers Union (ITGWU) in 1908, the Socialist Party of Ireland (SPI) in 1910, and the Independent Labour Party of Ireland in 1912. The formation of these new unions and political groups by radical leaders prompted the shift from 'old unionism' (characterised by moderation and negotiation with employers as a priority) to an Irish variant of syndicalism, a more revolutionary form of unionism.[2] This new unionism emphasised militant tactics such as strikes to progress the workers cause, and prioritised the organisation of low-skilled workers in order to achieve a wider political consciousness.[3] The organising of a wider range of industries meant a growth in membership and consequently, a growth in the strength of these unions.

The Irish suffrage movement had been re-energised by the formation of the IWFL during the same period. The IWFL was established in 1908, prompted

DOI: 10.4324/9780429344084-12

by the formation of the militant suffrage group in England, the Women's Social and Political Union (WSPU) in 1903. The founding members, Hanna Sheehy Skeffington and Margaret Cousins, established the IWFL to be militant and non-partisan. Based in Dublin, the IWFL had a membership of approximately 1,000 members by 1912, making it the largest suffrage organisation in Ireland at this time.[4]

The first half of this chapter considers the factors that enabled cooperation between these two movements. In particular, I consider the interchange of political ideas and strategies through friendships and networks of individuals, as well as the importance of militancy as a unifying form of action.[5] The second half of this chapter identifies the moments of practical support and solidarity demonstrated by the IWFL and the labour movement and interrogates the effect this had on groups and movements more generally.

The historiography of Ireland during this period has generally focused on the nationalist debate, which has also tended to dominate women's history. Literature concerning the Irish suffrage movement and Irish feminism has expanded since the 1980s, placing particular emphasis on understanding feminism within nationalism, and the female nationalists.[6] Limited historiography on the Irish labour movement during this period has also tended to emphasise the link with nationalism, focusing on individuals such as James Connolly, or considering labour in relation to the Irish revolution. Most of the literature concerning the Irish labour movement and Irish working class largely neglects the presence of women.[7] However, in recent years progress has been made to rectify this omission by scholars such as Mary Jones and Mary Daly.[8] Yet, even within work that has included the presence of women in class politics, there has been little analysis of women who partook in both suffrage and labour movements.

There were significant barriers to the alliance between the suffrage and labour movements, and it must be noted that the collaboration discussed within the chapter is not representative of the movements in their entirety. The most obvious barrier to cooperation was the difference in priorities. The reinvigorated labour movement prioritised class consciousness and unification of the (predominantly male) workers against capital, whereas the suffrage movement focused first and foremost on votes for women. Neither group would compromise their primary objective enough to ensure a lasting alliance between two movements of differing aims. Class difference was also an obstacle to a continued alliance between suffrage and labour. The suffrage movement was predominantly a middle-class venture, and the labour leaders were worried that if middle-class women achieved enfranchisement, their votes would be used against men of the working class. With property qualifications still in place, there existed a pervasive fear that the propertied classes would vote in their own interests and against those of the working class. This, in particular, resonated for the IWFL as their formative goal was for 'votes for women on the same terms as men'. To begin with, the IWFL had simply demanded the removal of the sex disqualification.[9] However, this goal changed as they began to collaborate closely with the labour movement in Dublin.

The Connections between Suffrage and Labour

The first key point of collaboration between the suffrage and labour movements in Dublin was through the support shown by the political wings of labour for women's suffrage. Both the SPI and ILP had universal adult enfranchisement as part of their formative agenda and actively supported votes for women from the outset. Additionally, the ITUC were arguably more progressive in their views on gender than their British counterpart, having voted Mary Galway onto its executive body, the parliamentary committee, in 1907.[10] This established her as the first woman in both the UK and Ireland to hold such a position. The British Trades Union Congress (TUC) parliamentary committee did not elect a woman member until over a decade later, in 1917. The close social networks of Dublin that straddled both movements are a key element to understanding this unique progression in terms of gender structures within the Irish labour movement.

There was an overlap in membership of political labour and suffrage, largely through the leaders of both movements. This led to the cross-fertilisation of political ideas and tactics and ensured both movements grew and developed in dialogue with one another. Rosemary Cullen Owens has stated that the IWFL was closest to formal alliance with labour through the beliefs of individual members if not official League policy.[11] I would go further to suggest that the beliefs of individuals when directed to another movement or organisation, had the capability to *influence* the policy and political affiliations of organisations. The influence of individuals in aligning movements is clear when considering Hanna and Francis Sheehy Skeffington. Hanna Sheehy Skeffington co-founded the IWFL in 1908 with Margaret Cousins, and espoused both socialist and nationalist political views. In particular, she was a member of the SPI and attended the inaugural meeting of the Irish Women's Workers' Union (IWWU) in 1911. Her husband, Francis, shared her political beliefs and was elected President of the SPI in 1912.[12] Francis Sheehy Skeffington was often requested to speak at SPI and ILP meetings and was very much a part of the network of labour leaders such as James Connolly, Walter Carpenter, and William O'Brien between 1911 and 1916.[13]

It is likely due to these personal connections that Hanna Sheehy Skeffington and Margaret Cousins were invited to address meetings of the SPI between April and June 1910.[14] Although both women kept to gendered topics such as 'Mary Wollstonecraft: A Pioneer Woman' and 'Sex Equality in Politics', speaking about these issues in a predominantly male-dominated political space ensured the intersection of political ideas and ideals, consequently helping educate and influence the politics of the men attending those meetings. In turn, individuals from the SPI such as Walter Carpenter spoke at IWFL meetings. In April 1917, Carpenter addressed a meeting of the IWFL concerning women's trades unions, and the following month addressed a meeting on the subject of housing.[15] This practice of speaking at meetings ensured exchange of political ideas between the IWFL and labour, and furthermore publicly cemented their relations. The close links between the SPI and the IWFL were evident, given that they shared rooms at the Antient Concert Rooms alternatively for their meetings.[16]

Sheehy Skeffington's personal connections arose from her middle-class status and education, having achieved a Bachelor of Arts and then a Master of Arts in Modern Languages from the Royal University of Ireland. Her father, David Sheehy, was an Irish Party MP and had taken part in the Irish Land War as a member of the Irish Republican Brotherhood (IRB).[17] Her university education and familial political reputation afforded her connections and a standing in the intellectual social network of Dublin. Despite this predominantly privileged background, she was clearly concerned with working-class politics and causes. Alongside ardent suffragism, Sheehy Skeffington's personal notebooks explored ideas for the '8hr working day' and 'the working-class value of the vote'.[18] Additionally, she was committed to trade unionism, and not only attended the inaugural meeting of the IWWU in 1911, but also shared the platform with socialists such as Constance Markievicz and James Larkin.[19] She spoke at the meeting, stating how proud she felt to be on the platform at such a momentous occasion, and felt it was 'desirable that men and women should work together for the welfare of both sexes'.[20] Furthermore, Sheehy Skeffington often spoke at meetings for the Irish Women's Reform League (IWRL), the only Irish suffrage society that placed equal emphasis on women's suffrage and trade union issues.[21]

Dublin-based labour leaders such as William O'Brien were supportive of the suffrage movement in Ireland. O'Brien was an influential figure within labour circles at this time and had close ties to Francis and Hanna Sheehy Skeffington. He was influential in successfully pressing the Dublin Trades Council to create a local Labour Party in 1911 and was a key player in ensuring women's suffrage was a policy of the newly formed party.[22] His own union, the Amalgamated Society of Tailors, admitted women as members.[23] Although William O'Brien was not as outspoken and outwardly passionate as James Larkin or James Connolly, he was known to be a 'useful though unobtrusive friend' of the IWFL and Irish suffrage movement.[24] His friendship with Hanna Sheehy Skeffington was sustained throughout the suffrage movement and beyond. This proved politically useful as he often wrote personally to Hanna Sheehy Skeffington from his position in the Dublin United

Trades Council and Labour League offering to send messages to individuals within labour circles and requesting and exchanging newspaper articles.[25]

James Connolly was arguably the most important individual from the labour movement to outwardly support the IWFL. I maintain that James Connolly was interested in the IWFL specifically because of their belief in militancy. It was reported that Connolly 'took an interest in women because they were in revolt, and as long as they were in rebellion, he would continue to take an interest in them'.[26] Sex equality featured strongly in his socialist ideology, and he supported this in practice. He famously wrote: 'the worker is the slave of capitalist society; the female worker is the slave of that slave'.[27] Connolly often expressed support for the women's cause in public forums, particularly in columns of the *Irish Citizen* newspaper. During the 1912 mass meeting of suffrage societies in Ireland, he stated that: 'A Home Rule Bill that excluded half of the people of Ireland from the franchise would be an anomaly in the age of progress'.[28] He also often travelled from Belfast to Dublin to speak at IWFL weekly meetings.[29] This action was largely appreciated by the League. Hanna Sheehy Skeffington stated that 'Connolly never once failed to respond to a call for a Mass Meeting, a Protest Demonstration; when he went to Belfast, he held meetings there for us'.[30] A letter from Louie Bennett, of the IWRL, highlighted Connolly's particular support for the IWFL. Bennett stated that Connolly, while 'a strong suffragist, he valued only the militant movement'.[31] It is difficult to determine if Connolly's relationship with Hanna Sheehy Skeffington came about as a result of militancy, or due to it. Either way, the shared appreciation for militant tactics ensured that the IWFL had a permanent ally in James Connolly.

Militancy

The shared appreciation for militant tactics was a key factor ensuring the connection between the IWFL and the labour movement in Dublin. Militancy distinguished the IWFL from the rest of the suffrage movement in Ireland, identifying them as 'social rebels', which ultimately made them a more interesting and worthwhile ally to the labour movement. Suffrage use of militancy had begun with the WSPU in 1905 and had rejuvenated the suffrage movement across the UK. Militant methods employed by suffragettes in both the UK and Ireland encompassed a broad range of behaviours and tactics, both legal and illegal. Although suffrage militancy has come to be recognised as synonymous with the arson and window-smashing campaigns of the WSPU, it also included various forms of direct action such as: selling suffrage literature in the street, heckling politicians and public meetings, holding open-air meetings, and generally challenging the political and social status of women in the public arena.[32]

The IWFL mainly utilised militancy in the form of holding open air meetings, heckling, and selling the suffrage newspaper, the *Irish Citizen*. They also, on one occasion in 1912, smashed the windows of the General Post Office (GPO), the Custom House, and Dublin Castle.[33] The labour movement utilised some of the same methods, and direct comparisons can be drawn. In a defiant shift away from 'old unionism', the proponents of the 'new unionism' of the late nineteenth and early twentieth century prioritised strike action, selling literature, and large-scale picketing. Dublin trade unionists regularly used militant methods in this period, holding large-scale meetings and protests, damaging or destroying blacklisted goods, and often physically attempting to prevent scab labour undermining strike action.[34]

This militant shift of both the suffrage rebels and Dublin trade unions occurred during the same period, which meant they experienced the same brutal repression from the state together. The shared experiences of police violence, arrests, prison sentences, hunger strike tactics, and general conflict with the government and local authorities brought the movements closer through shared struggle. When the Irish used militant forms of protest, it brought them into contact with a colonial state, rather than a domestic government. This distinction could explain why the Dublin labour movement and the militant suffragettes worked cooperatively more often than their English counterparts. Hanna Sheehy Skeffington stated that, the 'wiser male leaders' of the labour movement 'recognised the possibilities latent in the [suffrage] movement and welcomed women rebels wholeheartedly'.[35]

The militancy of the IWFL was arguably one of the most significant factors in gaining respect from trade unions and political labour. It set them apart from the other suffrage and women's groups of the era, as they violently defied the gender norms of their class with their methods. Their militancy gained them support from important labour bodies such as the ITUC. In 1913, the Liberal Home Secretary, Reginald McKenna, attempted to suppress the militant section of the women's movement in Ireland by banning the publication of their literature and the right to open air meetings. James Connolly moved a resolution at the ITUC meeting that year to condemn the 'cowardly and coercion-like methods' of McKenna in this suppression and asserted his personal support and acknowledgement of the militant women. He noted how the women had been 'driven to violence', and that they were reactive to British government policy.[36] The motion gained wider support from the congress, and Connolly stated he was 'glad the congress had spoken in support of the women and against those prosecutions'.[37] The motion was passed unanimously. The speech specifically referred to those militant suffragettes who engaged in the open-air meetings, which indicated Connolly's own interest in militant women, but also highlighted the wider support of the congress for militant suffrage activists. Holding open-air meetings and selling their literature in public were militant tactics also utilised by the labour movement in Dublin, and this commonality likely ensured their support for the women in this instance. This resolution and the support from the ITUC were well received by the IWFL who, in response, praised organised labour in the pages of the *Irish Citizen*, concluding with the hopeful statement, 'Ibsen said long ago that Europe would be saved by its women and its workmen. There is much hope that we might say the same of Ireland'.[38]

The ITUC supported the IWFL publicly on other occasions, often shunning non-militant suffrage groups in the process. In 1914, the ITUC report stated that having originally agreed to receive a deputation from the IWRL, it was deemed 'not necessary' because the resolution on adult suffrage had previously been passed.[39] The IWRL had been established in 1911 and was the only Irish suffrage organisation that explicitly united women's suffrage and trade unionism.[40] Despite the IWRL's aim of improved labour rights for women as well as equal franchise, the report states that the Chairmen observed, 'none of them would object to a militant suffragette, but they didn't want those humbugs who were not out for work'.[41] The disdainful phrase, 'not out for work', suggests that the Chairman, James Larkin in this instance, having noted their predominantly middle-class membership, assumed that they did not have to undertake waged labour to survive. The use of the term 'humbugs' further suggests that Larkin perceived the women to be deceptive or false in their aim in extending women's labour rights as well as achieving the franchise.

It is likely Larkin considered the IWRL to have ulterior motives, due to the fact that much of the early suffrage movement linked its call for the vote to property ownership.[42] Perhaps Larkin felt that the IWRL would gain support from working-class women in order to secure middle-class women the vote and neglect their aim of increased labour rights. Indeed, the conversation that followed considered the possibility of middle-class women using their vote against the interests of working-class men. This is interesting, as the IWFL were also an organisation who in the first instance had campaigned for votes for women on the same terms as men, i.e. with a property qualification. The Congress clearly believed they had already proved their support for the women's cause in 1912 by passing the resolution for adult suffrage, and therefore perhaps felt they had nothing more to offer the IWRL and decided there was no room for collaboration with this group. That the Congress would not object to a meeting with the militant suffragettes demonstrates their commitment to militancy, and respect for those women who utilised militant methods in their fight for suffrage.

Collaboration

It seems that at least on a few occasions, the support for the militancy of the IWFL was echoed in the streets as working men visibly supported, and occasionally aided, the women's movement. One example of this is recorded in Hanna Sheehy Skeffington's memoirs. When reminiscing about the smashing of windows in the GPO, the Custom House and Dublin Castle, she stated that the women were encouraged by a group of dock workers, 'who entered the spirit of the thing, cheering the ladies on and keeping a look-out!'[43] It must have been a surprising sight, predominantly middle-class women smashing the windows of several key institutions of the city, and this likely amused and enthused the working men who were present at the event. The militant action subverted gender and class norms, which arguably created a space in which the men could support the suffragettes without having to challenge their own gendered bias or support increased rights and opportunities for women of their own communities and movement.

Members of the ITGWU 'frequently interfered' at rowdy meetings of the IWFL in Dublin, protecting the women from violence.[44] In many instances, just the presence of these men at open-air meetings deterred violence against woman speakers.[45] It is unclear if these male trade unionists attended of their own accord or if they were prompted by the leadership sympathetic to the suffrage cause. The ITGWU had been founded in 1909 and from formation, its programme included adult suffrage and equal voting rights in parliamentary and local elections for all women and men over the age of twenty-one.[46] It was also led by James Larkin and James Connolly during this period so the leadership may have encouraged these interventions. It is most likely they were organised; a similar practice occurred in Britain, when WSPU members relied on male colleagues in the Labour Party to act as bodyguards at their meetings.[47]

While supporting militant tactics of the suffragettes, the labour movement was less inclined to support militancy from organised woman workers in their own communities. Leah Dowdall has pointed to the hostility of male trade unionists towards working women who were often used in industry to undercut men's wages. This hostility, as well as a reluctance to divert already stretched funds to organise women workers, meant that working-class women's participation in the movement was restricted.[48] I propose that middle-class suffragists in Dublin were given more support than their working-class counterparts due, in part, to being more removed from the lives of the working men. This meant their challenging of social norms did not directly affront the working-class male life view, as in most cases, it was not the women of their communities engaging in this behaviour.[49]

The most noteworthy example of practical solidarity between the labour movement and the IWFL can be found during the 1913 Lockout. Much has been written about the 1913 Lockout, and there are various interpretations of the politics behind the dispute and those enlisted to help, such as the IWFL members. The Lockout was a defining moment in the history of the labour movement in Ireland, and the participation of the IWFL in this infamous strike action can be seen as the culmination of years of collaboration. Padraig Yeates in his study of the Lockout, places importance on the roles of Hanna Sheehy Skeffington and Louie Bennett in aligning the movements during the struggle.[50] However this cooperation between the IWFL and labour in 1913 was not simply due to the relationships between individuals. The collaboration during the Lockout must also be understood in terms of the long-term broader commitments between suffrage and labour in the context of a visceral struggle that affected the entirety of Dublin.

The Dublin Lockout began in August 1913, with a strike undertaken by the ITGWU. By 4 September 1913, over 400 Dublin employers had locked out striking employees. The women at Jacobs' Biscuit Factory were among the most militant of the strikers, and the entire membership of the IWWU came out and shared the six months' struggle.[51] The industrial action gave the IWFL the chance to act on their political sympathies with the strikers. Within a few weeks from the beginning of the strike, over 15,000 workers had been locked out and were dependent on the British TUC food fund for survival.[52] The TUC sent concrete support in the form of food ships and money, however they were disinclined to sanction sympathetic industrial action in Britain.[53] The IWFL and a nationalist women's group, Inghinidhe na hÉireann (Daughters of Erin) united in manning the soup kitchens set up in Liberty Hall.[54] Leah Dowdall has argued that 'many rushed to charitable work during moments of class unrest, seeing these moments as prime opportunities to instruct working-class women on how to behave'.[55] However, Margaret Ward has argued to the contrary, that this gesture from the IWFL 'had nothing to do with charity and everything to do with the expression of solidarity in the class struggle between workers and employers'.[56] I agree that the IWFL came to the aid of the workers because they felt very strongly that the suffrage and labour struggles were interwoven, rather than acting out of charity. They felt that 'the Dublin Labour struggles are a fresh example of the need for the feminine point of view in politics', arguing that housing problems and cost of living affected women much more closely than men. The *Irish Citizen* stated, 'in seeking reforms, [the women of the working class] would have had the strong support of the more fortunate women' due to the claimed commonality of women's domesticity.[57]

The IWFL commenced their action at Liberty Hall in their capacity as a suffrage group, rather than as individuals. R.M. Fox reminisced that the 'soup kitchens were organised by the suffragettes and the sight of their green and orange colours as they ladled out soup was not forgotten by the strikers that winter'.[58] An onlooker described the scene:

> They talk together in low tones, and occasionally one hears scraps of conversation, in which the words, 'Suffragettes' and 'Votes for Women' occur with almost startling frequency, for members of the Irish Women's

> Franchise League are at work here, and the little orange and green button does not escape observation.[59]

At an IWFL meeting in September that year, it was noted that 'amongst the immense crowd which gathered round the speakers it was satisfactory to notice a number of the girls locked out in the present industrial struggle'.[60] The IWFL held meetings to spread their suffrage message to the strikers. An article in the *Irish Times* stated that at one meeting, 'several of the IWFL members and Constance Markievicz turned up early to a large crowd'.[61] The speakers for the IWFL declared, 'the women's cause was the same as that of the men now on strike, and they wished success to the workers in this struggle'.[62] It could be argued that the positive attitude of those locked out workers towards the IWFL was due to their noticeable participation in the soup kitchens. This action, therefore, helped ensure support and collaboration between the membership of the labour and suffrage movements on a larger scale after 1913, rather than simply cooperation and alliance between the leadership of the labour movement and IWFL. For the IWFL the link between the labour struggle and the women's movement was clear, and they supported the strikers with the belief that the outcome would be important for both movements.

Cissie Cahalan

Although referred to as a largely middle-class venture, the IWFL did have some working-class members who played a significant role in the group's political development. Cissie Cahalan was a member of both the IWFL and the Irish Drapers' Assistants' Benefit and Protective Union (also referred to as the Irish Drapers' Assistants' Union or IDAA). She often linked feminism and socialism in speeches she gave at IWFL meetings. She declared that the power of the vote could be wielded as a weapon in industrial life, and argued that if competition was replaced with cooperation, all of humanity would benefit.[63]

In August 1913, Cahalan delivered a speech that dealt with the conditions of women in the labour market.[64] Reports of meetings published in the *Irish Citizen* often specified who was present in the crowd, and for this speech of Cahalan's, it was many working-class women, 'with babies in their arms'.[65] At a meeting a month later, she dealt with the 'man in the streets' view that the suffrage movement was a 'fad', taken up by women with 'nothing better to do'.[66] She argued that the 'sweating of women' would continue, unchecked, unless they had the parliamentary vote. She further linked the systematic under-payment of women in all fields of work to their voteless condition.[67] The IWFL were keen to appeal to working-class women, partially for their own gain of increasing their membership and progressing their cause, but also due to the belief that working women must be empowered both politically and economically. Cahalan was able to embody and unite these goals of the IWFL and appeal to a broader audience. She was often the IWFL authority in matters concerning women in work, for example, presiding over a meeting on 'Women in Munition Work' in 1916.[68] Cahalan's working-class credentials gave her speeches more weight due to the fact that she had personally experienced the grind of low-paid labour.

In 1913, the *Irish Citizen* provided news coverage of the remaining speeches presented during the final days of Dublin Suffrage Week. Cissie Cahalan was one of the speakers on the 'Trade Unions and the Vote' panel and pointed out that women had been driven into factories through the decline in 'the home industry' but once there, the women had little opportunity for organisation and 'had not the means to make any organisation effective'.[69] In labour circles, capitalism was held accountable for forcing women out of domestic life and into paid employment. Socialist intellectuals such as James Connolly linked the women's movement with the appearance of women out on 'the Industrial field'.[70] Despite the negative implications about women in work, Cissie Cahalan fiercely believed that the position of women in the labour movement was not subordinate to that of men, and argued the case for mixed gender unions.[71] She concluded that organisation in industry is 'magnificent' but the vote is better, referring to how men achieved the weekly half-day holiday through voting.[72]

Cahalan was also largely influential in the IDAA and often used her IWFL connections to provide speakers from the suffrage movement to the union. This can be seen in a call for a women's only meeting of the IDAA in 1916, in which there was a discussion of the position of women in 'Shop and Commercial Life'.[73] The speakers at the meeting were Hanna Sheehy Skeffington, Louie Bennett, Helena Moloney, and Cissie Cahalan. These were all figures from the labour, suffrage, and nationalist movements in Ireland at this time. It is likely that Cahalan used her influence in the union to propose speakers already known to her through her engagement with the suffrage movement. Cahalan was elected to the Dublin branch executive committee of the IDAA in 1918, which provided a platform to continue pushing forwards a more equal agenda in labour politics.[74]

The use of Cahalan's contacts in both the suffrage and labour movements benefited both, as she was able to educate members of either movement to the other cause. This had the benefit of establishing similar political outlooks, but also aiding the movements in a material sense, when it was necessary to obtain practical support for militant action. Furthermore, it has been argued that the leader of the IDAA, Michael O'Lehane, brought about a new militancy amongst the shop assistants, and played a significant role in tipping the political balance in the ITUC towards the 'new unionism'.[75] It is important to recognise the part played by militant women who straddled the IDAA and the suffrage movement in progressing the IDAA's policies and outlook when it came to women. It is likely they were more influential in this shift towards militancy and gender equality than has previously been considered.

Conclusion

The collaboration and examples of solidarity revealed in this chapter suggest greater interconnection between the women's movement and the labour movement in Dublin. The history of the Irish labour movement and Irish suffrage movement have largely been written separately. The absence of historical consideration of the links between suffrage and labour stem from the assumption that the suffrage movement was largely a middle-class venture that lacked interest in industrial issues and that the labour movement was largely indifferent, and sometimes opposed, to female enfranchisement. The presence of the IWFL in labour disputes and key moments, and labour leaders and trade unionists in suffrage matters contradicts the acknowledged priorities, structures and politics of both movements. This chapter has attempted to show a more nuanced perspective. While class and gender-based issues provoked ruptures between suffrage and labour, there were times when the women of the IWFL successfully negotiated class tensions to champion the cause of the workers, and examples of times the labour movement overcame their gendered structures to provide support, defence, and solidarity to the suffragettes.

Historians of the suffrage movement in Britain have more recently begun to consider the complexities of class, race, and nationality within suffrage politics, but more work needs to be done to draw attention to these parallels and links in Ireland.[76] This case study has demonstrated that there is a benefit to examining the labour and suffrage movements in conjunction, as their similarities and mutual solidarity point to a broader picture of intricately intersecting political movements, individuals, and groups. It has shown that class politics made more space for militant feminist thought and politics than has previously been acknowledged by historians.

Notes

1 I use 'organised labour' to refer to trade unions, groups of workers, and trades boards. 'Political labour' refers to the political parties of labour. 'Labour movement' refers to both.
2 Emmet O'Connor, *A Labour History of Ireland 1824–1960* (Dublin, Gil & Macmillan: 1992), p. 68.
3 O'Connor, *A Labour History of Ireland 1824–1960*, p. 47.
4 *Irish Citizen*, 25 May 1912.
5 I draw upon June Purvis' broad definition of militancy as actions both legal and illegal, such as selling suffrage newspapers in the street, heckling politicians and interrupting meetings, strike action, and holding open air meetings. June Purvis, 'Did Militancy Help or Hinder the Granting of Women's Suffrage in Britain?', *Women's History Review* 28.7 (2019), p. 1201.

6 See: Rosemary Cullen Owens, *Smashing Times: A History of the Irish Women's Suffrage Movement 1889–1922* (Dublin, Attic Press: 1984); Margaret Ward, *Unmanageable Revolutionaries: Women and Irish Nationalism* (London, Pluto Press: 1989); and Senia Pašeta, *Irish Nationalist Women 1900–1918* (Cambridge, Cambridge University Press: 2013).
7 See: Arthur Mitchell, 'William O'Brien, 1881–1968, and the Irish Labour Movement', *Studies: An Irish Quarterly Review* 60.239/240 (1971), pp. 311–331; Peter Berresford Ellis, *A History of the Irish Working Class* (London, Gollancz: 1972). William K. Anderson, *James Connolly and the Irish Left* (Dublin, Irish Academic Press: 1994); Donal Nevin, ed., *Trade Union Century* (Cork and Dublin, Mercier Press in association with Irish Congress of Trade Unions & Radio Telefís Éireann: 1994); and Donal Nevin, ed., *James Larkin: Lion of the Fold* (Dublin, Gill & Macmillan: 1998) and Geoffrey Bell, *Hesitant Comrades: The Irish Revolution and the British Labour Movement* (London, Pluto Press: 2016).
8 Mary Jones, *These Obstreperous Lassies: A History of the IWWU* (Dublin, Gill & Macmillan: 1988). Mary Daly, *Women and Work in Ireland* (Dublin, Economic and Social History of Ireland: 1997) and Elaine Sugrue, 'Women and Irish Trade Unionism – A Case Study: The Irish Drapers' Assistants Association 1901–20', *Saothar* 42 (2017), pp. 65–74.
9 National Library of Ireland (NLI), Report of the Provisional Committee of the Irish Women's Franchise League for 1912.
10 ITUC Annual Report 1907, p. 36.
11 Owens, *Smashing Times*, p. 89.
12 Therese Moriarty, 'James Larkin and Women' in Donal Nevin (ed.), *James Larkin: Lion of the Fold* (Dublin: Gil & Macmillan: 2006), p. 94.
13 Letter from William O'Brien to Francis Sheehy Skeffington, 31 January 1912, NLI, Sheehy Skeffington Collection, MS 470, 7. Letter from William O'Brien to Francis Sheehy Skeffington, 30 November 1912, NLI, Sheehy Skeffington Collection, MS 470, 7.
14 Socialist Party of Ireland List of Lectures, April–June 1910, NLI Sheehy Skeffington Collection, MS 40,480/1.
15 'Irish Suffrage Activities: Irish Women's Franchise League', *Irish Citizen*, 7 April 1917. 'Irish Suffrage Activities: Irish Women's Franchise League', *Irish Citizen*, 5 May 1917.
16 Hanna Sheehy Skeffington, Unpublished Memoirs: Part III, in Margaret Ward, *Hanna Sheehy Skeffington: Suffragette and Sinn Feiner, Her Memoirs and Political Writings* (Dublin, University College Dublin Press: 2017), p. 12.
17 Margaret Ward, *Fearless Woman: Hanna Sheehy Skeffington, Feminism, and the Irish Revolution* (Dublin, University College Dublin Press: 2019), p. 2.
18 Loose notebook, NLI, Sheehy Skeffington Collection, MS 33, 615 (BOX).
19 Constance Markievicz was a well-known nationalist, suffragist and socialist who participated in all three movements, most notably fighting during the 1916 Easter Rising.
20 'Inaugural Meeting', *Irish Worker*, 2 September 1911.
21 On one occasion Sheehy Skeffington was invited to talk about prison reform having experienced incarceration herself. Letter from Helen Chenevix to Hanna Sheehy Skeffington, 12 February 1914, NLI, Sheehy Skeffington Collection, MS 33, 604 (4).
22 Mitchell, 'William O'Brien', p. 315.
23 Moriarty, 'Larkin and the Women's Movement', p. 95.
24 'Suffragists and the Strike', *Irish Citizen*, 6 September 1913.
25 Letter from William O'Brien to Hanna Sheehy Skeffington, 14 May 1914, NLI, Sheehy Skeffington Collection, MS 33, 604 (5). Letter from William O'Brien to

Hanna Sheehy Skeffington, 9 December 1915, NLI, Sheehy Skeffington Collection, MS 33, 604 (13).

26 'Irish Women's Franchise League: Mr. Connolly and the Power of the Workers', *Irish Times*, 12 November 1912.

27 James Connolly, *Labour in Ireland: Labour in Irish History: The Re-Conquest of Ireland* (Dublin, Maunsel: 1917), p. 292.

28 'Extracts from messages received about the recent Mass Meeting', *Irish Citizen*, 15 June 1912.

29 Rosemary Cullen Owens, 'Votes for Ladies, Votes for Women: Organised Labour and the Suffrage Movement 1876–1922', *Saothar* 9 (1983), p. 41.

30 Hanna Sheehy Skeffington, 'Reminiscences of an Irish Suffragette', in A. D. Sheehy Skeffington and Rosemary Cullen Owens (eds.), *Votes for Women: Irishwomen's Struggle for the Vote* (Dublin, Trinity College Library: 1975), p. 16.

31 R. M. Fox, *Louie Bennett, Her Life and Times* (Dublin, Talbot Press: 1958), p. 45.

32 June Purvis, 'Did Militancy Help or Hinder the Granting of Women's Suffrage in Britain?', *Women's History Review* 28.7 (2019), p. 1201.

33 Ward, *Fearless Woman*, p. 116.

34 Examples include the 1889 National Union of Gasworkers and General Labourers (NUGGL) Dublin strike, where pickets halted coal transportation, carts were overturned, and scabs assaulted, as well the 1911 ITGWU tramways strike in Dublin which came to be known as 'Bloody Sunday' due to the large-scale demonstration and rioting. O'Connor, *A Labour History of Ireland*, pp. 46, 50, 84.

35 Sheehy Skeffington, 'Reminiscences of an Irish Suffragette', p. 14.

36 Irish Trades Union Congress: Report of 1913, p. 67.

37 Irish Trades Union Congress: Report of 1913, p. 67.

38 'Labour Condemns Coercion', *Irish Citizen*, 24 May 1913.

39 Irish Trades Union Congress: Report of 1914, p. 78.

40 Maria Luddy, 'Introduction: An Overview of the Suffrage Movement', in Louise Ryan and Margaret Ward (eds.), *Irish Women and the Vote: Becoming Citizens* (Dublin, Irish Academic Press: 2007), p. xiii.

41 Irish Trades Union Congress: Report of 1914, p. 78.

42 Penny Holloway and Terry Cradden, 'The Irish Trade Union Congress and Working Women 1894–1914', *Saothar* 23 (1998), p. 55.

43 Sheehy Skeffington, 'Reminiscences of a Suffragette', p. 18.

44 *Irish Citizen*, 6 September 1913.

45 Margaret Ward, *Hanna Sheehy Skeffington: A Life* (Dublin, Attic Press: 1997), p. 115.

46 Moriarty, 'James Larkin and Women', p. 93.

47 Krista Cowman, '"Incipient Toryism" The Women's Social and Political Union and the Independent Labour Party, 1903–1914', *History Workshop Journal* 53 (2002), p. 137.

48 Leah Dowdall, 'A Tantrum in a Teacup: Women in the Irish Working Class Movement 1890–1916', *Soathar* 42 (2017), p. 31.

49 It must be noted that James Larkin and James Connolly were two male leaders who were interested in organising working women, the former having assisted the formation of the IWWU, and both demonstrated considerable support for locked out women during the 1913 Lockout.

50 Padraig Yeates, *Lockout: Dublin 1913* (Dublin, Gill & MacMillan: 2001), p. 367.

51 Margaret MacCurtain, 'The Vote and Revolution' in Margaret MacCurtain and Donncha O Corráin (eds.), *Women in Irish Society the Historical Dimension* (Dublin, Arlen House: 1978), p. 51.

52 Yeates, *Lockout*, p. 32.

53 Colin Whitston, 'The 1913 Dublin Lockout and the British and International Labour Movements' in Francis Devine (ed.), *A Capital in Conflict: Dublin City and the 1913 Lock out* (Dublin, Dublin City Council: 2013), p. 44.
54 Ward, Unmanageable Revolutionaries, p. 83.
55 Dowdall, 'Tantrum in a Teacup', p. 28.
56 Ward, Hanna Sheehy Skeffington, p. 62.
57 'Women's Suffrage and the Labour Troubles', *Irish Citizen*, 20 September 1913.
58 Fox, *Louie Bennett*, p. 52.
59 'Sunt Lacrimae Rerum', *Irish Citizen*, 4 October 1913.
60 'Irish Suffrage Activities: The Irish Women's Franchise League', *Irish Citizen*, 27 September 1913.
61 'Scenes in Beresford Place: School Boys Create a Diversion', *Irish Times*, 19 September 1913.
62 Ibid.
63 'Irish Suffrage Activities: Irish Women's Franchise League', *Irish Citizen*, 8 August 1914; 'Irish Suffrage Activities: Irish Women's Franchise League', *Irish Citizen*, 10 July 1915.
64 'Irish Suffrage Activities: Irish Women's Franchise League', *Irish Citizen*, 2 August 1913.
65 'Irish Suffrage Activities: Irish Women's Franchise League', *Irish Citizen*, 2 August 1913.
66 'Irish Suffrage Activities: Irish Women's Franchise League', *Irish Citizen*, 13 September 1913.
67 'Irish Suffrage Activities: Irish Women's Franchise League', *Irish Citizen*, 13 October 1913.
68 'Irish Women's Franchise League', *Irish Times,* 7 March 1916.
69 'The Conference Special Report', *Irish Citizen,* 20 December 1913.
70 Connolly, *The Re-Conquest of Ireland*, p. 290.
71 Holloway and Cradden, 'The Irish Trade Union Congress and Working Women', p. 47.
72 'The Conference- Special Report', *Irish Citizen*, 20 December 1913.
73 Irish Drapers' Assistants' Benefit and Protective Union letter, NLI, Sheehy Skeffington Collection MS 33, 604 (16).
74 Sugrue, 'Women and Irish Trade Unionism', p. 71.
75 Dermot Keogh, 'Foundation and Early Years of the Irish TUC 1894–1912', in Donal Nevin (ed.), *Trade Union Century* (Dublin: Mercier Press in association with Irish Congress of Trade Unions & Radio Telefís Éireann: 1994), p. 25.
76 For work on suffrage and labour see: Krista Cowman, 'Incipient Toryism', pp. 136–137; Denise Kleinrichert, 'Labour and Suffrage: Spinning Threads in Belfast', in Margaret Ward and Louise Ryan (eds.), *Irish Women and the Vote* (Dublin: Irish Academic Press), pp. 189–208 and Laura Schwartz, *Feminism and the Servant Problem: Class and Domestic Labour in the Women's Suffrage Movement* (Cambridge, Cambridge University Press: 2019).

10

BOOTSTRAPS AND BRAS

Maidenform, the International Ladies' Garment Workers Union, and the Creation of a New Export-led Economy in Puerto Rico

Natasha Synycia

'The goings-on in Puerto Rico no longer are of interest merely to the 2,300,000 islanders themselves or to specialists in underdeveloped countries. They are of deep concern to the officers and stockholders of the 550 companies that have nibbled on the Economic Development Administration's bait and opened plants here'.[1]

After the implementation of Operation Bootstrap in 1947, which incentivised American capital to manufacture on Puerto Rico through tax breaks and access to cheap labour, Maidenform, the US's largest brassiere company, became one of the earliest American companies to offshore its manufacturing. One might assume that a significant benefit of offshoring to Puerto Rico would be that Maidenform could rid itself of its powerful American labour union, the International Ladies Garment Workers' Union (ILGWU). It would also be reasonable to surmise that the ILGWU would vehemently fight against the offshoring of unionised 'American' jobs. As a result, such offshoring should have seriously strained the once cooperative and mutually beneficial relationship the union and company shared. And yet, it didn't.

This examination will demonstrate that Maidenform and the ILGWU largely continued their cooperation in Puerto Rico, highlighting the way in which labour history is connected to international politics and capitalist ventures, resulting in seemingly strange bedfellows. In an effort to thwart unionisation by more radical Puerto Rican unions, Maidenform encouraged the ILGWU to come to Puerto Rico. Together, Maidenform and the ILGWU prevented Puerto Rican unions from organising the company. Even after the ILGWU unionised Maidenform in Puerto Rico, the union worked against their Puerto Rican members' interests in Maidenform's favour.

DOI: 10.4324/9780429344084-13

The success of Operation Bootstrap was dependent on the American brassiere industry, as well as the cooperation between American business, American labour unions, and the Puerto Rican government. The brassiere industry was the foundation of Operation Bootstrap, and Maidenform became not only the largest brassiere company on the island but also Puerto Rico's second largest employer. While each institution – the Maidenform company, the ILGWU, and the Puerto Rican government – consciously worked towards their own self-interest, they also cooperated together, thereby buoying Operation Bootstrap and participating in the establishment of export-led industrialisation that has transformed global economics.[2] This study seeks to add to the scholarship on export-led industrialisation in Puerto Rico by analysing a key inchoate moment in this process in order to better understand how and why these various institutions worked together to implement this system.[3]

This study also reveals the contradictions in the US's Cold War modernisation programme. Operation Bootstrap was intended to demonstrate the superiority of US capitalism over Soviet communism. However, by the late 1970s, US businesses, including Maidenform, fled Puerto Rico, leaving scholars like Berrios Martinez to label Operation Bootstrap a failure.[4] This study demonstrates how the 'modernisation' of Puerto Rico was not a defeat of the Puerto Rican people or capitalism but the logical outcome of capitalism itself.

The Commonwealth of Puerto Rico

Operation Bootstrap or *Operación Manos a la Obra* was a Cold War modernisation programme meant to convert the largely agricultural economy of Puerto Rico into an industrial one. A newly modernised Puerto Rico could then be used as a symbol of the superiority of capitalism. To accomplish this 'economic miracle', the US government would require mainland industries to move to the island to displace the traditional sugar cane plantations. The government lured labour-intensive industries, like brassiere manufacturing, to Puerto Rico with promises of low-wage, compliant (and largely female) labour. The companies' profit margins would be additionally boosted by low rent, lucrative tax incentives, and duty-free access to mainland US markets. Essentially, US companies were offered cheap 'third world' production costs without having to pay 'first world' expenses. This profitable incongruency was only possible because Puerto Rico was a de facto US colony.

Puerto Rico became a US possession after it was 'liberated' from Spanish colonial rule during the 1898 Spanish American War. Spain's defeat simultaneously dissolved the Spanish Empire abroad and commenced the US's overseas empire. The 1898 Treaty of Paris allowed the USA to purchase the

Philippines from Spain, cede Guam and Puerto Rico to the USA, and make Cuba a US protectorate.

Half a century later, the post-Second World War decolonisation movement and the Cold War made the maintenance of colonies problematic for a country espousing democratic principles. However, the USA was not ready to let go of its Caribbean colony. With the help of the US-backed Puerto Rican politician Luis Muñoz Marín and his *Partido Populare Democratica* (Popular Democratic Party or PPD), the usefully ambiguous commonwealth status would be established in 1952.[5] Puerto Rico would have its own elected governor, legislature, and judiciary, although the USA maintained veto power and judiciary oversight, would be subject to the US draft and subordinate to the USA in defence and foreign relations, and, most significant for American investors, would not be subject to the federal minimum wage. The PPD supported Operation Bootstrap because it believed the programme would industrialise the island, provide local jobs, raise the standard of living, and last but not least, keep them in power. Puerto Rico's commonwealth status allowed the USA to maintain its colonial relationship and still project the outward appearance of granting self-determination.[6]

The new commonwealth status and the continuation of private American investment would allow Puerto Rico to be reinvented as an example of the power of US-style capitalism to transform a struggling region into a Caribbean paradise – or as *Business Week* called it, an 'Industrial Island in the Sun'.[7]

Operation Bootstrap and the Cold War

Operation Bootstrap was tied to American Cold War policy and the formation of 'development' strategies stressing export-led industrialisation, which would become a model for 'modernising' the globalised economy, spreading ideologies of 'free trade' and designations of 'export-processing zones' around the world.[8] Export-led industrialisation was implemented by business and government from developed countries who moved their manufacturing to developing states in order to take advantage of cheap, unorganised, and supposedly docile labour, as well as for advantageous tax benefits often offered by compliant foreign governments.[9]

Modernisation programmes had dual functions. First, they would boost the US economy by spreading a capitalist system advantageous to US business. Second, by improving the economies and standard of living in 'third world' countries, they would prove the superiority of capitalism, increase the US sphere of influence, and prevent the spread of communism. It was such a win-win for the USA in the global Cold War that Puerto Rico's experience would inspire President Harry Truman's 'Point Four' programme, economists W. Arthur Lewis's influential theory of surplus labour, John F. Kennedy's Alliance for Progress, Ronald Reagan's Caribbean Basin

Initiative, the 'Urban Enterprise Zones' for US inner cities, and 1998's 'AfricaNAFTA'.[10]

Especially after Fidel Castro's communist takeover of nearby Cuba in 1959, Puerto Rico became a symbol of the stability and prosperity possible with the American Way. In order to bolster Puerto Rico, the USA believed it was necessary to address four separate but overlapping areas: population control (involving a wide-spread sterilisation programme), a centralised state (via the PPD), export-led industrialisation (through American investment), and an increased standard of living (through Operation Bootstrap and emigration to the USA).[11]

The name Operation Bootstrap is associated with ideals of the Protestant work ethic and the American Dream. Pulling oneself up by one's own bootstraps refers to a person who lifts themselves out of poverty through hard work and self-reliance, as did characters in the novels by Horatio Alger.[12] This narrative took on renewed significance during the Cold War ideological battle between capitalism and communism. In the American Cold War rhetoric, Communists in the USSR relied on the government, resulting in an impotent populace who tolerated a simultaneously inept and all-powerful bureaucratic state capable of great evil. Alternatively, US democracy based on capitalism fostered a nation of bootstrappers whose self-reliance and God-given freedom made them a city-on-a-hill, single-handedly capable of improving the world. And so, the US government, would bring prosperity to Puerto Rico through Operation Bootstrap. That this was only possible with significant government intervention seemed beside the point.

This study also shows the rhetorical tension between capitalism and the role of the state during the Cold War. The US Cold War discourse promoted the role of the market fuelled by the private sector in contrast to the Soviet state-run model. Yet, as this study demonstrates, the role of the state was essential in creating the conditions necessary for American business to succeed. The American ideal of bootstrapping – of succeeding solely on one's own merits – which became even more symbolic in the war between capitalism and communism, was as much a myth for businesses as it was for individuals.

Maidenform Goes to Puerto Rico

The same year that the commonwealth status was approved, Maidenform opened its first of sixteen factories in Puerto Rico.[13] Numerous American undergarment companies followed over the next decade, but it was Maidenform who would become the second largest employer on Puerto Rico and the single largest employer of women on the island.[14]

The employment of women in brassiere and other apparel factories was the norm in the USA, but since Operation Bootstrap offered enticements for labour-intensive work, the apparel industry became one of the largest employers on the island, resulting in a large increase 21% of female employment in from 1940 to 1960.[15] In 1970, the total level of female employment was 30.8% but the participation of men in the labour force decreased from about 80% in 1950 to 60% in 1975.[16]

This new gender dynamic in the workforce caused a disruption of gender norms. *The Wall Street Journal* published an article whose headline said it all: 'Puerto Rican Menfolk Fret as Their Wives Bring Home the Bacon: Operation Bootstrap Creates New Jobs But the Ladies Grab Most of Them'.[17] The article cites a Puerto Rican Senator who states that women should be thanking Bootstrap for bringing them jobs and equality. One 'swarthy Puerto Rican' man did not agree. He 'grunted', and stated, '...some equality. It's the women who are running the whole country now'.[18] The shift in traditional gender norms made it so that men, when not employed in seasonal agricultural work, took care of the children.[19] Interestingly, this transformation was the opposite of the US Cold War ideology which encouraged women to be homemakers.[20]

Helen Safa argues that the increased female employment created more female empowerment as women no longer considered their income to be merely supplementary to that of their husbands'.[21] Alice E. Colon-Warren and Idsa Alegia-Ortega argue that the results of the gender power struggle were mixed: there was more divorce and more rights for women as the new constitution prohibited gender discrimination, but there were also higher instances of gender violence and the controversial sterilisation programme.[22] The empowerment brought with employment was the likely reason that when Puerto Ricans were surveyed as to which institution – their employers, the government or their union – was the most helpful, women clearly favoured their employers.[23] Maidenform, in particular, seemed to be well-liked in Puerto Rico. It had hundreds of employees who stayed with them over a decade and it also received an award from Fomento (the bureaucracy implementing Operation Bootstrap) honouring its contribution to the growth of the apparel industry.[24]

As one of the commonwealth's largest employers, Maidenform played a key role in how Puerto Rico's labour would be organised. When Maidenform first came to Puerto Rico, Maidenform managers spoke with managers of other American businesses to get a sense of the local situation. The manager of Consolidated Cigars, the largest company on the island, told a Maidenform representative that all Puerto Rican unions were substandard because they had 'ignorant leadership', and frequently split.[25] Maidenform seemingly agreed. Although it was technically illegal, as Puerto Rico was covered by American labour protections, Maidenform prevented at least two attempts by Puerto Ricans to unionise their plants.

Maidenform's behaviour was so egregious that in 1953 the National Labor Relations Board (NLRB) sanctioned them for violating the Taft-Hartley Act.[26]

According to the NLRB, Maidenform fired employee Angela Anglero because her father had made cursory attempts at organising and spoke against Maidenform's quota system.[27] Maidenform also fired another woman who was merely seen talking to Anglero's father.[28] Although the NLRB ruled against Maidenform, after much badgering, it only required Maidenform to write an unpublished letter stating that they would not discourage union formation or intimidate workers in the future.[29]

The lesson Maidenform learned from the NLRB was discretion and from then on, it went about its subterfuge more subtly. Maidenform headquarters on the mainland sent out memos reminding the Puerto Rico branch not to threaten the workers about unionising. Instead, they were to relate the positive things the company had done and emphasise that the management with its American connections (Maidenform managers in Puerto Rican factories were exclusively American men for more than a decade[30]), had more power to help them than would a Puerto Rican union, to whom they would have to pay additional dues.[31]

In the year following the Anglero case, Maidenform's interoffice communication between the mainland and Puerto Rico indicated that multiple unions had come around but their 'girls' were not interested. The Puerto Rican branch reported that some of the organisers were communists and that their employees had no interest in associating with them.[32] Perhaps the local Maidenform employees believed the company's claims that as a powerful American company, Maidenform held greater sway with the government who controlled the minimum wage rate than a small Puerto Rican-led union.

This claim probably seemed legitimate until April of 1954 when a Puerto Rican union the *Union de Trabajadores de la Industria del Brassiere*, which was affiliated with the powerful American Federation of Labor (AFL), came to Maidenform's factories. The higher ups in Maidenform suspected the head of the ILGWU, David Dubinsky, might be behind this new unionisation attempt. Dubinsky co-founded the Congress of Industrial Organizations (CIO) and worked with George Meany to unite the AFL and the CIO in 1955. The head of the NLRB – the same official who let Maidenform off the hook with an unpublished letter promising to be nice to unions – initially told Maidenform that he believed Dubinsky was connected and would eventually show up. A month later, the consensus seemed to be that Dubinsky may have given some funds but was not directly connected.[33]

This was unsettling for Maidenform, who seemingly believed that if it so desired, the ILGWU could successfully unionise their Puerto Rican plants. The likely reason why Maidenform was afraid of the ILGWU was that they had an exclusivity agreement.[34] Maidenform likely believed that the ILGWU would cause the company problems on the mainland if Maidenform refused to unionise with the ILGWU on Puerto Rico. The indirect attempts by Maidenform to see if the ILGWU had connections to the AFL-affiliated union's efforts hints at a mutual distrust as well as Maidenform's desire to avoid unionisation in Puerto Rico completely.

The *Union de Trabajadores de la Industria del Brassiere's* most tempting claim was that they could get the minimum wage pay raise granted by the NLRB faster.[35] Without their help, the union claimed, the workers would have to wait up to a year to see their wages increase. Maidenform countered that the union was lying and as a precaution, increased wages right before the vote to determine if the factory would be unionised. Maidenform felt so confident of their impending victory that they even encouraged their workers to vote. The vote was 42 in favour of the union and 77 against. In celebration, champagne was airmailed from the mainland with a congratulatory telegraph. Maidenform in Puerto Rico would remain union-free until the ILGWU showed up.

ILGWU and the Puerto Rican Government

With Operation Bootstrap attracting American apparel manufacturers to Puerto Rico, the ILGWU confronted a serious dilemma that threatened its very existence. If American business could generate larger profit manufacturing abroad, might enough union jobs move offshore, rendering the ILGWU obsolete? To support its American members and keep itself viable, should the union seek to discourage offshoring by attempting to raise the minimum wage on Puerto Rico? Or should the ILGWU expand beyond the continental US, thereby salvaging its overall membership?

The ILGWU head, David Dubinsky, was a pragmatist.[36] Ultimately, he would develop a mutually beneficial relationship with the Puerto Rican PPD government and Maidenform. Through various tactics, the ILGWU would rapidly unionise Puerto Rico and become one of, if not the most, powerful union on the island.[37]

The ILGWU and the PPD needed each other to survive the US government's modernisation programme. The PPD needed the ILGWU because American business preferred American unions because of unusually cooperative post Second World War relations and because they believed that Puerto Rican-run unions or 'independents' were prone to labour unrest.[38] The arrival of international unions (the name for mainland unions in Puerto Rico) undermined homegrown unions through their superior organisational and financial resources.[39]

By the early 1960s, two-thirds of the organised workers in Puerto Rico belonged to internationals,[40] and by 1964 an estimated 73% of organised labour was part of an AFL-CIO affiliate.[41] As hoped, American unions brought with them relatively harmonious relations with American business and many labour officials became fixtures in the PPD government.[42]

The ILGWU needed the PPD because it controlled the implementation of Operation Bootstrap, in particular unionisation, through Fomento. Puerto

Rican law defined collective bargaining as 'instruments by which to advance the public policy of the government in its efforts to stimulate production to the maximum, and thus it is declared they are vested with a public interest'.[43] In essence, the PPD would allow unionisation only if it benefited Operation Bootstrap. Encapsulating Governor Muñoz's philosophy towards labour was his motto: '[t]he worst wage is better than no wage'.[44] And the ILGWU had a huge role in deciding what that wage would be.

Originally, the 1938 Fair Labor Standards Act (FLSA) set a federal minimum wage which covered the entire US, including Puerto Rico. However, US businesses in Puerto Rico became furious at the wage hike and threatened to leave if the increase was enforced.[45] Therefore, Congress passed an amendment to the FLSA in 1940 which established a committee to set a minimum wage in Puerto Rico on an industry-by-industry basis.[46] Each committee would make a recommendation which they would then submit to the Administrator of the Wage and Hours Division of the US Department of Labor.[47] The goal of the annual and then biannual minimum wage hearings was to strike a balance – raise wages enough so that manufacturers in Puerto Rico were not given an undue advantage over mainland business, while at the same time keep wages low enough to prevent US business exodus from Puerto Rico. The result of the hearings kept wages on Puerto Rico far below wages on the mainland until the mid-1970s, only achieving wage parity in the 1980s.

Governor Muñoz and George Meany, head of the AFL and then the AFL-CIO, 'unofficially, but rigidly' delegated labour's position on the minimum wage in Puerto Rico to the ILGWU's head Dubinsky.[48] Prior to Dubinsky's incursion into Puerto Rico, he argued for wage parity, publicly decried the wage discrepancy, exclaiming that 'the presently unfair advantage enjoyed by Puerto Rican industrialists is becoming an ever-greater menace to certain mainland industries'.[49] However, by 1955, Dubinsky's rhetoric changed as he sent Robert Gladnick to unionise the island. The ILGWU released a statement to the Puerto Rican newspaper *El Mundo*, stating that the union eschewed wage parity claiming it, '...would ruin industry and leave many workers without jobs'.[50] Instead the ILGWU favoured a lower wage in Puerto Rico that would be raised with increased economic development.

Dubinsky's decision to promote incremental wage increase combined with his power on the minimum wage board, gave him the opportunity to play both sides. He would negotiate to set the minimum wage low enough to allow him to get his ILGWU members five cents above the minimum wage. This ostensibly made workers grateful they were members of the ILGWU but it also led to accusations that Dubinsky made 'sweetheart' deals with industry.[51] According to a 1965 article, claims were made that Dubinsky reached an agreement on the minimum wage from the comfort of the lavish Caribe Hilton hotel prior to the wage hearings even taking place. The article stated that '[o]ne high-placed Federal official in the Department of Labor here once described the hearings as a "farce"' and that 'Mr. Dubinsky seems to have had things pretty much his way'.[52] Maidenform interoffice correspondence confirms this scheming. A Maidenform manager in Puerto Rico wrote that Dubinsky was saving the higher wage for the ILGWU and instead proposing a lower minimum than what he could actually get because he 'must show the workers that he has been able to get something for them'.[53]

The ILGWU and Maidenform

The highly cooperative relationship between the ILGWU and Maidenform in Puerto Rico was first forged in the USA. Maidenform frequently renewed contracts earlier than required and with agreeable conditions.[54] When the ILGWU was approached by *Business Week* with the question, 'what is a day's fair wage?' – the ILGWU told the magazine to look no further than Maidenform.[55] Occasionally, ILGWU officials even defended the company against its own members. When Maidenform instituted a shorter workweek, members of local branch 420 were unhappy with the change. The ILGWU believed that the change would help issues of unemployment and told their members that, '[w]orkers in the Maiden Form Brassiere have been very fortunate'.[56]

Part of this cooperative relationship may have been formed by the shared experience of the leaders of Maidenform and the ILGWU. Both institutions were formed by Jewish immigrants fleeing persecution in the Russian Empire. Lucy Dawidowicz argues that Jewish workers and Jewish bosses felt a certain commonality, sense of a bound fate, and experience of anti-Semitism, which facilitated cooperative relationships.[57] This dynamic may have strengthened the remarkably amicable relationship between the business and union that continued in Puerto Rico.

The cooperation between union and business at the expense of ILGWU members in Puerto Rico may have also been influenced by racism. While there is no evidence of discrimination by Maidenform on the mainland, sources reveal bias within the ILGWU. Robert Gladnick, the most important ILGWU organiser in Puerto Rico, complained of difficulties in Miami in a letter to Dubinsky. 'There is nothing that can be done', he wrote, 'when Latins have a difference of a personal or political nature'.[58] An ILGWU organiser in Harlem stated:

> [t]his is a problem, you see, because they can't understand English, and we can't make them understand about the things they should have and why they should have a vision...But, you see, the Puerto Ricans, they don't have the education that we have...except for some elite like Miss Rodriquez here...But mostly they're just backward.[59]

The discrimination became such an issue that the US government got involved.[60] When called in front of a congressional committee to answer charges that the

ILGWU disallowed Latinos and blacks from attaining leadership positions, Dubinsky unwittingly showed his bias. When asked by the committee how many African Americans the 450,000 member ILGWU had above the position of business agent, Dubinsky replied, 'That's an unfair question'. When pressed further Dubinsky admitted that no African Americans held higher office but stated that it was their fault because of, 'their failure to put themselves forward'.[61] Dubinsky further insinuated that there were no qualified African Americans, Hispanics, or women in the ILGWU when he replied that he opposed the idea that 'a man should be a union officer because of his race, color or creed...he should be an officer based on his merits, ability, [and] character'.[62] Furthermore, Dubinsky claimed that he would absolutely be willing to promote minorities if the committee would, '[s]how me a colored or a Puerto Rican or Italian who is capable and I'll make him a business agent or vice president'.[63]

Dubinsky blamed any semblance of racial discrimination on the majority female membership. '80% of our members are women', Dubinsky stated, 'but we have only one woman vice president. Can we be charged with discrimination against women? No!'[64] Dubinsky believed that women should not serve in positions where they would need to leave their home to travel, which largely eliminated them from leadership roles. He claimed that family responsibilities and high turnover were responsible for women's low rate of leadership roles. That 90% of the black and Hispanic members were women explained the low rates of minorities in leadership positions.[65] The implication was that racial discrimination, if it existed, would be problematic, but gender discrimination, which admittedly did occur, was completely acceptable. Dubisnky felt the discrimination charges were utter nonsense because he himself was a minority and therefore could not possibly be guilty of discrimination. Those who spoke against the ILGWU and its leadership were denounced as anti-Semitic or Communists.[66] Nevertheless, the Congressional Committee chastised the union leadership for being cut off from their rank and file and reserving leadership positions for Jewish men.[67]

A newspaper reporting on the proceedings, referred to Dubinsky's own dubious Americanness, mocking his 'fractured English occasionally spiced [with] Yiddish'.[68] Media sources had also commented on Maidenform's founder Ida Rosenthal's Jewishness. *Fortune* wrote that the 'tiny (four-foot-eleven) lady from Minsk, who at sixty-four is...as nicely rounded as a bagel'.[69] The comparison of her figure to a bagel, which were specifically associated with Eastern European Jews, was almost surely a reference to her ethnicity.[70] Public comments like these likely reminded Dubinsky and Rosenthal that they were outsiders in a majority Protestant nation and perhaps they would do better sticking together.

Political leanings may have also played a role. Rosenthal and Dubinsky were both previously members of the Jewish Socialist Bund and, later, Cold War crusaders for the US government. Rosenthal became an informal diplomat with the USSR, while Dubinsky worked with the CIA to promote US style labour unions to suppress communism in Latin America.[71] The shared heritage and political transformations may have played a role in their interaction with the Puerto Rican labourers and the 'radical' left-leaning Puerto Rican unionisation movement.

As noted earlier, in the first couple of years on the island, Maidenform was able to thwart the formation of Puerto Rico-based unions. However, a unionisation attempt by Juan Carlos Citron probably would have succeeded if Maidenform had not sought out the intervention of the ILGWU. Maidenform recognised it would have to unionise, but with a familiar, American union. The ILGWU would be able to unionise the island by playing off employers' fears of the more radical Puerto Rican unions, allowing them to eliminate these 'independents'.[72] *The San Juan Star* stated that the ILGWU's point man on Puerto Rico, Robert Gladnick, had 'built the garment union here from scratch to a membership of 5,800 in 42 shops'.[73]

Citron was the most sophisticated independent organiser to attempt unionisation of Maidenform.[74] Ray Uszczak, the Maidenform manager at Ponce, feared Citron would succeed and so used current employees as spies to infiltrate Citron's organisation, finding fault with the work of those believed to be complicit in the unionising effort in order to terminate them.[75] Despite Maidenform's efforts, Citron gathered enough support for the NLRB to grant his *Union de Trabajodres de la Beatrice Needle Craft Inc, de Ponce* an election.[76] For Maidenform in Puerto Rico, the risk of their factories being unionised by independents was too great. The days of a union-free shop in Puerto Rico were over. From the mainland, word was sent that it was time to work with Gladnick and the ILGWU.[77]

Gladnick collaborated with Maidenform's Uszczak to form a strategy to defeat Citron.[78] Gladnick was eager to help as he believed that the real obstacle to unionising the island was not the PPD or resistance from American businesses but the independent Puerto Rican-based unions, whom he referred to as 'very unsavoury characters'.[79] Gladnick first attempted to get Citron to withdraw but he declined. However, Citron promised Gladnick that if he won the election, his union would become an ILGWU affiliate.[80] Gladnick refused. He felt that the real solution was an industry-wide NLRB vote to elect the ILGWU. Gladnick set up a third party in order to split the vote, hoping that Citron would lose the election and clear the way for Gladnick to organise Maidenform.[81]

A back and forth battle took place publicly and clandestinely. Gladnick placed an article in *El Mundo*, which recalled workers' heretofore unsuccessful attempts at organising with Puerto Rico-based unions, and urging them to join the ILGWU. Gladnick stated:

> [t]he majority of the leaders of your union are honorable and sincere and they will welcome the opportunity to be able to bring their little unions

into the folds of an Island wide powerful union and thus be able to put up a real solid front to your employers.[82]

The article also addressed fears that the real reason the American unions had come to Puerto Rico was to eliminate offshoring. It assured readers that the 'great American Labor Movement is built on economic common sense. It is also built on fraternal solidarity'.[83] In emphasising the belief that workers worldwide were part of a single brotherhood, Gladnick concluded his plea with the new ILGWU slogan for Puerto Rico, '*es union con Corazon*' (a union with heart).[84]

Gladnick also worked with Uszczak on a 'secret' Spanish-language anti-union flyer which was littered around the factory under the cover of night. Citron countered with his own inflammatory circular, warning workers that Uszczak was a 'foreigner'. The circular went on, 'to vote against the union is the equivalent of betraying yourself, and more so, to betray your own family'.[85] Citron's effort failed.

Elated that Citron's union had been defeated, Gladnick wrote to Dubinsky that 'this should take care of the Independents for a while', and that perhaps the effort by Citron had actually been a 'blessing in disguise'.[86] With the coast clear of independents, Gladnick was free to unionise Maidenform's Puerto Rico plants as well as the vast majority of the brassiere industry on the island.[87] Citron would later be elected as Mayor of Ponce and, according to Gladnick, would control all of the independent unions in the area and still desired to take over the ILGWU controlled shops.[88]

A decade later, Margarita Toro told a story on the radio of mistreatment by Maidenform and the ILGWU. Toro claimed that Maria Luisa Vigo was inappropriately fired from Maidenform by manager Paul Hammer after an 11-year tenure. Toro, as leader of ILGWU's local branch 600, came to her defence and was able to get Vigo reinstated at her job. However, Hammer demanded that Vigo switch duties from the ones she had performed for more than a decade. When Vigo refused, the manager and his assistant assaulted the her. Outraged, Toro sought the help of Jerry Schoen (Gladnick's replacement at the ILGWU). Rather than help, Schoen reportedly attempted to bribe Vigo into dropping the charges against Maidenform in exchange for her old position back. When Vigo refused, Schoen urged Toro to pressure Vigo into taking the deal. When Toro refused, she was fired from the ILGWU.[89] Toro decried the 'special relationship' between Maidenform and the ILGWU as detrimental to the workers, and urged the employees of Maidenform to form a new union.[90] In solidarity with Toro and Vigo, over one hundred Maidenform workers walked off the job in protest.

Toro then distributed a flyer at the Mayaguez plant urging the employees not to re-sign with the ILGWU. The handout claimed the ILGWU would soon distribute new cards for workers' signatures authorising the three dollar union dues which committed them to the union, a union which intended to impose on them a new business agent (to replace Toro) they did not know and who would not support them. The flyer went on:

> [f]ellow workers, don't let them fool you, knowing already the lack of backing you have. There is no law that forces you to belong to a Union you don't want. The moment has arrived to break the chains – Do not authorize your own slavery. Do not sign.[91]

Maidenform's lawyer contacted Jerry Schoen, warning him that the ILGWU members were violating their contract's no-strike policy. The attorney informed Schoen that he had twenty-four hours to fix the problem or else.[92] Considering the ILGWU's role in the incident, they probably did not require a threat to join the action, and join they did.

The story of two women fired and one assaulted was picked up by the newspaper *El Mundo*. In response to the bad publicity, vice president of the ILGWU in Puerto Rico denounced Toro in a 22-minute radio broadcast that ran over two days. Fearing that other local unions might smell blood in the water, the ILGWU sent out a warning threatening them 'to keep hands off and not support Margarita…if they felt they could "fish in these troubled waters" they would have a fight on their hands. The I.L.G. was not going to sit idly by with its "hands folded".'[93]

Maidenform did not sit idly by either. They were furious that their source of low-wage labour, which was not as low as it used to be, was impeding their production. Maidenform representatives met with the Mayor of Mayaguez and encouraged him to use his influence to stop the disruption.[94] Maidenform and the ILGWU sent ten spies to a meeting Toro hosted to discuss the formation of a new union.[95] Next, Maidenform managers began individually calling the protestors at their homes and warning them that if they did not return to work, they would be fired.

Their efforts were successful; the majority of the strikers returned to work. Those who did not were immediately fired.[96] Maidenform's actions made it clear that they would not tolerate disobedience in Puerto Rico. Neither would the ILGWU. Margarita Toro had been correct in her prediction. She was replaced by a union representative who lived more than one hundred miles from the Maidenform factory, severely hindering future efforts to effectively organise and protest.[97] Many of the women who were fired filed charges with the NLRB against Maidenform, citing violation of their right to strike. Maidenform countered that they had a no-strike clause in their agreement with the ILGWU that trumped the employees' right to strike. There is no evidence that the NLRB took any action.

As time passed and the women had no alternative income, their resolve faltered. One striker, Dolores Noriega, sent a letter to the ILGWU which was then forwarded to Maidenform.[98] In this letter Noriega blamed Toro and stated that she had no desire to continue the formal complaint and what she and many of the other women simply wanted were their jobs back.

A seemingly desperate Toro wrote to Ellis Rosenthal asking that he intervene on her behalf with the ILGWU and rehire her at Maidenform. There is no evidence of whether Toro received a positive response from Ellis but it is unlikely, as there is documentation that Maidenform refused to rehire Toro even though she apparently received at least nominal support from the ILGWU. Other women fired by Maidenform also attempted to return with the ILGWU's backing. None of the women were rehired.

The Aftermath of Operation Bootstrap

In 1970, Maidenform, the company that was so crucial to the success of Operation Bootstrap, began shutting down its manufacturing in Puerto Rico.[99] Maidenform was one of many American companies which left Puerto Rico and moved to Latin America and Asia in search of cheaper labour and larger profit margins.[100] As a result, hundreds of Maidenform employees in Puerto Rico lost their jobs with no other comparable employment to fill the void. The ILGWU complained that Maidenform refused to hand over its books, lied about having non-union shops, and discovered Maidenform brassieres made in Trinidad and Philippines with fraudulent union labels.[101]

Whether Operation Bootstrap was successful proved to be a matter of time and perspective.[102] American business, on the whole, did well. In 1965 it was estimated that American businesses in Puerto Rico were four times more profitable before taxes and eight times more profitable after taxes than businesses located on the mainland.[103] The island was industrialised and the standard of living on Puerto Rico increased, with income per capita rising from approximately $200 in 1950 to $1,200 in 1967.[104] These statistics point to a 'win' in one of the hottest times in the Cold War.

Some blamed the failings of Operation Bootstrap on the Puerto Rican people. Puerto Rico may have been seen as a 'laboratory for democracy' but it was also viewed as having a 'culture of poverty'.[105] In 1957, when *The Wall Street Journal* asked business owners about failings in Puerto Rico, four out of the five reasons given for the difficulty involved the Puerto Rican people. Businesses cited the costly training of unskilled and irresponsible workers, employee tardiness, increasing wages, and high shipping costs.[106] Essentially, when Operation Bootstrap was viewed as a success, it was as a victory for the USA and capitalism. When it was viewed as a failure, it was because of the inadequacy of the Puerto Ricans.

More recently, scholars have argued that Operation Bootstrap was a failure. Berrios Martinez argues that it did not generate enough jobs for the remaining population and because of the tax incentives, there was little funding for state programmes.[107] James Dietz argues that it relied too heavily on

US investment at the expense of local entrepreneurship, which resulted in a stilted dependent economy.[108] Despite over 50 years of US involvement and so-called development, Puerto Rico still lags behind comparable economies, is economically dependent on the USA, and has a serious debt crisis.[109]

Maidenform's exodus from Puerto Rico was not an instance of the failure of capitalism or of the Puerto Rican people. On the contrary, Operation Bootstrap worked just as capitalism was designed to work over the long term, and Puerto Rican workers performed with sufficient competency to generate business profit. What this analysis has shown is a conflict in capitalism and Cold War modernisation. The Cold War intent of Operation Bootstrap was to increase the Puerto Rican standard of living and therefore exemplify the superiority of American-style capitalism over Soviet style-communism to developing nations tempted to fall within the Soviet sphere of influence. However, as Puerto Ricans became more 'modern', they demanded higher wages. Unwilling to pay these higher wages, business offshored in search of less costly labour and increased profitability, leaving unemployment in its wake. In essence, as capitalism improved the living standards of 'developing' nations making them more like Americans, these workers then demanded higher wages, rendering themselves no longer sufficiently profitable in a competitive capitalist economy. Under the logic of capitalism, this succession of events will continue until new 'cheap' labour is no longer available.

Notes

1 Peter B. Bart, 'Puerto Rico Woes: Pay Boosts, Transport Troubles Drive Away Some Immigrant Firms. Unemployment Stays High; Island Pins Hope on GE and Other Big Newcomers. Cordero Clinks the Glasses', *The Wall Street Journal*, 22 March 1957. Series 10, Box 58, Folder 15, Maidenform Collection Archives Center, National Museum of American History, Smithsonian Institution.

2 Palmira Rios claims that Puerto Rico and not Hong Kong in the mid-1960s is the pioneer of the New International Division of Labor. Palmira N. Rios, 'Export-Oriented Industrialization and the Demand for Female Labor: Puerto Rican Women in the Manufacturing Sector, 1952–1980', *Gender and Society* 4.3, Special Issue: Women and Development in the Third World. (September, 1990).

3 Rios, pp. 323–332; Deborah Berman Santana D, *Kicking off the Bootstraps: Environment, Development, and Community Power in Puerto Rico* (Tucson, University of Arizona Press: 1996), pp. 88–92. Emilio Pantojas Garcia, *Development of Puerto Rico's Export-Led Industrialization Experience* (Boulder, CO, Lynne Rienner Publishers: 1990).

4 Rueben Berríos Martínez R. *Puerto Rico's Decolonization* (New York, Council on Foreign Relations: 1997). Berman Santana notes that there is disagreement over the success of Operation Bootstrap. Berman Santana, p. 89.

5 Rueben Berríos Martínez R. *Puerto Rico's Decolonization* (New York, Council on Foreign Relations: 1997). Berman Santana notes that there is disagreement over the success of Operation Bootstrap. Berman Santana, pp. 88, 110.

6 Berman Santana and Helen Safa, *The Myth of the Male Breadwinner: Women and Industrialization in the Caribbean* (Boulder, CO, Westview Press: 1995), p. 89.

7 'Puerto Rico: Industrial Island in the Sun: Economic Climate Still Beckons', 17 September 1964, *Business Week*, Series 10, Box 58, Folder 15, Maidenform Collection.
8 Rios, pp. 323–332.
9 Rios, pp. 321–337.
10 Santana, *The Myth of the Male Breadwinner*, pp. 90–92.
11 Laura Briggs, *Reproducing Empire: Race, Sex, Science, and U.S. Imperialism in Puerto Rico* (Berkeley, University of California Press: 2002), p. 18.
12 Noliwe M. Rooks, 'The Myth of Bootstrapping: Politicians Love to Portray Themselves as Horatio Alger Characters, But They Aren't Talking about How Social Mobility Is All But Impossible for the Many These Days', 7 September 2012, *Time Magazine*. https://ideas.time.com/2012/09/07/the-myth-of-bootstrapping/
13 'Puerto Rico: Industrial Island in the sun', 17 September 1964, *Business Week*, Series 10, Box 58, Folder 15, Maidenform Collection. '30 Years Selling to Puerto Rico, 10 years on Puerto Rico', Maidenform's 40th Anniversary. 1 August 1963, Series 10, Box 58, Folder 19, Maidenform Collection.
14 '30 Years Selling to Puerto Rico, 10 years on Puerto Rico', Maidenform's 40th Anniversary. 1 August 1963, Series 10, Box 58, Folder 19, Maidenform Collection.
15 Briggs, pp. 113–114.
16 Briggs, pp. 113–114; Rios, pp. 322–323.
17 'Puerto Rican Menfolk Fret as Their Wives Bring Home the Bacon: Operation Bootstrap Creates New Jobs but the Ladies Grab Most of Them', 19 February 1957, *The Wall Street Journal*, Series 10, Box 58, Folder 15, Maidenform Collection.
18 'Puerto Rican Menfolk Fret as Their Wives Bring Home the Bacon: Operation Bootstrap Creates New Jobs but the Ladies Grab Most of Them', 19 February 1957, *The Wall Street Journal*, Series 10, Box 58, Folder 15, Maidenform Collection.
19 'Puerto Rican Menfolk Fret as Their Wives Bring Home the Bacon: Operation Bootstrap Creates New Jobs but the Ladies Grab Most of Them', 19 February 1957, *The Wall Street Journal*, Series 10, Box 58, Folder 15, Maidenform Collection.
20 Elaine Tyler May, *Homeward Bound: American Families in the Cold War Era* (New York, Basic Books: 1988).
21 Safa, p. 27.
22 Alice E. Colon-Warren and Idsa Alegia-Ortega, 'Shattering the Illusion of Development: The Changing Status of Women and Challenges from the Feminist Movement in Puerto Rico', *Feminist Review*, No. 59, Rethinking Caribbean Difference (Summer 1998), pp. 101–117, 103–106.
23 It was found that men had a slight preference towards their unions (Galvin, p. 148).
24 'Founder of Maidenform to be Feted at Party Here', 18 January 1966, *The San Juan Star*, Series 10, Box 58, Folder 15, Maidenform Collection.
25 Series 10, Box 58, Folders 16–17, Maidenform Collection.
26 Series 10, Box 57, Folders 5–7, Maidenform Collection.
27 Series 10, Box 57, Folders 5–7, Maidenform Collection.
28 Series 10, Box 58, Folder 16–17, Maidenform Collection.
29 Series 10, Box 57, Folders 5–7, Maidenform Collection.
30 '30 Years Selling to Puerto Rico, 10 years on Puerto Rico', Maidenform's 40th Anniversary. 1 August 1963, Series 10, Box 58, Folder 15, Maidenform Collection.
31 Interoffice Correspondence, Series 10, Box 58, Folders 16–17, Maidenform Collection.

32 Interoffice Correspondence, Series 10, Box 58, Folders 16–17, Maidenform Collection.
33 Interoffice Correspondence, Series 10, Box 58, Folders 16–17, Maidenform Collection.
34 Box 25, Folders 15–23, 25–26, ILGWU Collection, Kheel Center, Cornell University.
35 Series 10, Box 58, Folder 17, Maidenform Collection.
36 Robert Parmet, *The Master of Seventh Avenue: David Dubinsky and the American Labor Movement* (New York, New York University Press: 2005), p. 80.
37 Hernandez-Diaz, 19.
38 Alex W. Maldonado, *Teodoro Moscoso and Puerto Rico's Operation Bootstrap* (Gainesville, University Press of Florida: 1997), pp. 138–140.
39 Many Puerto Rican union members also migrated to the U.S. mainland during this period.
40 Arleen Hernández-Díaz, *Labor-Management Relations in Puerto Rico during the Twentieth Century* (Gainesville, University of Florida Press: 2006), p. 21.
41 Caban-1984, p. 162.
42 Caban-1989, p. 562. Miles Galvin, *The Organized Labor Movement in Puerto Rico* (Teaneck, Fairleigh Dickinson University Press: 1979), p. 153.
43 Caban-1989, p. 562. Miles Galvin, *The Organized Labor Movement in Puerto Rico* (Teaneck, Fairleigh Dickinson University Press: 1979), p. 153.
44 Galvin, *The Organized Labor Movement in Puerto Rico*, p. 136.
45 Leo C. Brown, 'Tripartite Wage Determination in Puerto Rico', 19th Annual Meeting – National Academy of Arbitators, 1966, naarb.org/proceedings/pdfs/1966-1.PDF, pp. 1–2.
46 David Card and Alan B. Krueger, *Myth and Measurement: The New Economics of the Minimum Wage* (Princeton, NJ, Princeton University Press: 1995), p. 243.
47 Card and Krueger, *Myth and Measurement*, p. 243.
48 Card and Krueger, *Myth and Measurement*, p. 161.
49 Caban-1984, p. 163.
50 Translation of ILGWU statement in *El Mundo*, 23 December 1955, Box 351, David Dubinsky 57800/002, ILGWU Collection.
51 23 December 1965, *Women's Wear Daily*, 'Puerto Rico – where the profits are', Series 10, Box 58, Folder 15, Maidenform Collection.
52 23 December 1965, *Women's Wear Daily*, 'Puerto Rico – where the profits are', Series 10, Box 58, Folder 15, Maidenform Collection.
53 1954 NLRB Hearings, Letter from Hammer to Rosenthal, Series 10, Box 57, Folder 5–7, Maidenform Collection.
54 *Justice*, January 1954, Series 10, Box 71, Folder 9, Maidenform Collection.
55 *The Maiden Forum* described the article in *Business Week* and reprinted the photographs, which ran on 27 October 1951. October 1951, 6, *The Maiden Forum*, October 1950, 1, Series 4, Subserise B, Box 21, Maidenform Collection.
56 Box 13, Folder 13–16, Upper South Department Records, 5780/039, ILGWU Collection.
57 Lucy S. Dawidowicz, 'Jewish Labor Movement', *The American Jewish Experience* 1997/1986, pp. 191–193.
58 Robert Cassanello, Melanie Shell-Weiss, eds. *Florida's Working-Class Past: Current Perspectives on Labor, Race, and Gender from Spanish Florida to the New Immigration*. Working Americas Series. (Gainesville, University Press of Florida: 2008).
59 Robert Asher and Charles Stephenson, *Labor Divided: Race and Ethnicity in United States Labor Struggle 1835–1960* (Albany, New York State University Press: 1990), pp. 118–119.
60 Herbert Hill, Labor Secretary of the NAACP, in a 14 page memo submitted to the subcommittee.

61 Herbert Hill, Labor Secretary of the NAACP, in a 14 page memo submitted to the subcommittee.
62 'Why Hasn't It Been Said Before?' 29 September 1962, 4, *The Nashua Telegraph.*
63 'Why Hasn't It Been Said Before?' 29 September 1962, 4, *The Nashua Telegraph.*
64 'Dubisky Right, Only Merit Significant', by David Lawrence, 29 August 1962, *The Evening Independent.*
65 Green, pp. 89–90.
66 Parmet, p. 308.
67 Parmet, p. 310.
68 'I Explain You, Mr. Congressman', 22 September 1962, 1, *The Victoria Advocate.*
69 'Maidenform's Mrs. R', *Fortune* 42 (July, 1950), pp. 75–76, Series 2, Sub C, Box 68, Folder 1, Maidenform Collection.
70 Maria Balinska, *The Bagel: The Surprising History of a Modest Bread* (New Haven, CT, Yale University Press: 2008).
71 Emily Rosenberg, 'Another Mission to Moscow: Ida Rosenthal and Consumer Dreams', in Choi Chatterjee and Beth Holmgren (eds.), *The Russian Experience: Americans Encountering the Enigma, 1917-Present* (New York, Routeledge: 2013), pp. 127–138. Parmet, pp. 234–235.
72 Box 350, Folder 3a–3c, David Dubinsky 5780/002, ILGWU Collection.
73 'Lingerie Worker Will Receive More Pay: New Pact Imminent', 17 August 1960, *San Juan Star*, Series 10, Box 58, Folder 15, Maidenform Collection.
74 4 June 1955 and 15 July 1955 Correspondence between Ray Uszczak and Ellis Rosenthal. Series 10, Box 58, Folder 17, Maidenform Collection.
75 28 July 1955, Correspondence between Ray Uszczak and Ellis Rosenthal. Series 10, Box 58, Folder 17, Maidenform Collection.
76 8 September 1955, Correspondence between Ray Uszczak and Ellis Rosenthal. Series 10, Box 58, Folder 17, Maidenform Collection.
77 18 October 1955 and 21 October 1955, Correspondence between Ray Uszczak, Metzger, and Ellis Rosenthal. Series 10, Box 58, Folder 17, Maidenform Collection.
78 24 October 1955, Correspondence between Uszczak and Metzger, Series 10, Box 58, Folder 17, Maidenform Collection.
79 17 October 1955 Correspondence between Lazare Teper and David Dubinsky, Box 351, Folder 1a–1c, 2a–2b, 3,4, 5a–5c, David Dubinsky 57800/002, ILGWU Collection.
80 17 October 1955 Correspondence between Lazare Teper and David Dubinsky, Box 351, Folder 1a–1c, 2a–2b, 3,4, 5a–5c, David Dubinsky 57800/002, ILGWU Collection.
81 21 October 1955, Correspondence between Metzger and Uszczak, Series 10, Box 58, Folder 17, Maidenform Collection.
82 Underline in the original article. A note included told Dubinsky that the underlined section was the 'real' reason he ran the ad. 'To the Workers of the Brassiere and Needle Industry of Puerto Rico', *El Mundo*, October 1955. Translation of article included in correspondence between Gladnick and Dubisnky, 7 October 1955, Box 351, Folder 1a–1c, 2a–2b, 3, 4, 5a–5c, David Dubinsky 57800/002, ILGWU Collection.
83 'To the Workers of the Brassiere and Needle Industry of Puerto Rico', *El Mundo*, October 1955. Translation of article included in correspondence between Gladnick and Dubisnky, 7 October 1955, Box 351, Folder 1a–1c, 2a–2b, 3, 4, 5a–5c, David Dubinsky 57800/002, ILGWU Collection.
84 October, 1955, Correspondence between Gladnick and Dubisnky; *El Mundo* interview (6 October 1955). Box 351, Folder 1a–1c, 2a–2b, 3, 4, 5a–5c, David Dubinsky 57800/002, ILGWU Collection.
85 24 October 1955, Correspondence between Uszczak and Metzger, Series 10, Box 58, Folder 17, Maidenform Collection.

86 24 October 1955 and 3 November 1955 Correspondence between Gladnick and Dubisnky. Box 351, Folder 1a–1c, 2a–2b, 3, 4, 5a–5c, David Dubinsky 57800/002, ILGWU Collection.
87 'Puerto Rico – where the profits are', Roy Brown, *Women's Wear Daily*, 23 December 1965, Series 10, Box 58, Folder 15, Maidenform Collection.
88 Correspondence between Gladnick and Stulberg, Box 111, Folders 1a–1c, Dubinsky 57800/002, ILGWU Collection.
89 Correspondence between Gladnick and Stulberg, Box 111, Folders 1a–1c, Dubinsky 57800/002, ILGWU Collection.
90 Certified transcript of speech, Series 10, Box 58, Folder 22, Maidenform Collection.
91 Translation of flyer sent 17 March 1965 to Maidenform's Mayaguez factory, signed by Margarita Toro, Series 10, Box 58, Folder 22, Maidenform Collection.
92 Letter from Vicente J. Antonetti, JD, to Jerry Schoen, 11 March 1965, Series 10, Box 58, Folder 22, Maidenform Collection.
93 'Notes Re: Mayaguez Work Stoppage 3/6 – 3/23/65', 2–3, day-to-day break down of activity sent to Maidenform Headquarters. Series 10, Box 58, Folder 22, Maidenform Collection.
94 'Notes Re: Mayaguez Work Stoppage 3/6 – 3/23/65', 2–3, day-to-day break down of activity sent to Maidenform Headquarters. Series 10, Box 58, Folder 22, Maidenform Collection.
95 'Notes Re: Mayaguez Work Stoppage 3/6 – 3/23/65', 2–3, day-to-day break down of activity sent to Maidenform Headquarters. Series 10, Box 58, Folder 22, Maidenform Collection.
96 'Notes Re: Mayaguez Work Stoppage 3/6 – 3/23/65', 2–3, day-to-day break down of activity sent to Maidenform Headquarters. Series 10, Box 58, Folder 22, Maidenform Collection.
97 Copy of US NLRB 'Charge Against Employer' filed by Dolores Noriega, Francisca Martell de Alegain, Inocencia Santiago, Ramona Figueroa, and Angelica Arroyo Hernandez, 30 March 1965. Series 10, Box 58, Folder 20, Maidenform Collection.
98 Letter from H. Lieberman containing the content of the letter from Dolores Noriega, 12 April 1965. Series 10, Box 58, Folder 20, Maidenform Collection.
99 Folder 15–23, 25–26, Box 25, Wilbur Daniels 5780/084, ILGWU Collection.
100 Safa, p. 26.
101 Folder 19, Box 9, Gus Tyler 5780/88 and Folder 15–23, 25–26, Box 25 and Folder 3–5, Box 26, Wilbur Daniels 5780/084, ILGWU Collection.
102 Berman, p. 89.
103 'Puerto Rico – Where the Profits Are', 23 December 1965, *Women's Wear Daily*, Series 10, Box 58, Folder 15, Maidenform Collection.
104 Berrios Martinez.
105 Rexford Tugwell, the New Dealer and one-time Governor of Puerto Rico during the 1940s is credited for the first quote, while the second quote is from anthropologist Oscar Lewish in his 1966 book *La Vida*. Lapp, 170.
106 Bart, 'Puerto Rico Woes', 22 March 1957, *The Wall Street Journal*, Series 10, Box 58, Folder 15, Maidenform Collection.
107 Bart, 'Puerto Rico Woes', 22 March 1957, *The Wall Street Journal*, Series 10, Box 58, Folder 15, Maidenform Collection.
108 James L. Dietz, *Economic History of Puerto Rico: Institution Change and Capitalist Development* (Princeton, NJ, Princeton University Press: 1986).
109 Pantojas-Garcia, pp. 170–171. See Michelle Kaske and Martin Z. Braun, 'Puerto Rico's Slide', 4 December 2015, *Bloomberg;* Benjamin Zycher, 'For Puerto Rico Debt Crisis, the Can Hits the End of the Road', 10 December 2015, *The Hill*; Gillian B. White, 'What's Really Happening in Puerto Rico?' 29 June 2015, *The Atlantic*; Richard Finger and Justin Velez-Hagan, 'Default: Puerto Rico's Inevitable Option', 1 December 2015, *Forbes*; The Editorial Board, 'Puerto Rico Needs Debt Relief', 1 July 2015, *The New York Times*.

11

PATRIOTISM AND THE ENGLISH WORKING CLASS, C. 1902–1929

David Swift

The recent increased scholarly interest in class has coincided with the growth of nativist and anti-immigrant sentiment in the UK and elsewhere. This has in turn led to a heightened interest in the relationship between class, nationalism, and patriotism. In terms of historical scholarship, there is a rich literature concerning working-class patriotism in the early decades of the twentieth century. Book-length works, such as Richard Price's *An Imperial War and the British Working Class* and Paul Ward's *Red Flag and Union Jack*, have examined working-class and left-wing reactions to the South African and First World Wars, while Marc Mulholland and Mathew Morris have recently published on the left-wing debates around militarism in the lead up to August 1914. There is also a great deal of literature concerning support – and opposition – to the First World War, both local studies and work that encompasses the whole of the United Kingdom.[1]

Yet any attempt to analyse the sentiments of the 'working class' is fraught with both conceptual and methodological difficulties. First, who or what was the 'working class'? Can one accurately speak of *the* English working class, or was such a class in reality riven by hierarchies of income and craft, and by regional and ethno-religious differences? If the latter is true, then how does this affect our ability to gauge the patriotism of this class? Second, how should we attempt to capture and measure these patriotic sentiments? Given the political disenfranchisement of many working-class men and – in terms of national elections – of all working-class women; the lack of working-class voices in media and literature; and the arduous struggles to simply survive from one week to the next, it is difficult to take an accurate measurement of their patriotism. Finally, what exactly do we mean by 'patriotism'? Is it merely 'love of one's country', and if so, what about their country warranted

DOI: 10.4324/9780429344084-14

this affection? Alternatively, is it something more sinister, a symptom of national chauvinism, which held that one's own country was intrinsically greater than other nations?

A thorough treatment of these methodological and theoretical concerns that did justice to the complexity of these issues would constitute an essay in itself, and leave no room for any analysis of the past. For that reason this chapter will be based on a specific terms of reference that, while imperfect and contestable, will at least allow for an understanding of the nature of patriotism for some of the English working class in this period. The concept of 'patriotism' here is a broad one, encapsulating both chauvinistic nationalism and the sense that community and nation were essential prerequisites to social justice. In terms of methodology, the chapter will draw on the lives of labour leaders, the utterances and activities of ordinary workers and women, the trade union and labour press, and the speeches and debates at the Labour Party's annual conferences.

Certainly, not every member of the working-class was of the Left, and not everyone on the Left was working-class. To ameliorate these issues, the chapter will avoid more avowedly middle-class left-wing organisations such as the Fabian Society, and will concentrate more on trade unionists than Labour MPs, in particular those who self-consciously identified as faithful representatives of working-class sentiment – including conservative sentiments. Furthermore, the use of trade union newspapers, in addition to providing a decentralised picture, will also include the views of Liberal or Conservative working people.

The chapter will also move away from traditional areas – such as South Wales, East Lancashire and the Durham coalfields – and consider London, the Midlands and West Lancashire. Similarly, there is less of a reliance upon coal miners and textile workers, with increased attention given to unskilled or general labourers. The first section focuses on the period in-between the South African and First World Wars, and assesses the complicated relationship between many workers and patriotism: sceptical of jingoism, but often economically dependent on the military and on Empire. The second section concerns the reaction of workers to the First World War, and the outpouring of patriotic sentiment this induced. The final section addresses the 'pacifistic turn' in the 1920s and examines its limits, while analysing exactly what kind of working-class internationalism deve1oped in this decade.

Between the South African and First World Wars

The notion that nations were meaningless was almost entirely absent across the Edwardian working class, yet there was often an ambiguous attitude towards nationalism and patriotism. For many, war weariness after three years of a gruelling conflict in South Africa, a distrust of imperialists, and an abstract, often vague internationalism, co-existed with a banal nationalism, belief in Empire and support for the military.[2] For many in the labour movement, their commitment to internationalism and pacifism were superficial at best. Indeed, very often their left-wing views were based around an idea of community and nationhood that belied any internationalism.

The British National Committee, set up in 1905 to represent British workers at the Second International, consisted of politicians Arthur Henderson, John Hodge and Will Thorne, and the trade unionist Ben Tillett, all of whom would fall into the 'patriots' camp during the First World War.[3] Yet this tenuous and abstract internationalist stance was not supported by a pragmatic scheme of co-operation between the labour movements of different European nations, nor did it preclude a certain chauvinism on behalf of British trade unions. For example, it was only in 1913 that the representatives of the French and German trade unions were invited to the TUC's annual conference, while American delegates had been invited since 1894.[4] Although there would have been practical concerns with language difficulties, assumptions of greater cultural connections and kinship with Americans vis-à-vis French and Germans may have been a factor in this.[5] Regardless, the fact that representatives from the two leading Continental economies did not attend the British TUC until the year immediately before the war gives an idea of the limited extent of actual co-operation between different European workers. Furthermore, elites of the labour movement were more advanced than ordinary workers in this respect; as Douglas Newton has argued, 'most trade unionists were undoubtedly quite unaware that, through their affiliation to the [Labour Representation Committee], they had become enrolled in something called the Second International'.[6]

Labour MPs representing workers who benefitted from increased naval funding felt this took precedence over any pacifistic or internationalist sentiment. John Jenkins and Alexander Wilkie of the Shipwrights' Union (MPs for Chatham and Dundee, respectively) and Charles Duncan of the Engineers (MP for Barrow-in-Furness) rebelled against their party line and voted with the government on increases to naval spending.[7] Meanwhile, Will Thorne MP continued to press for the introduction of compulsory military service designed on the Swiss system.[8] For Thorne this would ensure the permanent defeat of militarism, as every man would be trained and equipped to defend himself against both external aggression and internal oppression. Thorne felt that his 'citizen's army' would have a democratising effect on society as a whole, and awaken working people to their true power.[9] Similarly, in 1906 seven Labour MPs – including future prominent patriots John Hodge and Charles Duncan – signed a petition calling for the introduction of compulsory military training in schools.[10]

Soon after the conclusion of the South African War, German expansionism and sabre-rattling prompted many trade union leaders and socialist writers to claim that, while they had opposed the war against the Boers, a conflict with Germany would be another matter. As early as 1903, *Justice* – the newspaper of the Social Democratic Federation – welcomed the *entente cordiale*, and claimed that it and the SDF had never been 'peace at any price'.[11] Although for most on the Left, Russia remained a paradigm of despotism – as evidenced by the outrage over the visit of the Tsar in 1906 – by 1907 *Justice* was warning that the Kaiser was the real menace to Europe, and that only the German Social Democratic Party could act as a restraining influence.[12] Ben Tillett, also writing in 1907, claimed that the Boer War had been fought 'for a rich gang of thieves and a khaki mad crowd', yet the attitude expressed towards Germany in its pages suggested that war with that country would be a different matter altogether.[13] By 1910, H.M. Hyndman of the SDF wrote of:

> the right and duty of this nationality to maintain its independence, even under capitalism...There is no mistake about that. If this is to be a jingo, then I am a jingo; if this is to be a bourgeois, then I am a bourgeois, if this is to be an opponent of organized Socialist opinion, then I am an opponent of organized Socialist opinion.[14]

Therefore, by the time of the crisis of the summer of 1914, there was a substantial section of organised working-class opinion that, while theoretically internationalist and anti-imperialist, believed their nation to be a tangible community, with real claims on the lives and labour. The events of August 1914 were to force millions of British workers to make a decision: to protest against war foisted on them by forces beyond their control, or to support their country in its hour of need. The overwhelming majority chose the latter option.

The First World War

Most leading individuals in the labour movement remained firmly against the war in the days preceding the start of the conflict. For much of the leadership – as with ordinary trade unionists, Labour supporters and the British population at large – the German invasion of Belgium and the subsequent ultimatum to withdraw served as a turning point, and gave a stamp of morality to the conflict.

The invasion of Belgium confirmed that Britain had no honourable option other than to fight. Since the war was pitched as a question of morality, public opinion quickly painted complex issues in stark, contrasting colours. Whereas only months previously British attitudes towards Germans had been rather ambiguous, soon – aided by tales of atrocities committed in Belgium – Germany became the symbol of everything immoral, and everything un-British. In the words of Adrian Gregory, 'it was the war that massively increased anti-Germanism' and popular militarism – rather than these sentiments pushing the country into the conflict.[15]

As Arthur Marwick claimed, there was a great sense of 'relief' when the Germans ignored the ultimatum to withdraw (as, of course, everyone knew they would), and while 'the opposition to the war was striking, [it was] no more striking than the speed with which the bulk of it dissolved'.[16] In the Imperial War Museum's audio archive of interviews with war veterans collected in the 1980s, Raynor Taylor – a trade unionist born in Oldham 1898-concurred with this view: 'Strangely enough I think before war broke out we sensed it, everybody sensed it, that war would break out because the newspapers...were full of it...As I remember it there was a sense of...relief...it sounds strange to say, but it's true'.[17] William Gillman – who would later go on the be a prominent Labour and trade union activist in West Ham – recalled how he 'thought it was great' when war broke out, as he 'wanted to fight the Germans', 'like we all did, us youngsters'. He did not realise at the time how long the war would last, nor the number of casualties; he 'look[ed] at it in a different way', when he was eighteen, and saw only the possibility for adventure and heroism.[18]

In his 1992 book *Labour at War,* John Horne spoke of the 'choice of 1914'; the idea that the British labour movement ultimately judged its country and its society preferable to that of Germany, and so committed itself for the duration of the conflict.[19] Yet Professor Horne understated the extent to which this choice was made for the labour elites by working-class opinion. The mainstream of the labour movement were well aware that they could not afford to oppose the war once British entry was a reality. At the first Labour Party conference held since the outbreak, in January 1916, dockers' leader James Sexton put forwards a resolution, passed by 1,502,000 votes to 602,000:

> That this Conference, whilst expressing its opposition (in accordance with previously expressed opinions) to all systems of permanent militarism as a danger to human progress, considers the present action of Great Britain and its Government fully justified in the present war, expresses its horror at the atrocities committed by Germany and her ally by the callous and brutal murder of non-combatants, including women and children, and hereby pledges the Conference to assist the Government as far as possible in the successful prosecution of the War.[20]

J. Stokes of the London Trades Council, supporting the motion, argued that 'If...the resolution was turned down what would be the position of the Labour Movement so far as the great mass of the British people were concerned...they would say that the Conference was against the country'.[21]

It is important not to underestimate the prevalence of nationalism in Britain at the start of the twentieth century. Many Britons not only believed themselves to be culturally and 'racially' separate to others; they considered themselves markedly superior, and this attitude was found among those on the Left just as on the Right. An October 1914 edition of the *Wheatsheaf*, a cultural periodical attached to the Co-operative movement, featured a 'Map of Racial Europe'. The map is notable for its specificity; it delineates between not only 'French' and 'German' peoples, but also 'Western Slavs', 'Eastern Slavs', 'Anglo-Irish', and 'Irish'.[22]

Nor was this nationalism necessarily incubated by the government or youth movements such as the Boy Scouts. E.H. Reisner, an American historian of nationalism and education, claimed in the 1910s that the English hardly used schools at all as a means of incubating nationalist sentiment.[23] At least two of the labour activist ex-servicemen in the Imperial War Museum's archive were members of youth groups: Frederick Orton was born in Nottingham in June 1892, the youngest of ten children, and would later go on to become a leading trade unionist. He was in the Boy's Brigade from age twelve, trained with wooden rifles and lances, and noted it was very religious and 'definitely militaristic'.[24] Contrastingly, Jack Dorgan, born in Ashington in 1893, joined the Church Lad's Brigade aged fourteen, mainly because his friends had joined. He recalled that there was no religious instruction, just constant drilling, with very few overtly militaristic aspects.[25]

That a great mass of the population were willing to fight was demonstrated by the hundreds of thousands of men who came forwards, both during the opening weeks and months of the conflict, and in a more or less steady stream throughout, until the introduction of conscription. As Anne Summers has argued, if 1.5 million volunteers could be found in a period of little over a year, there must have been a deep-seated comfort with militarism and warfare.[26] While some men enlisted to escape unemployment and absolute poverty, this cannot be said of any more than a minority, and volunteers came from buoyant industries as much as from depressed trades, including many from protected occupations where demand for labour was high, jobs secure and wages competitive.[27]

In his study on working-class enlistment, David Silbey argued that a broad spectrum of motivations caused men to volunteer, but one cannot help notice that many of the reasons given – 'I got patriotic', or 'We were being patriotic. Or young and silly', are very similar to the motivations for marriage described in music hall comedian Dan Leno's sketch *Young Men Taken in and Done For.* For example, one man woke after a night of drinking to find that he had pledged himself to a woman, although he did not have any memory of this: 'She said, "Yes you do, you spoke about it last night, when you'd had a little drink." Well, I thought, if I did say so, I suppose I did, so I came downstairs half asleep (in fact I think every man's asleep when he going to be married)'.[28] People joined the Army for much the same range of reasons that led to marriage: an initial burst of excitement; a courage and sense of purpose born of alcohol; a vague sense of duty; peer pressure; financial pressures; a desire for adventure. Whatever their original motivations – and these soon faded into irrelevance – men were resolved to see through their obligations until the end, and knew full well that they were involved 'for the duration'.

Frederick Orton recalled that his friends' joining up was important to his decision to enlist, but the most attractive factor was a week's holiday once a year. He also noted that the medical examination was very 'sketchy' and not particularly thorough; Orton's parents owned a sweet shop and were none too strict on young Frederick sampling their wares – by the time he enlisted he had lost all his teeth, yet was still passed as fit to serve.[29] Jack Dorgan was a particularly militant worker; as a teenager he earned a reputation for standing up to pit bosses when older men were afraid to do so, yet he joined the Territorials three years before the war: 'We were intensely loyal, you know, nationalistic...the Union Jack was something to be treasured in those days'. He recalled that he and his friends 'never knew or cared about Germany... didn't really know or care [about] anything outside of Northumberland'. They understood and accepted that 'the people in charge of the country' had declared war on Germany; there were no celebrations or outbursts of patriotic fervour, 'it was just accepted'.[30]

An example of the intersection of patriotism and self-interest can be found in the formation in March 1915 of the Liverpool Dock Battalion. This group consisted of trade unionists willing to submit themselves to organisation along military lines in exchange for a guaranteed minimum of 35s. per week and the promise from Lord Derby that 'the force will adhere strictly to Trade Union rules and under no circumstances will be used as a strike breaking battalion'.[31] While this may not have been possible in more militant areas such as the Clyde or the Tyne, it does show how many workers were willing to make temporary sacrifices in respect of their power to strike for reasons of patriotism and material gains, and the battalion was vastly oversubscribed.

By 14 August 1914 it was estimated that fifteen thousand postmen had left for the services,[32] and by January 1915 *The Post* calculated that fifteen thousand gasworkers and general labourers, thirty thousand Durham miners and 1,434 postal sorters of the Fawcett Association had enlisted.[33] By mid-1915 around 230,000 miners had volunteered nationwide.[34] In addition to organised workers in regular employment, casual labour also streamed forwards to enlist, with John Ward of the Navvies' Union raising four battalions; in Birmingham alone it was thought that one thousand navvies [general labourers] had joined up: 'I often feel proud to know that I am an old navvy's son', claimed one, 'because I know that there is not another class who have answered the call to the flag for home and beauty as our navies have done'.[35] Similarly, in Merseyside, as many as eight thousand dockers, the majority of whom were members of the Dockers' Union, joined the Army between August 1914 and March 1915. Given that so many of their members joined-up, some trade unions immediately decided that they would not be eligible to pay subscriptions during their time with the colours.[36]

In *Armies of Freeman*, Tom Wintringham paid tribute to the Amalgamated Society of Engineers (ASE) members who piloted the tanks in the last years of the war:

> A high proportion of the officers were rankers, but not just any sort of ranker. Skilled engineers to the last finger-nail, men who had come out of the shipyards and fitting-shops in the middle years of the war, they had taken to the new mechanical soldiering the minute it offered. With the matehood of the lathe and bench and the union branch in them, regarding a man as worthy or unworthy according as he turned out his job of work, watching for weakness or inefficiency with eyes trained to the micrometer, riding to death-tests with their men in their early "suicide-club" machines.

'They came from Birmingham and Liverpool and Sheffield', wrote Wintringham, 'from the big centres of the engineering industry and the engineering unions, and they didn't care a damn for anyone'.[37]

Of the 461 young men in the Bradford Independent Labour Party, by the introduction of conscription, fully 113 were already in the trenches, 118 were in training in England, six were in the Navy and 207 had attested under the Derby Scheme. By 1918 of 442 members eligible for service, 351 were serving while 48 were conscientious objectors or doing national war work. This was from a political group generally sceptical of the war, in a city and region more hostile than most to the conflict.[38]

Soon enough notices of the death or wounding of working-class activists and trade unionists began to appear in the left-wing papers. Private Jones of the Bedford Regiment fought in five large engagements in the autumn and winter of 1914, including twelve bayonet charges, until being wounded in the head and neck. His comrades said of him:

> He was a very active and loyal member of the [Manchester No. 4] branch [of the National Union of Railwaymen], and if he proves as good a soldier as he was a Trade Unionist the Germans will not land in England yet. We are proud of our comrade and wish him God speed and a safe and glorious return to his country, wife and children.[39]

A letter in *The Clarion* of November 1915 told of the death of another activist with the colours:

> Clarionettes in South London will be grieved to learn that our dear comrade Jack Reed has been killed in action. His genial kindness and serenity

> endeared him to all, and there are some who knew him intimately who will learn of his death with a dreadful pang. We loved old Jack.[40]

A further missive of August 1916 lamented:

> My only chum is gone: "Alec," as he was affectionately known in the old West London Fellowship, is on the Roll of Honour…Once – how incredibly long ago it seems – he stood up manfully against a special meeting of the branch and defended his position as a Socialist and a Territorial. To think that in those days some of us considered the two things incompatible![41]

An edition of the *Railway Review* of June 1917 told the story of Sergeant Harry Cator, a member of the Yarmouth branch of the NUR and a Lewis gunner in the East Surrey Regiment, who had been awarded the Victoria Cross.[42] Meanwhile, two NUR men had won the Military Medal: W.H. Binge, one time secretary of the South Eastern District Council and Hither Green branch, and A. Lodge, member of the Manchester No. 5 branch and formerly a carter of the Lancashire and Yorkshire railway.[43] Sergeant H. J. Sheppard, formerly Secretary of the Barry Socialist Society, was awarded the DCM in November 1916.[44] The journal of the ASE reported in January 1917 that Sergeant A. Warham of Crewe No. 4 Branch and the Royal Engineers had been given the Military Medal; while from the same regiment Lance-Corporal James Coupe of Barrow Fifth Branch was mentioned in dispatches and presented with the French Medaille Militaire.[45] In January 1918 the engineer Harry Coverdale – a sergeant in the Manchester Regiment who had enlisted in September 1914 – was awarded a Victoria Cross to complement his Military Medal won earlier in the war.[46]

A Glaswegian ASE member and Lance Corporal in the Royal Scots' Fusiliers won the DCM; as did Sergeant Major John Broderick (of Jarrow No.3 Branch), for carrying a wounded officer on his back to safety whilst under heavy fire near Armentieres on 9 December 1915; and the following year Joseph Wilson, a riveter of Hebburn No. 2 Branch became another ASE man honoured with the DCM. Corporal C. Andrews, a stretcher bearer of London No. 11 Branch and the Royal West Kent was also garlanded with the Belgian Croix-de-Guerre to complement his DCM.[47] The Military Medal was awarded to Private W.C. Orr of South Shields No. 1, Jack Naden of Sunderland, Joseph Vaughan of Gateshead and Joshua Horsley of Hartlepool.[48] The final year of the war saw Corporal Ernest Goulding of the 7th Lincolns and Lincoln No.1 Branch, who had enlisted in August 1914, awarded the Military Medal for conspicuous conduct and gallantry in bombing a pill-box.[49]

The issue of war badges, which men in 'reserved' occupations would wear to demonstrate their contribution to the war effort, serves as another demonstration of the concern of the average worker to appear patriotic. For example, one correspondent to the *Railway Review* of May 1915 inquired:

> In many of the munition factories the men have been supplied with these badges; then why have not the railwaymen been supplied with them? We have been stopped from enlisting, and told we are doing just as much to help our country by sticking to our jobs. If this is so, I think we deserve to have such a small form of recognition extended to us.[50]

Meanwhile a column in that newspaper from October of that year complained:

> It has been mentioned in these columns that war badges are indiscriminately distributed to all and sundry employed in railway shops, without regard to age or ability to serve in H.M Forces, and it certainly does seem unnecessary and incongruous that greybeards should be seen proudly disporting themselves in this decoration, and thus claiming immunity from the blandishments of the recruiting sergeants.[51]

Furthermore, a leaflet circulated in 1915 by the Workers' National Committee (which coordinated the response of trade unions and socialist groups to the War) explained how men who had attested under the Derby Scheme but not yet called up could 'show his friends that he is a soldier' through an armlet marked with the Royal Crown.[52] Many of these survive to this day, and there are several in the collections of the People's History Museum, Manchester.

Above all, it was felt imperative not to be seen as a 'shirker'; in August 1914, the politicians George Wardle, Arthur Henderson, and George Roberts, and the trade unionists William Mosses of the Patternmakers, James Brownlie of the Engineers, and Frank Smith of the Cabinet Makers visited France and Belgium, and upon their return assured the workers that:

> It is upon them, as well as upon the men at the front, that the responsibility for procuring victory rests. The lives of our own kith and kin, the desolated homes, the devastated villages, the ruined towns cry aloud for a supreme effort to end quickly this horrible nightmare, and the way to end it is to speed up the supply both of guns and ammunition, until the invader has been driven from his trenches and chased across the Rhine.[53]

Writing from the Front to *Co-Partner's Magazine*, a correspondent named 'F.C.B.' claimed:

> I would rather risk it all again than be a slacker. I rejoice to think that I am not that. We are at present resting in a dear little village; as I write I am sitting in comfortable room, with a full belly and a nice cigar; and if

> it was not for the thoughts of my dear old pals we have left behind I would be perfectly happy. I understand some of the boys of East Ham are knocking things about. It would be better for everyone if they came out here. If I had a brother, and he was a slacker, I would never speak to him again.[54]

There was a widespread hostility towards those suspected of not pulling their weight: discussing the Middlesex Appeals Tribunal, David Langrish has claimed that the tribunal received unsolicited letters from people accusing their neighbours of shirking and demanding that they not be exempted.[55]

In terms of the First World War, the overwhelming majority of British workers were willing to support their country with their lives and labour. They may not have appreciated the intricate system of alliances and intrigues that had led to the conflict, but most appreciated that it had to be fought until the end. Support for the war remained steady throughout the conflict, even as the death toll and cost of living rose beyond anything imagined in 1914. The more severe the conflict grew, the more imperative it became that Britain must not lose. This is not to say that support for the war equated to support for the government; on the contrary, the war years witnessed a great deal of working-class agitation against the state. Yet most workers made a distinction between their country and the government of the day. When the war finally ended, many were determined that the country should never again be entrusted to the same people.

The 'Pacifistic Turn'? 1919–1929

The decade following the Armistice witnessed a stark repudiation of the war – and the nationalism that had led to it – from a broad swathe of the working class. In keeping with this reaction against the conflict, there was a concerted effort from across the Left to foster internationalism and pacifism. Publications such as the *Labour Woman* and the Birmingham Labour Party's *Town Crier* contained numerous reports on working-class lives across Europe and the wider world, and urged the compulsory teaching of Esperanto in schools.[56] These accompanied advertisements for tours of German industrial districts, and of German music groups touring Britain.[57] Under pressure from local trade unions, Birmingham city council removed war relics from its parks, and left-wing newspapers criticised the continuation of military parades.[58] There was sense – present throughout much of British society in the inter-war period – that the next war would result in near total annihilation of the combatant nations. A 1929 edition of the *Town Crier* reported the remarks of Reverend Leyton Richards, speaking at Carr's Lane Church: 'Even admirals and generals had admitted that the next war, should it come, would end in the mutual destruction of both sets of combatants and the probable obliteration of the very civilisation for which the war would be fought'.[59]

The Parliamentary Labour Party systematically opposed increases in the military estimates, endorsed the 1924 Geneva Protocol renouncing the use of force in arbitrating international disputes, and strongly condemned the fostering of a 'militarist or narrowly national or imperialist outlook' in schools.[60] At the 1926 Party conference, Fenner Brockway MP moved a resolution on working-class war resistance:

> so that they would not be placed in the position they were placed in 1914, when, on the Sunday before the war was declared they were speaking of war resistance, but by the middle of the week their arguments had been shattered and resistance made impossible.[61]

In 1928, the TUC joined Labour in welcoming the United States' proposed 'Peace Pact', which had the stated aim of removing war from national policy. That same year Oswald Mosley MP condemned 'the terrible work' of the government in:

> undermining, if not destroying, that great heritage of peace which was bequeathed to it by the Labour Government...so strong was the demand for peace to-day that even the men of war, the men whose policies had brought war again and again in the tragic history of the last generation-even those men, when they presented themselves before the electorate, were dressing up in the white robes of peace. But lift the corner of the robe and they would see the jack-boots.

This pacifistic and internationalist sentiment sometimes extended to criticism of imperialism. The *Labour Woman* was particularly supportive of Irish independence and had a great deal of concern for conditions in Europe, beset during this time by disease and starvation. However, this stance was not necessarily reflective of the significance accorded these issues by the working class more broadly, nor even representative of their readers: in August 1924, the paper held an essay-writing competition for children on the British Empire Exhibition in London. The winning entry, by a 14 year old from Barnet, decried the Empire, although its provenance may have been dubious; the judges noted it was 'very imaginative...just a bit too flowery'. However, none of other essays – including the second and third prizewinners – criticised the Empire, instead focusing on more prosaic points, such as the low wages of the Lyons' coffee house waitresses. The editors concluded that sadly, 'some of them...were greatly impressed by the size of the Empire' and appeared filled with 'a dangerous kind of Imperial swelled-headedness'.[62]

Even socialist publications were equivocal about condemning imperialism. The *Town Crier,* reviewing a book on Empire by socialist J.F. Horrabin, claimed the author 'ought to be ashamed of himself. The tone of the book is deplorable'. Not only did the Marxist writer get his facts wrong – his 'picture of the [1857 Indian Rebellion] is as one-sided as a Tory book on Russia' – and he did 'the movement great discredit with his careless and intemperate' book. A few months later, the same paper reported with pride on the Labour government's investment in colonial infrastructure, particularly in the bridge over the Zambesi.[63]

At the 1925 party conference, Jack Jones MP argued that 'whether for good or ill, they had an Empire...and the problem was...what was the best use they could make of it'. In this he was supported by Haden Guest MP who claimed that to 'smash' the Empire was a Communist solution; their aim instead should be to 'socialise' it. At the same time, the trade unionist C.T. Cramp spoke out against imperialism in Egypt and the Sudan.[64] Perhaps the most surprising interjection at that year's conference was the resolution moved by Ben Tillett, condemning the behaviour of foreign powers in China, and calling for the revision of Treaties granting extra-territoriality to Britain: 'Even if it was true that the British military and fighting forces were necessary to hold our place among the nations', Tillett stated, 'that was no reason why they should be utilised to uphold the most degrading forms of slavery and utilised effectively from a purely economic and capitalist standpoint against the interests of the workers at home'. Here we can see the compatibility of support for Britain during the First World War and criticism of capitalist exploitation of foreign peoples.[65]

Labour called for immediate self-government in India, and fought against any prolonged involvement in Iraq.[66] At the 1928 party conference, Brockway put forwards a motion, subsequently carried, calling for the release of political prisoners in India. This was supported by Mrs L. Cohen of the General Municipal Workers, who noted that she had a particularly sympathy as she had been imprisoned for supporting a policy [equal suffrage] that was 'one of the main planks on which the Tory Party was going to face the next General Election'. She further claimed that 'England was the Mother Country, and being the Mother Country she ought at least to stand for justice for her children'.[67]

Nonetheless, the anti-imperialist and pacifistic sentiments which dominated the labour movement during the 1920s were often unreflective of wider working-class opinion.[68] For some labour leaders and writers, the idea of a difference between the 'working-class Left' of the pre-war years and the *arriviste* middle-class intellectuals using the movement for their own gain continued after the war. The pages of the *British Citizen and Empire Worker* (BCEW) denounced the 'long-haired brigade' and 'un-English methods', and warned that if Labour 'was successful in attracting a large following from the better educated middle classes, to say nothing of countesses from the ranks of the aristocracy' the proletarian character of the party might be lost forever.[69]

Speaking at the 1919 party conference, Mary Bamber a British Socialist party delegate from Liverpool (and mother of Bessie Braddock) claimed:

> If the Labour Party…would stop trying to be statesmen, and get on with the work which the rank and file were doing outside, they would be surprised at the support they could get from the country…With one or two exceptions it had not been possible in most of the labour speeches to draw a dividing line between the speeches of Labour Members and some of the advanced Liberals in the House of Commons…Speaking as a woman of the working class, but a woman who understood the whole international position, she declared that there was a mighty difference in being a Labour Member and understanding the international situation. If they were going to build up a Party to dominate the thinking of workers of this country, they would have to go on definite working class lines.[70]

In a similar vein, at the 1925 annual conference, the dockers' leader James Sexton noted how:

> It might be refreshing, but not encouraging, to hear the robust revolutionary principles advocated from aristocratic Richmond…Thirty or forty years ago he was where their young friend from Richmond was, but time and experience and responsibility had somewhat tempered the wind to him as it has done to others' and mocked the paltry contribution of the Richmond CLP to the Party's funds.

At the same conference, Robert Williams of the Transport Workers noted that the most pacifistic and internationalist delegates

> came from Croydon and from the Ancient and Royal Borough of Richmond' – that is to say, suburban, rather than industrial, districts. At the 1927 conference, Jimmy Thomas MP responded to calls for a general strike to prevent a future war by claiming that such talk came from 'people who have nothing to lose [and who] would not make any contribution towards it.[71]

Another continuity with the war years was the manner in which the Left utilised the language of patriotism to call for radical socioeconomic change. In January 1919 the *Labour Woman* attacked the £25 'Peace Frock Allowance' for the women typists at the Paris Peace Conference: 'Working girls have had to stand throughout the war continued comments upon their extravagance in dress. The munition worker's fur coat has been a constant gibe'. The author noted that West End shops had run out of evening dresses and sarcastically claimed that 'the patriotic munition worker has been dropped her overall and taking to chiffons…what must the munition girl on 25/- unemployment allowance' think about 'the new dance frocks so widely advertised in the media'. Further extolling the virtues of patriotism, the newspaper claimed in December 1919 that 'as soon as the people of this country became conscious of their existence as a nation, they understood that certain things are best done by the community for the community'.[72]

In Bradford, trade unionist Mrs M. Brock claimed that 'the country needed women who would interest themselves in the government of the country' and called for 'national control of industries vital to the national safety, the national assistance for industries essential to national interests, and, finally, the demand that discharged soldiers and sailors be given an opportunity to go on to the land'.[73] The *Town Crier* newspaper spoke of 'Britain's shame... we used to have great prestige as an industrial nation...[now] even Spain is ahead of us' and claimed that Prime Minister Stanley Baldwin's negotiation of debt repayments was 'bleeding the British people'.[74] 'The greatest crime' of the Tory Party, claimed a resolution passed at the 1927 Labour conference, 'is that they have frittered away the magnificent spirit which possessed the nation at the end of the war'. The following year Oswald Mosley called for Britain to 'once again resume her great task as the natural leader of the nations'.[75]

The new-found worldwide enthusiasm for pacifism and internationalism did not extent to immigration. C.T. Cramp attended the World Migration Congress in June 1925, and spoke to the Labour Conference of the:

> Deep cleavage of opinion between the emigrant countries with large surplus populations and a low standard of living, and the immigrant countries who desire both to maintain their higher standards of living and to prohibit in practice the immigration of workers of different races and even nationality.[76]

For many British workers, it was clear with which peoples their destiny belonged. J.T. Walton Newbould MP, while protesting that 'none one wanted more a United States of Europe' than he, argued that Labour should try to make a 'League of Atlantic Powers rather than make a hotch-potch arrangement trying to get a League of European and Asiatic Powers [by which he meant the League of Nations] that would never come in'. The British Left 'must look to the West rather than the East; to their own folk across the seas in the great Republic of the United States'.[77]

In 1925, the organ of London Labour criticised the Municipal Reform Party for 'inflaming the blind passions of certain sections of the public against the so-called "alien"', before proceeding to do exactly that, noting that the Reform Party chair was 'a gentleman with the rather exotic name of Jessel'. It continued that the Party did not

> even keep its platform above suspicion. Thus, at a women's gathering in Brixton in support of [their] candidates, one of the speakers was Baroness de Knoop, who said she had Relatives in Russia...The following

> names are borne by members of the [party] on the L.C.C.: Sir Philip Henriques, J.M. Gatti, C.H.M. Jacobs, C.B. Levita, H.B. Lewis-Barned, E.L. Meinertzhagen, Isidore Salmon, O.E. Warburg.

It concluded by noting that 'it should be remembered that practically the only found from which Tories draw inspiration nowadays is a man whose father was named D'Israeli'.[78] Thus, merely seven years after the end of the war, the official newspaper of London Labour was using xenophobia and antisemitism as a means to attack political opponents, while at the same time organising tours of German cities and other goodwill ventures.

While less openly bigoted, the *Labour Woman* newspaper did not attempt to escape racial stereotypes. An article on 'Working Women at Geneva' noted how

> the tiny Chinese delegate, Miss Zung, with her voice like the tinkling of the finest porcelain, was perhaps the most interesting figure present. She spoke with great care and delicacy in excellent English, and gave a very clear account...then there were the two Italian delegates, in exhaustible in enthusiasm and vivacity.[79]

At the end of the 1920s, the organ of the Birmingham Labour Party printed a satirical article 'The Banana. As a Jap Boy Sees It', making racial slurs against Japanese people, and re-printing the infamous article 'Does Jazz Serve Us Right? The Negro's Revenge!'; clearly the paper saw no contradiction between printing these articles and running pieces about Esperanto and visits by German singing groups.[80]

For *Justice,* the guns had barely fallen silent before they were criticising the 'international Jews who master [David Lloyd George] and his associates', and talking about the 'Jewish problem' in Czechoslovakia.[81] By March 1921, the *BCEW* called for workers to 'make our unions too hot to hold, in any official capacity whatsoever, a single one of the white-livered Labour-fakers who stayed at home, truckling with the Huns, job-snatching, strike-wangling, and hob-nobbing with the alien scum of Europe'.[82] In *Justice,* now controlled by the patriotic wing of the former SDF, there was a continuation of the pre-war argument about the need for working-class control over the military. Writing in January 1919, Lieutenant S. Howard Withey argued that 'never against must we support a policy which would mean the serious reduction of our means of national defence and strength'. There were also continued calls for a citizen army.[83] As late as 1928 some Labour members criticised calls for disarmament at conference due to the economic dislocation it would cause, not merely to shipbuilders and steel workers, but 'even the hundreds of girls employed making buttons for uniforms of our soldiers'.[84]

Justice continued to attack the pacifist Left, long after the guns had fallen silent, claiming that the pacifist E.D. Morel's view of the Treaty of Versailles was undeniably 'pro-German'.[85] The *BCEW*, discussing the situation in East Prussia said that 'if [socialist President] Herr Winning weren't a Hun we would offer him our sympathies'. Two years after the end of the war, that newspaper's 'Mainly for Women' column urged their readers to buy 'British toys for British boys and girls', and chided that a 'Hun-filled stocking... would be nearly as bad as an unfilled one to the patriots of the nursery', complaining that 'enormous quantities of German-made goods [had] already been dumped into the country'.[86]

The *BCEW* went as far as to admonish Arthur Henderson for calling for the expulsion from the British Army of General Dyer – perpetrator of the 1919 Amritsar Massacre.[87] That newspaper claimed that 'the British Empire is no unnatural system of one dominant and many enslaved states', but rather 'a great spiritual partnership'.[88] In May 1920 James Seddon MP gave a speech to his constituents in which he claimed that Sinn Fein

> was a movement for setting up a Republican Government in Ireland, and he was prepared to resist that to the uttermost. (Hear, hear.)...If those who belonged to the Labour Party were going to support a Republican form of government in Ireland, they would make vain the sacrifice of those who had died for this country.[89]

By the end of the 1920s there were distinctly different visions of left-wing 'internationalism'. *Justice* was more internationalist than the *BCEW*, but what kind of internationalism? It was virulently antisemitic and anti-capitalist. This was not too far from the views of many in the Labour Party itself. At the 1925 conference, J. Adams of the Woolwich Trade and Labour Council claimed that the League of Nations was set up by capitalists, and that he 'did not feel confident' it would 'be of [any] service to the working class'. At the same conference Willie Gallacher – notably for his opposition to the First World War and denounced by Labour patriots as pro-German – criticised the Dawes' Plan as a bankers' scheme to enslave the workers of Europe, while the Geneva Protocol was set up by 'representatives of High Finance'.[90]

Thus, while the First World War caused a repudiation of nationalism and militarism among much of the working class, this was often rather superficial. In many ways, from the Empire to race to national identity, patriotic sentiment remained the rule, rather than the exception.

Notes

1 See R. Price, *An Imperial War and the British Working Class* (London, Routledge: 1972); P. Ward, *Red Flag and Union Jack: Englishness, Patriotism and the British Left, 1881–1924* (London, Boydell: 1998); J. Stapleton, 'Citizenship versus Patriotism in Twentieth-Century England', *The Historical Journal* 48 (2005), pp. 151–178; M. Mulholland, '"Marxists of Strict Observance"? The Second International, National Defence and the Question of War', *Historical Journal* 58

(2015), pp. 615–640; M. Morris, 'Peace, But Not at Any Price: British Socialists' Calls for Peace on the Eve of World War One' in L. Bland and R. Carr (eds.), *Labour, Radicalism and World War One* (Manchester, Manchester University Press: 2017), pp. 17–34; C. Pearce, *Comrades in Conscience: The Story of an English Community's Opposition to the Great War* (London, Francis Boutle Publishers: 2001); C. Pennell, *A Kingdom United: Popular Responses to the Outbreak of the First World War in Britain and Ireland* (Oxford, Oxford University Press: 2012); A. Gregory, *The Last Great War* (Cambridge, Cambridge University Press: 2008); and D. Swift, *For Class and Country: The Patriotic Left and the First World War* (Liverpool, Liverpool University Press: 2017).

2 On 'banal' nationalism see M. Billig, *Banal Nationalisms* (London, Sage: 1995).

3 Whilst Henderson had no truck with the jingoism which came to characterise Hodge, Tillett, and Thorne, he took up chairmanship of the Parliamentary Labour Party after MacDonald's resignation, and was instrumental to the war effort.

4 Douglas Newton, *British Labour, European Socialism* (Oxford, Clarendon Press: 1985), p. 71.

5 Neville Kirk has written about the comradeship between British, Australian and American trade unionists. See N. Kirk, *Comrades and Cousins: Globalization, Workers and Labour Movements in Britain, the USA and Australia from the 1880s to 1914* (London, Merlin: 2003) and 'Transnational Labour in the Age of Globalization', *Labour History Review* 75 (2010), pp. 8–19.

6 Newton, *British Labour, European Socialism*, p. 49.

7 H. Weinroth, 'Left-Wing Opposition to Naval Armaments in Britain before 1914', *Journal of Contemporary History* 6 (1971), p. 116.

8 *Justice*, 5 December 1903.

9 Ward, *Red Flag and Union Jack*, p. 112.

10 Newton, *British Labour, European Socialism*, p. 157.

11 *Justice*, 7 November 1903.

12 *Justice*, 9 February 1907.

13 *Justice*, 18 May 1907. See the coverage of the Kaiser's visit to Britain in 7 September 1907 edition for anti-Prussian sentiment.

14 *Justice*, 3 September 1910.

15 Gregory, *The Last Great War*, p. 39.

16 Marwick, *Deluge*, pp. 72–73.

17 Imperial War Museum, Catalogue No. 11113, Raynor Taylor, interviewed 1990–1992.

18 Imperial War Museum, Catalogue No. 9420, William Gillman, interviewed 1986.

19 J. N. Horne, *Labour at War. France and Britain 1914–1918* (Oxford, Clarendon Press: 1991).

20 Report of the Fifteenth Annual Conference of the Labour Party.

21 Report of the Fifteenth Annual Conference of the Labour Party.

22 *Wheatsheaf*, October 1914.

23 According to E. H. Grainger, *Patriotisms. Britain 1900–1939* (London, Routledge Kegan Paul: 1986), pp. 30–31.

24 Imperial War Museum, Catalogue No. 10411, Frederick James Orton, interviewed 1988.

25 Imperial War Museum, Catalogue No. 9253, Jack Dorgan, interviewed 1986.

26 A. Summers, 'Militarism in Britain before the Great War', *History Workshop Journal* 2 (1976), p. 105.

27 Wilson, *The Myriad Faces of War*, p. 519.

28 Quoted in G. Stedman Jones, 'Working-Class Culture and Working-Class Politics in London, 1870–1900: Notes on the Remaking of a Working Class', *Journal of Social History* 7 (1974), p. 492.

29 Imperial War Museum, Catalogue No. 10411, Frederick James Orton, interviewed 1988.
30 Imperial War Museum, Catalogue No. 9253, Jack Dorgan, interviewed 1986.
31 K. Grieves, 'The Liverpool Dock Battalion: Military Intervention in the Mersey Docks, 1915–1918', *Transaction of the Historical Society of Lancashire and Cheshire* 131 (1982), p. 148.
32 *The Post*, 14 August 1914; Co-Partners' Magazine, March 1916.
33 *The Post*, 29 January 1915.
34 R. Holmes, *Tommy. The British Soldier on the Western Front 1914–1918* (London, Harper Perennial: 2005), p. 149.
35 D. Sullivan, *Navvyman* (London, Coracle: 1983).
36 See the *Railway Review*, 21 August 1914.
37 T. Wintringham, *Armies of Freemen* (London, Labour Book Club: 1940), pp. 126–127.
38 K. Laybourne and Reynolds, *Liberalism and the Rise of Labour* (London, Croom Helm: 1984), pp. 184–189.
39 *Railway Review*, 29 January 1915.
40 Letter from Jack Wilmot, *The Clarion*, 5 November 1915.
41 Letter from W. G. N., *The Clarion*, August 1916.
42 Letter from W. G. N., *The Clarion*, 15 June 1917.
43 Letter from W. G. N., *The Clarion*, 8 June 1917.
44 Letter from W. G. N., *The Clarion*, 10 November 1916.
45 ASE Monthly Journal and Report, January 1917.
46 ASE Monthly Journal and Report, January 1918.
47 Boilermakers' Reports, April 1918.
48 ASE Monthly Journal and Report, March and May 1917.
49 ASE Monthly Journal and Report, May 1918.
50 Letter from G. White, *Railway Review*, 7 May 1915.
51 *Railway Review*, 22 October 1915.
52 LHASC, WNC.8/8/8/24: The Group System. Questions and Answers.
53 *Railway Review*, 10 September 1915.
54 Co-Partners' Magazine, July 1915.
55 D. Langrish, 'Conscription, Tribunals and Sacrifice: The Papers of the Middlesex Service Appeals Tribunal', paper given at 'Labour and the First World War' Conference at Anglia Ruskin University, 3 May 2014.
56 See, for example, *Labour Woman*, February 1923 and *Town Crier*, 18 January 1929.
57 See review of German signing group in Birmingham, *Town Crier*, 28 September 1928.
58 See *Town Crier*, 8 February 1929 and 19 July 1929.
59 *Town Crier*, 15 February 1929. On fear of the destructive capacity of air power before the Second World War, see M. Smith, '"A Matter of Faith": British Strategic Air Doctrine before 1939', *Journal of Contemporary History* 15 (1980), pp. 423–442 and B. Holman, 'The Air Panic of 1935: British Press Opinion between Disarmament and Rearmament', *JCH* 46 (2011), pp. 288–307.
60 Labour Party Annual Conference Reports, 1925 and 1927.
61 Labour Party Annual Conference Report, 1926.
62 *Labour Woman*, August 1924.
63 *Town Crier*, 15 March 1929 and 26 July 1929.
64 Labour Party Annual Conference Report, 1925.
65 Labour Party Annual Conference Report, 1925.
66 Labour Party Annual Conference Reports, 1925 and 1926.
67 Labour Party Annual Conference Report, 1927.

68 For Labour's criticism of 'Prussianism at home' during the 1920s see J. Lawrence, 'Forging a Peaceable Kingdom: War, Violence, and Fear of Brutalization in Post-First World War Britain', *The Journal of Modern History* 75 (2003), p. 585.
69 *BCEW*, 31 January and 12 February 1920.
70 Report of the Eighteen Annual Conference of the Labour Party.
71 Labour Party Annual Conference Report, 1925 and 1927.
72 Labour Woman.
73 *BECW*, 25 February 1920 and 29 April 1920.
74 *Town Crier*, 5 April and 26 April 1929.
75 Labour Party Annual Conference Report, 1927 and 1928.
76 Labour Party Annual Conference Report, 1926.
77 Labour Party Annual Conference Report, 1927.
78 *London News*, March 1925.
79 *Labour Woman*, 1 November 1921.
80 *Town Crier*, 9 August 1929 and 27 September 1929.
81 *Justice*, 13 February 1919 and 2 October 1919.
82 *BCEW*, 5 March 1921.
83 *Justice* 2 January 1919 and 13 March 1919.
84 Major Leigh Aman of Fareham DLP, Labour Party Annual Conference Report, 1928.
85 *Justice*, 26 June 1919.
86 *The British Citizen and Empire Worker*, 24 January 1920 and 27 November 1920.
87 *BCEW*, 3 January 1920.
88 *BCEW*, 11 March 1920.
89 Reported in *BCEW*, 13 May 1920.
90 Labour Party Annual Conference Report, 1925.

12

MEDICAL CARE FOR WORKING-CLASS CHILDREN IN THE LATE EIGHTEENTH AND EARLY NINETEENTH CENTURY

Claire Phillips

Dispensaries, voluntary infirmaries, and domestic medicine were all used in order to care for sick children in the period c. 1770–1834. Each of these institutions had their own entry requirements, and a large number of dispensaries and voluntary infirmaries demanded recommendation from a governor or subscriber. A governor, or subscriber, paid a set amount to the institution in order to help it remain financially viable. In return, each was allowed to have one patient on the books – more if they were paying a substantial sum in subscriptions. Patients had to petition a local governor in order to be accepted into the institution. This was important for several reasons. First, it meant that if a disease was spreading through a family, a choice had to be made as to who would receive treatment. It also meant that the patient, or the parent of the patient, needed to have access to a governor willing to petition for their admission to the institution. Second, the patients, and their families, had to adhere to strict conditions of entry. These included presenting themselves at a specific place and time, ensuring that all prescribed medications were only taken by the patient, and attending all follow up appointments as required. Third, once restored to health, the patient had to write to the governor to express their thanks for the assistance they had provided.

This chapter discusses the various avenues open to the working class and the poor in terms of medical care for their sick children in four sections. First, it examines institutions that only permitted admission on the receipt of recommendations, and considers how this affected the treatment of the poor. Second, it analyses institutions, such as a number of dispensaries, where no recommendations were required. Third, although their location in London ensured they were available only for a relatively small proportion of the population, institutions that were specifically established to treat sick children

DOI: 10.4324/9780429344084-15

will be examined. Fourth, the remaining option for those who could not – or did not wish to – access medical care from an institution was domestic medicine. Treatment administered within the home provides the final avenue to be examined here.

The parents of sick children had a number of options available to them, and parents were aware of these options. In particular, parents were willing to use any networks that they may have had to ensure their child was provided with care in voluntary infirmaries and dispensaries. They also travelled long distances to access medical care that was provided without restrictions. Where medical care for children was not available in institutions, it was provided within the home. Much of the evidence for this treatment is contained within middle- and upper-class domestic receipt books; the women who owned these books could provide assistance to their poor neighbours. In instances where parents did not have access to domestic receipt books, they provided their children with basic medical care derived from oral tradition passed down through family members.

Recommendation-required Institutions

Recommendation proved the main barrier between working-class children and medical care in the late eighteenth and early nineteenth century. The sick were not simply able to go to an infirmary or dispensary and request medical care. Governors, or subscribers to these institutions, were permitted to recommend a number of patients according to the value of their annual subscription. At Alnwick Dispensary in Northumberland, every subscriber of one guinea per year was allowed to have one patient constantly on the books. Annual subscriptions larger than one guinea allowed the subscriber to recommend patients 'in proportion to the sum subscribed'.[1] At the Dispensary and Infirmary at Sunderland, one guinea bought the subscriber three patients annually, whilst two guineas bought six patients annually.[2]

Whilst blocking medical care for all but a select few, infirmaries and dispensaries ensured that they were working closely with the 'indigent sick'. The Resolutions of the Alnwick Dispensary illustrate that the governors had the poor at heart when establishing their institution:

> That institutions having for their object the relief of the indigent sick have ever had, in this country, the sanction of the humane and charitable, and have invariably met with the most liberal and benevolent support; and as the utility of dispensaries in general has been fully evinced by long experience, the establishment of a charity of that kind, for the purpose of administering advice and medicines, gratuitously, to the poor of these districts is a measure which has the unanimous approbation of this meeting.[3]

Many institutions that only permitted entry upon recommendation developed a series of rules and regulations. These rules and regulations changed according to the date, area, and the nature of the infectious diseases present in the vicinity at the time. However, they also contained many similarities. The rules and regulations at Liverpool Infirmary, for example, included a number of restrictions that prevented patients from seeking care:

> That no woman big with child, no child under seven years of age, except in extraordinary cases; no persons disordered in their senses, suspected to have the small-pox, the itch, or other infectious distemper, or that are apprehended in a dying condition or incurable, be treated as in-patients.[4]

The rules at the Sunderland Infirmary – but crucially not at the Sunderland Dispensary – insisted that patients be above the age of seven years unless they needed an operation.[5] Thus, children under the age of seven (or nine in some other institutions) were not allowed to be admitted. This meant that parents of children below the minimum age – or parents whose children were suffering from smallpox, the itch, or any other infectious disease – did not have the option of having their children treated at an infirmary. The exceptions were usually children who needed emergency surgery or who had broken a bone. Similarly, the dispensaries at Alnwick and Sunderland, amongst others, accepted the need to treat those who had suffered from accidents and/or broken bones, and were able to accept these individuals as patients.[6]

The combination of rules for the Sunderland Infirmary and Dispensary demonstrate a clear difference between how the two institutions were run, despite the fact that they were operated in conjunction with one another. The Infirmary, as an in-patient institution, did not accept children nor those with infectious diseases as individuals in both of these categories could cause problems for other patients. However, as an out-patient institution, the Dispensary was able to accept both children and patients with infectious diseases as the dispensary operated in much the same way as a modern-day pharmacy. Patients attended on specified days and took their medication home with them. Therefore, the dispensary acted as a link between traditional domestic medicine and emerging forms of institutional care.

Dispensaries, particularly those set up with charitable provisions, were created to benefit the poor. Yet how much they were actually able to help the poor is debatable. The recommendation system blocked all but a select few of the working class from receiving care. Patients needed to have access to a governor or subscriber, and that person needed to have a free bed in the dispensary at the time. Even if all the stars aligned, and a poor mother was able to gain the help of a subscriber, the condition suffered by the sick child had to be within the boundaries of the rules. Therefore, children suffering from many common childhood diseases were automatically excluded, as were younger children. Parents invariably also faced the choice of which sick child to help, particularly during times of epidemic. Deborah Brunton argues that only those who were able to support their families, but unable to then pay for medical care, were eligible for sponsorship into one of these institutions.[7] Thus, those who were not able to support their families – the destitute – were unable to access medical care in such institutions. However, despite this, dispensaries offered assistance, regardless of age, gender, or background, for emergency treatments.[8]

Although not discussed specifically in either the Old or the New Poor Laws, medical care was regarded as a necessity for those unable to pay for a physician.[9] The workhouse was the only option available to those without the ability to gain access to an infirmary, as they accepted anyone presented at their doors. Although not a dedicated medical institution, the workhouse did provide medical care for inmates who suffered from infectious diseases, children, and the undeserving poor.[10] However, the standard of that care was comparatively poor and susceptible to influence from those who paid for the institution through Poor Law subscriptions. As Frank Compton has suggested, 'the speed of medical treatment development and the order in which the alleviation of diseases were tackled, depended upon the perceived threat to the ruling elite'.[11]

Children were regularly present at the Chelsea Union workhouse in London. Whilst the majority of children were either born in the workhouse, entered with their parents, or arrived following the deaths of their parents, the surviving records indicate that a number of children were admitted to the workhouse due to illness. Henry Magraw, aged eleven, was admitted to the Chelsea Union workhouse on 20 September 1794. He was 'taken out by his mother having gotten well' one month later, on 21 October. Similarly, Isabela McKenzie, aged twelve, was admitted into the same workhouse at Chelsea on 1 June 1796. She was the only individual recorded as having been admitted to the workhouse that day. She was listed as 'not well' and remained in the workhouse until 22 June. Her discharge notes recorded that she was 'taken out by her mother, having gotten better'. That both of these children were in the workhouse for more than three weeks demonstrates that, whatever the causes of their illnesses, their care needs were substantial. Although the records do not contain sufficient information to be certain, five-year-old John Joyce may provide another example. On 26 July 1743, John was described as 'sick' and admitted to the workhouse. He remained in the workhouse until 19 August, when he was retrieved by his mother. Yet he returned to the workhouse in December, when he was re-admitted because 'his mother could not keep him'. Whether this was to do with John's earlier illness or not is unclear, but in January 1744 his mother was 'ordered to keep him'. This command suggests that John was re-admitted due to a chronic illness rather than because of poverty.[12]

Being removed by a mother was not an uncommon discharge notice in workhouses during the eighteenth and nineteenth centuries. Many children were placed into the workhouse whilst their parent, or parents, secured work and accommodation. However, the fact that sick children were placed in the workhouse to receive medical care demonstrates that poor and working-class parents understood how to access medical care – albeit with the workhouse acting as a place of last resort. In contrast to many dispensaries and voluntary infirmaries, parents could guarantee that the workhouse would provide medical care for their sick children for a number of conditions. The dispensary and voluntary infirmary movement of the late eighteenth and early nineteenth century provided medical care to those able to gain recommendations, which gave them with an alternative to the workhouse. The dispensary movement added a further layer to the medical care available to the poor and working classes, which ensured that the deserving poor could be – in a limited number of cases – treated for their illnesses.[13]

The inoculation of children with smallpox was one area of dispensary medical care that was offered both free of charge and with incentives. Not all of the records for the treatment of smallpox within dispensaries have survived, but those for the Dispensary at Newcastle provide evidence of preventative medicine and the importance attached by the institution to ensuring that all children were provided with treatment. Opened in 1777, the Newcastle Dispensary opened its services to 'the diseases of children, and to every distemper'.[14] It aimed to 'restore the families of the poor to health, and usefulness' – the latter a clear indication of the important role played by children as financial contributors to the family home during the late eighteenth century.[15] Yet, despite the dangers of death, disability, and disfigurement, children who played a vital role in the household economy were frequently not inoculated as the child would not be able to work for a number of weeks during the inoculation process.[16] Therefore, the dispensary at Newcastle was one of a number across England that offered financial incentives to poor parents in an attempt to increase the number of poor children being inoculated. Parents were offered five shillings for the inoculation of one child, seven shillings for the inoculation of two children, and nine shillings for the inoculation of three children. Families that had four or more children inoculated received ten shillings.[17] It is unclear from the surviving records precisely how many families took the dispensary up on their offer of payment, but 788 individuals were inoculated by Newcastle Dispensary between 1786 and 1789. The first batch of inoculations were carried out in April 1786, and further procedures were undertaken 'every spring and autumn' henceforth – taking into account the periods during which smallpox infection was recognised to be at its most dangerous.[18] A total of 215 patients who had caught smallpox naturally were admitted in the first twelve years of the dispensary's existence, and 161 were discharged cured.[19] The payments issued to the parents would have been more than enough to cover the lost wages of a child absent from work for the duration of the procedure, and the inoculation ensured the child would not succumb to the disease during a future outbreak.

The system in place at Newcastle and other dispensaries changed in 1801. They no longer offered inoculation against smallpox using their previous method. Instead, Newcastle Dispensary followed the guidance of Edward Jenner and began to vaccinate using cow-pox.[20] The governors at Newcastle noted that the cow-pox vaccination was cheaper, safer, and easier than the inoculation process. As children were no longer carrying around a live case of smallpox, they did not need to be placed in isolation to prevent the disease's spread. Therefore, it took less time to treat the children and the dispensary no longer needed to offer financial incentives to parents. Furthermore, progressively fewer patients required treatment for smallpox at the dispensary following the introduction of vaccination. Between the years 1812 and 1817, just fifty-six individuals with smallpox contracted in the natural way were admitted to the Newcastle Dispensary; forty-six were discharged cured.[21] The surviving documents do not record the ages of those treated. However, as smallpox was largely a disease of childhood we can assume that the majority of those vaccinated were children. From 1840, the poor were required to vaccinate their children and the costs were covered by the government.[22] Compulsory vaccination was not universally popular, but by the time Great Ormond Street Hospital opened in 1852 comparatively few children were treated for smallpox contracted in the natural way than had been the case in the eighteenth and early nineteenth centuries.[23]

Unrestricted Access Institutions

Bamburgh Castle Dispensary treated all patients in need, as the funding for the institution was provided by a general charitable trust established by Nathaniel Lord Crewe. Dr John Sharpe, who worked within the trust and founded the dispensary, was responsible for the dispensation of money earmarked for 'charitable use'.[24] Patients were still required to demonstrate they were worthy of medical care. However, all that was required was a signature from a member of the clergy.[25]

Although the records do not contain details of the treatment provided to poor, sick children at the Bamburgh Castle Dispensary, the admissions records for the institution are enlightening. The admissions records begin from 1777, and they record the date, the name of the patient, the parish from which they originated, their age, how long they had been ill prior to seeking treatment at the dispensary, when they were discharged from their treatment, and how they were discharged. The data has been examined for patterns that provide information about how the poor accessed medical care when it was freely available. They demonstrate that a wide cross-section of society was admitted to, and received care from, the dispensary. Sibling and family groups are present in the records – all suffering from the same disease. Thus, the fact that Bamburgh Castle Dispensary did not operate under the same rules and regulations as other institutions permitted whole families to be present on the dispensary books at the same time. This would have made life far easier for poor families that had, for example, three children concurrently ill with a serious disease such as whooping cough.[26] In March and April 1781, a large number of children who suffered from whooping cough or 'hooping cough' were admitted to the care of the dispensary.[27] Two brothers, Adam and James Telford, aged five and three years old respectively, were among them. They were admitted on 24 March and had been suffering from whooping cough for a week prior to their admission. They were both discharged, listed as 'cured' on 31 March.[28] The Reikaby siblings – four-year-old twins George and Dorothy, and eighteen-month-old Henry – were admitted on the same day as the Telford brothers. They were also listed as having suffered from the disease for a week prior to admission. However, their recovery took longer. They were discharged cured a full two weeks after the Telford brothers, on 14 April.

Conditions such as fever were also prevalent among sibling groups treated at Bamburgh Castle Dispensary. On 4 April 1778, William and Sarah Hunter, aged eighteen and eleven respectively, were admitted to the dispensary having suffered from fever for the previous twenty days. Both were discharged cured almost a month later, on 2 May.[29] David and John Henderson, aged four and two respectively, were patients of the Dispensary for seven days with their fevers. Admitted on 16 May, they were discharged cured on 23 May, suggesting that those fevers had not been as severe as that suffered by the Hunters.[30] The Henderson brothers had only been suffering with fever for a week prior to their admittance. This could suggest that swifter medical treatment led to shorter recovery times, but it may also infer that they suffered from a different, milder type of fever.

Highly infectious diseases, such as the itch, caused the admittance of entire family groups to the Bamburgh Castle Dispensary. The itch was an uncomfortable skin disease; whilst not life threatening it could lead to scarring. Children with scars from the itch were more likely to be passed over by potential employers. Therefore, there were clear economic and medical motivations behind the decision to seek treatment for the disease. In August 1793, George Cuthbertson was admitted to the dispensary along with his children, Isabel (19), Barbara (17), and Robert (14). They had been suffering from the itch for one week prior to their admittance, and were discharged 'relieved' on 27 August. Had the Cuthbertson family only been allowed to admit one sick member to the dispensary – as was the practice elsewhere in the country – which one of the children would have been chosen? Would the medicine that child received have been shared around the family? Would the entire family have been 'relieved' of the condition?

As the itch, as with whooping cough and fevers, was an infectious disease, curing one child did not mean that the entire family was protected. Four siblings from the Young family, listed in the admission registers as hailing from Durham – far outside Bamburgh Castle Dispensary's catchment area – also suffered from the itch. John, Elizabeth, Mary, and Eleanor, aged two, thirteen, ten, and seven respectively, were all discharged 'cured'.[31] Why the Youngs travelled such a distance to Bamburgh Castle is not noted in the surviving records. However, it is possible that all four children required medical care and their parents were unwilling – or unable – to decide which of their children should receive priority over their siblings.

Institutions for the Treatment of Sick Children

There were few institutions in late eighteenth- and early nineteenth-century England that focused specifically on the care of sick children. The Foundling Hospital and its associated branches and the Dispensary for the Infant Poor were the two most prominent, whilst Christ's Hospital in London acted as a type of orphanage. However, both Christ's Hospital and the Foundling Hospital only treated sick children that were under their care; they were not open institutions for the provision of general medical treatment to children. The parents who gave up their children to the institutions were aware that the children would receive medical care, despite their lowly status in life. The Foundling Hospital treated all of its sick children in-house, and when children were sick whilst out at nurse in the first five years of life their care was provided through the Hospital.

However, children at the Foundling Hospital were in a delicate position. They had been abandoned by their parents to the care of an institution. Therefore, they had little access to domestic medicine. Yet they were treated by some of London's best physicians without having to rely upon securing a recommendation or referral. This access came at a cost: children at both the Foundling Hospital and the Dispensary for the Infant Poor were used as subjects in medical trials, with few adult voices advocating on behalf of the children's rights. These children, through their participation in medical experiments, provided the patient base that stimulated the development of paediatrics as a medical specialism in the eighteenth century, rather than the nineteenth century as previously thought.[32]

Skin conditions were among those to be the focus of medical trials at the Foundling Hospital. Despite their access to some of the most advanced treatments and skilled physicians of their day, many of the children within the Foundling Hospital suffered from skin conditions. The hospital apothecary, Robert McClellan, treated forty children at the hospital with Powis

Wells Water in an attempt to cure conditions of the head, skin, and eyes.[33] Although this particular experiment was not harmful, it did not prove to be a success. Many of the children who were treated for scald head recovered well enough, but some had relapses and the cure could take months or years to be effective.[34]

Foundling children were also used in experiments for smallpox inoculation. Physician William Watson used a number of foundlings in his quest to identify the most efficient method for smallpox inoculation, despite the risks this may have posed to the children. In Watson's experiments, children were separated into groups and prepared for the inoculation procedure in different ways – Watson then observed and recorded the children's progress over the course of the inoculation process.[35] However, the experiments at the London Foundling Hospital were not as dangerous as that undertaken by George Armstrong at his Dispensary for the Infant Poor. Armstrong wrote several texts on the care of sick children and was a recognised authority on the subject.[36] He became one of the first physicians to explicitly acknowledge that children were a different 'species' from adults.[37] Yet his experiments on children with whooping cough drew ire from his fellow physicians over his use of hemlock.[38] Of all the experiments examined for this chapter, Armstrong's was arguably the most dangerous; hemlock is a poison. Despite its potential risks, Armstrong demonstrated that using hemlock as part of the treatment for whooping cough proved more successful than previous treatments for the disease. Yet for the purposes of this chapter, the efficacy of the solution is less important than the means by which it was identified. Poor and working-class children were offered medical care for free if they participated in the trial – care they desperately needed as they were suffering from a life-threatening disease. But they were used as test subjects, and given no say in the nature of their treatment. The use of children in medical experiments placed them at the forefront of medical science and helped bring about substantial improvements in children's medicine,[39] but it also underscored another dilemma faced by poor and working-class families: accept, for free, experimental forms of treatment with potentially fatal outcomes, or refuse to allow their children to become 'guinea pigs' and thereby lose access to a potential source of medical treatment.

Domestic Medicine

The home was always an option for children who required medical care in the late eighteenth and early nineteenth centuries – for many, it was the only option. Medical care entered the home in a number of ways, the most obvious being domestic medicine. Domestic receipt books were prevalent throughout the period. However, it is important to note that the poor did not possess the means to purchase copies of such texts, nor perhaps the ability to read them.

Treatment was passed down from grandmother, to mother, to daughter, with the women of the family acting as the source of medical knowledge and treatment.[40] Neighbours, friends and relatives may also have been in a position to refer the poor to individuals with access to these texts, and thus the domestic medical marketplace and 'kitchen physic' came into its own.[41] Whether directly or indirectly, parents were able to access the assumed knowledge contained within domestic receipt books to provide care for their sick children.[42]

Domestic receipt books were often written by women for women during the eighteenth and nineteenth centuries. Frequently, they were written and handed down through the family, and a difference in hands can often be seen, such as in the book ascribed to Hannah Sheppard.[43] Some of these texts are known only by the name of the woman whose name is written in the front, such as Sheppard's, Mary Anne Fawcett's book, or the book entitled Sarah Ellis and Others.[44] These books comprised both cookery and 'physic', or medicine. The combination of these subjects within the same books, which more often than not belonged to women, show how intertwined medicine and cookery were during the period. Indeed, foodstuffs were frequent ingredients in the remedies contained within the books, whilst a good diet was often recommended as one of the keys to good health. The remedies that were noted in the domestic receipt books have a distinctly domestic feel to them. They include elements of cookery, such as using a serving pan and simmering on the stove – methods that were largely linked with women's work. As women were largely in charge of the cooking, so they were in charge of caring for the sick within their families.[45] These links between cookery and medicine permit women's medical work within the home to be rendered visible.[46]

The fact of illiteracy among the poorer classes means that we have no way of knowing for sure how they treated their sick children in the late eighteenth and early nineteenth centuries, unless they attended an institution or were attended by a physician. Physicians attended poor children at home during the period, but it is unclear how many parents paid for this medical care. There is no mention of payment in the records of William Hey, a surgeon from Leeds, but he did attend children at home – particularly apprentices who were cared for by their masters.[47] Similarly, Thomas Giordani Wright also treated children within their homes from his practice in early nineteenth-century Newcastle Upon Tyne.[48] Like Hey, Wright rarely mentioned the social standing of his patients, preferring to focus on their conditions and medical treatment. However, as Wright largely cared for patients in the coal mining towns in the vicinity of Newcastle, it is more than likely that he treated the poor. It is unclear whether he treated the poor for free, drawing from his richer patients as a way of covering his costs, or whether the managers of the mines took responsibility for the sick in their employment. Wright appears to have been a much-valued member of the community, willing to help the poor and the sick in early nineteenth-century Newcastle, hence why he was treating the poor with little mention of payment.

Conclusion

Medical care was available for the children of the poor and working classes in the late eighteenth and early nineteenth centuries. However, the nature of that care was dependent upon a range of factors. Children's access to care was limited by where they lived. Although the records demonstrate that families travelled from Newcastle Upon Tyne and Durham to obtain medical care at the Bamburgh Castle Dispensary, such examples are rare. Working-class children were usually treated within walking distance of their homes; children who lived in Newcastle did not benefit from the medical experiments undertaken by physicians in London. Therefore, the care of sick, working-class children, was primarily dependent upon local amenities.

Poor and working-class children's medical care also depended to a large extent upon the wealthy. The rich subscribers and governors of dispensaries and infirmaries controlled access to their institutions, and denied access to children based on age and the nature of their illness. Children under the age of seven and those with infectious diseases were barred from many institutions, whilst entry to others was dependent upon securing a recommendation from a subscriber. Therefore, even if children lived in close proximity to a dispensary or infirmary they were not guaranteed treatment.

Access was also a challenge within the home. Many poor and working-class families did not contain members who could read, and even those who could may not have had sufficient money to purchase medical texts such as William Buchan's *Domestic Medicine*.[49] Therefore, many sick children had to rely upon their mother's acquired knowledge, or upon the availability of medical knowledge within the community. Similarly, paying for a physician to visit the home was beyond the reach of many poor and working-class families – they were reliant upon men such as William Hey and Thomas Giordani Wright to provide them with treatment.

Theoretically, the poor and working classes in the late eighteenth and early nineteenth centuries were presented with a range of options for the treatment of their sick children. Yet the reality was somewhat different. Individuals did not always have access to the governors able to recommend them to institutions. Parents could not always permit their children time away from work to ensure they were protected against smallpox, and parents did not always possess the ability to treat their sick children within the home.

Notes

1 The Alnwick Dispensary Minute Book, August 1815–October 1870, 3650/1, Northumberland Record Office (NRO), Woodhorn.
2 Royal Infirmary of Sunderland, *The Constitution and Rules of the Infirmary, Dispensary, House of Recovery for the Cure of Contagious Fever, and Humane Society, for the Towns of Bishop Wearmouth, Sunderland, Monk Wearmouth, and Their Immediate Vicinities* (Sunderland, J. Hatchard and Son: 1824), p. 18.
3 The Alnwick Dispensary Minute Book, 3650/1, NRO.

4 Governors, *Rules and Orders of the Public Infirmary at Liverpool* (Liverpool, A. Williamson: 1781), p. 13.
5 Royal Infirmary of Sunderland, *Constitution and Rules of the Infirmary*, p. 22.
6 Royal Infirmary of Sunderland, *Constitution and Rules of the Infirmary*, p. 20 and Governors, *Rules and Orders of the Public Infirmary at Liverpool*, p. 13.
7 Deborah Brunton, *Medicine in Modern Britain 1780–1950* (London, Routledge: 2019), p. 64.
8 Dispensary Annual Reports, 1777–1872, HO.ND, Tyne and Wear Archives (TWA), Newcastle Upon Tyne.
9 Samantha Shave, *Pauper Policies: Poor Law Practice in England, 1780–1850* (Manchester, Manchester University Press: 2018).
10 Shave, *Pauper Policies*, pp. 199–202 and Frank Crompton, *Workhouse Children* (Stroud, Sutton: 1997).
11 Crompton, *Workhouse Children*, p. 74.
12 Peter Higginbotham, 'Chelsea Workhouse Admissions and Discharges, 1743–1799', *The Workhouse: The Story of an Institution...*, accessed 1 May 2014, http://www.workhouses.org.uk/Chelsea/Chelsea1743.shtml.
13 Brunton, *Medicine in Modern Britain*, p. 64.
14 Governors, *An Account of the Newcastle Dispensary, for the Relief of the Poor, From Its Commencement in 1777, to Michaelmas 1789* (Newcastle, Hall and Elliot: 1789), p. 6.
15 Governors, *An Account of the Newcastle Dispensary*, p. 6.
16 Claire Rennie, 'The Care of Sick Children in Eighteenth-Century England' (PhD dissertation, University of Leeds, 2017), p. 110.
17 Governors, *An Account of the Newcastle Dispensary*, p. 7.
18 Governors, *An Account of the Newcastle Dispensary*, p. 6.
19 Dispensary Annual Reports, 1777–1872, HO.ND, TWA.
20 Dispensary Annual Reports, 1777–1872, HO.ND, TWA.
21 Dispensary Annual Reports, 1777–1872, HO.ND, TWA.
22 Deborah Brunton, *The Politics of Vaccination: Practice and Policy in England, Wales, Ireland, and Scotland, 1800–1874* (Woodbridge, Boydell and Brewer: 2008), p. 2.
23 Historic Hospital Admission Records Project, accessed 29 August 2017, http://www.hharp.org/.
24 Alun Withey, 'Medicine and Charity in Eighteenth-Century Northumberland: The Early Years of the Bamburgh Castle Dispensary and Surgery, c. 1772–1802', *Social History of Medicine* 29.3 (2016), p. 471.
25 Withey, 'Medicine and Charity in Eighteenth-Century Northumberland', pp. 467–468.
26 Anne Hardy, *The Epidemic Streets: Infectious Disease and the Rise of Preventative Medicine, 1856–1900* (Oxford, Clarendon Press: 1993), p. 9.
27 Dispensary Register of Patients, October 1777–January 1784, 452/D/8/2/3, NRO.
28 Dispensary Register of Patients, 452/D/8/2/3, NRO.
29 Dispensary Register of Patients, 452/D/8/2/3, NRO.
30 Dispensary Register of Patients, 452/D/8/2/3, NRO.
31 Dispensary Book Similar, Register of Patients, April 1793–June 1816, 452/D/2/4, NRO.
32 Elizabeth Lomax, *Small and Special: The Development of Hospitals for Children in Victorian Britain* (London, Wellcome Institute for the History of Medicine: 1996); Ashley Mathisen, 'Treating the Children of the Poor: Institutions and the Construction of Medical Authority in Eighteenth-Century London' (PhD dissertation, University of Oxford, 2011) and Ashley Mathisen, 'Mineral Waters, Electricity and Hemlock: Devising Therapeutics for Children in Eighteenth-Century Institutions', *Medical History* 57.1 (2013), pp. 28–44.

33 Mathisen, 'Mineral Waters, Electricity, and Hemlock', p. 35 and Mathisen, 'Treating the Children of the Poor'.
34 Apothecary's Notes (in English) on treatment with the use of Powis Wells Water, 1759–1762, A/FH/A/18/009/001, London Metropolitan Archives, London.
35 Rennie, 'Care of Sick Children'.
36 George Armstrong, *An Essay on the Diseases Most Fatal to Infants: To Which Are Added Rules to Be Observed in the Nursing of Children, with a Particular View to Those Who Are Brought up by Hand* (London, T. Cadell: 1767); George Armstrong, *An Account of the Diseases Most Incident to Children, from Their Birth Till the Age of Puberty; With a Successful Method of Treating Them. To Which Is Added, an Essay on Nursing. Also a General Account of the Dispensary for the Infant Poor, from Its First Institution in 1769 to the Present Time* (London, T. Cadell: 1777) and George Armstrong, *An Account of the Diseases Most Incident to Children, from the Birth Till the Age of Puberty; with a Successful Method of Treating Them. To Which Is Added, an Essay on Nursing: With a Particular View to Children Who Are Brought up by Hand. Also a Short General Account of the Dispensary for the Infant Poor. A New Edition, with Several Additions. This Edition Contains, amongst Other Additions, Three Cases of the Hydrocephalus Internus, Successfully Treated.*, 2nd edition (London, T. Cadell: 1783).
37 Armstrong, *An Account of the Diseases Most Incident to Children*, 1783, p. vii.
38 Armstrong, *An Account of the Diseases Most Incident to Children*, 1783; Mathisen, 'Mineral Waters, Electricity, and Hemlock' and Claire Rennie, 'The Treatment of Whooping Cough in Eighteenth-Century England', *Ex-Historia* 8 (2016), pp. 1–33.
39 Andrea Tanner, 'Choice and the Children's Hospital: Great Ormond Street Hospital Patients and Their Families, 1855–1900', in Anne Borsay and Peter Shapely (eds.), *Medicine, Charity and Mutual Aid: The Consumption of Health and Welfare in Britain, c. 1550–1950* (Aldershot, Ashgate: 2007), p. 136.
40 Leigh Ann Whaley, *Women and the Practice of Medical Care in Early Modern Europe, 1400–1800* (Basingstoke, Palgrave Macmillan: 2011), p. 150.
41 Anne Stobart, *Household Medicine in Seventeenth-Century England* (London, Bloomsbury Academic: 2016), p. 103.
42 Edith Snook, '"The Women Know": Children's Diseases, Recipes and Women's Knowledge in Early Modern Medical Publications', *Social History of Medicine* 30.1 (2017), pp. 1–21.
43 Hannah Sheppard, 1818–1863, MS. 4520, Wellcome Library, London.
44 Mary Anne Fawcett, 1795–1832, MS. 2339, Wellcome Library; Sarah Ellis and Others, c. 1820, MS. 2291, Wellcome Library.
45 Whaley, *Women and the Practice of Medical Care*, p. 196; Rachel G. Fuchs, 'Charity and Welfare', in David I. Kertzer and Mario Barbagli (eds.), *Family Life in the Long Nineteenth Century, 1789–1913* (London, Yale University Press: 2002), p. 155.
46 Owen Davies, 'Female Healers in Nineteenth-Century England', in Nigel Goose (ed.), *Women's Work in Industrial England: Regional and Local Perspectives* (Hatfield, Local Population Studies: 2007), p. 229.
47 William Hey, Notebooks of Medical and Surgical Case Histories, 1763–1809, MS 1991/1/2, Brotherton Library Special Collections, Leeds.
48 Thomas Giordani Wright, *Diary of a Doctor: Surgeon's Assistant in Newcastle upon Tyne, 1826–1829*, ed. Alistair Johnson (Newcastle upon Tyne, City of Newcastle upon Tyne: 2008).
49 William Buchan, *Domestic Medicine Or, a Treatise on the Prevention and Cure of Diseases by Regimen and Simple Medicines*, 17th edition (London, 1800).

13

'I HAVE TOLD HER THAT IT WAS NEGLECTED, AND ASKED HER WHY'

Working-class Women and Discourses of 'Bad Motherhood' in England and Wales, 1870–1939

Daniel J.R. Grey

On 20 November 1871, Susan King, aged 44, was tried at the Central Criminal Court in London for the manslaughter of Alice Butcher, a seven-month-old infant who had been left in her care.[1] The child's mother, a single woman named Annie Butcher, testified that the baby had been entrusted to King since she was a fortnight old. Butcher had been given an allowance by the child's father that covered the six shillings a week charged for Alice's care, as well as the offer to provide any new clothing that might be required.[2] Despite this, however, and the fact that Butcher was always careful to keep up with maintenance payments, Alice was appallingly neglected. Far from providing the loving and attentive environment that Butcher had hoped for her daughter, Susan King seems to have become infamous within her neighbourhood in Islington for alcohol abuse, a foul temper, and – above all – because she continually failed to provide the infant with either adequate food or even the most rudimentary care, generally leaving the baby in the charge of one of her own preadolescent daughters while she went out drinking.[3] Although King insisted at her trial that Alice had been well-looked after and that the charges had been trumped up out of spite, courtroom testimony proved damning. Emma Mills, a married mother of five children who had lodgings in the same house as King, had been so appalled by the way the baby was treated that she had argued vehemently with the other woman more than once about the matter: 'I have told her that it was neglected, and asked her why […]'.[4] So too had Emma Watson, another neighbour who had warned King more than once that the baby was visibly emaciated. Watson had been roundly abused in response. When these exchanges had no effect, Mills reported the matter to the authorities, and when the Islington relieving officer visited King's home on 18 September he immediately removed Alice from the house and placed

DOI: 10.4324/9780429344084-16

her with an another local foster mother, Mrs Jane Wells.[5] Wells was so outraged by Alice Butcher's condition – by this time, so underweight her bones were visible beneath the skin, she had been covered in excrement, and left in clothing so foul it had to be burned – that the morning after having taken the baby in, she went round to berate King herself.[6] Despite her best efforts to nurse the baby back to recovery over the following three weeks, Wells was unable to restore her to health, an experience which still distressed her deeply when she was giving witness testimony at the subsequent trial. On 13 October, Alice died from inflammation of the lungs, exacerbated by her emaciated state and by King's neglect over the preceding months.[7] Convicted of manslaughter, Susan King was sentenced to 18 months' imprisonment with hard labour at Westminster Prison.[8]

In many ways, the 1871 trial of Susan King embodies the competing and contradictory discourses that surrounded working-class motherhood in Britain during the late nineteenth century, and particularly those that related to the highly contentious subject of 'baby farming', a term which was often (but not inevitably) used as a pejorative description for a range of childcare practices that a twenty-first-century reader might separate out into the distinct categories of paid childminding, foster care, or even an informal 'adoption', since while the circulation of children within and sometimes beyond immediate kinship groups had a long history, child adoption had no legal status or protection until 1926 in England and Wales.[9] In the most sensational instances of baby-farming during the late nineteenth and early twentieth century that came to public attention, this term was used to refer to criminal activity that – on the surface – deliberately mimicked any of the preceding 'normal' childcare or parenting practices, but was in fact deployed as a cover by some women for extreme cases of fraud, child neglect, and even premeditated murder, sometimes with multiple infant victims.[10] Brief reports – often no more than a sentence in length – of King's trial and conviction made their way into newspapers published across the country. Yet in some senses it is surprising that the case did not attract more public attention than it did. After all, only fourteen months earlier, the notorious baby-farmer Margaret Waters had been convicted, also in the Central Criminal Court, of the murder through deliberate neglect of a baby boy that she had been paid to look after. Waters was subsequently executed, and her trial provoked national disquiet about the perils of untrustworthy foster carers and the potential for other, similar instances to go undetected.[11]

What is also significant about the Susan King trial is how it demonstrates the everyday nature of foster care and other forms of paid childcare in working-class communities, especially for illegitimate children, even at the height of the 'infanticide panic' that spread across Britain during the 1860s and 1870s.[12] Across these two decades, it was regularly alleged in the press and other forums that cases of infant homicide were frequently practices by women who had become pregnant outside of marriage, but it was also simultaneously believed that the crime was only rarely detected and even more seldom appropriately punished.[13] Nobody queried that Alice's mother had needed to find a foster placement for her baby, rather than attempt to keep the child with her. Even the most sympathetic of employers who were willing to hire women they knew to be unmarried mothers still expected that some form of long-term care and accommodation arrangement would be made for their child. Nor did King's neighbours – or even the Islington relieving officer – disapprove of foster mothers *in general*, hence the immediate relocation of Alice to the home of Jane Wells, who from the brief context of the case seems to have enjoyed an excellent local reputation for her work in this role. Rather, what was important was the degree to which biological mothers or foster carers were perceived as providing the *right* sort of care for children, and what this 'good mothering' or its converse was held to consist of during a period of relatively rapid and significant changes in the construction and understanding by both expert commentators and by the general public of parenting, of childhood, and of youth.[14] This chapter focuses on three key themes – ignorance, neglect, and maternal violence – to interrogate cultural narratives of what constituted 'bad motherhood' in England and Wales between 1870 and 1939.[15]

'Ignorance'

One major cultural and social shift that occurred in the period covered by this chapter was a new and steadily increasing emphasis in England and Wales on working-class motherhood as being in constant need of surveillance and education to improve the wellbeing of the family, and, by extension, of the nation.[16] Working-class families were often perceived as being unduly influenced by older relatives (especially parents and grandparents), and as having childcare practices that were at best dated and at worst actively harmful.[17] This dovetailed with other, broader critiques of the standard of living in working-class communities and the dire impact of poverty that were levelled during the late nineteenth century in a range of mediums, such as the extensive social investigations of philanthropist Charles Booth, first published in 1889 but extending to multiple volumes in later editions, and (sometimes directly inspired by the former), polemical texts such as *In Darkest England and the Way Out*, written by William Booth, founder of the Salvation Army, which drew explicit and racist parallels between white working-class communities in England and the behaviour of supposedly 'uncivilised' Black African colonial subjects.[18] Such attitudes were significantly bolstered by critical events such as the South African War (1899–1902) and the findings of the subsequent Inter-Departmental Committee on Physical Deterioration in 1904, where the poor physical condition of many potential recruits to fight in South Africa was explicitly blamed by politicians on the lasting physical damage done during childhood by ignorant and feckless working-class mothers.[19] If such perspectives and the corresponding processes were relatively informal and ad hoc in the 1870s, and could vary significantly from region to region, by the 1930s this view had effectively become both systematic and national. By the interwar years this formed a cultural consensus that was rarely questioned by a range of professions (including medicine and nursing), and was buttressed by a wide range of services, legislation, and initiatives that had been introduced to try and improve standards of maternal and infant welfare across the country.[20] Taken as a whole, these practices all strongly emphasised the need for scientific knowledge and social policy to work in concert, and were increasingly bolstered by legislation to either support or mandate such reforms, such as the Maternal and Child Welfare Act 1918, which established infant welfare centres and an expectation that prenatal and postnatal services would henceforth be delivered by local authorities as a standard practice for pregnant women and nursing mothers.[21] This steadily increasing emphasis on the need to 'educate' working-class mothers had also led to the creation of new professional opportunities for women, such as health visiting.[22] Health visiting had its roots in an earlier initiative, that of 'sanitary reform', a broadly defined scientific field which filtered through all aspects of public health, social policy, nursing and medical reforms that were enacted in Britain between the 1830s and the 1880s.[23] The first women's organisation dedicated to such reforms, the Ladies Branch of the Manchester and Salford Sanitary Association, had been founded in Manchester in 1862. From the late 1860s onwards, the group employed 'upper' working-class women to visit local homes and to help in bringing the house up to what was considered a 'good' sanitary standard. Importantly, as Vanessa Heggie has illustrated, the decision to employ working-class women was rooted in the resistance middle-class women had faced from working-class communities: it was recognised that only suitable women of a similar class background would be able to gain access and dispense advice or assistance in these neighbourhoods.[24] In 1890, Manchester's Medical Officer of Health began to pay the salaries of six visitors, and other areas began to consider whether a similar scheme might be worth adopting in their own area.[25] Following the recommendation of Florence Nightingale, the first three paid health visitors outside Manchester were appointed by Buckinghamshire County Council in 1892 after a two-year course of study.[26] Other local authorities swiftly followed suit: Lara Marks has noted that by the outbreak of the First World War, 195 different areas employed 470 salaried health visitors.[27] Already dealing with a heavy workload that demanded extensive weekly reports, that their own home act as a model for others in their community of good practice, and undertaking classes in hygiene as well as their practical duties, the requirements for becoming a health visitor also became increasingly strict as their focus moved from a wider range of health and domestic-related duties to prioritise infant wellbeing.[28] After the passage of the London County Council (General Powers) Act 1908, a prospective health visitor in the metropolis now had to possess a midwifery certificate, and to have also either undergone three years hospital training as either a general or children's nurse, or had to have studied a two year public health diploma.[29] There was also an increasing effort by health visitors to demarcate their own professional boundaries from other similar roles, emphasising the specifics of their training and knowledge. When Miss Steele, the Infant Life Protection Visitor for Swansea, applied to join the Health Visitor's Association in December 1918, despite the significant degree of overlap between these professional responsibilities, the committee refused her request as she was not a holder of either a nursing qualification or a sanitary inspector's certificate.[30] This rule remained in effect until 1921, when it was overturned by a vote at a special general meeting of the Health Visitor's Association.[31]

Beyond these formal qualifications, it was also (just as with nursing or midwifery) considered essential for the health visitor to possess the right personal qualities, and health visiting was frequently framed in terms of an explicitly feminine spiritual calling.[32] Lily Skene impressed upon the reader in her 1923 textbook that:

> To us women who have been called into this glorious field of labour for our Empire, a field so brimming over with golden opportunities and unknown possibilities of usefulness, the words- Ideal Health Visitor- set our hearts on fire with enthusiasm and the desire that we may indeed be ideal helpers to the Mothers of our future men and women.[33]

Commentators were also much more likely to assert after the turn of the century that the best background for a potential health visitor was 'from the families of those who have a recognised professional or mercantile position'.[34] By 1917, the significant reduction in rates of infant mortality and morbidity during the preceding decade and a half was being ascribed directly to the work and influence of the health visitor.[35] As the status of the health visitor rose, so too did the expectation that she would come from a middle-class background. While in the late nineteenth century it was believed to be a shared set of experiences and values that would allow a health visitor to gain admittance to the home, now, it was personal charisma and tact which (both literally and metaphorically) unlocked these doors. As one author put it:

> They are curious people- pitiably ignorant and superstitious, full of prejudices, and often stuffed with dreadful advice from terrible old gamps and dowagers in their immediate vicinity. But if they *like* you, and if you can

succeed in impressing them with your air of experience, you can do anything you like with them.[36]

Significantly, too, this trend also coincided with the increased targeting by health visitors and childcare experts during the interwar years of middle-class mothers, in addition to maintaining the surveillance and policing of working-class ones. Even those well-off families who were able to benefit from employing a nanny or, for those with colonial connections or who had spent time in South Asia, an *ayah*, and so with much less care directly provided by mothers, were now seen as being able to benefit greatly from specialist advice.[37] As Katharina Rowold has demonstrated with regard to advice on breastfeeding and the rise in publication of advice manuals of infant care and parenting classes aimed specifically at middle-class audiences, this placed a new emphasis on the importance of *all* mothers learning from the 'right' experts.[38] The explicit expansion of the categories of mothers who might be deemed 'in need of advice' to include middle-class women during the 1920s and 1930s, however, further reinforced class-based assumptions and prejudices about the degree and type of interventions (the more extensive interventions becoming more likely the more deprived the mother's background and circumstances, and the converse applying to mothers from prosperous middle-class families) that might be required to achieve the best results.

Neglect

The subject of child neglect, and its causes and the best means of prevention, detection, and punishment, lay uneasily in the minds of late nineteenth- and early twentieth-century commentators between ignorance and deliberate, sustained cruelty. Widespread attitudes which condemned working-class mothers as liable to be ignorant (while insulting and inaccurate) nevertheless did not automatically presume malice on the part of those families. Indeed, the entire point of many health visiting or childcare textbooks was the firm belief that despite potential hostility at the outset, any such mothers would be immensely grateful to the health visitor once they saw the positive impact of her advice on their subsequently thriving infants. Allegations of failing to provide sufficient care, however, potentially fell into an uneasy and increasingly criminalised border category during the period covered by this chapter. As Robert J. Parr of the National Society for the Prevention of Cruelty to Children (NSPCC) warned his readers in 1910, 'Cases of cruelty are not rare'.[39] The successful passage of the Protection from and Prevention of Cruelty to Children Act 1889, and the related formation of various campaign allies into the new NSPCC shortly afterwards, was seen by contemporaries as a major legal landmark which would enable the criminal justice system to more effectively prevent and punish parents from neglecting or abusing their children.[40] Indeed, the conservative judge Viscount Alverstone, a keen supporter of the NSPCC right from its formation, believed that helping to pass and later enforce the 1889 Act was the crowning glory of his career.[41]

The judge and legal authority Sir William Blackstone had first described the duty of parents to adequately care for their children in 1770 as 'a principle of natural law, which the municipal law enforces'.[42] Indeed, for illegitimate children, who in addition to the stigma this condition imposed upon them were also treated differently to children born within marriage in regard to rights such as inheritance and parental custody, this was held by Blackstone to be 'the only duty of parents...which the law recognises'.[43] However, the interrelated issues of parental duty to maintain and what then constituted parental neglect were profoundly gendered, a pattern of unequally apportioning blame on mothers which Margaret Arnot has demonstrated was a central feature of all child neglect cases that came before the Central Criminal Court between 1840 and 1880.[44] While in theory it was held that in cases where a man and woman were jointly indicted for neglect 'the man is equally guilty with the woman if he has seen what was going on', the application of this principle was highly uneven, and rarely were men held to the same expectations of care provision.[45] In order to help explain why this was so, I briefly explore below the joint trial of Alfred Sansome and his partner Julia Kinch.

In February 1908, Alfred Sansome, a 46-year-old carter, and Julia Kinch, a 46-year-old field worker, were jointly indicted at the Hampshire Winter Assizes for the manslaughter of their ten-week-old son Alfred Joseph Kinch. They were also jointly charged with criminally neglecting Alfred and his three older sisters: Edith, age 12, Ellen, age 8, and Selina, age 4.[46] The case turned on what steps should have been taken by the parents when their children's welfare began to suffer. Evidence was given during their trial by a neighbour that Sansome was a loving father who paid the rent on their home and, in addition to this, always gave Kinch 12s. a week (just over half his weekly wage) for meeting the housekeeping costs.[47] In contrast, Julia was depicted in witness testimony by both the anonymous neighbour and the NSPCC inspector who had visited the house as a feckless alcoholic. Yet, although Mr. Justice Coleridge 'pointed out that the father of the child had duties beyond merely providing money', in his summing up, the jury acquitted Sansome of all charges while convicting Kinch of manslaughter and leaving the charge of neglect to remain on file.[48] She was sentenced to serve twelve months hard labour, which Mr Justice Coleridge noted wryly would 'keep her from drink for some time'.[49]

To the jury, Sansome, described in the *Hampshire Chronicle* as 'sober and hardworking', and who provided his long-term partner with funds for food, clothing and shelter, had undoubtedly met the key requirements of being a 'good father'.[50] As Timothy Fisher has pointed out, even the most routine of childcare tasks relating to babies like their infant son were considered outside a father's sphere in the early twentieth century.[51] Since Sansome was competently acting as the breadwinner for his family, the jury saw no reason to agree with the judge that if Kinch's neglect had been long term, since they were living together as a family unit, then Sansome should have taken more direct action to prevent it.[52] Kinch was a heavy drinker who had apparently ignored Sansome's suggestion that Alfred should be taken to see a doctor.[53] Given Bronwyn Morrison's observation that alcoholism and maternal neglect were invariably associated in fictional, medical and social discussions of both subjects between 1870 and 1920, this meant the jury was much more likely to consider her both inherently 'unrespectable' and as posing a danger to her children.[54] Respectability was a complicated, nebulous and highly relational concept in nineteenth- and early twentieth-century England and Wales. It was all too frequently assumed by commentators to be a self-evident and 'common sense' category that required no explanation, yet it did not map neatly on to divisions and categories such as class background, and it might be experienced by men and women in working-class communities as either a coercive and undermining way of being policed by others, or conversely as a deep-rooted source of personal and familial pride. What does seem to be clear, however, is that instances in Victorian and early twentieth-century courtrooms where a defendant was perceived by the court as being a 'respectable' woman or man meant that the accused stood a much better chance of receiving lenient and potentially even overtly sympathetic treatment by the judge, the jury, and by those newspapers that reported the trial.[55]

Maternal Violence

Then as now, the idea that a mother might be willing to *deliberately* harm her own children seemed particularly shocking when reported in the press or brought before the courts, a contravention of all the much-vaunted ideals which represented (married) motherhood as the epitome for English and Welsh women of their biological and spiritual destiny during the late nineteenth and early twentieth century.[56] A variety of explanations might then be sought as to what could have led to instances of maternal violence, which by definition was understood to be a disturbing and unnatural aberration. One possibility was that, like the Brixton 'baby farmer' Margaret Waters in 1870, mentioned at the start of this chapter, such women might be simply depicted as monstrous – in Waters' case, this was underscored by the fact the child who died was not her biological son, despite witness testimony that suggested she had cared for this fostered infant deeply.[57] Another, particularly when this was combined with allegations of child neglect, might be addiction to drugs or alcohol. Beyond this, suggestions of mental and physical fragility or illness as a potential mitigating – or at the very least explanatory – factor in such instances of maternal violence could appear even when cases of abuse seemed to have been both premeditated and systematic, as indicated by the short newspaper article reporting the trial of Elizabeth Smith for the assault of her adolescent daughter in December 1910 at the Welsh town of Pembroke Dock.[58] Smith, described in the press as a married woman, had taken back custody of her 14-year-old illegitimate daughter (also Elizabeth) Epsworth from the local workhouse about a year prior to her appearance before the Pembroke Dock Petty Sessions.[59] The magistrates heard Smith used to routinely send Elizabeth to the local barracks to beg from the marines stationed there, and while the specific attack that had led to Smith's arrest was striking her in the head with 'a heavy pint cup' that November, she was known to have previously hit the girl in the back with a poker, and was also charged with 'ill-treating her on other dates'.[60] Despite this demonstrable history of abuse, as the *Cardiff Times* reported, Smith's ill-health precluded the possibility of a prison sentence: she was instead bound over (in effect, a suspended sentence), and her daughter removed from her custody and sent to a children's home.[61]

Perhaps surprisingly, given that it was not only the most extreme possible act of maternal violence but also a crime that was overwhelmingly associated with working-class women who had 'fallen' through an illicit sexual relationship and subsequent pregnancy, infanticide cases were routinely reported sympathetically in newspapers and received lenient treatment from the courts in England and Wales during the period covered by this chapter.[62] A cultural consensus had been established at least as far back as the 1860s that infanticide was associated with a form of temporary mental illness by the mother (complicated by shame, fear, and the pain of childbirth) that did not necessarily correspond to either legal or medical definitions of 'insanity', and in the overwhelming majority of cases, witness testimony heard at the assizes and reported in the press demonstrated that such defendants had previously conformed to all societal expectations of 'respectability'.[63] Women charged with having killed their infants (particularly if death had occurred close to the time of delivery) were thus frequently acquitted or convicted on a lesser charge than murder, particularly 'concealment of birth', which could be an alternative verdict in newborn murder cases as well as a separate charge.[64] Technically punishable by up to two years imprisonment with hard labour, by the 1920s the sentence imposed for concealment of birth was often as short as a few days.[65] The passage of the Infanticide Act 1922, which meant that cases where a woman found guilty of killing her baby while 'the balance of her mind was disturbed' as a result of childbirth were no longer subject to the mandatory death sentence imposed for murder, effectively wrote this cultural consensus into the statute books.[66] It has remained there ever since, despite periodic criticisms that the Act is not fit for purpose.[67] This rapidly became a preferred option for juries even on those occasions when the interwar authorities tried to pursue an indictment for murder instead.

Ena Garwood, who had been abandoned by her boyfriend while pregnant and subsequently killed her newborn son at Brighton in March 1931, had the bill for murder rejected by the Grand Jury when she came for trial at the Lewes Assizes.[68] Charged instead with infanticide, Garwood plead guilty, and was released on her own recognisance for the sum of £5.

Cases where working-class women killed their older children, however, seem to have stood a much greater likelihood of harsher representation in the press and more severe treatment by the criminal justice system: clemency was not guaranteed. Selina Wadge, a 28-year-old single woman from Launceston charged with the murder of her two-year-old son Harry at the Cornwall Assizes in 1878, was described in witness testimony as always having been a kind and loving mother to both of her young sons.[69] The killing did not seem to have been premeditated, and her subsequent behaviour after the crime at least suggested the possibility that an insanity plea should be considered.[70] Despite this, a clear recommendation to mercy from the jury following her conviction, and petitions on her behalf from the local community, Wadge's sentence of death was not commuted to life imprisonment by the Home Office, which was the usual practice in child murder cases.[71] Instead, represented by the judge as a calculating killer, she became one of the very few women to be executed in late nineteenth-century England and Wales.

Conclusions

Ideas about what constitutes 'good motherhood' are not only culturally, regionally, and chronologically specific, but twenty-first-century mothers themselves are often only too aware of how easily one can be labelled a 'bad mother' through failing to conform to these ideals, and the pernicious impact that such labelling is likely to have on their lives and those of their children.[72] They are also painfully conscious of the degree to which constructions of race and class further mediate these representations, making it much more likely for working-class and/or ethnic minority women who are already marginalised to be made scapegoats for a variety of social ills.[73] As the sociologist Imogen Tyler has compellingly argued, such discourses in the British media often take an explicitly misogynistic and class-prejudiced line to particularly single out young mothers from working-class backgrounds as objects of disgust and vilification.[74] Key elements of these contemporary discourses are significantly different from their precedents in the late nineteenth and early twentieth century, having been reshaped by the significant political, cultural, social, economic, and legal developments in England and Wales since the Second World War. But in many respects, the surveillance, stereotyping and policing (both literal and metaphorical) of working-class mothers in 2024 represents a depressing continuity with the years between 1870 and 1939.

Notes

1 The National Archives [henceforth TNA] CRIM 4/797/48; *Old Bailey Proceedings Online* (www.oldbaileyonline.org, version 9.0, accessed 6 January 2024), November 1871, trial of SUSAN KING (44) (t18711120-38).
2 *The Morning Post*, 23 November 1871, p. 7.
3 *The Morning Post*, 23 November 1871, p. 7.
4 Old Bailey Proceedings Online (t18711120-38).
5 *The Times*, 23 November 1871, p. 12.
6 Old Bailey Proceedings Online (t18711120-38).
7 *The Times*, 23 November 1871, p. 12.
8 TNA CRIM 4/797/48.
9 Stephen Cretney, *Family Law in the Twentieth Century: A History* (Oxford, Oxford University Press: 2003), pp. 596–627; Jenny Keating, *A Child for Keeps? The History of Adoption in England, 1918–45* (Basingstoke, Palgrave Macmillan: 2009); Ginger S. Frost, *Illegitimacy in English Law and Society, 1860–1930* (Manchester, Manchester University Press: 2016), pp. 216–222.
10 Margaret L. Arnot, 'Infant Death, Child Care and the State: The Baby –Farming Scandal and the First Infant Life Protection Legislation of 1872', *Continuity & Change* 9.2 (1994), pp. 271–311; Ruth Ellen Homrighaus, 'Wolves in Women's Clothing: Baby-Faming and the *British Medical Journal*, 1860–1872', *Journal of Family History* 26.3 (2001), pp. 350–372; Ruth E. Homrighaus, 'Baby Farming: The Care of Illegitimate Children in England, 1860–1943' (PhD dissertation, University of North Carolina at Chapel Hill, 2003); Daniel Grey, '"More ignorant and stupid than wilfully cruel": Homicide Trials and "baby-farming" in England and Wales in the Wake of the Children Act 1908', *Crimes and Misdemeanours: Deviance and the Law in Historical Perspective* 3.2 (2009), pp. 60–77; Jim Hinks, 'Other People's Children: Representations of Paid-Childcare in Britain, 1867–1908' (PhD dissertation, University of Liverpool, 2015); Joanne Pearman, 'Bastards, Baby Farmers, and Social Control in Victorian Britain' (PhD dissertation, University of Kent, 2017); Shirley A. Smith, *'Out of Sight, out of Mind': Infanticide, Baby Farming and Abortion in South and West Wales, 1870–1922* (Cardiff, Rowanvale Books Ltd: 2021), pp. 51–99; Joshua G. Stuart-Bennett, *Motherhood, Respectability, and Baby-Farming in Victorian and Edwardian London* (Abingdon, Routledge: 2023); Catherine Elkin, 'Childcare and Criminality: Representations of Baby-Farming 1834–1908' (PhD dissertation, Manchester Metropolitan University, 2023).
11 TNA MEPO 3/93; TNA HO 12/193/92230; *Old Bailey Proceedings Online* (www.oldbaileyonline.org, version 9.0, 6 January 2024), September 1870, trial of MAGARET WATERS (35) SARAH ELLIS (28) (t18700919-769); *Illustrated Police News,* 16 June 1870, p. 3; *Reynold's Newspaper*, 19 June 1870, p. 6; *The Era*, 26 June 1870, p. 9; *Lloyd's Weekly Newspaper*, 3 July 1870, p. 4; *The Times*, 24 September 1870, p. 11; *British Medical Journal*, 1 October 1870, pp. 362–363; *Illustrated Police News*, 1 October 1870, p. 3; *Lloyd's Weekly Newspaper*, 9 October 1870, p. 3; *The Times*, 12 October 1870, p. 9; *Illustrated Police News*, 15 October 1870, pp. 1–2.
12 As Jim Hinks has observed, despite their ubiquity in working-class communities, paid childcare arrangements have left almost no traces in the archival record, bar when something (as in this case) went so badly wrong that the authorities then became involved. See Hinks, 'Other People's Children'.
13 Margaret L. Arnot, 'Gender in Focus: Infanticide in England, 1840–1880' (PhD dissertation, University of Essex, 1994); Annie Cossins, *Female Criminality: Infanticide, Moral Panics, and the Female Body* (Basingstoke, Palgrave Macmillan: 2015), pp. 57–167.

14 See especially Ellen Ross, *Love and Toil: Motherhood in Outcast London, 1870–1918* (Oxford, Oxford University Press: 1993). Note too parallel shifting discourses of fatherhood during the same period: See especially Julie-Marie Strange, *Fatherhood and the British Working Class, 1865–1914* (Cambridge, Cambridge University Press: 2015); Laura King, *Family Men: Fatherhood and Masculinity in Britain, 1914–1960* (Oxford, Oxford University Press: 2015); and Jessica Butler, 'Representations of Paternal Child Killers in the English National Press, 1900 to 1939' (PhD dissertation, University of Liverpool, 2018).

15 Although beyond the scope of this chapter, it is essential to recognise – particularly because so many authors in this period drew racialised parallels between the imagined values and experiences of a supposed homogenous and monolithic white working-class community in England and Wales and a similarly imagined Black or Asian colonial Other overseas – that people of colour, both migrants and those who were themselves English or Welsh, were *also* members of these communities between 1870 and 1939. See for instance Caroline Bressey, 'The Next Chapter: The Black Presence in the Nineteenth Century' in Gretchen H. Gerzina (ed.), *Britain's Black Past* (Liverpool, Liverpool University Press: 2020), pp. 315–330; Laura Tabili, *Global Migrants, Local Culture: Natives and Newcomers in Provincial England, 1841–1939* (Basingstoke, Palgrave Macmillan: 2011).

16 Ross, *Love and Toil.*

17 Siân Pooley, 'Grandfathers, Grandmothers and the Inheritance of Parenthood in England, c.1850–1914' in Siân Pooley and Kaveri Qureshi (eds.), *Parenthood between Generations: Transforming Reproductive Cultures* (Oxford, Berghahn: 2016), pp. 135–159.

18 Charles Booth, *Life and Labour of the of the People in London*, 2nd edition, 9 volumes (London, Macmillan: 1892–1897); William Booth, *In Darkest England and the Way out* (London, Salvation Army: 1890). On the impact and context of these sorts of commentaries and investigations, including their voyeuristic and exploitative potential see especially Judith R. Walkowitz, *City of Dreadful Delight: Narratives of Sexual Danger in Late Victorian London* (Chicago, IL, University of Chicago Press: 1992) and Seth Koven, *Slumming: Sexual and Social Politics in Victorian London* (Princeton, NJ, Princeton University Press: 2004).

19 'Report of the Inter-Departmental Committee on Physical Deterioration: Vol. I: Report and Appendix', *Parliamentary Papers*, 1904, Cd. 2175, Vol. XXXII, pp. 1–144.

20 See for instance Jane Lewis, *The Politics of Motherhood: Child and Maternal Welfare in England, 1900–1939* (London, Croom Helm: 1980); Lara Marks, *Model Mothers: Jewish Mothers and Maternity Provision in East London, 1870–1939* (Oxford, Clarendon Press: 1994); Lara Marks, *Metropolitan Maternity: Maternal and Infant Welfare Centres in Early Twentieth Century London* (Amsterdam, Rodopi: 1996); Ross, *Love and Toil.*

21 Anna Davin, 'Imperialism and Motherhood', *History Workshop Journal* 5 (1978), pp. 9–65; Deborah Dwork, *War is Good for Babies and Other Young Children: A History of the Infant and Child Welfare Movement in England 1898–1914* (London, Tavistock: 1987).

22 Celia Davies, 'The Health Visitor as Mother's Friend: A Woman's Place in Public Health, 1900–14', *Social History of Medicine* 1.1 (1988), pp. 39–59; Alice Reid, 'Health Visitors and "Enlightened Motherhood"', in Eilidh Garrett, Chris Galley, Nicola Shelton and Robert Woods (eds.), *Infant Mortality: A Continuing Social Problem* (Aldershot, Ashgate: 2007), pp. 191–212; Vanessa Heggie, 'Health Visiting and District Nursing in Victorian Manchester; Divergent and Convergent Vocations', *Women's History Review* 20.3 (2011), pp. 403–442. This period also saw significant (albeit relative) expansion of other professional opportunities for

women: see especially Helen Glew, *Gender, Rhetoric and Regulation: Women's Work in the Civil Service and the London County Council, 1900–55* (Manchester, Manchester University Press: 2016).

23 See Alison Bashford, *Purity and Pollution: Gender, Embodiment and Victorian Medicine* (Basingstoke, Macmillan: 1998).

24 Heggie, 'Health Visiting', p. 408.

25 Davies, 'The Health Visitor as Mother's Friend', p. 42.

26 Florence Nightingale, *Reproduction of a Printed Report Originally Submitted to the Bucks County Council in the Year 1892, Containing Letters from Miss Florence Nightingale on Health Visiting in Rural Districts* (London, P.S. King & Son: 1911).

27 Marks, *Metropolitan Maternity*, p. 171.

28 Heggie, 'Health Visiting', pp. 409–410.

29 Lucy Ridgely Seymer, *A General History of Nursing* (London, Faber & Faber Limited: 1932), pp. 172–173.

30 Wellcome Library SA/HVA/ B1/6. Minute Book: Sessional Meetings, December 1915–April 1919. See notes regarding General Meeting, 4 December 1918, p. 111.

31 Wellcome Library SA/HVA/ B1/7. Minute Book- Sessional Meetings, 30 May 1919–11 March 1927. See Special General Meeting, 28 October 1921, p. 23.

32 On the complicated relationships between personal qualities and the professional training of nurses, see Daniel J. R. Grey, 'Murder, Mental Illness, and the Question of Nursing "Character" in Early Twentieth Century England', *History Workshop Journal* 80 (2015), pp. 183–200.

33 Lily Skene, *The Ideal Health Visitor* (London, John Bale, Sons & Danielsson, Ltd: 1923), p. 1. Capitals in original.

34 E. M. Evans, 'The Essential Qualities of a Lady Health Visitor', *Journal of the Sanitary Institute* 24.3 (1903), p. 306.

35 E. W. Hope, *Report on the Physical Welfare of Mothers and Children: England and Wales*, Vol. 1 (Liverpool, The Carnegie United Kingdom Trust: 1917), p. 17.

36 Emilia Kanthack, *The Preservation of Infant Life: A Guide for Health Visitors* (London, H.K. Lewis: 1907), p. 4.

37 On the history of these respective groups of paid women child carers see Arunima Datta, *Waiting on Empire: A History of Indian Travelling Ayahs in Britain* (Oxford, Oxford University Press: 2023); Katherine Holden, 'Nanny Knows Best? Tensions in Nanny Employment in Early and Mid-Twentieth-Century British Childcare Magazines', in Rachel Ritchie, Sue Hawkins, Nicola Philips and S. Jay Kleinberg (eds.), *Women in Magazines: Research, Representation, Production and Consumption* (Abingdon, Routledge: 2016), pp. 148–164.

38 Katharina Rowold, 'Modern Mothers, Modern Babies: Breastfeeding and Mother's Milk in Interwar Britain', *Women's History Review* 28.7 (2019), pp. 1157–1176.

39 Robert J. Parr, *Wilful Waste: The Nation's Responsibility for Its Children* (London, NSPCC: 1910), p. 52.

40 On the history of the NSPCC and its influence, see variously George K. Behlmer, *Child Abuse and Moral Reform in England, 1870–1908* (Stanford, CA, Stanford University Press: 1982); George K. Behlmer, *Friends of the Family: The English Home and Its Guardians, 1850–1940* (Stanford, CA, Stanford University Press: 1998). For a valuable comparison with how the organisation developed in Ireland, see Sarah-Anne Buckley, *The Cruelty Man: Child Welfare, the NSPCC and the State in Ireland, 1889–1956* (Manchester, Manchester University Press: 2013).

41 Alverstone seems to have been extremely irritated by the degree of attention and praise heaped on the Children Act 1908, which despite covering a vast array of matters relating to child welfare and introducing several totally new practices – such as the creation of juvenile courts – he considered a trifling extension of the 1889 Act.

See Viscount Alverstone, *Recollections of Bar and Bench* (London, Edward Arnold: 1914), pp. 180–181.

42 R. M. N. Kerr, *Blackstone's Commentaries on the Laws of England*, 9th edition (London, William Clowes and Sons: 1885), p. 97.

43 Kerr, *Blackstone's Commentaries*, p. 99. On the legal and social context of illegitimacy in this period see especially Frost, *Illegitimacy in English Law and Society.*

44 Arnot, 'Gender in Focus', pp. 201–244.

45 W. Clarke Hall, *The Law Relating to Children* (London, Stevens and Sons, Limited: 1894), p. 43.

46 The National Archives (henceforth TNA) ASSI 21/80. See 7 February 1908 (unpaginated); TNA ASSI 25/73/5/42; TNA ASSI 25/73/5/43.

47 *Hampshire Chronicle*, 8 February 1908, p. 5.

48 *Hampshire Chronicle*, 8 February 1908, p. 5.

49 *Hampshire Chronicle*, 8 February 1908, p. 5.

50 *Hampshire Chronicle*, 8 February 1908, p. 5. See also Strange, *Fatherhood.*

51 Timothy J. Fisher, 'Fatherhood and the Experience of Working-class Fathers in Britain, 1900–1939' (PhD dissertation, University of Edinburgh, 2006), pp. 193–196.

52 See broader context of these attitudes in Hilary Land, 'Overshadowed by the Male Breadwinner: Care in 20th Century Britain', in Janet Fink and Åsa Lundqvist (eds.), *Changing Relations of Welfare: Family, Gender and Migration in Britain and Scandinavia* (London, Routledge: 2016), pp. 17–38; Jane Humphries and Ryah Thomas, '"The Best Job in the World": Breadwinning and the Capture of Household Labor in Nineteenth and Early Twentieth-Century British Coalmining', *Feminist Economics* 29.1 (2023), pp. 97–140.

53 *Hampshire Chronicle*, 8 February 1908, p. 5.

54 Bronwyn L. Morrison, 'Ordering Disorderly Women: Female Drunkenness in England, c.1870–1920' (PhD dissertation, Keele University, 2005).

55 See for instance Carolyn A. Conley, *The Unwritten Law: Criminal Justice in Victorian Kent* (Oxford, Oxford University Press: 1991); Alison C. Pedley, *Mothers, Criminal Insanity and the Asylum in Victorian England: Cure, Redemption and Rehabilitation* (London, Bloomsbury: 2023) throughout but especially 3–7; Daniel J. R. Grey, '"A hard-working and nice person"? Respectability, Femininity, and Infanticide in England and Wales, 1800–2000' in Stacy Banwell, Lynsey Black, Dawn Cecil, Yanyi Djamba, Sitawa Kimuna, Emma Milne, Lizzie Seal, and Eric Tenkoran (eds.), *International Handbook of Feminist Perspectives on Women's Acts of Violence* (Bingley, Emerald Publishing Ltd: 2023), pp. 33–45.

56 Focusing on the American context, Barbara Barnett demonstrates that idealised narratives of motherhood as inherently fulfilling, wondrous, and similarly 'natural' remain a core facet of contemporary media, and this trope continues to influence journalistic and popular responses to cases of women who kill their children. See Barbara Barnett, *Motherhood in the Media: Infanticide, Journalism, and the Digital Age* (Abingdon, Routledge: 2016).

57 Arnot, 'Infant Death, Child Care and the State'.

58 *The Cardiff Times*, 31 December 1910, p. 12.

59 Even if Smith had later married Epsworth's father (which seems unlikely from the circumstances here) before her current marriage, her daughter would have retained this stigmatising and public 'illegitimate' status, as the law in England and Wales refused to allow subsequent legitimation by parents who married after their child's birth until new legislation was introduced in 1926. See Frost, *Illegitimacy*, pp. 146–174.

60 *The Cardiff Times*, 31 December 1910, p. 12.

61 *The Cardiff Times*, 31 December 1910, p. 12. Frustratingly, no details are given in the article as to what this health complaint was.

62 Smith, *'Out of Sight, out of Mind'*; Grey, '"A hard-working and nice person"?' It is important to note this leniency did also extend to married and widowed women, even though such cases did not fit the popular stereotype.
63 Pedley, *Mothers, Criminal Insanity and the Asylum.*
64 See especially Emma Milne, 'Concealment of Birth: Time to Repeal a 200-year-old "convenient stop-gap"?', *Feminist Legal Studies* 27.2 (2019), pp. 139–162.
65 Daniel J. R. Grey, 'Representations of Infanticide in England, 1880–1922' (PhD dissertation, Roehampton University, 2008).
66 1922 12 & 13 Geo. 5 c.18. The amending Infanticide Act 1938 (1938 1 & 2 Geo. 6 c.36) replaced the deliberately vague criteria agreed as a compromise by legislators in 1922 for the child to have been 'newly born' with an age limit of 12 months. This Act remains in force in England and Wales.
67 Daniel J. R. Grey, '"Sometimes the Worst Happens": Newspaper Reportage of Infanticide and the Law in England and Wales Since 1922' in Karen Brennan and Emma Milne (eds.), *100 Years of the Infanticide Act: Legacy and Impact* (London, Bloomsbury: 2023), pp. 91–115.
68 TNA ASSI 31/58. See 7 July 1931 (unpaginated); TNA ASSI 36/44. *R.* v. *Garwood.*
69 See TNA ASSI 26/14. *R* .v. *Wadge* and TNA HO/45/9464/75879.
70 Tamar Hager, 'Justice, Morality or Politics: Why Did the British Legal System Execute Selina Wadge?', *Women's History Review* 26.3 (2017), pp. 455–476.
71 Arnot, 'Gender in Focus'.
72 See for instance Cath Sullivan, '"Bad Mum Guilt": The Representation of "work-life balance" in UK Women's Magazines', *Community, Work & Family* 18.3 (2014), pp. 284–298; Sarah Pedersen, 'The Good, the Bad and the "good enough" Mother on the UK Parenting Forum *Mumsnet*', *Women's Studies International Forum* 59 (2016), pp. 32–38.
73 Val Gillies, *Marginalised Mothers: Exploring Working-class Experiences of Parenting* (London, Routledge: 2007); Jessica White, 'Child-centred Matriarch or Mother among Other Things? Race and the Construction of Working-class Motherhood in Late Twentieth-century Britain', *Twentieth Century British History* 33.4 (2022), pp. 498–521.
74 Imogen Tyler, '"Chav Mum, Chav Scum": Class Disgust in Contemporary Britain', *Feminist Media Studies* 8.1 (2008), pp. 17–34.

14

UNORGANISED WORKERS

Wool Textile Workers and Class Identities in Twentieth-century Yorkshire

Laura Christine Price

The workers of the Yorkshire wool textile industry had limited involvement in trade union activity, from the earliest days of trade unionism to the collapse of the industry in the late twentieth century. In this, they were very similar to many other occupational groups in twentieth-century Britain. Whilst the focus of a great deal of labour history on organised workers has much to tell us about the lives of some working-class people, there remains great scope for the exploration of the lives of workers who tended not to join trade unions, including the identities they possessed. Patrick Joyce warned, as long ago as 1991, that class is not, and has never been, the only significant way to understand working people, which this chapter acknowledges.[1] However, as Joyce also stated, 'Class will not go away'.[2] Other chapters in this volume will examine the working-class experience through different lenses, but this chapter interrogates how a group of working-class people conceived of their own class. Histories of British wool textile workers are scant, but there is much to learn about work, class and deindustrialisation from the example of a traditional workforce whose industry was in decline for much of the twentieth century.

The purpose of this chapter is to understand how a group of workers who had limited connections to trade unions – membership of which is so often considered a barometer of class consciousness – conceived of and expressed their identities in relation to class, trade unionism and politics. This is in order to redress the balance of labour history and focus attention on an under-represented group. Historians such as Selina Todd have sought to challenge the emphasis on 'affluent workers' seen in some areas of post-war British history, and this chapter is written in the same spirit.[3] It also draws on the work of Mike Savage, and in particular his examination of the

DOI: 10.4324/9780429344084-17

Affluent Worker Study of the 1960s, challenging some of the conclusions he reached about working-class people's difficulties in giving coherent answers to officially posed questions about class.[4]

This chapter uses oral histories recorded by the Bradford Heritage Recording Unit (BHRU) in the 1980s to illustrate how wool textile workers thought about class in the twentieth century. At a time when oral history was growing as a field, the BHRU collected around 800 oral testimonies in the mid-1980s on a range of topics including childhood, wool textiles, work more broadly, and the experiences of immigrants to Bradford. The purpose of the project was to collect the life stories of typical Bradford residents. This is beneficial to the historian attempting to learn more about class identities: questions about class were asked, but were not the entire focus of the interview, meaning that narrators were presumably not forewarned that the interview would be about class. As such, responses on the theme of class were likely to be unrehearsed and spontaneous – and, therefore, based on initial feelings rather than using rehearsed narratives around class – giving us insight into how people in the woollen district thought about and articulated their class identities.

The chapter makes use of the work of Penny Summerfield and her concept of 'discomposure': the idea that, in oral histories, some interviewees struggle to construct coherent narratives when recalling their past.[5] We will see that, when discussing class, many oral history narrators gave discomposed accounts of their identities. The chapter also considers the position of Jon Lawrence, who argued that there was a significant difference between everyday usage of the language of class and how officials and professionals used language around class.[6] Given the volunteer-led nature of the BHRU's recordings, this issue seems to be less relevant to our focus than it is to, for example, the Affluent Worker Study.

There are three key research questions for this chapter. The focus is to establish how Yorkshire wool textile workers expressed their class identities, and whether there was any relationship between work and class for this group of people. Further to this, I will examine how much meaning class had for the interviewed workers, and whether there was any relationship between the class identities expressed in oral histories and workers' own involvement with trade union or political activity. This will allow me to draw conclusions about the relationship between trade unionism and class for twentieth-century wool textile workers. We will see that there is a great deal of complexity in how wool textile workers expressed their class identities, and that Summerfield's concept of 'discomposure' can be used as a way to understand how twentieth-century workers conceived of their class identities.

Class Identities

Like other workers, the class identities of wool textile workers in the post-war woollen district of Yorkshire were far from uncomplicated. Although the overwhelming majority of respondents in oral history interviews were able to identify where they felt they belonged in the class system, few were able to elaborate on their class in any detail, and when they did discuss class, there were regular pauses, breaks in sentences and filler words such as 'er' or 'um' punctuating sentences. Penny Summerfield described this phenomenon in oral history as 'discomposure', a process whereby oral history narrators struggle to compose a coherent narrative about the topic of discussion.[7] This is the opposite of 'composure', where 'narrators draw on public discourses in constructing accounts of their pasts for their audiences'.[8] Summerfield stated that discomposure may occur when the oral history narrator has an audience that struggles to understand or sympathise with them, or when their own personal narrative deviates from social norms.[9] Summerfield argued that if no public discourse exists for an oral history narrator to draw upon, composure will be difficult to achieve.

This is perhaps why wool textile workers often found it difficult to talk about class and trade unions with reference to their own personal experiences. If there were few public narratives specifically about the class identity of wool textile workers with which they could identify and use in their own tellings of their experiences – such as those that might be provided by trade union membership and involvement in discussions around class – then composure would be hard to achieve.

Wool textile workers did not struggle to identify their own class in simple terms, in common with many other groups of twentieth-century workers. James Hinton's research on class identities in responses to Mass-Observation directives before 1939 demonstrated that 'Hardly anyone proved unable to think in the language of class'.[10] In response to questions asked about the class identity of Mass-Observers, Hinton pointed out that 87% were able to assign themselves to a conventionally recognised class group, and he stated that class 'provided a meaningful identity' to British people.[11] In a survey taken in 1950–1951 and published in *The People*, 90% of 11,000 people were able to assign themselves a class, though it is necessary to note that such a survey may have provided respondents with a list of class groups to choose from, therefore making the process of ascribing oneself to a group somewhat easier.[12] In the oral histories examined for this article, all respondents were able to describe their own class in conventional terms, but lacked fluency in doing so.

Many of the interviews with former wool textile workers recorded by the BHRU in the 1980s contain discomposure when the subject of class is raised. A male narrator born in 1934 responded to a question about his class thus:

> Oh yes, I wouldn't think there were any… I don't think there's anything wrong with being in – coming from a working-class background, that's – I mean we all work, depending whichever management level you look at, but we're all working class.[13]

The breaks in the middle of sentences and abrupt changes in tack suggest a lack of composure in this former wool worker's narrative. This was common throughout the sample of interviews examined. The reference to 'management level' is particularly interesting, given that it would be unusual to consider someone in a managerial position to be working class.

Another example is from a female narrator born in 1927. This woman tells of her shame at her family's poverty in childhood, and similarly displays the characteristic trailings-off and use of filler words such as 'er' that mark discomposure:

> Well actually we were about the poorest. We were the only ones who were called "being on the Town". Because most people, I think, the man worked from what I can remember... er... I don't remember anybody else being in our position. And I can remember feeling ashamed. You know I'd think "Oh we are so poor" you know... er... I remember feeling that.[14]

She goes on to stress her father's respectability, apparently keen to emphasise that despite their poverty, they did not deviate from social norms:

> Well it used to cause arguments I think, my mother and dad used to have arguments and it was always... because of... I mean my father didn't drink.[15]

It is interesting that this narrator makes links between poverty and respectable behaviours, and, despite some discomposure, is able to elaborate somewhat on that link. When asked about her class, however, she is less able to elaborate:

Interviewer: I mean do you think that the people who lived in that area... would they call themselves working class?

Narrator: Yes. Yes. Mmm.[16]

This suggests that the narrator either had little to say about the matter of her class – which is unlikely, given that she was able to talk at length, albeit falteringly, about other issues such as poverty – or that she lacked access to a narrative that would have helped her frame her own responses about class at greater length. Possibly, poverty is an easier concept to explain and elaborate on than class, given the incredibly obvious and direct effects of it that the narrator experienced. Class, perhaps, is a more intangible idea to explain.

Another narrator tells an interesting story about moving house as a child. He discusses his move from what he describes as a working-class area,

Thornton, to a more middle-class area, Heaton, and in the telling of it produces a narrative that is somewhat difficult to follow:

> Well, I left there when I was nine because we moved across to Heaton, and then I went to St. Barnabas School, which I wasn't particularly happy at because I, I came out of a strictly working-class environment, and Heaton at that time was a little bit, or at least, they thought they were a little bit better, you know.[17]

What is interesting in this interview is that when discussing schooling, the narrator remains composed – possibly because his schooldays gave him a clear framework with which to discuss his memories – but when he goes on to explain the link to his class, he becomes more discomposed, repeating words and speaking sentences that were more difficult to follow. He continues with more discomposure when discussing the impact he felt the move had on him:

> I always believed, wrong… rightly or wrongly, probably wrongly, but I was believed it that er… it set my education back a little bit at the time.[18]

Again, this suggests that the narrator – a former wool worker – was speaking these thoughts aloud for the first time, and that he could not draw on other, public narratives that he understood and related to in order to tell his own story.

A focus on so-called 'affluent workers' has been a significant agenda in research on class since the 1960s. In the mid-twentieth century, earnings for manual workers were increasing, when some saw their pay double.[19] Mike Savage's reconsideration of the Affluent Worker Study led by John Goldthorpe in the early 1960s suggested that there was a gap in understanding between the way the researchers and the respondents understood and thought about class.[20] Savage argued that the reason that some respondents stumbled over their words and struggled to form a coherent answer was this difference in their understandings of class. Jon Lawrence has also argued that there was a 'gulf between official and vernacular understandings of social class in twentieth-century Britain' which could well have led to the participants in the Affluent Worker Study to face difficulty in forming fluent responses to questions on class.[21] However, this could also have been a form of discomposure, either based in the lack of understanding the audience (the researchers) had of the respondent's conceptions of class, or because the respondents lacked a meaningful public discourse through which to tell their story. In examining the oral history interviews conducted by the BHRU, there is no indication that there was a gap in understanding class between the interviewers and the interviewed, given that interviewees were able to understand what interviewers meant in their questions. Furthermore, the BHRU interviews were carried out by oral history volunteers who appear to have been local to the area, rather than professional sociologists, making a gap in understanding less likely.

One narrator spoke of class in terms that was more reminiscent of the responses given in the Affluent Worker Studies that made pains to stress the respondent's 'ordinariness'. Although, when prompted, she said her family was 'definitely working class, yes', she also commented on the idea of ordinariness.[22] When asked about her neighbourhood, she said:

> The neighbourhood, there was very cramped living quarters, and there was no secrets because you could hear everything through the walls, you know, literally. But there again you didn't sort of need that privacy because you were all the same. Er... there were only two class distinctions then and that was the poor class and the very rich ones. There didn't seem to be anything in between as far as we were concerned.[23]

Notably, this respondent gave her opinion on class when asked a question about neighbourhood, suggesting that, for this woman, a link existed between the two. More interesting is the fact that she deviates from what the rest of the narrations surveyed for this article said about class. Whilst she confirmed she viewed herself as working class when prompted, she went further in offering her own analysis of the class system that existed when she was growing up in the first half of the twentieth century. This analysis is much more in line with what Savage found in his reappraisal of the Affluent Worker Study.

Savage argued that 'most respondents [in Goldthorpe's study] do not see class as being about clusters of occupational groups... Class performs other features in their thinking. It defines ideas of individuality and authenticity'.[24] For the workers interviewed in the Affluent Worker Study, Savage argued that to be working class was to be ordinary, rather than to be part of a particular occupational group. Indeed, Savage maintained that for this group of workers, ideas about class did not come from 'the social relations of work and community', but from 'people's understandings of what it is to be an "ordinary" individual'.[25] This may be because the particular group of people that Goldthorpe and his associates interviewed, well-paid workers from three workplaces in Luton at the beginning of the 1960s, had a different understanding of class to workers in lower-paid and more traditional industries earlier in the twentieth century. Indeed, Hester Barron noted in her history of the 1926 miners' lock-out in County Durham that though there was rarely one dominant occupational culture in pit villages, there were very few middle-class people living alongside miners and others in these areas, which could have helped build a strong working-class identity.[26] Additionally,

Helen Jones's research on the work identities of civil defence workers during the Second World War found that the strong bonds formed by ARP wardens was supported by wardens working with people of the same class as them.[27]

As one of the younger participants in the oral history project, however, it is possible that the interviewee who distinguished between 'ordinary' and 'rich' had different views than the older participants because of her age. David Kynaston argued that there was a generational dimension to class identities in the 1950s, but warned that it is too simplistic to suggest that the Second World War was responsible for such changes, given that much of life reverted back to pre-war ways at the end of hostilities.[28] Indeed, Selina Todd commented that 'class relations were a highly significant continuity in twentieth-century British history'.[29] This is at odds with what Goldthorpe and his colleagues described in Luton, but based on the rest of the oral testimonies used in this article, Kynaston and Todd have given a more accurate analysis of generational differences in class identities.

Todd's argument is exemplified in the interview of a woman born in 1910 and interviewed in 1983. The oral history interviews examined for this article include reminiscences from across the twentieth century, with several respondents having worked in wool textiles as early as the 1920s. This participant was asked whether her neighbours and co-workers would have considered themselves working class, and she replied:

> Well, they'd have to, wouldn't they? We were working class. I mean, myself, I never wore a pair of clogs, but when I was little most of the children wore clogs... I can remember people going to the mill with their shawls on, you know.[30]

This respondent was clearly able to describe the class of people in her neighbourhood in terms of the traditional symbols of working-class wool textile operatives, highlighting the particular shoes and garments such a person would be likely to wear and clearly linking them to their class identity. Whilst Goldthorpe's analysis of affluent workers stated that they did not think about class in terms of work relations or the traditional symbols of class, it is clear that some working-class people well into the twentieth century did conceive of their class by using readily understood symbols to convey meaning. Crucially, the symbols they used to explain the class of those around them were typical of wool textile workers whose use of clogs and shawls, whilst not exclusive to them, was certainly seen as a hallmark of their appearance. The interviewer did not prompt the respondent on this issue, suggesting that they understood what the respondent meant by referencing clogs and shawls despite, presumably, being younger than them. Perhaps an understanding of such visual cues assisted some interviewees in composing a somewhat more coherent narrative of their class identity. For some people, then, symbols of working-class life related to occupation still held meaning late into the twentieth century, confirming Todd's analysis of the continuity of conceptions of class across the century.

Trade Unions and Class Identities

Although the industry was in decline throughout the twentieth century, wool textiles remained a significant employer in the West Riding of Yorkshire until the later decades of the century. The 1961 census indicated that, in a 10% sample of West Riding workers, a total of 922 per 10,000 were employed in textiles and related trades.[31] Wool textile workers' numerical significance can be compared against a total of 714 per 10,000 people in the West Riding employed in coal mining and 456 per 10,000 in the iron and steel industries.[32] Although it is not possible to say that the West Riding, and later West Yorkshire, was dominated by wool textile workers, they comprised a large part of the region's workforce.

Wool textile workers were poorly organised into trade unions throughout their history, with limited numbers joining the many unions open to wool textile workers, including the largest such organisation from the 1930s onwards, the National Union of Dyers, Bleachers and Textile Workers (NUDBTW). Calculating an exact percentage of union members in wool textiles is a difficult task: there were many small craft unions for skilled wool workers, and the NUDBTW itself admitted workers in other textile trades such as cotton and jute. However, using the NUDBTW figures, it is possible to discern a rough estimate of union membership in wool. The majority of NUDBTW members were from the Yorkshire woollen district, and as wool dominated in this area, with very few other types of textile manufacturing taking place, we can assume that the figures of the NUDBTW are at least in some way representative of the wool workforce, which was mainly based in Yorkshire. In 1957, there were 155,865 wool operatives in the United Kingdom, and 68,596 members of the NUDBTW – this suggests that 44% of wool textile workers were members of the NUDBTW, but as the NUDBTW was home to more than just wool workers, it is not possible to be entirely certain of this figure.[33] By 1964, there were 130,842 UK wool textile workers and 57,306 NUDBTW members, a percentage of 43.8.[34]

Other labour historians have commented on the relationship between trade union membership and identities in other British industries. For example, Charlie McGuire argued that building workers in post-war Stevenage constructed identities based on membership of the Amalgamated Union of Building Trade Workers (AUBTW).[35] McGuire used oral histories to assess the relationship between trade unions and identities, and one of the interviewed builders said that he felt like a part of the local community through his involvement in trade unionism, with McGuire arguing 'the aims of building worker trade unionism in Stevenage went beyond a struggle for better wages and conditions on the sites'.[36] The situation of Stevenage building workers was very different to Yorkshire wool workers: nearly all Stevenage builders had been trade unionists before beginning work on building Stevenage New Town, and many building sites required their workers to be trade union members before they were given work.[37] Despite the differences, however, it is important to note that membership of a trade union has been linked to broader identities in other twentieth-century workers.

George Stevenson's research on the strike at the Trico windscreen-wiper factory in Brentford in the summer of 1976 focused on the involvement of women in industrial action. Stevenson argued that, in this case, it was the women's class identities, rather than gender, that shaped their understanding of the strike, which was eventually successful in gaining the women equal pay.[38] The women on strike were reported to have said that the lessons they learned from their involvement in the action were about the importance of workers' collective organisation and class solidarity.[39] Again, this demonstrates that there was a link between trade union membership and class for some twentieth-century British workers.

Several of the oral histories deposited in Bradford contain reference to trade union activity. Many contain indications of discomposure when discussing their role in trade unions, suggesting that although some of the workers interviewed had some level of involvement in trade unionism, few of them had access to a narrative that could help them frame confident and coherent responses to questions about this involvement. It is clear from many of the interviews that despite membership, the union did not play a large role in their lives, for example through attendance at union meetings or the provision of union-only leisure facilities. Furthermore, there is a large degree of difference in attitudes towards unions and accounts of their operation in wool textiles in the oral histories.

For example, the interviewees made a range of different comments on whether trade union membership was an expected part of work in the wool textile industry. A female narrator born in 1908 stated that 'my father was a very keen trade unionist, and I had to join the textile union when I went half-time', referring to the time she started working in the mill half of the day and attending school for the other half.[40] She noted that 'they weren't all [her fellow operatives] in it, but I was', and that 'I was in the textile union all the time I worked in the mill'.[41] Another woman narrator commented that, 'I've only ever been once in a union and that was at Drummond's, and I had to be in a union then', implying that her membership was solely because of the closed-shop arrangement that was in place at Drummond's.[42] A male narrator described how he joined the union in April 1941, and that 'At the time I was about the only one in my trade [textiles engineering] that was in the union'.[43] A woman narrator born in 1903 commented that she had been in a union at one point in her working life, but that dissatisfaction led to many at her mill to withdraw, saying 'we gave up paying union money then, threw out of it'.[44]

Several interviewees referred to their fathers' involvement in trade unionism. A woman worker born in 1910 stated that her father 'had his union card till he died', and a male worker born in 1911 said that his father 'was very interested in trade unions', commenting that he was 'very concerned with his work too, that played a very important part in his life, politics and trade unionism came a good second I would say'.[45] Another female worker reported that her father 'was a very keen trade unionist', but that he was a gas worker.[46] This particular interview was notable for its narrator's composure when discussing trade unions and work. For example, when asked why she wanted to join a trade union, she gave a long response outlining her motivations:

> Well, because the, *the people had been so oppressed* you know, by, in those days, *there was slave labour* you see, my grandfather, my mother told me that my grandfather was carried to work on his father's back to work down the pit at seven years of age, and of course you see, my father'd worked in the pit when he was a very young boy, and his father'd been in the pits and they worked for next to nothing you know.[47]

Although this narrator took few pauses for breath, and stumbled somewhat at the beginning, the narrative becomes increasingly composed as it goes on:

> And of course, my Uncle Arthur, he was my mother's brother, he was a real politician you know, I mean he was one of the founders of the ILP in Bradford, in fact at Dudley Hill and Tong Socialist Club his photograph is up there as the founder.[48]

It is unclear who Uncle Arthur was, but he obviously was locally important in Bradford. This woman talked with ease in the language of the labour movement, referring to the end of the 1926 General Strike by saying 'they were forced back you know, the unions had to go back… there were so many blacklegs'.[49] Wool textile workers with family members involved with trade unions may have had greater knowledge of the labour movement in general, and may have been able to discuss class with greater ease. Frustratingly, this particular interviewee was not asked outright about her class identity, but her references to 'blacklegs', 'oppression', and 'slave labour' mean that it is likely that she would have considered herself to be working class.

A male interviewee born in 1911 whose father was involved in trade unions had much to say about class. Again, this narrator appears not to have been asked about his class identity outright, perhaps because the interviewer felt that it was obvious that he would identify as working class. He stated that he was born in a 'very working-class area, slum area in fact', and that he attended a Socialist Sunday School in 'one of the biggest slum areas of Bradford'.[50] He noted his shock on picking up a copy of *Reynolds News*, saying:

> I was greatly surprised at the different kind of information that paper gave about working class people, about the way they were living, just the same as we was in our street, and it was the same throughout Great Britain, the working class people, workers of this country going through a very rough time and there was no need for it, it could be improved.[51]

Like the female narrator quoted above, this narrator was able to compose his narrative about the working classes of Britain clearly and with no hints of discomposure through pauses, stumbles and breaks in speech. Such reminiscences are particularly marked when compared against the majority of other recollections of trade unionism, which indicated a lack of familiarity in discussing the topic. His father's class consciousness and union involvement are factors that distinguish him from most other interviewees.

A woman born in 1907 gave her account of a strike that had occurred at her mill in 1929. She stated that 'It must be over a pay rise' but she couldn't recall exactly the reason for the strike, adding, 'it weren't a firm where they had to be in the union, if you know... one or two were in the union and others weren't'.[52] This part of her narrative was relatively composed, but when it came to discussing how her family managed financially during the strike, she found it very difficult to compose a coherent narrative:

> Well – er... How did...? I don't really know. I supposed we'd have to do without owt, wouldn't we? My dad would be working, you see, and we'd have to manage... I don't know... I don't know how long we...[53]

It is possible that the narrator misunderstood the question, or that her memories of this particular aspect of the strike experience were dim, given the passage of fifty-four years and the fact that she was aged seventy-six at the time of her interview. But compared with the previous, reasonably full description of the activities of the strike, it is curious that she could not give a clear answer on an issue that presumably would have left strong memories of hardship and struggle.

Another female narrator displayed discomposure when asked if she was a union member. The question was simply put: 'Were you in a union?' Her response is stumbling:

> Not then... I was in when I worked up at Wibsey, at Greenwoods at Wibsey and er... there were, everybody was in like, they are now you know.[54]

This kind of response is more typical in this set of interviews than the more composed and coherent narratives offered by a small number of the interviewees. This links with narrators' difficulty in composing clear descriptions of their class, especially given that when asked to talk about other issues – where they grew up, schooling, leisure activities – they were able to give clearer and more composed accounts. It is particularly notable that those whose parents had been involved in trade unions and the labour movement were those most able to compose clear narratives.

Another narrator displaying discomposure had been an overlooker and spoke negatively about trade unions. Born in 1934, this man was at pains to emphasise that his family had always worked hard, and gave the opinion that all wool textile workers were working class.[55] He went on to say that:

> at that time wages structures were more governed by social needs rather than – there were no union agitators, there were nothing you see, so there were nothing really.[56]

His repetition is interesting. He expressed the view that unions were 'agitators' in the matter of wage structures, which perhaps tallied with his role as an overlooker who helped establish a mill in Peterlee, County Durham, but is interesting in relation to his professed membership of the working class. When asked about his role in arbitrating between the shop-floor workers and the management, he gave another answer which is riddled with discomposure:

> Now then it does help labour insofar as – they might not accept the amount that they get, I'm not saying it's right, I think it's too low but – they might not accept the rate that they get, but at least they know that everybody else has got the same. Now then, then it's up to managers like me to maintain the work rate. Now you've got to do that by getting rid of the wrong uns... workers have got to accept that whoever pays their wages calls the bloody tune.[57]

As well as breaking off several times and repeating himself, this narrator literally contradicted what he said were his beliefs within one response. Beginning with the position that the wages textile workers received may not be 'right', he went on to say that workers should accept the conditions they are given by their employers. His responses sound like a desperate attempt to reconcile his identity from childhood with his current position and beliefs. This may be why discomposure was so prevalent in his response.

Strikes and industrial actions were generally few and far between in the twentieth-century wool textile industry, the most long-running being the lock-out at William Denby & Sons of Baildon, beginning in 1963 and ending in 1965. However, some narrators were able to give their recollections of industrial unrest, with varying degrees of detail provided.

A female narrator born in 1924 discussed her memories of the lock-out at Denby's. She gave the opinion that wool workers had 'never been really militant in unions', but that 'the dyehouse was militant'.[58] She reported that she was 'afraid' to join a union 'because my father never belonged to a union, and he always said the unions never did anybody any good, because people would come out on strike'.[59] Her statement about Denby's contained a deal of discomposure:

> I've never known textiles to be out on strike, only one firm, that was Denby's, I've only ever known one firm be – come on strike.[60]

She recalls that the lock-out 'never really officially ended' – this is not the case, as the NUDBTW did call an end to the dispute in February 1965.[61] It is interesting that she said that 'your unions can sort of blackmail you into coming out', and 'So it was a form of blackmail'.[62] There were other narrators who expressed negative opinions of striking. A female narrator born in 1907 told the story of a strike in Denholme in 1929 in which four overlookers broke the strike and, according to this account, caused bad feeling in the area – 'it spoilt Denholme altogether'.[63]

Whilst there were several narrators who told stories about strikes and union membership, there were more who made no or limited comments on this topic. Most said they could not recall strikes in the industry beyond wool workers' involvement in the 1926 General Strike, and few had any direct involvement in strikes themselves. It is telling that the narrators whose families before them had been involved in trade unionism were generally more able to construct coherent narratives regarding trade unionism, and that those who were not trade union members, or who were members but had little involvement in their unions, were more likely to give a discomposed answer. This tells us much about how working-class people who were not committed trade unionists thought about and related to industrial organisation. Whilst trade unions were important institutions for some working-class people, they were not significant to others, to the extent that many former wool workers were unable to compose clear responses to questions about them. From the small sample of interviews analysed for this article, it appears that trade unionism played a limited role in wool workers' identities of class and work.

Politics and Class Identities

In the testimonies examined for this article, the only political parties referred to were the Independent Labour Party (ILP) and the Labour Party, save for a few disparaging remarks about the Conservative Party. The interviewers often asked questions about the ILP, though perhaps somewhat mistakenly: the majority of those interviewed were too young to have many memories of the ILP. It is telling, of course, that parties representing working-class people were those former wool workers referenced in their accounts, and that comments on the Conservative Party were negative. Some of those interviewed had possibly voted Conservative or supported the Conservative Party, but no such comments could be found in the transcripts. It is unlikely that all those interviewed voted Labour, but perhaps social expectations and attitudes prevented these people from voicing their support for a party that was, at the time in the 1980s, deeply unpopular with many working-class people.

A male narrator born in 1946 who had 'always been a trade union member' and became an assistant shop steward in 1977 discussed his reasons for joining the Labour Party:

> I used to go along to [union] meetings and whatever, and the thing that really turned me ultra-active if you like, was Margaret Thatcher coming to power. I think it decided me that I had to become a member of the Labour Party as well because I detest the damn woman, all she stands for, every cretin she has in her Cabinet I detest.[64]

Clearly this narrator's views on the Conservative Party of the mid-1980s were incredibly negative, but it is interesting that he confuses his memory of joining the Labour Party with greater involvement with his union: 'So I joined the branch, or the union executive committee... I was secretary within a few months'.[65] This narrator has conflated his memories of Labour membership and involvement in the union, linked perhaps by Thatcher's well publicised views on trade union power.

Other narrators were involved in the Labour Party. Another male union member, born in 1922, told of his joining Labour:

> Being a believer in the Labour Party, and for the first few years I wasn't very active and then I did become active and I became Chairman of the Allerton Ward Labour Party in 1969, and this was a position I held for thirteen years.[66]

As with the narrators who were committed trade unionists, those who told of commitment to the Labour Party were fewer in number than those who simply said they supported Labour, or who said little or nothing about party politics at all. For some wool textile workers, an association with Labour was likely part of their class identities.

This was no more obvious than in an interview with a man born in 1911. He talked about growing up in 'a very working-class area, slum area in fact', and his father's interest in trade unionism.[67] He talked about campaigning in his locality and attending a Socialist Sunday School where he learned that 'if we had a proper bringing up, as we called it, we would have a good education and we would be more secure in our way of life'.[68] His narrative is the most politically aware of those surveyed, and his discussion of politics is remarkably composed in comparison to others' testimonies. He spoke of being involved, as a child, with collecting packages to send to the poor in the Soviet Union, and of supporting the Republic in the Spanish Civil War.[69] He confessed regret at not joining the International Brigades, saying 'I should have gone across to Spain, I was of age, fit enough, right enough'.[70] In this interview, identification with the labour movement and working-class politics was clear, composed and coherent, much more so than in any other interview. Despite the other interviewees' tendency towards discomposure, when political views were expressed they were clearly aligned with the labour movement. For this group of disorganised workers at least, non-involvement in trade unionism did not equate to a lack of support for working-class political movements and the Labour Party.

Conclusion

Interviews with former wool textile workers from the Yorkshire woollen district demonstrate that they identified with being working class. Some participants expressed this clearly and were able to elaborate on it; others were able to state which class they felt they belonged to, but either chose not to elaborate or were not able to; some were able to associate their class with traditional symbols of working-class people and wool textile workers in particular, such as the clogs that many wore to work in the nineteenth and early twentieth centuries.

What became clear was that those interviewees who had meaningful connections to trade unionism or were politically engaged through the Labour Party, for example, were more able to express their views on class, work, trade unionism and politics with greater clarity than most of those who did not cite any such connections. It is possible, then, that people associated with trade unions and political parties had access to clear narratives about class and work that others lacked, which in turn led to greater composure in oral history interviews. Conversely, those without links to trade unions and political parties tended to give interviews which contained discomposure.

Whilst the sample size of interviews is not large enough to make definite claims about the link between membership of an organisation and the ability to articulate views on class, it is telling that in this sample, discomposure tended to appear more in interviews with those who were not members of organisations. Interestingly, it was also evident that people who joined trade unions or political parties tended to have family members whose example they emulated – in this set of interviews, it was most often parents.

This short article demonstrates the broad scope available to historians who wish to delve deeper into the histories of workforces that were largely disengaged with trade union activity. In order to produce histories that are truly representative of the working-class people of the past, we must strive to focus more on those about whom sources may be more difficult to locate, but whose lives tell us much about the thoughts, feelings and actions of the working classes more broadly.

Notes

1 Patrick Joyce, *Visions of the People: Industrial England and the Question of Class, 1848–1914* (Cambridge, Cambridge University Press: 1991), p. 1.
2 Joyce, *Visions of the People*, p. 1.
3 Selina Todd, 'Affluence, Class and Crown Street: Reinvestigating the Post-War Working Class', *Contemporary British History* 22.2 (2008), p. 501.
4 Mike Savage, 'Working-Class Identities in the 1960s: Revisiting the Affluent Worker Study', *Sociology* 39.5 (December, 2005), p. 937.
5 Penny Summerfield, 'Dis/composing the Subject: Intersubjectivities in Oral History' in Tess Cosslett, Celia Lury and Penny Summerfield (eds.), *Feminism and Autobiography: Texts, Theories, Method* (London, Routledge: 2000), pp. 92–93; Penny Summerfield, 'Culture and Composure: Creating Narratives of the Gendered Self in Oral History Interviews', *Cultural and Social History* 1.1 (January, 2004), p. 69.
6 Jon Lawrence, 'Class, "Affluence" and the Study of Everyday Life in Britain, c. 1930–64', *Cultural and Social History* 10.2 (2013), p. 273.
7 Summerfield, 'Dis/composing the Subject', pp. 92–93; Summerfield, 'Culture and Composure', p. 69.
8 Summerfield, 'Culture and Composure', p. 65.
9 Summerfield, 'Culture and Composure', pp. 69, 74.
10 James Hinton, 'The "Class" Complex: Mass-Observation and Cultural Distinction in Pre-War Britain', *Past and Present*, 199.1 (May, 2008), p. 208.
11 Hinton, 'The "Class" Complex', pp. 209, 212.
12 David Kynaston, *Family Britain, 1951–57* (London, Bloomsbury: 2009), p. 135.
13 Interview A0008, Bradford Heritage Recording Unit, male, born 1934, recorded 24 November 1983 by Ali Hussein.
14 Interview A0011, Bradford Heritage Recording Unit, female, born 1927, recorded 28 November 1983 by Ali Hussein.
15 Interview A0011, Bradford Heritage Recording Unit, female, born 1927, recorded 28 November 1983 by Ali Hussein.
16 Interview A0011, Bradford Heritage Recording Unit, female, born 1927, recorded 28 November 1983 by Ali Hussein.
17 Interview A0040, Bradford Heritage Recording Unit, male, born 1946, recorded 30 January 1984, no note of interviewer.
18 Interview A0040, Bradford Heritage Recording Unit, male, born 1946, recorded 30 January 1984, no note of interviewer.
19 Selina Todd, *The People: the Rise and Fall of the Working Class, 1910–2010* (London, John Murray: 2014), p. 253.
20 Savage, 'Working-Class Identities in the 1960s', p. 937.
21 Lawrence, 'Class, "Affluence" and the Study of Everyday Life in Britain, c. 1930–64', p. 273.

22 Interview A0018, Bradford Heritage Recording Unit, female, born 1924, recorded 12 December 1983 by Ali Hussein.
23 Interview A0018, Bradford Heritage Recording Unit, female, born 1924, recorded 12 December 1983 by Ali Hussein.
24 Interview A0018, Bradford Heritage Recording Unit, female, born 1924, recorded 12 December 1983 by Ali Hussein, p. 937.
25 Interview A0018, Bradford Heritage Recording Unit, female, born 1924, recorded 12 December 1983 by Ali Hussein, p. 942.
26 Hester Barron, *The 1926 Miners' Lockout: Meanings of Community in the Durham Coalfield* (Oxford, Oxford University Press: 2010), p. 42.
27 Helen Jones, 'Civil Defence in Britain, 1938–1945: Friendship during Wartime and the Formation of a Work-Based Identity', *Labour History Review* 77.1 (April, 2012), p. 124.
28 Kynaston, *Family Britain, 1951–57*, p. 138.
29 Selina Todd, 'Class, Experience and Britain's Twentieth Century', *Social History* 39.4 (2014), p. 489.
30 Interview A0005, Bradford Heritage Recording Unit, female, born 1910, recorded 22 November 1983 by Ali Hussein.
31 Table 4, *Census 1961: West Riding County Report* (London, 1963), pp. 33–38.
32 Table 4, *Census 1961*, pp. 33–38.
33 *Monthly Bulletin of Statistics*, Wool Industry Bureau of Statistics – the Wool Textile Delegation, January 1960, no. 121 (relating to the month of November 1959), p. 7; West Yorkshire Archive Service (Bradford), WYB123/1/4/1/6, Transport and General Workers' Union records, Minute Book of the Executive Committee, National Union of Dyers, Bleachers and Textile Workers (hereafter NUDBTW Minutes), 13 September 1958.
34 *Monthly Bulletin of Statistics*, Wool Industry Bureau of Statistics – the Wool Textile Delegation, January 1970, no. 241 (relating to the month of November 1969), 7; West Yorkshire Archive Service (Bradford), WYB123/1/4/1/8, Transport and General Workers' Union records, Minute Book of the Executive Committee, National Union of Dyers, Bleachers and Textile Workers, 20 March 1965.
35 Charlie McGuire, '"Through Trade Unionism You Felt a Belonging – You Belonged": Collectivism and the Self-Representation of Building Workers in Stevenage New Town', *Labour History Review* 81.2 (December, 2016), p. 211.
36 McGuire, 'Through Trade Unionism You Felt a Belonging – You Belonged', p. 232.
37 McGuire, 'Through Trade Unionism You Felt a Belonging – You Belonged', pp. 217–218.
38 George Stevenson, 'The Forgotten Strike: Equality, Gender and Class in the Trico Equal Pay Strike', *Labour History Review* 81.2 (July, 2016), pp. 141, 145.
39 Stevenson, 'The Forgotten Strike', p. 161.
40 Interview A0023, Bradford Heritage Recording Unit, female, born 1908, recorded 19 December 1983 by R W Jones.
41 Interview A0023, Bradford Heritage Recording Unit, female, born 1908, recorded 19 December 1983 by R W Jones.
42 Interview A0005, Bradford Heritage Recording Unit, female, born 1910, recorded 22 November 1983 by Ali Hussein.
43 Interview A0020, Bradford Heritage Recording Unit, male, born 1922, recorded 12 December 1983 by I M Horbury.
44 Interview A0017, Bradford Heritage Recording Unit, female, born 1903, recorded 8 December 1983 by I M Horbury.
45 Interview A0005, Bradford Heritage Recording Unit, female, born 1910, recorded 22 November 1983 by Ali Hussein; Interview A0012, Bradford Heritage Recording Unit, male, born 1911, recorded 1 December 1983 by Robert B Perks.
46 Interview A0023, Bradford Heritage Recording Unit, female, born 1908, recorded 19 December 1983 by R W Jones.

47 Interview A0023, Bradford Heritage Recording Unit, female, born 1908, recorded 19 December 1983 by R W Jones. Author's italics.
48 Interview A0023, Bradford Heritage Recording Unit, female, born 1908, recorded 19 December 1983 by R W Jones. Author's italics.
49 Interview A0023, Bradford Heritage Recording Unit, female, born 1908, recorded 19 December 1983 by R W Jones. Author's italics.
50 Interview A0012, Bradford Heritage Recording Unit, male, born 1911, recorded 1 December 1983 by Robert B Perks.
51 Interview A0012, Bradford Heritage Recording Unit, male, born 1911, recorded 1 December 1983 by Robert B Perks.
52 Interview A0019, Bradford Heritage Recording Unit, female, born 1907, recorded 12 December 1983 by I M Horbury.
53 Interview A0019, Bradford Heritage Recording Unit, female, born 1907, recorded 12 December 1983 by I M Horbury.
54 Interview A0017, Bradford Heritage Recording Unit, female, born 1903, recorded 8 December 1983 by I M Horbury.
55 Interview A0008, Bradford Heritage Recording Unit, male, born 1934, recorded 24 November 1983 by Ali Hussein.
56 Interview A0008, Bradford Heritage Recording Unit, male, born 1934, recorded 24 November 1983 by Ali Hussein.
57 Interview A0008, Bradford Heritage Recording Unit, male, born 1934, recorded 24 November 1983 by Ali Hussein.
58 Interview A0018, Bradford Heritage Recording Unit, female, born 1924, recorded on 12 December 1983 by Ali Hussein.
59 Interview A0018, Bradford Heritage Recording Unit, female, born 1924, recorded on 12 December 1983 by Ali Hussein.
60 Interview A0018, Bradford Heritage Recording Unit, female, born 1924, recorded on 12 December 1983 by Ali Hussein.
61 West Yorkshire Archive Service (Bradford), 5D82/1/3, National Union of Dyers, Bleachers and Textile Workers Bradford No. 1 Branch records, Minute Book of the Executive Committee, National Union of Dyers, Bleachers and Textile Workers, 20 February 1965.
62 Interview A0018, Bradford Heritage Recording Unit, female, born 1924, recorded on 12 December 1983 by Ali Hussein.
63 Interview A0019, Bradford Heritage Recording Unit, female, born 1907, recorded 12 December 1983 by I M Horbury.
64 Interview A0040, Bradford Heritage Recording Unit, male, born 1946, recorded 30 January 1984, no note of interviewer.
65 Interview A0040, Bradford Heritage Recording Unit, male, born 1946, recorded 30 January 1984, no note of interviewer.
66 Interview A0020, Bradford Heritage Recording Unit, male, born 1922, recorded on 12 December 1983 by I M Horbury.
67 Interview A0012, Bradford Heritage Recording Unit, male, born 1911, recorded on 1 December 1983 by Robert B Perks.
68 Interview A0012, Bradford Heritage Recording Unit, male, born 1911, recorded on 1 December 1983 by Robert B Perks.
69 Interview A0012, Bradford Heritage Recording Unit, male, born 1911, recorded on 1 December 1983 by Robert B Perks.
70 Interview A0012, Bradford Heritage Recording Unit, male, born 1911, recorded on 1 December 1983 by Robert B Perks.

15

'WHERE THE BRASS BAND IS BELOVED', BRASS BANDS AND WORKING-CLASS CULTURAL IDENTITY

Inventing a Musical Metonym in the Southern Pennines, c.1840–1914

Stephen Etheridge

In 1898 the *Pall Mall Gazette* featured an article about northern bandsmen.[1] The author emphasised the leisure pursuits of northern working-class bandsmen and their followers, writing:

> The brass band is not the object of every man's adoration, nor its music of the kind which sooths every savage breast. But with the north-country man the love of the brass band is a passion ... These bands are composed of workmen, without exception, and workmen are their chief admirers. The workmen in these regions must have a hobby, if it is only dog-racing or rat-worrying; but when he makes music his hobby there is no limit to his ambition. Weber is not too exacting for him, nor Wagner too abstruse. Coal-grimed pitmen leave the mines and hurry away in their dirt to practice a selection from Mozart; and mill-workers leave the discordant roar of spinning and weaving sheds to study Gounod.[2]

For this author bands were fixed within the *culture* of their wider working-class audience. The rise of brass bands coincided with a period when social reformers were taking an increased interest in emerging working-class leisure.[3] The journalist Thomas Wright, for example, gave the middle class what were effectively a series of written guides to a working class that was becoming increasingly visible. The market for Wright's *Some Habits and Customs of the Working Classes* (1867) and *The Great Unwashed* (1868) reflected an increasing interest in observing and understanding the lives of the working class.[4] Even though want and poverty were present, from around 1873 to 1896 there was an improvement in average wages during a

DOI: 10.4324/9780429344084-18

period when living costs fell, meaning that a number of affordable working-class pastimes emerged.

The Southern Pennines: A High Density of Brass Bands

The *Pall Mall Gazette*'s emphasis on the North was not unusual. Bands were a national pastime, yet reporting highlighted the 'crack' (most successful) bands of the North. There was a high density of bands concentrated in the Southern Pennines. In 1903, the band commentator 'Shoddythorpe' estimated that there were at least 250 bands in West Yorkshire alone.[5] Around the Lancashire side of the region the brass band historian Arthur Taylor illustrated the density of brass bands in this period by saying the whole area of Saddleworth 'could almost be designated a national park for brass bands, with Dobcross as the centrepiece'.[6]

These bands gained dominance over others as a result of training and contest success: together with elements of instrumental tradition, such as internal mentoring, and the semi-oral transmission of technique. In the first edition of the *Amateur Band Teacher's Guide and Bandsman's Adviser*, published in 1899, the editors advocated the training methods in use among northern bands: theirs was 'a synthesis of the systems on which the celebrated prize bands of Lancashire and Yorkshire [were] taught'.[7] This period saw a national consistency of technique that was influenced by the imitation of the playing styles of the championship bands, which were often conducted by the northern triumvirate of band trainers from the region, John Gladney (1839–1911), Alexander Owen (1851–1920), and Edwin Swift (1843–1904). From 1875 to 1895, there were few major contests when one of them did not conduct one of the winning bands.[8] Hence the dominance of bands from the Southern Pennines created an arena to examine the development of a working-class leisure pursuit that was to become a powerful metonym of working-class cultural identity.

This chapter examines elements in how bandsmen and bands strengthened their working-class cultural identity in a period after mid-century when the development of working-class culture had a definable chronology – the rise of football, the seaside holiday, allotments, and naturalist societies, for example, became popular. Bandsmen developed a cultural identity when a distinct opinion of what it meant to partake in working-class leisure was becoming fixed within the national consciousness[9] This 'measuring' takes the form of press correspondence that concentrated on the triangular dialogue between internal and external reporters and the bandsmen. First, I explore the internal reporting of class: how editors of band periodicals reflected on the rational recreation ethos to reprimand bandsmen on the dangers of bringing the movement into disrepute. Next comes the external view of bandsmen from outside the movement, and, finally, how did working-class bandsmen interpret these views of their music-making?

Bands and Rational Recreation

Bandsmen were encouraged by social reformers to engage themselves in the concept of rational recreation. Rational recreation in its simplest form matches the *Oxford English Dictionary's* definition of the words. Rational: 'sensible, sane, moderate, not foolish, absurd or extreme', together with recreation: 'the process or means of refreshing or entertaining oneself'.[10] To the Victorian mind, the ethos was a way of *refreshing* the worker with moderate, improving and sober pastimes. In the eyes of middle-class reformers workers had a duty to use leisure time responsibly. Music was arguably the best of all rational recreations, many believing that the appreciation of music could lead to social harmony and have a refining influence upon people.[11] The result of this reliance on rational recreation created a dialogue between the bandsmen, who often drew attention to themselves because of perceived bad behaviour, the external observers, who were quick to notice this behaviour, and the band movement's internal periodicals, where editors constantly emphasised the desire for bandsmen to act like gentlemen when under scrutiny from these observers.

To understand how publications represented bands we need to understand the nature of the media. People loved to read and write about music, this was reflected in journals – around 200 titles – that gave substantial column space to music.[12] From local newspapers to scholarly journals there were huge differences in quality of writing, regional bias, and depth of knowledge. Journals were known to copy articles from each other without acknowledgement. The press published articles verbatim from the band periodical the *British Bandsman* during the first 20 years of its publication from 1887.[13] In spite of this replication the press remains an important site for exploring the representation of bands and their followers. Writing in this period showed observations of the band movement from a middle-class position; the writing was quasi-anthropological in nature, resulting in studies of working-class music-making that engaged with, and complemented, observations of the changing nature of leisure in this period. For the press it was band contests that became central events in the representation of working-class cultural identity.

The Brass Band Periodical Editor's View

The band contest became the key observation point for both internal and external reporters. It should be noted that local contests were being held regularly from the 1840s, and, by 1853, contests were held at Belle Vue Gardens in Manchester. By 1860 the first national contest was held at Crystal Palace. Contests attracted crowds in their thousands, which resulted in a range of behaviour from bandsmen and their supporters, much of it considered unsuitable by observers. For the editors of band periodicals, and others, it was clear that the brass band movement was linked with sporting prowess, and the notion of good 'sportsmanship'. Reporting of band contests frequently included comparison with football's major competitions, and they likened the audience enthusiasm to a championship match. In 1898 the *Pall Mall Gazette* showed how easy it was for the reporter to link bands and sport, writing that:

> There is a brass band contest season, just as there is a football season; there is a brass band public just as there is a football public, as enthusiastic, opinionated, and observant. That season is now at its height, and is about to culminate in the great contest by which the champion amateur brass band of the year is chosen. This is more than an incident in north-country life: it is an event of vast moment. It excites as much excitement as an English Cup Tie, and if any matter takes as deep hold of the public mind of Lancashire as a football match it is indeed important.[14]

In 1899, the editors of *Wright and Round's Amateur Band Teacher's Guide and Bandsman's Adviser* expanded this theme explaining that competition was a national trait acquired at birth, found in empire building, industry, music, and sport. They wrote:

> Competition is born in an Englishman, whether it is building up the greatest empire, sinking the deepest mine, or singing the best song. Of course, he does not always succeed, but he never gives it up. Thus it happened, that when the village bands pleased the villagers the villagers praised them, and boasted they were better than any other. In this way band contests originated ... On average some 200 band contests take place annually in the United Kingdom, and they are the very best means of developing and retaining a standard of good playing, just as cricket matches keep up the standard of good cricket. Not only do they who take part in either benefit by the rivalry, but all who listen and watch are having a grand object lesson.[15]

These observations were replicated in other periodicals. Writing in 1901, for example, T.W. Wilkinson wrote in *Good Words* that, 'brass band contests evoked white-heat enthusiasm in local people; they were important factors in the social life of the people, thousands of people took the keenest interest in them'.[16] Significantly, Wilkinson noticed that the audience 'follow the playing with intelligent approval or censure according to its quality; and as a successful body of musicians, on returning home, receives an ovation similar to that accorded to the winners of a football cup'.[17] The growth of football was synchronous with the band contest so reporters naturally compared football crowds with band supporters. In other words, as an emerging phenomenon, reporters wanted something to compare bands to; they searched, and found symmetry, in wider working-class leisure.

The View of the Local Press

The local press also relied on sporting imagery to understand local brass bands. By the 1870s newspaper reading had become established in the provinces, creating interest in local journalism.[18] As Lucy Brown noted, 'the reading of newspapers became central to the daily routine, becoming part of the normal furniture of life for all classes'.[19] The local press was complicit in creating local heroes. The press would often lionise a local sporting team or sports person who had been successful. Hence, when a local brass band won a contest, the writing mirrored this lionisation of sporting success. The choice of stories, the position taken and the language used, created legends about people and places. When the text is approached from this perspective an array of ideas about space, place and region emerge. As Jeff Hill has argued, 'the press is not just a passive reflector of local life and thought, but an active source in creating local feeling'.[20] As with sport, supporting a band was, 'an expression of a town identity, an association with others from the town that asserted a collective geographical allegiance'.[21] The band contest gave working people a sense of class consistency that was expressed through musical performance.

Large numbers of people travelled from their towns and villages by train to support their bands. By 1850 much of the country was linked by rail with London. Rail travel gave thousands mobility within the north and beyond. A clear example of this mobility was when a large proportion of east Lancashire's Rossendale Valley travelled to the 1857 Belle Vue Contest to support Bacup Band. The trains stopped at each station along the Rossendale Valley and took on significant numbers of passengers. In 1908, Isaac Leach reminisced about the contest:

> The excitement of the neighbourhood was intense, and for days before the contest the fate of the band at Belle Vue was almost the sole topic of conversation. The practice of the band in the mill yard at Broudclough, on the Sunday previous to the fateful day, was attended by thousands of persons. On the morning of the contest, the Belle Vue excursions from Bacup were packed with people, and most of the mills were obliged to stop. Two special trains were run, the local bookings being as follows: Bacup 1093, Stacksteads 200, Newchurch 519, and Rawtenstall 323.[22]

These numbers were made possible by the affordability of rail fares for labouring people. Hugh Cunningham argued that 'brass band contests … were possible only because of cheap rail fares; by 1888 there were fifty excursion trains for the Belle Vue contest in Manchester'.[23]

In public view, then, it followed for the movement's journal editors that bandsmen and their followers should not be seen as rough. For editors, roughness fell into three broad areas: drunkenness, disputing contest results – which could lead to threats of violence to supporters of other bands and the adjudicators – and swearing. These areas often all came together at one pivotal moment such as when the contest results were announced. The editorial tone of band periodicals tried to distance bandsman from rougher elements of working-class life. Inevitably, because of the nature of its social networks, the brass band movement became a visible extension of larger working-class leisure habits that could not remove itself from its own class, rough or not.

For example, in February 1900, the *Cornet* wrote about the importance of the contest in promoting the positive aspects of the movement. It was each bandsman's duty to ensure they did not behave in a way that could upset a range of middle-class benefactors. In other words, each bandsman had accountability to represent the movement. Moreover, it was the financial benefits that came from the sponsorship of people with significant disposable incomes that was important. The alcohol induced social side of the contest was viewed as a negative activity. The *Cornet* wrote:

> This being a subject of importance to the whole "live" brass band fraternity, there is no need to apologise for laying a growl before the numerous readers of the "Cornet." There is urgent need for improvement in the manner most contests are carried out … It is a fact that brass bands are placed at a low estimate by a majority of people occupying the best social positions, whose influence would be enough to guarantee the success of any band, and would undoubtedly be glad to subscribe to the funds. They are deterred, however, by the line of conduct adopted by many bandsmen… especially on the contest field. It is no uncommon occurrence at band contests to find, after the decision, men who have drunk well, if not wisely, making all kind of insinuations against committees and adjudicators, and using language of the vilest description, because their favourite band has not been placed in the prize list. None will deny this, yet there are some that say, "Take no heed; they have had too much John Barleycorn, and are to be excused. No one need accept their opinions." Perhaps not, but this kind of thing drives away many people, and also tends to keep them; and their friends away from the next contest; besides, they are likely to withdraw their influence and support from the village or town band.[24]

Two months later, the *Cornet* was moralising again. The editor condemned bandsmen when they drank, argued, and made a great deal of comment over contest results, the rationale being that it would deter the people from subscribing to band funds. Such drunken behaviour would counteract the positive work that the movement had achieved in bringing working-class musical performance to the fore. They wrote:

> Bandsmen should learn to control their feelings, a great deal more than they are accustomed to do. There is not a bandsman I know… who would like to be called "low" or "vulgar" and yet, to exhibit, so openly the uppermost feelings in one's mind, is nothing short of the essence of vulgarity. The natural consequence of these exhibitions of feelings, is that the gentry and upper-class people will have nothing to do with contests not because they object to where bandsmen are – but because they are never safe to being a witness to one of these questionable scenes, which almost invariably take place at contests. No, if bandsmen only knew, it does not pay; and they are performing the peculiar feat of raising themselves with one hand, and knocking themselves down with the other.[25]

Editors did not recognise that contests were an extension of older labouring-class traditions: as such the event reflected communal holiday revelry. The dislike of bad behaviour at contests, and the suggestion of revulsion at this behaviour, indicated a clash of cultures. Hence, the band contest became an arena for working-class display. It was this traditional revelry that the editors of the brass band periodicals were fighting against. When the bands played in public it was a festive event, and, as such, bandsmen could not avoid mixing with the wider working class, who some commentators saw as rough and detrimental to the band movement. In *Wright and Round's Amateur Band Teacher's Guide and Bandsman's Adviser*, for example, the editors featured a letter from F. C. B., who wrote:

> I have much to say in favour of our amateur bandsmen… and hope I may live to laud them as gentlemen…. Of what value is the "divine art" to them if it does not refine their tastes, and subdue evil passions, and enkindle good passions? Next to hearing a band play well, I like to see a band behave well, and not indulge in rough horse-play and vulgar talk at every opportunity. Again nothing can be more fatal to a band's interest than for the members to make too familiar with the clowns that always crowd around them when fulfilling and engagement.[26]

Often held in wakes weeks contests drew upon traditions that were common in northern manufacturing districts. Particularly tenacious in Lancashire, the wakes week was the culmination of a full calendar of traditional celebrations.

The wakes was originally a religious festival, held on the saint's day of the local church, which centred on the rush bearing festival.[27] This festival was part of the cycle of historical time. Individual and collective memory became essential in marking historical meaning and continuity.[28] The appreciation of brass band music, and its importance to local memory, depended upon a complex process of memory, recalling past events and experiences. Audiences did not enter an event that featured a brass band with an open mind but brought with them extensive musical and social experience. Much of the meaning of the event relied upon what happened in the past, the brass band taking on elements of older rituals.

The contests were days of carnival, mill owners often giving workers the day off.[29] In April 1868, for example, Accrington hosted a contest that reinforced the carnival atmosphere, the contest becoming central to the day's events: The *Accrington Times* wrote:

> This year's exhibition had brought into the town visitors so numerous as to surpass the most sanguine anticipations, tradesmen made great preparations. The lovers of the marvellous too had ample opportunities of gratifying their tastes, for in Church Street, there were exhibitions of the most curious and rare freaks, that nature ever produced. At the top of Union Street, there was a boxing booth, featuring the thorough bulldog type of facial beauty ... Blackburn Road was crowded with people from nine o'clock in the morning until noon, witnessing the arrival of the various bands, intending to take part in the days contest.[30]

External Views

As such, brass band contests came to the attention of commentators. One example, called 'Musical Prize Fight', appeared in November 1859, in the journal *All Year Round,* which was written by John Hollingshead, a theatre impresario working with Gilbert and Sullivan. He was also a London journalist under the tutelage of Charles Dickens, and, as such, the piece is often attributed to Dickens.[31] The writing resonated with the cultural identity of the labouring people who lived around Redcar, a place that Hollingshead, who wrote in a pseudo-anthropological way, thought few London frequenters of spas and watering places would know. Hollingshead's attention fixed on a 'Grand Village Band Contest', being held in Lofthouse, halfway between Redcar and Whitby.

Hollingshead encountered a brass band in the taproom of the Golden Lion Public House, 'very busily engaging in the Lofthouse rum and ale: hanging up by the hooks from the ceiling... were several cornopeans to be used in the harmonious fight'.[32] He noticed the habit of every band to play a march when approaching the Golden Lion, forming a circle, and finishing off with a defiant tune to say that we are here, 'beat that if you can'. They would retire to one of the drinking rooms, 'where the landlord gazed upon them with a silent but fatherly interest, having more regard to what they drank, than to what they played'. Hollingshead noticed the attention that the spectators gave the bands. 'The whole village ... was quite willing to stand still... and give itself up to gazing at everything and everybody'. He noticed that even though music was a rational recreation – implying bandsmens' respectability – the bandsmen, and their followers, could be rough:

> It was a hopeful sight for those who travel through the moorland district in the constant fear that some ruffian will 'fettle their mouths with a brick.' I do not pretend to say, that because Ah, ehe la morte! is blown upon a Yorkshire trumpet, fighting is altogether a stranger to Yorkshire fists, but I think that the man who conducts the melodies of Bellini, although in a crimson waistcoat and corduroys, is not likely to bite off his neighbour's ear, or to gouge out his neighbour's eye, and is very likely to have a humanising influence on some of his less cultivated brethren, besides.[33]

Contest results, he observed, still roused 'cheers and groans [that] were sufficiently loud and antagonistic to warrant the presence of police officers, who had come from every village within twenty miles'.[34]

Such events were duplicated in districts where labouring people were in the majority. Reporting on a Yorkshire band contest at Easter 1901, for example, the *Musical Standard* reinforced the points that Hollingshead had highlighted. They decided, 'the brass band is to country musicians what Paderewski is to the ordinary run of piano players and to belong to one, and share in its glories is a great thing'.[35] They noticed the locality of regional contests, together with the habits of the working people who followed them: 'most of the bands came from colliery villages, and it was therefore not unnatural that the admirers should in many instances be accompanied by dogs'.[36] The reporter also noted the public house as a meeting place for discussion of the contest: 'there was naturally much consumption of ale over all these matters ... it was something more than ludicrous to hear two colliers dressed in their Sunday best, and washed very cleanly, discussing Chopin as against Handel, over their pots'.[37]

Antipathy towards Adjudicators

The police were often present at band contests to control dissent towards adjudicators. Adjudicators were aware they were under scrutiny by not only the bands, but also the supporters in the audience. In 1896, the *Magazine of Music* found that the contest judge 'was as sanguine, sober and sophisticated as they imagined'. In this 'chat with a judge' the writing not only revealed the authority of adjudicators, but they also found that the audience could have the potential to argue. The reporter began with the judge's clear authority:

> He sat in his tent, with a table well filled with papers and a closely marked score before him, while outside, preparations were busily going forward for the great contest… I enquired as to the success of brass bands in other parts of the country, and was informed they were invariably popular. "English people love a brass band," explained the judge … they are not always reliable critics, though, and it is no very uncommon experience for a judge in a competition like this to be told pretty plainly that his verdict is not the popular verdict.[38]

Disagreements over adjudicators' comments were common. They could spill over into threats of violence. A contest, for example, was held on Keighley Cricket and Football Club's field, on the 30 May 1886. The judge was Mr. E. Holland, bandmaster of the 1st Northampton Regiment. He gave first prize to Leeds Forge Band, second to Irwell Bank, third to Wyke Old, fourth to Wyke Temperance, and fifth to Kingston Mills. He stated that there was only five marks difference between the first three prizes. Black Dyke Mills and Honley did not receive a prize[39]: The *Manchester Times* reported:

> [The] decision gave a good deal of dissatisfaction, and a most unseemly disturbance followed. Dike Band behaved in an unruly and even threatening manner. One man suggested that they should play the "*Dead March*", and this was no sooner said than several of the players struck up a dirge in front of the judge's tent. It was found necessary for three police constables to escort the judge to a cab in waiting, and then police-constable Newhill proceeded with him to the railway station. When the cab drove off there was mingled hooting and cheering, and one enthusiast threw a stone after the departing vehicle, but no damage was done. Arrived at the station, Mr. Holland had to wait several minutes for a train to Preston… and in the meantime some of the members of Black Dike and Honley bands had come on to the platform and these began to taunt and hoot again. Mr. Holland was afraid that bodily harm would be done to him … he was accompanied by a police constable as far as Skipton.[40]

The contest day was a period of time when the labouring people could challenge decisions made by people in authority. As features of the local holiday day the bands represented a temporary suspension of deference to authority; nevertheless, this was only brief, as figures of authority quickly re-established order. The editors of band periodicals may well have been constant in their pleas for gentlemanly conduct, but when bands gathered together the joint force of the bandsmen and their supporters gave dissent a currency – however briefly – that was associated with groups of working-class people. We can see in thc audience the notion of moral economy, whereby, as E. P. Thomson argued, that in the eighteenth century:

> The men and women in the crowd were informed by the belief that they were defending traditional rights and customs; and, in general, they were supported by the wider consensus of the community. On occasion this popular consensus was endorsed by some measure of license afforded by the authorities. More commonly the consensus was so strong that it over-rode motives of fear or deference.[41]

These events meant working people, through their support of the bands, had cultural autonomy. The displeasure at these results from the bandsmen, and their supporters, legitimised the culture of bands within the landscape of working-class leisure. Contests were not the food riots of the eighteenth century; nevertheless, grievances brought about by the actions of the crowd on the contest field highlighted what was expected of a judge within the social norms of the contest. Any outrage against the moral assumptions of the crowd, which band should win, for example, was the occasion for direct action, from silence at the announcement of a result, to threats of violence.[42]

Bandsmen as Viewed by Other Working-class People

Musical journals centred the bandsmen in a working-class environment visible from the outside. How did locals view the bands? The evidence suggests local people did not see band members as different from normal working people. Jean Mills remembered seeing Bacup Band march through the town; she recalled that they were all working lads from the factory.[43] The bands also used this same colloquial language when describing themselves. In September 1911, Helmshore Band's committee decided that they should advertise in the Post Office window for, 'lads', who wanted to play the cornet'.[44] This language defined the class the bandsmen came from, and the class to which they wanted to appeal for their members.

One exception to this picture was the way that children perceived bandsmen. Some children saw band members as heroic figures, adding colour to the lives of the working class. As a child, the author Ben Brierley remembered watching Hollinwood Band. He wrote, 'the uniform adopted by these musical gentlemen was a blue swallow-tail coat, with brass buttons, white trousers, and a black beaver with a yellow band. They were in our eyes princes who had condescended to come amongst poor people'.[45] For some children, bands were role models, who were considered *outside* their class, they were perceived as gentlemen.

The brass band perpetuated its working-class association with activities outside music. Fundraising was something that every band did. In 1869, for example, Westhoughton Old Band held a prize draw to raise money for uniforms. The prizes were a harmonium, a fat pig, a sack of flour, a cheese, an iron bedstead and a fat duck.[46] The prizes showed that value was placed on goods that could make working-class life easier, in short, food, leisure, and rest. Protein-rich food was seen as essential in the working person's diet that sustained a person who arrived home after a day's manual labour. In this way these prizes enhanced the relationship between bands and the day-to-day working-class experience. In 1910, Helmshore Brass Band, from east Lancashire's Rossendale Valley, held a prize draw for the July holidays. The first prize was a ten-day ticket to Blackpool with two-pound spending money. The second prize was a five-day ticket to Blackpool and one-pound spending money. The third prize was a day ticket and five-shilling spending money. There were also five other one day tickets.[47] These prizes associated the brass band with the northern working-class sea-side experience.[48]

By offering these prizes the bands were confirming their social place in the community amongst other organisations from other social classes that offered prizes for fundraising. The bands did not consider any prizes that would appeal to the middle class; or rather just people with money, they knew the audience to which the band appealed, and the scope of that appeal. Despite gaps in the internal class membership of bands, the activities of the bands showed that they understood that the audience to whom they appealed, and from which they came.

Conclusion: 'How Others See Us'

How did bands respond to external reporting that singled them out as being working class? The bands' own periodicals provide the best place to explore this question. In 1901, the *Cornet* was asking the question, 'How Others See Us?'[49] This column did not cite the newspapers reporting on the bands: the significance, however, was that bands were collecting observations about brass bands that were external to the movement to highlight how others *observed* and sometimes *judged* bandsmens' activities. What was apparent was that forty-two years after Hollingshead described the local brass band contest at Redcar the same themes were evident and were being transferred to the London stage to describe bandsmen from the north. First, there was the notion that the bands were all working people from mills, factories or mines. Hence, a reporter on the 1901 Crystal Palace Contest wrote:

> The brass band contest is a function that on no account should be missed by the Londoner in search of excitement and novelty. Apart from the delight which it gives the sympathetic student of humanity to see thousands of

> hard working northerners, men of the pit and men of the mill steeped to the soul of melody.[50]

Second, commentators were happy to point out that the supporters were not only educated in the style of music, but at the core of their identity were elements of a rougher type of working-class leisure. The essence of this was rooted in the whole working-class experience. One commentator, writing to the *Musical Standard*, in 1867, felt that choirs would be much better, and agreeable, than bands, mainly because bandsmen were, in their opinion, authors of their own fate. In an attack on rough behaviour the author felt that choral music would be a gentler form of competition. Being working class inevitably led bandsmen to the beer shop after playing. The author wrote:

> Would it not be far more agreeable ... to organize choirs in our large business establishments? Musical instruments are expensive; they are also very noisy... Brass bands have become a perfect nuisance of late years; blowing away with all their strength; they are always followed by some immense crowd, composed of an admixture of almost all grades of the lower society – "Tagrag and Bobtail." The greatest objection to these noisy bands will be found in the demoralizing influence upon the members: practices are generally held in the public-house. The exhaustion in blowing a wind instrument for any length of time in the street naturally leads the members of a band to a beer shop, where they too frequently indulge to excess; eventually becoming worthless members of society, instead of finding their music a source of pleasure to them.[51]

Yet, what commentators expected from working people – to be rough and possibly violent – was in contrast to what they witnessed. The main comment was that, even though they contained rough elements, working people were prepared to travel long distances to spend free time following a band. One author in the *Cornet* wrote:

> When the bands are playing the "testpiece" the great audience, mostly from Yorkshire and Lancashire, or Wales, sits score in hand, following every note. Men of whom you would hesitate to ask your way, in a dark lane, sit listening for a fault of execution, in a selection from *The Martyr of Antioch*. They have come up, most of these musicians from the bowels of the earth, and lost a day's pay, and two days rest, simply for the sake of art. When I listened to a gigantic miner, roaring as gently as a sucking dove upon the bombourdon, I felt my cheeks tingle with shame at the remembrance that I once tried to play *Pop Goes the Weasel* on the mouth organ and failed.[52]

When the press referred to the communal group as 'they' or 'them', bandsmen became the representation of the other, the anthropological, and the not fully understood social phenomenon. Even in the band periodicals commentators defaulted to rational recreation when faced with uncomfortable elements found working-class life. One commentator wrote:

> In these amateur bands composed of working men of the north, you have not only technical skill, you have the tenderness which is the soul of music. When you look at them, when you hear them talk, when you know amid what surroundings they pass their lives and earn their bread, you come to one conclusion. That conclusion is that of all the arts music must be the one that comes most naturally to the great mass. It would, I take it, be impossible to get a similar assemblage to show such technical skill and perfection of execution in painting or in sculpture, or even in poetry, which is the music of words.[53]

As a result of these magazines and journals, which were largely published in London, bandsmen were seen as the epitome of the working-class autodidact. Underlying this image of respectable musicianship lay the potential for rough behaviour, often viewed by the press as prevalent amongst the bands' supporters. As the *Manchester Guardian* highlighted, at the Belle Vue Contest in 1893, 'each particular band had its party of friends, and the applause when a difficult passage was achieved was deafening'.[54] Yet, if others disturbed the concentration of the audience who followed the band, the *Pall Mall Gazette* was keen to point out a 'torrent of rude Lancashire [would be brought down] upon your head'.[55] These 'men who you would hesitate to ask the way in a dark lane', then, for the press, were undeniably people who were respectable, but had the potential for disorderly conduct. The London press held the belief that followers of bands were working class and, as such, these people naturally followed other male working-class leisure pastimes, such as horseracing, dogs, gambling and drinking. Yet the brass band was the ideal pastime to confirm and embrace the idea that the working class had a respectable leisure activity, but, bands provided a highly visible field for working-class roughness and, on occasion, delinquency. In the final analysis, for the external reporters, in the London press, bandsmen were always the working class with all the prejudices and views of them intact. Together with the band movement's own periodicals defence of bandsmen this reporting provided significant amounts of material that created a metonym of northern working-class culture that remains with us today.

Notes

1 Anon, 'Where the Brass Band Is Beloved', *Pall Mall Gazette*, 2 September 1898.
2 Anon, 'Where the Brass Band Is Beloved', *Pall Mall Gazette*, 2 September 1898.

3 The development of bands is too lengthy a discussion for this chapter. Bands emerged from the 1820s from a mix of woodwind and brass instruments, through a number of phases, to, by the 1870s, the standard band instrumentation seen today. Key stages were the invention of the keyed bugle (1820s); the invention of the piston valve (invented no later than 1814 and developed through 1827–1850) and the development of the saxhorn, invented by Adolph Sax in the 1840s and 1850s.
4 Alistair J. Reid, 'Wright Thomas' (1839–1909)', *Oxford Dictionary of National Biography* (Oxford, Oxford University Press: 2006) accessed, 1 August 2013, http://www.oxfordnb.com/view/article/4426.
5 *British Bandsman*, 23 May 1903, p. 264.
6 Arthur R. Taylor, *Brass Bands* (St Albans and London, Hart-Davies MacGibbon: 1979), p. 211.
7 Wright and Round's *Amateur Band Teacher's Guide and Bandsman's Adviser* (Liverpool, Wright and Round: 1889), front cover.
8 J. L. Scott, 'The Evolution of the Brass Band and Its Repertoire in Northern England', unpublished PhD thesis, University of Sheffield (1970), p. 248.
9 Jose Harris, *Private Lives: Public Spirit: Britain 1870–1914* (London, Penguin Books: 1994), pp. 93–95.
10 R. E. Allen, ed., *The Concise Oxford Dictionary* (Oxford, Oxford University Press: 1964, this edition, 1990).
11 In its most elaborate form the notion of music as a rational recreation was developed by the High Church Theologian Hugh Reginald Haweis. His influential book, *Music and Morals*, was published in 1871 and by 1903 it had reached its twentieth edition.
12 Leanne Langley, 'The Musical Press in Nineteenth-Century England', *Notes,* 2nd Series, 46.3 (1990), p. 583.
13 Alf Hailstone, *The British Bandsman Centenary Book, A Social History of Brass Bands* (Baldock, Egon: 1987), p. 95.
14 *Pall Mall Gazette,* 2 September 1898.
15 Wright and Round's *Amateur Band Teacher's Guide*, 2.
16 T. W. Wilkinson, 'Brass Band Contests', *Good Words* 42 (December, 1901), p. 593.
17 Wilkinson, 'Brass Band Contests', p. 593.
18 Richard D. Altick, *The English Common Reader* (Chicago, IL, Chicago University Press: 1957), p. 356.
19 Lucy Brown, *Victorian News and Newspapers* (Oxford, Oxford University Press: 1985), p. 273.
20 Jeff Hill, '"Rite of Spring": Cup Finals and Community in the North of England', in Jeff Hill and Jack Williams (eds.), *Sport and Identity in the North of England* (Keele, Keele University Press: 1996), p. 86.
21 Jack Williams, '"One Could Literally have Walked on the Heads of the People Congregated There": Sport, the Town and Identity', in Keith Laybourn (ed.), *Social Conditions Status and Community, 1860-ca.1920* (Stroud, Sutton Publishing: 1997), p. 123.
22 Isaac Leach, *Bacup Old Band* (Bacup, L.J. Priestly: 1908), p. 6.
23 Hugh Cunningham, *Leisure in the Industrial Revolution* (London, Routledge: 1980), p. 159.
24 *Cornet*, 15 February 1900, p. 4.
25 *Cornet*, 19 April 1900, p. 6.
26 F. C. B., 'Appearance and Behaviour of Bandsmen', *Brass Band News*, n.d., ca. 1899. Cited in, *Amateur Band Teacher's Guide*, p. 75.
27 Robert Poole, 'Lancashire Wakes Week', *History Today* 8.34 (1984), pp. 22–23.

28 Peter Borsay, *A History of Leisure, The British Experience Since 1500* (Basingstoke, Palgrave Macmillan: 2006), p. 208.
29 Chris Aspin, *The First Industrial Society, Lancashire, 1750–1850* (Preston, Carnegie Publishing Ltd: 1995), p. 229.
30 *Accrington Times*, 11 April 1868.
31 Bob Nicholson, 'Musical prize fight, accessed 07 April 2014, http://www.digitalvictorianist.com/2014/02/musical-prize-fight/ and John Hollingshead, 'Musical Prize Fight', *All the Year Round*, 12 November 1859, pp. 65–68. (Quotes about the contest are from this article.)
32 The cornopean was an early piston-valved instrument that was one precursor of the modern cornet.
33 Hollingshead, 'Musical Prize Fight', pp. 65–68.
34 Hollingshead, 'Musical Prize Fight', pp. 65–68.
35 Anon, 'Makkin Mewsic', *Musical Standard* 15.381 (1901), p. 247.
36 Anon, 'Makkin Mewsic', p. 247.
37 Anon, 'Makkin Mewsic', p. 247.
38 Anon, 'Brass Band Contests: A Chat with a Judge', *Magazine of Music*, October 1896, p. 646.
39 *Manchester Times*, 5 June 1886.
40 *Manchester Times*, 5 June 1886.
41 E. P. Thompson, 'The Moral Economy of the Crowd in the Eighteenth Century', *Past and Present* 50 (1971), p. 78.
42 Thompson, 'The Moral Economy of the Crowd in the Eighteenth Century', p. 78.
43 Arthur R. Taylor, *Labour and Love an Oral History of the Brass Band Movement* (London, Elm Tree Books: 1983), p. 9.
44 Accrington Local Studies Library, *Helmshore Brass Band Minute Book*, 13 September 1911.
45 Ben Brierley, *Home Memories and Recollections* (Manchester, n.p., 1862), p. 17.
46 'Westhoughton Old Band', accessed, 26 February 2010, www.boltonrevisited.org.uk/a-whband.html.
47 Helmshore Brass Band Minute Book (31 May 1910).
48 For the working-class Blackpool experience see, for example, John K. Walton, *The Blackpool Landlady: A Social History* (Manchester, Manchester University Press: 1978) and, John K. Walton, *The British Seaside: Holidays and Resorts in the Twentieth Century* (Manchester, Manchester University Press: 2000).
49 *Cornet*, 15 October 1901, p. 6.
50 *Cornet*, 15 October 1901, p. 6.
51 *Musical Standard*, 7 December 1867, p. 359.
52 *Cornet*, 15 October 1901, p. 6.
53 *Cornet*, 15 October 1901, p. 6.
54 *Manchester Guardian* 15 September 1893.
55 *Pall Mall Gazette*, 2 September 1898.

16

STREET LIFE

The Leisure Spaces and Places of Working-class Youth in Britain, c. 1870–1960

Laura Harrison

One Sunday in early January 1954, the Rev. Peter Stanley, senior curate of St. Augustine's Roman Catholic Church in Darlington, County Durham, pronounced in his weekly sermon that the young people parading in the Darlington main streets on the 'monkey walk' had turned the town into a 'flaming jungle'. Father Stanley described to his congregation how 'every night, and Sundays in particular, the parade starts – with young men and women, mostly teenagers, walking up and down', going on to proclaim: 'if you know of a more hybrid collection of spivs, bohunks and yahoos; listless, shifty-eyed, tailor-dummied youths and painted trollops – you would surprise me'.[1] In response to these comments, the *Daily Mirror* sent their reporter Keith Waterhouse for an evening out in 'jungle town', resulting in an article for the paper headlined: 'Why all the fuss, Father Stanley?' Waterhouse explained to readers of the *Mirror* how the town's 'monkey walk' proceeded:

> To do the Monkey Walk you stroll along High Row, up Post House Wynd, past the Friends' Meeting House in Skinnergate and the funfair in Bondgate. The round tour takes about twenty minutes. If you are a girl, you walk the opposite way. The result, of course, is as old as creation – boy meets girl.[2]

While in Darlington, Waterhouse spoke to a number of residents in the town, including local publican Harry Ellis who told the reporter he himself used to parade up and down on the monkey walk when he was young: 'I met my wife there, if you want to know'. Waterhouse observed that while he witnessed a significant group of rather flashily dressed young people gathering in the streets, they certainly did not appear to be 'yahoos' or 'spivs', with many of

DOI: 10.4324/9780429344084-19

the young men having come from an 'honest day's work in the railways or in the mills'. As for the 'painted trollops', Waterhouse noted disdainfully; 'I think Father Stanley must mean that the girls wore make-up'.[3]

Waterhouse was particularly interested in the enduring popularity of the monkey walk, even in the face of increasing competition from commercial leisure opportunities and other provisions for working-class youth, including Darlington's five cinemas, a theatre, two dance halls, forty-seven pubs, a funfair, twenty-four dramatic societies and seventy youth clubs. He spoke to a number of young men and women on the parade:

> I stopped one and asked him why he chose to do so. 'Seventy youth clubs are there?' said eighteen-year-old Frank Webley, a clerk. 'Well, THIS is our club – those streets here. We meet each other and walk round ... we just like to be out on the streets, strolling, talking, meeting friends. What's wrong with that?'.[4]

Out and about in the streets, young people moved around and across the urban environment in search of sociability, fun and relationships, and used central streets and public spaces to meet with friends and potential partners. Informal street-based leisure continued to play a central role in the social lives of many of the young working class, and offered an alternative to an evening at the cinema or a night of dancing. Focusing on the importance of the street as a site of youthful working-class social interaction, this chapter takes one particular social activity, the monkey walk, to examine how the young working class were able to carve out a space of their own in the face of ongoing hostility from other residents and observers. The monkey walk, also known as the 'monkey parade', was a popular youth custom that saw young working people gather and walk up and down particular streets in the evening, socialising with friends, and showing off in front of the opposite sex. In 1936 the *Sheffield Independent* noted: '"monkey parades", I may say for the edification of readers who may be mystified by the term, is a commonly used description of those stretches of streets, to be found in all towns, where youths and girls parade up and down each Sunday night', and certain streets and public spaces gained semi-official recognition as a place for young people to gather and parade.[5]

The monkey parades have received far less attention than the well-publicised fears about the street gangs of the late nineteenth century. Those 'boys and ruffians' who were said to 'possess' the streets garnered numerous column inches, and have been the subject of a significant amount of both popular and academic interest.[6] They have also received less consideration than the media-driven panics about the state of youth in the post-war years, where Teddy Boys were blamed for the outbreak of violence in Nottingham and Notting Hill in 1958. Across the period, debates raged over the best way to deal with young working people and their behaviour on the streets, and anxieties about urban space, masculinity, crime, race, and class were all mapped onto the figure of the hooligan, the delinquent gang member, and the Teddy Boy; though the vast majority of young working people did not join these more formalised youth gangs. As Melanie Tebbutt and others have highlighted, in much of the considerable literature on British youth, the focus has primarily been on the spectacular and the subcultural, rather than the lives and experiences of the majority of young working people.[7]

Much of the work on working-class youth across the period has also overwhelmingly focused on the lives, experiences and regulation of boys and young men. Carol Dyhouse's pioneering work was one of the first to address the distinctive experiences of both working and middle-class girls and young women in the Victorian and Edwardian period, while more recently, Pamela Cox has examined how young women were seen as posing an increasing threat to the social order across the first half of the twentieth century.[8] In the early work on mid-century youth pioneered by sociologists associated with the Centre for Contemporary Cultural Studies (CCCS) in Birmingham, girls were often absent from accounts of what were described as masculine subcultures, an absence not always overtly acknowledged, and something explicitly challenged by feminist scholars at the time.[9] Angela McRobbie suggested that the predominantly masculine narrative of youth in the post-war period was a result of the gendered ownership of cultural space, with young men in the 1950s taking ownership of the public sphere, including the street. Girls, in contrast, created a space for leisure and consumption within the private sphere, which was not a site of compliance but one of subcultural resistance.[10] This suggestion has subsequently been challenged by historians who have highlighted the active participation of girls and young women in a range of public arenas, including the street.[11] By focusing on the street behaviours of young working people, and how young working-class men and women interacted with each other in public spaces, this chapter considers how experience was shaped by gender. Focusing on the everyday experiences of working-class youth culture, it also attempts to shed some light upon what Paul O'Leary described as 'one of the most elusive aspects of urban history'; what actually went on in the streets, and situates the everyday movements of working-class youth as essential to youth culture.[12]

Definitions and descriptions of youth, and the lives and experiences of young working people changed dramatically between 1870 and 1960, reflecting wider developments in the legal, social, and economic status of young people, but over these years, age continued to define working-class experience. The time between starting work and getting married was seen as one of the most prosperous stages of life for the working classes, and youth was marked by a degree of personal independence. In his second social investigation, *Poverty and Progress: A Second Social Survey of York,*

B. Seebohm Rowntree highlighted the affluence of young workers, and oral history respondents and autobiographers have recalled their increased spending money and improved leisure opportunities after starting work but before the responsibilities of a family.[13] Relative freedom allowed young working people to take advantage of leisure opportunities, though material, moral and gender constraints were also central in shaping their experiences and access to the streets. Throughout the period, however, the street continued to be a site for developing working-class youth cultures, and there were continuities both in young people's leisure experiences, and in how this street-based leisure remained a pressing concern for moral reformers and educationalists.

Alongside greater leisure opportunities, courtship also helped to further distinguish young people from their parents or younger siblings; it was an important part of youth, a transitional stage between childhood and adulthood. For young women in particular, courtship represented a negotiation to the next life-cycle stage of marriage, and courting formed a core part of the social activities of the young working class throughout the period discussed in this chapter.[14] As Claire Langhamer has argued, the realm of leisure was particularly correlated with boy-girl, heterosexual, relationships, and courtship was considered a significant rite of passage for both young men and women, especially within a society where marriage was expected.[15] Pearl Jephcott wrote of the one hundred and three girls whose lives formed the basis of her 1946 study *Rising Twenty: Notes on Some Ordinary Girls* that 'boys were their third major preoccupation', noting that 'the first spontaneous subject that the girls bring up, the thing that they want to talk about, and the one topic that is included in even the briefest of their letters has some bearing on a boy friend'.[16] Courtship was, however, to stop short of sexual intercourse, certainly for young women, and anxieties were also expressed about inter-racial relationships.[17] Heterosexual identity as expressed through marriage remained central to constructions of adolescence throughout the period, and as a result courtship, and the social activities associated with it, played a significant role in the lives of many young working-class men and women.

Drawing upon press reports, policing records and institutional documents, this chapter traces the series of contestations between young working people and adult observers that surrounded the monkey parades. These records can shed light on the experiences of the young working-class who gathered in the streets, even as they reveal much about the adults and authorities who interceded in their lives. Descriptions of obstruction, disorderly behaviour and nuisance cases can all give an insight into how young working people utilised the street, and reports of police and juvenile court proceedings often appeared daily in local and regional newspapers. The history of young working people has largely been told through this prism of adult perspectives, and young people's voices can be hard to uncover in the past, especially those of young working-class women. This chapter also draws upon a number of oral history interviews and working-class autobiographies to illuminate the remembered experience of those who were themselves young working people in the very last years of the nineteenth century and first half of the twentieth. This includes interviews from York Oral History Project (YOHP), a collection of over 600 interviews gathered by the York Oral History Society, a group of local historians who have carried out interviews with York residents since 1982.[18] Additional interviews have also been consulted, including the over 450 interviews collected by Paul Thompson as part of his project 'The Edwardians: Family Life and Work Experience Before 1918'.[19] Utilising a range of existing oral history testimony and autobiography has allowed me to examine the memories and recalled experiences of men and women who socialised on the monkey parades, and to consider how adult narrators formed their own understandings of growing up in the streets.

'All dressed up and nowhere to go': The Monkey Parade and Its Critics

> 'Idle promenading in the streets cannot fail to leave its effects on the body and mind. Without suggesting that the results are always grave, I hold that the Sunday "monkey parades" do lead to a considerable amount of immorality. Cases at the City Police Court testify to the fact. The "all dressed up and nowhere to go" feeling is bound to be harmful to young minds.'
>
> *'Monkey parades and morals',* Hull Daily Mail, *4 February 1926*

Town and city centre thoroughfares were the setting for everyday social activities, and young working-class men and women took to the streets to saunter, gossip with companions, window shop, and flirt with one another. Streets offered a number of advantages both for younger teens and young wage earners in their early twenties; they were accessible, useful meeting places – both pre-arranged and spontaneous – and they were important routes between sites of both work and pleasure. Social commentators across the period recognised the importance of the streets for working-class youth. In 1886, Walter Besant noted the 'new pleasures' of the streets, where young people could 'talk and play, unrestrained, left wholly to themselves'.[20] In his early twentieth-century investigation, S. F. Jackson argued that as adolescents began to develop their own private lives, they increasingly looked towards the streets: 'life throbs in the streets! It is there the new born social instincts can find satisfaction'.[21] In the 1950s, T. R. Fyvel noted that the Teddy Boys he observed in his neighbourhood were not too interested in television, and instead spent their leisure time on the streets.[22] At the same time, youthful behaviour in these public streets could appear to adult observers as incomprehensible, unsuitable, and even threatening. There were certain street activities which drew the direct attention of the authorities, with tensions between adults and working-class youth that were a product of class and age, as well as gender. In the course of their leisure time, some young people found themselves in the path of the policeman walking his beat, and young working-class men and women appeared before the magistrates charged with a variety of offences; obstruction of a footpath, using obscene language, playing football in the street, being drunk and disorderly, fighting, using insulting behaviour, or assaulting a police officer, resulting in punishments ranging from a small fine to incarceration with hard labour.[23] Some young women found themselves approached by a middle-class rescue worker, or escorted by a police constable or moral welfare officer to one of the many charitable and state female reform homes across Britain.[24] Other reformers hoped to divert young working people away from street life and commercial leisure venues altogether, by providing alternative 'rational' and 'improving' recreation, and promoting membership of uniformed youth organisations and youth clubs. Despite these efforts, town and city centre streets were populated by young working people who gathered outside cinemas, dance halls and coffee bars, and socialised and flirted on the monkey parade. The street was an accessible, convenient place, and continued to be an important leisure space for the young; it was one autonomous space that young working people were able to carve out for themselves.[25]

The monkey parades saw working-class youth gather on particular central streets across Britain to parade, socialise with friends, and show off in front of the opposite sex. In the middle decades of the nineteenth century, the young working class of Liverpool gathered on the Landing Stages at George's Pier on the Mersey to promenade, much to the disgust of a local journalist who wrote of the 'permitted indecency and immorality on the Landing Stage'. Almost one hundred years later, a correspondent complained about the parades in the *Liverpool Evening Express,* noting that 'surely the young people must be lacking in imagination if all they can think of is to "mooch" about the streets'.[26] In the 1870s the *East London Observer* discussed the monkey parade on Bow Road, describing scenes of 'vulgarity, rudeness, and immorality', and providing one of the earliest uses of the term 'monkey parade' in the press.[27] By 1904, one journalist noted how 'it has grown into a weekly institution in all large towns has this social parade on Sunday night', and oral history respondents also emphasised the dominance of the 'monkey parade' in the working-class social calendar.[28] In his second social investigation of York, Rowntree highlighted how:

> The main street was so thronged with [young working people] that it was difficult to make one's way through it and a number of policemen were required to keep people moving and to prevent the horseplay between

> youths and girls becoming too obstreperous. Youths used to boast about how many girls they had 'got off with' during the evening.[29]

In 1956, the *Edinburgh Evening News* continued to report on the 'Sunday night spectacle' of 'hundreds of teenagers' parading the streets on the 'monkey parade', and Maureen Reynolds, who grew up in post-war Dundee, recalled the 'hundreds of people' that walked up and down Overgate.[30]

The parades were an early form of identifiable youth culture, with young working-class men and women differentiating their behaviour from adults by gathering in particular public spaces.[31] The *Oxford English Dictionary* defines 'monkey parade' as 'an evening parade of young people especially for the purpose of meeting members of the opposite sex' and notes it was chiefly a dismissive term.[32] The use of 'monkey' certainly implies mischievous behaviour, and perhaps murkier connotations of young people behaving in a way that was seen as debasing or regressive, with hints towards racial degeneration. This reading is supported by some discussions of the term in the press, with the *Birmingham Daily Gazette* arguing in 1932 that taking a stroll along one of the city's parades confirmed that 'both sexes had degenerated since the war' and where the 'silly inane chatter reminds one forcibly of the zoo'.[33] The *Yorkshire Evening Post* commented that the term 'monkey parade' was 'rather an insult to the well-behaved members of the simian species'.[34] The 'monkey parade' was also known by a range of alternative names, including 'monkey run', 'monkey walk', 'bunny run', 'chicken run', and 'hen walk', and these local variations similarly imply mischief making on the part of the paraders.[35] While these terms were used by the parades' critics, they were also regularly used by the participants themselves. Mrs Radnell discussed the parade in Arnold, Nottingham where she met her husband; 'it used to be called the "monkey run", down there'. John Allan told the YOHP that 'you just simply walked up and down the "monkey run"' and in her memoir of growing up in Dundee, Maureen Reynolds recalled her fondness for the 'monkey parade' every Sunday night.[36] Naming their activities was an important means by which young working people were able to claim possession, of both the act of promenading, and the street itself.

The parades could simply be a means of socialising with friends, but they were often seen as a useful way to meet a potential partner. Commentators discussed the centrality of the parades to working-class courtship, with Arnold Freeman noting in 1914: 'we should remember that it is nearly always in the street that the working boy makes the acquaintance of the girl he will afterwards marry'.[37] Unlike dance halls or coffee bars, participation was free, as long as a parader was already in possession of suitable clothing. The prevalence of unattached members of the opposite sex made parading better for picking up than the cinema, and it was a definite focus: 'many a romance started from raiking' [Yorkshire dialect word for parading].[38] For

Matt Houlbrook, the 'monkey parade' was the heterosexual equivalent of homosexual cruising, predicated as it was on moving through defined city spaces, gazing and searching for contact.[39] Many couples, once courting, drifted away from the parades and walked out together in different parts of the city: 'later on, when it sort of developed as something more serious then we used to meet and go to the pictures'.[40]

The monkey parades were subject to sporadic police attention from their outset, and faced criticism from a range of observers. As J. B. Priestly observed in *English Journey*, 'ever since I can remember, elderly citizens have been protesting against this practice of promenading on Sunday nights. They have always been disgusted by the sight of young people "monkey parading" in this fashion'.[41] Young men and women on the parades were observed; by the policeman stationed to keep them moving, by 'concerned' citizens and ratepayers, by journalists, and by representatives of the civic authorities. Other users of the street could find themselves jostled off the footpath, witness coarse behaviour, or be exposed to obscene language. The *Daily Telegraph and Courier* reported on the 'fine art' practised by young paraders in 'pushing people off the pathways, or bumping them against the shutters, or suddenly swinging from a lamppost and butting a pedestrian in the stomach'.[42] The 'idle and senseless' nature of 'loafing up and down' busy central streets attracted the attention of concerned 'ratepayers', who wrote to the local press complaining about the state of central streets on Saturday and Sunday evenings, and the activities of the young people gathered there.[43] Commenting on the 'disgraceful proceedings' of young men and women in the central streets of York, the Lord Mayor noted that the young working class 'seemed to think that they could take the streets under their control. They must be taught that they could not do so, and the citizens must be protected against the nuisance'.[44] In Burnley, the local press asked their readers to consider the town's central streets on a Sunday night: 'hundreds of young people wandering aimlessly for hours, handicapping pedestrians, police, and even vehicular traffic'.[45] For these commentators, the streets were no longer thoroughfares, but spaces in which young working-class men and women could gather and flout conventions.

The parades also exerted an element of fascination for local journalists, and others who felt the need to witness the parades with their own eyes. These accounts demonstrate an intermingling of disgust and attraction over youthful use of space, particularly on the part of those who spent numerous evenings observing working-class behaviour on the parades. In 1937 one Mass Observer diarist wrote at length about his local parade in Bedford, which he declared 'worthy of a special Mass Observation'.[46] As with concerned residents and correspondents, many press reports focused on young people's behaviour on the parades as being out of place. Young working-class men and women were condemned for 'invading' the 'principal and most respectable thoroughfares'.[47] In 1895, the *Yorkshire Evening Post* commented on the ability of the young paraders to turn a respectable, central thoroughfare into 'a howling wilderness', and another journalist reported how young people in 1904 '*converted* Robertson Street into a kind of social centre on Sunday night' [emphasis added].[48] These concerns about the ability of young people to compromise space continued later into the twentieth century, and journalists maintained their observations of the streets. In 1939, one journalist who styled himself as 'onlooker' argued that the 'hobble-de-hoy' type of young people were 'uncouth' anywhere, but that in the 'public streets' they were 'particularly obnoxious'.[49] By 1957, a journalist for the *Burton Observer and Chronicle* reported on the 'gangs of youths and girls who on Sunday evenings *take possession* of the High Street', complaining that at times it was difficult to pass through the streets 'due to the surging throng' [emphasis added].[50] Young men and women were 'taking over' city centre streets and claiming public space in a way that challenged adult middle-class perceptions of it. Criticisms of their behaviour suggest a lack of understanding of, or appreciation for, the importance of the street to the social lives of young working people.

'Not fit for decent girls': Young Working-class Women and the Parades

> It is very unbecoming of the young women who race backwards and forwards [on the monkey run], giggling and behaving like lunatics rather than respectable young ladies, and I think they ought to be thoroughly ashamed of themselves.
>
> Sheffield Evening Telegraph, *2 February 1909*

While criticisms of the parade were clearly both class and age based, and focused on specific spatial practices, they were also gendered. The potentially sexualised nature of the interactions between young men and women made the parades seem particularly threatening to many observers, and expectations and concerns about youthful use of space reflected the prevailing gender ideology. Young women were in the minority of those who appeared before the courts charged with offences, yet their behaviour in the streets was closely monitored, and female delinquency continued to be stereotyped in sexual terms in the middle decades of the twentieth century, much as it had at the start of the period. Expressions of sexuality among young women were perceived to transgress both gender and class boundaries, with regulatory strategies that 'aimed to moralise rather than criminalise'.[51] Jenny Birchall has examined criticisms of young women on the Oldham Street parades in nineteenth-century Manchester, and the apparent eagerness of young women to contribute to ribald jests in their interactions with young men were a particular worry to middle-class moralists across Britain in this period.[52] In 1954, Father Stanley's remarks focused particularly on what he described as the 'open, unashamed and deplorable ... flaunting of sex' on the evening parades, and the young female participants came in for particular criticism, for wearing 'enough paint on to paint a battleship and enough powder to blow us to smithereens'.[53] Young working-class women were subject to forms of policing and surveillance that were specific to them, and often regarded as both more vulnerable than boys, and therefore in need of protection, but also more morally deviant and disorderly.

Letters of complaint and police reports on the monkey parade suggest that young women's behaviour was under constant scrutiny, and Father Stanley's comments in 1954 were reminiscent of earlier complaints about the behavior of young women on the parades. In Liverpool, Hugh Shimmin noted that the young women who were attracted by 'the game of the Landing Stage' with 'their gaudy dress, rude speeches and unseemly conduct' were not yet 'social evils', but were well on their way to becoming outcasts from decent society. Concerns were expressed about young women gleefully embracing the bad language of boys, reflecting the opportunities the parades presented for 'unladylike' behaviour. One aggrieved correspondent wrote to the *Hull Daily Mail* about his 'annoyance and disgust' over the 'bad language used by girls' on the parades, and young female paraders in Sheffield were described as 'lunatics' who ought to be 'thoroughly ashamed of themselves'.[54] Young working-class women were seen as employing masculine characteristics, swearing and instigating sexualised encounters. The *Daily Herald* wrote of the girls wandering up and down, 'their eyes flashing invitation to the young men as they brushed by'.[55] In Plymouth, one member of the Board of Guardians declared: 'the devil, it is said, finds work for idle hands to do, and many of the promiscuous acquaintances formed during those idle perambulations are responsible for the troubles with which we, as members of the Board of Guardians, are confronted'.[56] The language used to describe these young female paraders reinforced the perception of them as lacking respectability, and confirmed that their presence in the streets was seen as threatening to the social and moral order. Others focused on the moral dangers for young women represented by the parades. In Harrow, local residents petitioned the council to put a stop to the 'unseemly behaviour' on the parades, complaining that 'it really was not fit for decent girls to go along the road on a Sunday night'.[57]

The parades were a form of performance; one which involved particularly gendered routines and displays. Andrew Davies found in Manchester and Salford that girls were far from passive in the process of 'clicking', and it was the displays put on by young women and girls that provoked the harshest criticism.[58] For young men, disorderly offences could be overlooked, or put down to youthful high spirits. It seemed inevitable that boys would be 'a nuisance', and seek female companions, but the behaviour of young women was seen as more subversive. In Manchester, Charles Russell described the young men who took part in the parades as merely adhering to 'what is the fashion of their kind' and that 'making an acquaintance' with a girl was a 'feather in their caps'.[59] This attitude remained remarkably persistent, and was apparent among some police officers in the later twentieth century: 'a lad should be allowed to sow his wild oats'.[60] In addition to anxieties about their own behaviour on the monkey parades, female paraders were also held responsible for the conduct of the young men they associated with. In Clapham, one police constable complained about the parade on St John's Road, arguing that 'the lasses incited the lads to make a disturbance', while in Hull, 'Tracker' claimed that 'the influence of a girl who possess a bad character will drive a boy to further harm.[61]

'Was it fun? I'll say it was!' The Parades as an Everyday Social Activity

> We walked up and down the Overgate along with hundreds of people, just looking and speaking to folk. It was stupid really but we loved it.
>
> *Maureen Reynolds,* Voices in the Streets, *p. 236*

Journalists, the police and concerned observers continued to question the monkey parade and young people's use of the streets throughout the period, though into the twentieth century increasingly more balanced voices were also heard. George A. Greenwood followed parades in Leeds, Wakefield, Dewsbury and Batley in the early 1920s, and concluded 'nothing I saw among the enormous crowds in those four towns struck me as being either improper or indecent'. Though the young men and women on the parades were a 'formidable block' to other pedestrians, 'the suggestion that these young men are all libertines and those young women are all unfortunates is a foul aspersion upon thousands of clean-minded and clean-living mill workers, shop assistants, clerks, teachers and the like'.[62] As Charles Russell noted of the parades in Manchester: 'sometimes there is an element of roughness, sometimes there is a measure of disorder, sometimes a considerable degree of coarseness in the remarks which are passed, on the other hand, there is much harmless enjoyment'.[63] 'Fancy Free' in the *Burnley Express* argued in 1936 that the parades had been taking place 'for many a generation', and criticised the 'wholesale and indiscriminate, and often unfair' condemnation of the paraders. While promenading may indeed have been senseless and a waste of leisure time, he reminded his readers that that many of the parades most vocal critics may even have 'done a bit themselves', concluding that paraders were simply 'merry and thoughtless'.[64] The *Leeds Mercury* reported in 1938 that 'some people call it monkey parading, but why use such a scoffing expression? Why should young people not enjoy seeing each other in their finery and getting to know each other?'[65] Keith Waterhouse's contemptuous reporting of Father Stanley's comments, particularly about young women on the parade, suggest that the strict gendered classification of behaviour on the parade were also becoming increasingly difficult to maintain.

The behaviour of young men and women on the monkey parades evidently provoked concerns and criticisms, but the condemnation of the parades expressed in newspaper correspondence, proclaimed by middle-class observers, and heard at court was not the only narrative of this social activity. Despite criticisms of their behaviour, young people continued to use the streets as a venue to parade and socialise, and a participant-based viewpoint offered by oral history respondents, autobiographers, and those young paraders who wrote to the press provides an alternative version to the use of this space. Fred Milburn, who paraded in his youth, and later was responsible for observing the parades as a police constable in York recalled:

> I was one of them, oh yes, as I say, until you were sixteen or eighteen or nineteen [Coney Street] was where everybody congregated. All the youths and lasses used to congregate there. That was, as I say, the main parade ground, especially on a Sunday.[66]

Young working-class residents often felt a clear sense of attachment to, and ownership of, the streets, and their occupation of these spaces was both an act of identification and differentiation. This ownership was often temporary, could be fragile, and was often disrupted by other users of the street, but it is important to briefly imagine the streets through the eyes of the young men and women who used it in this way.

Many of the young working class did not see the parades as sensational or scandalous, but simply as an everyday social activity. They made use of the streets and central thoroughfares in their daily lives. In 1910 following a spate of letters and commentaries on the parades in Sheffield, one young woman wrote to the *Sheffield Evening Telegraph* to call out the unfair criticism: 'we work hard during the week and want a bit of a run round on Sundays'.[67] One correspondent, signed 'A Young Person', argued that the attempts by the police to move paraders on was having a detrimental effect on the relationship between young working people and the police: 'instead of making the rising generation look up to and respect the police, it is making us hate them'.[68] In 1939 one young man wrote to the *Northants Evening Telegraph* to 'state the case for the defence' of the parades, arguing that it was 'the most natural thing in the world' for young people of both sexes to meet together 'unrestricted and quite apart from their elders'. One ex-parader argued 'I don't walk the "bunny run" as there is no need, for I am married and have a car these days, but I remember all too well the time I used to, and was it fun? I'll say it was!'.[69]

Young people did not lack self-regulation on the parades. They developed their own rules of participation and entry. Care was taken over appearance and dress. What constituted respectability for the young men and women involved in the parades may not have been recognised by outsiders, but young people were adhering to their own values. One correspondent to the *Sheffield Evening Telegraph* commented sneeringly on the 'girls with their cheap and gaudy dress, and men in the latest cut of the 20s and a "perfect fit" suit'. However, for the young working-class men and women involved, wearing 'Sunday Best', doing hair and wearing make-up helped to address the sense of performance of the monkey walk, and one young parader responded to these complaints noting: 'we shop girls dress as we can afford and be as bright as we can be'.[70] Behaviour considered too rough was not accepted by the other paraders, and the parades offered a chance to flirt and socialise, in a way that was not taken altogether seriously. As Mrs Allan cheerfully recalled to the YOHP, she went to Coney Street 'looking for some talent (laughs)!' Mrs Duckers, who promenaded in her youth, noted that in Highgate young people would walk around the bandstand, 'give one another the eyes you know – a bit of fun, that's all'.[71] Brad Beaven has noted that male youths demonstrated a remarkable propensity to manipulate and customise their surroundings, gathering in city centre spaces to flout moral codes.[72] The behaviour of young women, however, was clearly seen as more subversive, and thus their ability to manipulate their surroundings must also be highlighted.

By continuing to occupy the space of the monkey parade, young working-class men and women engaged in an ongoing process of establishing claims to the use and enjoyment of public space, and increasingly challenged outsiders' interpretations of it. The young working class saw these central thoroughfares as sites of social engagement, and the streets formed an important, if not central, element of their social lives. These streets and public spaces could be a space over which young people had a powerful influence. The young working class claimed these central streets as their own on Saturday and Sunday evenings, and paraded up and down, away from parental supervision, often under the watchful eye of a police constable or two, or perhaps a local journalist, noting down street customs and commenting on their behaviour.

Conclusion

Young people traversed the central streets of the city in ways that differentiated them by both class and age, carving out spaces of sociability which they increasingly defined as their own. The central districts of larger towns and cities remained increasingly significant to youthful working-class leisure across the period, and young people negotiated their transition to adulthood in the streets. Alongside class and age, experiences of and access to the streets was also shaped by gender, and young women could be particularly vulnerable to moral regulation. Like their male counterparts, they had to contend with the spatial constraints imposed by adults and moral reformers, but unlike male youths they also had to deal with gendered ideals of femininity that further restricted their public behaviour. Despite this, girls and young working-class women continued to socialise and flirt on the monkey parade, and it was their behaviour – seen as especially subversive – that demonstrated the remarkable abilities of the young working class to manipulate their surroundings.

Much historical work on working-class youth has focused on the more spectacular confrontations over space, but this chapter has considered how the young working class who paraded up and down used city centre streets and spaces in the course of their more everyday experiences. By demanding central streets as their own on Saturday and Sunday evenings, and using the monkey parade as a venue to socialise with friends, display fashion and independence from parental authority, as well as search for a potential partner, young people made a distinct claim on these spaces. They used central streets and public spaces in a particular way, and in doing so differentiated their behaviour from adults. Young working-class men and women on the parades were able to make their own conventions, and the monkey parades are an important example of young working people creating their own, distinct, culture of the street, representing the spatial autonomy of working-class youth.

Notes

1 'Parade of Wrath', *Yorkshire Evening Post,* 6 January 1954; 'Youth "at shrine of Ava Gardner"', *Daily Mirror,* 6 January 1954 and 'Why All the Fuss, Father Stanley?', *Daily Mirror*, 9 January 1954.
2 'Why All the Fuss, Father Stanley?', *Daily Mirror*, 9 January 1954.
3 'Why All the Fuss, Father Stanley?', *Daily Mirror*, 9 January 1954.
4 'Why All the Fuss, Father Stanley?', *Daily Mirror*, 9 January 1954.
5 'Monkey parades', *Sheffield Independent,* 17 November 1936.
6 In Birmingham the town clerk suggested that 'the town was in the possession of boys and ruffians'. *Birmingham Daily Gazette*, 14 March 1874. See Philip Gooderson and Carl Chinn for work on the sloggers and Peaky Blinders of Birmingham, Andrew Davies for work on the Scuttling gangs of Manchester and Salford, Rob Sindall for gangs of Liverpool, and Davies for Glasgow gangs. Geoffrey Pearson and Drew Gray have written about the London hooligan gangs. Philip Gooderson, '"Noisy and Dangerous Boys": The Slogging Gang Phenomenon in Late Nineteenth-Century Birmingham', *Midland History* 38.1 (2013), pp. 58–79; Carl Chinn, *Peaky Blinders: The Real Story of Birmingham's Most Notorious Gangs* (London, John Blake Publishing: 2019); Andrew Davies, 'Youth Gangs, Masculinity and Violence in Late Victorian Manchester and Salford', *Journal of Social History* 32.2 (1998), pp. 349–369; Andrew Davies, *The Gangs of Manchester: The Story of the Scuttlers – Britain's First Youth Cult* (Manchester, Milo Books: 2011); Rob Sindall, *Street Violence in the Nineteenth Century: Media Panic or Real Danger?* (Leicester, Leicester University Press: 1990); Geoffrey Pearson, *Hooligan: A History of Respectable Fears* (Basingstoke, Macmillan: 1983) and Drew Gray, 'Gang Crime and the Media in Late Nineteenth-Century

London: The Regent's Park Murder of 1888', *Cultural and Social History* 10.4 (2013), pp. 559–575.

7 Melanie Tebbutt, *Being Boys: Youth, Leisure and Identity in the Interwar Years* (Manchester, Manchester University Press: 2012). See also Laura Harrison, *Dangerous Amusements: Leisure, the Young Working Class and Urban Space in Britain, c.1870–1939* (Manchester, Manchester University Press: 2022) and Sarah Kenny, *Growing Up and Going out: Youth Culture, Commerce, and Leisure Space in Post-War Britain* (Manchester, Manchester University Press: forthcoming).

8 Carol Dyhouse, *Girls Growing Up in Late Victorian and Edwardian England* (London, Routledge: 1979) and Pamela Cox, *Gender, Justice and Welfare in Britain,1900–1950: Bad Girls in Britain, 1900–1950* (Basingstoke, Palgrave Macmillan: 2003).

9 For example, John Clarke and Tony Jefferson, 'Working Class Youth Cultures', in Geoff Mungham and Geoff Pearson (eds.), *Working Class Youth Culture* (London, Routledge & Kegan Paul: 1976), pp. 138–158; Stuart Hall and Tony Jefferson, eds., *Resistance through Rituals: Youth Subcultures in Post-War Britain* (London, HarperCollins Academic: 1975); Dick Hebdige, *Subculture: The Meaning of Style* (London, Methuen: 2002. Originally published 1979); P. Rock and S. Cohen, 'The Teddy Boy', in Vernon Bognanor and Robert Skidelsky (eds.), *The Age of Affluence: 1951–1964* (London, Macmillan: 1970).

10 Angela McRobbie, *Feminism and Youth Culture: From Jackie to Just Seventeen* (London, Macmillan: 1991), p. 14.

11 Bill Osgerby, *Youth in Britain since 1945* (Oxford, Blackwell: 1998), p. 57 and Louise A. Jackson, 'The Coffee Club Menace: Policing Youth, Leisure and Sexuality in Post-War Manchester', *Cultural and Social History* 5.3 (2008), p. 292.

12 Paul O'Leary, *Claiming the Streets: Processions and Urban Culture in South Wales c.1830–1880* (Cardiff, University of Wales Press: 2012), p. 6. See also Leif Jerram's call to write history through street life. Leif Jerram, *Streetlife: The Untold History of Europe's Twentieth Century* (Oxford, Oxford University Press: 2013).

13 B. Seebohm Rowntree, *Poverty and Progress: A Second Social Survey of York* (London, Longmans: 1941), pp. 329–449.

14 Claire Langhamer, 'Love and Courtship in Mid-Twentieth Century England', *The Historical Journal* 50.1 (2007), p. 175 and Harrison, *Dangerous Amusements*, pp. 46–56.

15 Claire Langhamer, *Women's Leisure in England, 1920–1960* (Manchester, Manchester University Press: 2000), p. 113.

16 Pearl Jephcott, *Rising Twenty: Notes on Some Ordinary Girls* (London, Faber: 1948), pp. 17, 65.

17 For example, when discussing the causes of rioting in Liverpool in 1919, *The Times* closed their description of the 'recrudescence of the racial fights' with a consideration of relationships between black men and white women: 'the intermarriage of black men and white women, not to mention other relationships, had excited much feeling'. 'Black and white at Liverpool: Sunday night outbreak', *The Times,* 10 June 1919. In 1954, one 15-year-old girl appeared before the Lambeth Juvenile Court for associating with a '19-year old coloured man, in spite of her parents' objections', 'Girl, 15, went out with colour youth', *South Western Star,* 8 October 1954.

18 'York Oral History Society', accessed 9 April 2021, www.yorkoralhistory.org.uk.

19 The Edwardians: Family Life and Work Experience Before 1918, 1870–1973.

20 Walter Besant, 'From Thirteen to Seventeen', *Contemporary Review*, 49 (1886), p. 417.

21 S. F. Jackson, 'The New Scholar' in J. J. Findlay (eds.), *The Young Wage Earner and the Problem of His Education, Essays and Reports* (London, Sidwick and Jackson: 1918), pp. 50–52.

22 T. R. Fyvel, *The Insecure Offenders: Rebellious Youth in the Welfare State* (Middlesex, Penguin: 1964), p. 76.
23 For example: 'The juvenile offender', *Globe*, 26 July 1884; *Kilburn Times*, 'The pests of the street', 19 August 1898; 'Sunday night obstructions', *Nelson Leader*, 20 February 1920; 'Young woman's drunkenness', *Hartlepool Northern Daily Mail,* 21 August 1929; 'Young Chester offenders: fines on youths who threw stones and kicked doors', *Liverpool Echo,* 26 November 1930; interview with Charles Mulligan, born 1902, 2000int257, The Edwardians; 'A gang of 30 youths armed with bottles', *South London Observer,* 12 August 1954; York Explore Archives (YEA): Police Files, Service and Character Books, Acc. 236.23.12.13, Henry Barker.
24 In 1915 the York Penitentiary Society sheltering home noted 'by far the greater number of those [young women] being dealt with have been brought by the police having been found wandering about late at night'. YEA, York Penitentiary Society, PEN/3/4, Loose Annual Reports, 1915.
25 Gill Valentine, *Public Space and the Culture of Childhood* (Aldershot, Ashgate: 2004), p. 85.
26 Hugh Shimmin, 'Sunday Night on the Landing Stage' in John K. Walton and Alastair Wilcox (eds.), *Low Life and Moral Improvement in mid-Victorian England: Liverpool through the Journalism of High Shimmin* (Leicester, Leicester University Press: 1991), p. 88 and 'Church commentary: "the monkey parade"', *Liverpool Evening Express,* 21 March 1940.
27 'The Mile End Boulevard on Sunday Night', *East London Observer*, 23 August 1879.
28 'On Parade: A Sunday Night in Burnley', *Burnley Express,* 13 February 1904. For example: 'that was, as I say, the main parade ground, especially on a Sunday'. Interview with Fred Milburn, born 1894, YOHP.
29 B. Seebohm Rowntree, *Poverty and Progress: A Second Social Survey of York* (London, Longmans: 1941), p. 469.
30 'For Teenagers', *Edinburgh Evening News,* 10 May 1956 and Maureen Reynolds, *Voices in the Street: Growing up in Dundee* (Edinburgh, Black & White: 2006), p. 236.
31 Harrison, *Dangerous Amusements*, pp. 181–214.
32 *OED,* 'monkey parade'.
33 *Birmingham Daily Gazette*, 1 March 1932.
34 'What about Briggate?', *Yorkshire Evening Post*, 26 May 1896.
35 For example, see 'Hear All Sides: Is Youth Being Kept under?', *Birmingham Daily Gazette,* 4 March 1932; 'Doom of the "bunny run"', *Shipley Times and Express,* 29 August 1924, 'Sunday Night Parades', *Burnley Express,* 26 May 1937.
36 Interviews with Mrs Radnell, 2000int220, The Edwardians and John Allan, born 1912, YOHP. Reynolds, *Voices in the Street*, p. 236.
37 Arnold Freeman, *Boy Life and Labour: The Manufacture of Inefficiency* (London, P. S. King & Son: 1914), p. 152. Andrew Davies notes that in Manchester and Salford, the 'monkey parades' were without parallel as a means of meeting unattached members of the opposite sex. Andrew Davies, *Leisure, Gender and Poverty: Working-Class Culture in Salford and Manchester, 1900–1939* (Buckingham, Open University Press: 1992), p. 102.
38 Interview with Vera Tomlinson, born 1916, YOHP.
39 Matt Houlbrook, *Queer London: Perils and Pleasures in the Sexual Metropolis, 1918–1957* (Chicago, IL, University of Chicago Press: 2006), p. 67.
40 Interview with Alice Hick, born 1901, YOHP.
41 J. B. Priestly, *English Journey* (London, Gollancz: 1934), p. 183.
42 'London Day by Day', *Daily Telegraph and Courier*, 25 December 1897.

43 'Correspondence', *York Herald*, 21 November 1890.
44 'Sunday Evenings in York: A Caution to Youths', *York Herald*, 24 March 1882.
45 'Burnley's Monkey Parade', *Burnley Express*, 19 September 1936.
46 Mass Observation, Day Survey Writer 249, Day Survey for Sunday 18 September 1937.
47 'The Monkey's Parade – Disgraceful Scenes', *East London Observer*, 3 March 1888.
48 'Yorkshire Echoes', *Yorkshire Evening Post*, 2 April 1895 and 'On Parade: A Sunday Night in Burnley', *Burnley Express*, 13 February 1904.
49 'Out and about', *Uxbridge and West Drayton Gazette*, 28 April 1939.
50 *Burton Observer and Chronicle*, 31 October 1957.
51 Cox, *Gender, Justice and Welfare in Britain*, p. 55.
52 Jenny Birchall, '"The carnival revels of Manchester's vagabonds": Young Working-Class Women and Monkey Parades in the 1870s', *Women's History Review* 15.2 (2006), p. 235.
53 'Parade of Wrath', *Yorkshire Evening Post*, 6 January 1954; 'Youth "at shrine of Ava Gardner"', *Daily Mirror*, 6 January 1954 and 'Why All the Fuss, Father Stanley?', *Daily Mirror*, 9 January 1954.
54 'Letters to the Editor: Hull Street Scenes', *Hull Daily Mail*, 19 February 1923 and *Sheffield Evening Telegraph*, 2 February 1909.
55 'Tales That Enthral', *Daily Herald*, 24 May 1928.
56 'No Sunday Kinemas', *Western Morning News*, 24 January 1929.
57 YEA, York Penitentiary Society, PEN/3/3 Annual Reports 1886–1906, 1902 and 'Station Road: Sunday night scenes', *Uxbridge and West Drayton Gazette*, 23 December 1921.
58 Davies, *Leisure, Gender and Poverty*, 103.
59 Charles Russell, *Manchester Boys: Sketches of Manchester Lads at Work and Play* (Manchester, Manchester University Press: 1905), p. 116.
60 Miss Barker, Chief Superintendent of the Metropolitan Women Police, September 1962, cited in Louise. A. Jackson and Angela Bartie, *Policing Youth in Britain, 1945–1970* (Manchester, Manchester University Press: 2014), p. 66.
61 'The Monkey Parade at Clapham Junction', *South London Press*, 18 April 1896 and *Hull Daily Mail*, 27 October 1917.
62 'An Impression of Sunday Night Parades in West Riding', *Yorkshire Evening Post*, 26 October 1922.
63 Charles Russell, *Social Problems of the North* (London, Garland Publishing Inc: 1980 [1913]), p. 102.
64 'Random Reflection by "Fancy Free"', *Burnley Express*, 3 October 1936.
65 'It Seems to Me', *Leeds Mercury*, 25 January 1938.
66 Interview with Fred Milburn, born 1894, YOHP.
67 'The Monkeys Parade', *Sheffield Evening Telegraph*, 20 September 1910.
68 'Letters to the Editor', *Hull Daily Mail*, 28 October 1907.
69 'Rushden Youth: Safety Valve of the Parade', *Northants Evening Telegraph*, 1 February 1939 and 'Married Woman's Reminder', *Northants Evening Telegraph*, 26 January 1939.
70 'The Monkeys Parade', *Sheffield Evening Telegraph*, 17 September 1910; 'These Commons! Discoveries at the Avenue at Clapham', *Norwood News*, 16 May 1930 and *Sheffield Evening Telegraph*, 20 September 1910.
71 Interviews with Mrs Allan, born 1912, YOHP and Mrs Duckers, born 1892, 2000int003, The Edwardians.
72 Brad Beaven, *Leisure, Citizenship and Working-Class Men in Britain, 1850–1945* (Manchester, Manchester University Press: 2005), pp. 117–118.

17

COAL MINERS IN THE INDUSTRIALISATION AND DEINDUSTRIALISATION OF FRANCE AND GERMANY

A Comparative Synthesis of the Nord/Pas-de-Calais and the Ruhr

Brian Shaev

About a month before the 2017 German federal elections, *The Financial Times* published a long article, titled 'Germany: the hidden divide in Europe's richest country'. The article profiled Gelsenkirchen, a former coal city that lies almost exactly in the centre of the de-industrialised Ruhr valley, the former epicentre of Germany's coal economy. Gelsenkirchen, the article points out, had a 14.7% unemployment rate, nearly triple the national average, and among the lowest household incomes and health standards in the country.[1] Four day later, the FT followed up with another article about Gelsenkirchen. The German Social Democratic Party (SPD), which has long been the dominant party in local and national elections in the city, had lost the credibility to defend a message based on reducing social inequalities according to former coal miners interviewed for the story. In regional elections, the SPD vote sank from 57% in 2012 in Gelsenkirchen to 38% in 2017, while the far-right Alternativ für Deutschland (AfD) scored 15%, among its largest successes at that time outside of the states of the former Eastern Germany. The FT quotes a former coal miner who switched from the SPD to the AfD, and who is a local official down the road in the Ruhr city of Essen. He exaggerated the shift by stating that, 'The SPD was no longer the party of the workers – the AfD is'.[2]

While 15% of the vote is a significant local success for a far-right party in Western Germany, the political transformation from left to right of the Nord/Pas-de-Calais, the principal mining region of France, has been developing for a far longer period of time and has advanced much further, particularly in the Pas-de-Calais. Socialist Party strongholds until the 1930s and then Communist Party fiefdoms for much of the postwar period, the far-right

DOI: 10.4324/9780429344084-20

Front National made major gains in the area beginning in the 1980s. In the second round of the 2017 presidential elections, the Pas-de-Calais was the only department of France other than the nearby Aisne in which FN leader Marine le Pen defeated now-President Emmanuel Macron (she expanded on her success in the region in 2022).[3] In the legislative elections that followed, the FN won four of the ten districts in the area, half of its total victories in all of France.[4] Marine le Pen entered the National Assembly for the first time as a representative of Hénin-Beaumont, formerly Hénin-Liétard, which includes Courrières, once the site of the largest mining company in France. Perhaps even more emblematic of the changes that have occurred, the district to the west, which includes the famous former mining town of Lens, was picked up for the FN by José Évrard, a former communist party official who bears the family name of several generations of mining leaders who directed the Lens region in local and national office until the Second World War under the ticket of the Socialist Party.

As the coal mines of France and Germany closed in jolting stages from the 1960s to 2000s, there has been a sense that these former mining communities, once almost synonymous with the working class and with national industrial power, have exited history. At the least, they have largely exited public consciousness, until recently. Before the coal industry entered a period of terminal decline in the 1960s, these communities were not only at the forefront of domestic politics, for instance the development of social welfare institutions and labour politics, but also were at the heart of geopolitical conflict because the material miners were extracting, coal, fueled the engines of industrialising economies. Considerable hardship and pain came to the regions, traumas that amplified the periodic tragedies of what was already a dangerous and sometimes deadly occupation. The German occupation of the French mining basin during the First World War, the French occupation of the Ruhr area during the invasion of 1923–1924, a second and more brutal German occupation of the French northern mines in the Second World War, all opened wounds between peoples and nations and, in France, between employers and employees. The geopolitical conflict remained during the Allied occupation of Germany and was finally more or less resolved by the Schuman Plan of 1950 and the creation of the European Coal and Steel Community, the objective of which was to assure peace within the Western bloc and ensure lower costs and prices for the production of energy.

This is how I came to study these coal regions of France and Germany, as objects of geopolitical ambition, conflict and, eventually compromise. As I read local and regional histories as well as sociological studies, many of which are referenced here, I realised workers often were conscious of being treated as objects of policymakers pursuing goals far afield from mining.[5] The objective of this chapter is not to survey again the geopolitical context, the national policies for industrialisation or the restructuring that occurred during de-industrialisation. Rather it is to explore some of the central themes scholars have examined to try to understand the lived experiences and daily life of miners from the end of the nineteenth century until the de-industrialisation of the 1960–1980s. The chapter is therefore a comparative synthesis, as incomplete as it may be, of the historiography on miners in the Nord/Pas-de-Calais and the Ruhr, first, in a traditional sense as agents of trade union militancy and launchers of strikes, second, as communities shaped by a tradition of paternalism, migration, and gender norms and roles and finally, as people who experienced the dislocation and sense of loss that came with the collapse of king coal. Having exited history, perhaps, former mining communities appear to be re-entering it again, with potentially tumultuous consequences for national and European politics.

Strikes, Trade Unions, and Welfare: Coal Mining in French and German Industrialisation

The privatisation in the 1860s of Prussian coal mining, which included the Ruhr area, set the stage for the mass industrialisation of the sector in the last decades of the nineteenth century. In France, the three largest mining companies were all in the Nord/Pas-de-Calais, located in Anzin, Courrières, and Lens. Much of the early work of social historians investigated the 'making of the working class', emphasising the formation of political class consciousness, whether or not they explicitly evoked this phrase. This older focus can still be observed in Klaus Tenfelde's 1985 chapter 'Comparative Research in the History of Mining Workers', in which he writes that,

> In labour history we are dealing with the process of economic, social, and political formation of the working-class and, at the core of the question, we are asking how structural—that is economic as well as social and political—changes work together to generate something like the working class.

This leads him to suggest 'four major fields of comparative research': 'socialisation and labour history, radicalisation and labour history, rationalisation and labour history, state interference and labour history'.[6] A mere four years later, Tenfelde reflected the change in historiography that had gathered steam in the 1980s, writing that 'Arbeitsgeschichte, "labour history" and "histoire du travail" should not be limited to trade union and workers' movement history'.[7] Though labour history has moved on, any history is incomplete without some mention of the important role strikes played in labour and cultural history.

Trade unionism developed early in the northern French mines, where close-knit communities facilitated the launch of trade unionism in the 1880s, which developed into the *Vieux Syndicat*, France's storied coal miners' union of the first half of the twentieth century. In the more heterogenous Ruhr area, trade unionism was slower to take off due to linguistic and cultural differences between Poles and local workers and the heavy sway of Catholicism. Nonetheless, Ruhr coal miners launched massive strikes in 1889, 1905 and 1912. The 1889 strike was the largest workers' strike in Germany in the nineteenth century and made a deep impression on German public opinion.[8] The mass strike in Ruhr mining in 1905 began as a spontaneous revolt against the imposition of a new work order at one mine but it quickly spread across the basin, fueled by discontent over wages, working conditions and daily experiences of labour relations. Though the Ruhr was by no means the centre of the German Revolution of 1918–1919, tens of thousands of coal miners went on strike in Dortmund and Essen in 1917, followed by large strikes in summer 1919 in Hagen and in the outskirts of Essen.[9] In France, massive and violent coal miners' strikes occurred in the 1860s in Anzin in the Nord and Valenciennes in the Pas-de-Calais.[10] The Anzin strike of 1884 was soon mythologised in Émile Zola's *Germinal* and launched the career of Émile Basly, who was depicted in the novel and later became the most powerful actor on the local political scene as mayor of Lens, as well as a socialist deputy in the National Assembly. Despite its importance and resonance, the Anzin strike ended in failure but the Lens strike of 1889 achieved a resounding victory. In Lens whole families came to rallies, crying 'Vive la république' and presenting their *cahier de doléances*, or list of grievances modelled on events in the early stage of the French Revolution. There followed a basin-wide strike in 1891, which prompted the first set of collective bargaining between employers and trade unions, resulting in the Convention d'Arras, which introduced a new form of industrial relations in French mining.[11] Later, massive strikes accompanied the victory of the Popular Front coalition in 1936, including the illegal confinement (sequestration) of managers at the Anzin mine.[12] The striking miners achieved almost all of their demands, though these were then progressively chipped away after the left-wing coalition collapsed.[13]

Mining was central to the development of workplace safety standards and hygiene in France and Germany. Judith Rainhorn recently edited a comparative book on health and safety in mining.[14] One of the contributions by Lars Bluma, a scholar at the German Coal Mining Museum (*Deutsche Bergbau-Museum*) in Bochum, applies recent historical approaches on the importance of concepts of the human body to analyse scientific and managerial disputes surrounding the role of hygiene in curing a worm disease [anchlostomiasis] that broke out in Ruhr mining in 1900. In his analysis, 'The miner's body, considered at a social level...is an object of knowledge and politics – or rather of power – constructed by actors...concern[ed with] his health, his efficiency, his productivity and his endurance'.[15] A prolonged debate among elite figures revolved around the biological and, by extension, moral (and perhaps financial) responsibility for the affliction. An actor network of scientists and managers that stressed miners' hygiene practices prevailed over those who blamed miners' environments, i.e., the extremely hot underground temperatures and humidity that provided an ideal setting for the larva and eggs of the parasite to propagate.

During the height of turn-of-the-century industrialisation, deadly explosions rocked a number of mines, most tragically in Courrières in 1906 where 1,099 miners died in the worst mining disaster in modern European history. Despite the spectacular size of this tragedy, safety conditions were generally worse in the Ruhr. The accident rate in German mining had more than twice the ratio of deadly accidents as French mining in 1898, with nearly 3 in 1,000 workers dying annually on the job.[16] Explosions attracted a great deal of press and attention but more deadly in cumulative terms were the quotidian experiences of falling rocks and cave-ins.[17] Deaths on the job decreased with increasing safety precautions and hygienic measures but increased again during the rationalisation campaigns of the mid-1920s. The new freight cars and rail systems introduced underground were especially prone to accidents. Explosions and cave-ins continued through the twentieth century, gaining a new resonance with the introduction of television which allowed the public to witness in horror the mining disasters in Hamm and in the Saar that killed a combined 320 workers in 1961–1962. Worm disease and accidents were the major health and safety problems in turn-of-the-century French and German mining but, as the mines were modernised in the 1920–1950s, new drilling techniques greatly increased the amount of dust coal miners swallowed, leading large numbers of underground workers to develop black lung disease (silicosis), especially during the postwar 'battle for coal' where safety standards were often shirked and miners forced to work exceptionally long hours despite the 1946 nationalisation of the French coal industry.[18] A study at one mine in the Ruhr in 1935 revealed that 25% of coal miners displayed early signs of silicosis while 20% were already fully afflicted by the illness.[19] It was a decade-long battle for miners to attain recognition and (partial) compensation for this chronic and often fatal illness. Widespread consciousness of the syndrome gained public prominence only in the 1970s and 1980s, partially due to poignant televised images of a northern French miner giving a tour of a graveyard in which he pointed out the gravestones of his colleagues who had died prematurely from silicosis.[20] The often fatalistic perspective many miners adopted towards their chronic afflictions can be seen in this 1975 quotation of a retired French miner, who reflects here on de-industrialisation as well:

> The miner has no future (...). In my view, [mining] has only 10 or 15 years left....I am sure that I will die of silicosis; I have thought about it but I tell myself that one will always die anyway of one thing or another.[21]

Paternalism, Hierarchies at Work, and the Social Position of Miners

The isolation of mining communities has drawn a large amount of scholarly attention but such a focus has also at times been disputed. David F. Crew criticises early literature on the history of mining communities for propounding a 'isolated mass perspective [in which] miners as an occupation group [displayed a] unity, homogeneity and physical isolation from other workers [that] predisposed them to militancy and to radicalism'. Nevertheless, the 'isolated mass hypothesis' has had a long scholarly life.[22] Olivier Schwartz encapsulates the isolation of French mining communities by referring to them as 'islands' of 'social seclusion' in his 1990 book on the Nord region.[23] He draws a line directly from the paternalist system of the nineteenth century in which mining communities 'were cut off from the external world' to the 'closed world in the heart of the [twentieth century]'.[24] German scholars, for their part, often referred to coal communities as 'colonies'. Unique to these communities was that, often separated from the cities, there were few if any 'bourgeois' or even 'petty bourgeois' inhabitants in the mining towns of France and Germany.

Olivier Kourchid states that, 'Paternal control over work and life were very important to the point that we consider the mining world the archetype of what we call paternalism'.[25] The famed Anzin mine company in the Nord opened a long stretch of company housing in the 1820s, a model that companies in the Pas-de-Calais copied during their period of expansion in the 1850s. By the First World War, 40% of Anzin employees lived in housing owned by firms while in the Pas-de-Calais, about 50% of the total mining workforce lived in some sort of company housing. In 1846 Alfred Krupp ordered the construction of company housing for coal miners in Oberhausen, beginning a long tradition of paternalism in the Ruhr.[26] German company housing took off later, with only 10% of coal miners living in such housing in the 1890s but this figure increased to 35% by the First World War.[27] Michel Joël points out, though, that, 'Everything seems to indicate that company housing first came about due to economic pressures [the difficulty of attracting labor to the mines] and less from the intention of *social control*' but, once they were built, the owners did attempt to exercise such control, for instance by favouring married workers with better housing and other benefits to promote reproduction. Miners who quit or were laid off lost not only their jobs but also their homes and some companies in the Pas-de-Calais even required a recommendation from a priest for employment.[28] Joël designates such control in mining towns as 'impersonal patriarchalism', highlighting that mine owners, management and engineers lived elsewhere. Company charities, schools, and churches were core social structures of mining communities but companies increasingly faced pressures and demands from their inhabitants that yielded success, such as the opening of dance halls, community gardens, and the like. To management's frustration, miners often sought to emancipate their communities from company control and place welfare and community building in the hands of municipal and national governments, efforts that were often successful.

Scholars writing on the history of Ruhr and Nord/Pas-de-Calais mining appear unanimous in their assessment that relations between foremen and workers were generally dismal and daily interactions above and below ground aggravated social tensions in mining. Helmuth Trischler argues that foremen and miners in the Ruhr had inhabited the same social universe up to the 1860s, sharing much of their leisure and free time together. Foremen even behaved like 'father figure[s]' to workers before the great industrial transformation of the late nineteenth century.[29] However, the long Great Depression of the 1870s uprooted social relations as owners pressured foremen to squeeze every profit they could from labour and also instituted a system of fines and punishments that foremen were required to enforce. Disputes over the measurement of piecework were especially acrimonious. Miners were incensed by the frequency with which foremen disqualified returning wagons of coal if they contained rocks or other items, a process known as 'Nullens' that would nullify miners' wages for the entire labour that went into filling the wagon.[30] Hans-Christoph Seidel describes the relations this way:

> As delegated representative of the "Master-in-House" viewpoint the foreman often appeared to the worker to make arbitrary use of the extensive instruments of company strictures for punishment, [and] also gave orders in a dictatorial tone and carried these through by use of corporal beatings and punishment.[31]

Despite the institution of co-determination in German mining in the 1950s, complaints about the 'arbitrary, dictatorial, [and] lack of respect' of foremen towards their workers remained a marked feature of workplace life.[32] In France, meanwhile, foremen 'who had emerged from the ranks' of the workers 'were virtually considered to be traitors'.[33]

Societal perceptions of the mining profession were poor. Karl Lauschke writes about Bochum after the Second World War that, 'Mining was looked upon terribly and the opinion was widely shared that only those of below average intelligence and children from socially marginalised sectors went' into the mines.[34] Popular sayings in the Ruhr like 'Nothing learned, go to the pit' and 'nothing in the head and thick arms' encapsulate the derogatory attitude many had of the occupation.[35] In an oral history project interviewing women born in the 1920–1930s, mining women recalled how their fathers and mothers did not want their daughters to marry coal miners.[36] In another interview, a Ruhr miner recalled that under National Socialism:

> Us young people of course realized that the armaments industry was growing. And for us fellows that meant: Escape from the pit! – When we would meet girls back then, we did not say "We are from the pit", rather we said, "Yes, yes, we work in the factory". The first question from the girls was always: "Do you have work" and "What do you do?" The pit – they wanted nothing to do with that. For this reason alone many of us wanted to escape.'[37]

Clear-cut hierarchies also existed within the mining occupation itself. In the Nord/Pas-de-Calais a 'real miner' (*vrai mineur*) meant someone directly involved in extracting coal, 'the king occupation in the mines, considered as crown of a career underground', and, to a lesser extent, those who cleared the passages and tunnels to prepare extraction.[38] Opportunities for career advancement and ascension were meagre in Ruhr mining.[39] As coal miners aged, their productivity declined, and they were compelled to leave the 'front line' positions for more rearguard positions, becoming dusters, handymen, or working in other less strenuous technical positions. According to Michael Zimmermann, this had 'considerable psychic and financial consequences' for Ruhr miners, with a substantial loss of income and prestige that generated further discontent.[40] Kourchid sees a similar development in the Nord/Pas-de-Calais: 'The resurfacing to day work came with a diminution of salary and the sentiment of a considerable loss of identity'.[41] De-skilling was another threat that especially affected the generation of workers who reached the peak of their careers in the 1920s when Taylorist modernisation programmes rendered many semi-skilled occupations obsolete.[42] Miners also fiercely resisted the switch from compensation by teamwork to individual piecework that was instituted in the Ruhr and Nord/Pas-de-Calais in the 1930s, which they blamed for destroying the solidarity and comradery of workers underground.

Themes in Miners' History: Migration, Sport, and Gender

Turnover was a massive headache for management during the entire history of mining in the Nord/Pas-de-Calais and Ruhr. For instance, of the 730,000 new miners who worked underground in West German mines from 1946 to 1956, 580,000 left the industry.[43] Constant turnover also gave rise to conflict between an old-guard of steady coal miners who had developed their own traditions and expectations and the more transient (and often short-term) miners who entered for shorter periods.

An important feature of mining culture was therefore the high numbers of migrants who came to work in the mines. By 1914, 300,000–350,000 inhabitants of Germany's three eastern provinces with predominantly Polish populations had moved to the Ruhr. An estimate from 1906 has 80%–90% of Poles in the Ruhr toiling in coal mines.[44] Historians have drawn parallels between the migrant experience of Poles in the Ruhr and Nord/Pas-de-Calais before the First World War and Turkish 'guest workers' in Germany and Maghreb migrants in France during the postwar period.[45] Like most Turkish migrants, Poles came predominantly from rural areas and met religious and ethnic discrimination in the Ruhr, which amplified both ethnic communities' tendencies to build their own community organisations to use their native language and represent their own customs and traditions.[46] Poles developed the concept 'Hakatismus' to describe the manifold targeted efforts of German officials, the press and politicians against the Ruhr's Polish population.[47] Poles were overwhelmingly Catholic and initially gave their votes to the Catholic Centre Party in the 1890s, before increasingly supporting the campaigns for office of Polish politicians at the turn-of-the-century and, finally, after 1907, voting for the SPD.[48] With the creation of a Polish state after the First World War, and an active recruitment campaign of French mining officials who set up offices in Poland and in the Ruhr city of Duisburg, a large exodus of Poles gathered steam in the early 1920s. By 1929 the Polish population in the Ruhr had shrunk by an estimated 50%–60% to 150,000.[49] A transnational history of this migration of Poles to the Ruhr and then on northern France would be a significant contribution to existing scholarship.

During the rapid phase of industrialisation in the last decades of the nineteenth century, most new workers to the northern French mines came from nearby rural communities. The largest immigrant group were Belgians, often coal workers from the Borinage, which was experiencing economic difficulties. In 1886, about 10% of coal mine workers in the northern mines were Belgian.[50] In 1892, 600 additional Belgians arrived from the struggling Borinage after having been recruited by mining companies. The local population subjected them to taunts, beatings and other abuse that prompted their mass departure and an international incident between the French coal mining unions, which had adopted a passive or even anti-Belgian attitude during the incidents, and Belgian trade unions.[51] After 1900, about 5,000 Kabyles were recruited from Algeria to the Nord/Pas-de-Calais, with many of them working in the coal mines. In France, mine owners founded an immigration service in 1924 that attracted 400,000 foreigners to the French mines by 1930.[52] These efforts began as soon as the war ended, in part out of a need to reconstruct mining infrastructure that had been systematically destroyed during German occupation. The change in workforce composition was dramatic: the Courrières mine employed only 469 foreigners in 1921 but this number jumped to 10,859 by 1924. In that year 73% of underground mine workers in the Nord were immigrants, of which 70% were Poles.[53]

By 1931, the Pas-de-Calais and the Nord were the third and fourth departments with the highest absolute numbers of immigrants, behind only the Paris and Marseilles areas.[54] Poles were disproportionately assigned to work underground, where they constituted about 50% of the workforce in the northern coal basin.[55] Within Polish communities, leadership was generally taken by the 'Westphalians', the group of Poles that had lived and trained in Ruhr coal mining. The mine companies sponsored an elaborate set of Polish clubs, churches, and residential segregation in the region. Philip H. Slaby argues that this phenomenon of 'ethnic paternalism' of which 'no other immigrant group interwar France possessed' succeeded initially in 'hamper[ing] the operation of working-class institutions to incorporate immigrants' and also their social integration with native mine communities.[56] Still, it is notable that, unlike in Germany, efforts to found a Polish trade union failed and Poles instead joined (though slowly at first) the major French unions, the CGT and the communist-aligned CGTU.[57] The Great Depression had a devastating impact on Polish workers as they were laid-off *en bloc* and lived in fear of receiving mandatory deportation notices to embark on trains specially commissioned by the mining companies to transport them back to Poland, especially in 1934–1935.[58]

A unique and tragic form of labour was the forced labour employed by Ruhr mines during the First and Second World Wars. The only (loose) equivalent to this in the Nord/Pas-de-Calais was the forced labour of German POWs in the northern French mines for several years following the Second World War. The 1916–1917 forced deportations from occupied Belgium and later Russia to the Ruhr mines led to massive international and internal protest until most of them were released in summer 1917. Labour shortages during wartime also led to restrictions on the freedom of movement of Polish coal miners in the Ruhr. In October 1918 70,000 POWs and 20,000 mostly Belgian and Russian civilian workers were labouring in Ruhr coal mines. By the end of the year, almost all of them returned home.[59] An even larger number of forced labourers left the region after the Second World War, leading the British occupiers to employ rather desperate measures to conscript German POWs into the mines to replace them, a largely unsuccessful endeavour as over 70% of these workers left the industry by early 1946.[60] Conflicts between new and old miners were endemic yet again, particularly due to the willingness of the generally younger class of new miners to agree to the individualised piecework rates shunned by the solidarity-oriented corpus of miners who had been socialised within mining communities.[61]

Migration from North Africa and Turkey in the 1960s–1980s was shaped by the context of the industry's terminal decline. There was only a small presence of foreigners in the Ruhr mines through the 1950s but this rapidly changed after structural crisis hit the industry in 1958. The proportion of foreigners among new hires in the Ruhr rose from 10% in 1958 to almost 40% in 1964.[62] Migrant coal miners were mostly Yugoslavs and Italians before the coal crisis, and then large numbers of Spanish and Greeks were employed in 1961–1962, before Turks became the primary migrant group in the mid-1960s, joined also by Moroccans. Though IG Bergbau und Energie, the German mining and energy union, initially had difficulty recruiting the new foreign workers, as the coal crisis deepened and layoffs accelerated, unionisation rates of foreigners rose dramatically from about 36% at the end of 1965 to 82% at the end of 1969.[63] Unlike previous periods, Ruhr municipal governments and non-governmental organisations 'took care of the social and economic needs of migrants [and] viewed education and further training as a tool for integration'. Sara-Marie Demiriz writes that 'the old paternalistic approach gave way to a more participatory one' and the '*Ruhrgebiet* thereby became an experimental ground for foreign education policy…'.[64]

In the Nord/Pas-de-Calais, the Algerian presence in the region steadily increased into the 1980s. During the Algerian War, Algerians in the region were particularly engaged in supporting Algerian independence, which brought down upon them the heavy hand of the state as well as the incomprehension and anger of many of their fellow workers. Violence broke out between Algerian demonstrators and the police on multiple occasions in mining towns but also between Algerians because northern France was a bastion of support for Massili Hadj, whose cadres were systematically destroyed in the FLN's 'battle of the cafés'.[65] French mine recruiters also panned out through rural Southern Morocco in the early 1960s, organising humiliating spectacles in which they observed semi-nude young men lined up in a row and designated them with red or green dye to signal their rejection or acceptance for employment. Once in France, Moroccans had inferior social and employment rights until a mass strike in 1980 in the industry led them to obtain 'the miners' statute' enjoyed by French miners since 1946. Thereafter Moroccan miners were entitled to social security and housing as well as family reunification rights.[66]

A brief yet important mention must be made of sport, which was central to culture in French and German mining. Football threw down roots in the Nord/Pas-de-Calais in the early twentieth century, sponsored and financed by the paternalist system. The region became an incubator for talented working-class youth, especially of youth from Polish families. Raymond Kopa (short for Kopaszewski), born in Nouex-les-Mines in 1931 in the Pas-de-Calais, was among the best-known football players in the world in the 1950–60s and a hometown hero. He spent his youth working in the mines and had disfigurements to show for it: two amputated fingers from an accident at the age of 16.[67] The famed football team Schalke 04 had its home in Gelsenkirchen. It was the first team founded by workers that achieved a place in the national league. Schalke gained a storied place among Ruhr youth when it defeated Nuremburg in 1934 to win the German championship.[68] And it hardly needs mention that the successful Borussia Dortmund football team, founded in 1909 and Schalke's sworn rival, has been enormously important for leisure and culture in the Ruhr, especially in the second half of the twentieth century.

Gender has traditionally been a rather neglected feature of mining history but important scholarship has emerged to build a more comprehensive panorama of life in coal mining communities. David F. Crew wrote in 1992 about mining historiography that, 'Because mining appears to be a quintessentially "masculine" industry, employing few women underground, it has been rather easy for labor historians to equate the history of mining communities with the history of their male members'.[69] In 1981, Marcel Gillet published an article titled, 'The Women of the Nord have no history?'[70] This gap in historiography has been partially filled by recent works, assisted by the turn from the late 1980s to gender and cultural history, though there are also illuminating oral history studies conducted in the early 1980s, some of which we reference here.

Women had been employed underground in French mining in the nineteenth century but were gradually pushed out before an 1892 law banned underground female mine labour.[71] A similar development occurred in Germany. By the 1910s women employed in Ruhr mining all (or almost all) had surface jobs in administrative or service positions. When management at the Germania mine in Dortmund proposed employing women underground because of acute labour shortages during the First World War, workers launched a spontaneous strike that beat back the effort. In most mines, it appears, management did not dare to propose recourse to female labour underground. Still, 9,000 women had employment in Ruhr mining at the end of the First World War but, according to Dieter Ziegler, almost all of them were laid off in or before 1920. Some women were retained for cleaning, cooking, and first aid occupations. Scholars have noted that women often played the most prominent roles in protest movements in mining areas, including during much of the unrest that took place in the Ruhr in 1917–1922.[72]

Mining communities were socially conservative on issues of gender: women were expected to stay home and care for their family after they married and overwhelmingly they did so. Schwartz writes that, in the Nord, 'at five o'clock in the morning, every miners' wife prepared a coffee for her husband'.[73] Much of the social life of married women revolved around community rituals in which women would stop by each others' dwellings unannounced and enjoy long chats over coffee together while their kids were at school and husbands at work. In an oral history study by Anne-Katrin Einfeldt, German women born during the 1920–1930s from mining backgrounds reported that as girls they were expected to stay inside and help their mothers. Their fathers, they said, generally showed little interest in their upbringing compared to their sons. In the Nord/Pas-de-Calais and the Ruhr there were few jobs available for women. French women in the northern coal industries often worked in textile plants before their marriage but few other opportunities existed.[74] In the Ruhr, women often took small side-jobs, like washing linen and cleaning houses and churches. Einfeldt interviewed 15 self-identified 'housewives' of coal-mining families in Gelsenkirchen for the first volume of Lutz Niethammer's oral history of the Ruhr. Einfeldt found that the women downplayed the time they spent on household cleaning and shopping and emphasised instead the pains-taking labour they exerted cleaning and mending the clothing of their coal miner husbands.[75] She describes the family division of labour thus: 'The economic foundation of the family is constructed by the work of man *and* woman, in which the man first and foremost earns money through his work while the woman generally saves money through her work'.[76]

Deindustrialisation and Generations in Mining History

Lutz Niethammer's oral history of the Ruhr emphasises the different perspectives and distrust between workers who came of age during Weimar and the Hitler Youth generation. Zimmermann's contribution highlights various elements that were at play in generational conflicts, for instance, travel and sports. Politics and psychology combined in the opportunity afforded by National Socialist organisations to challenge the authority of the 'red' paternal figure, leading to 'trench warfare between father and son in numerous families over requests for the son to join the Hitler Youth'.[77] Nonetheless, Zimmermann argues that Ruhr youth became increasingly disenchanted and largely abandoned the Hitler Youth by 1939/1949, 'indicating the failure of the NS-Youth policy in coal-mining communities'.[78] Generation became an even more poignant factor during deindustrialisation as new generations grew up with little to no prospect of working in the mines.

Deindustrialisation has hit no region of France and Germany harder than the Ruhr and Pas-de-Calais. The high costs of mine labour and, even more so, the steady increase in petroleum supplies and the collapsing prices of freight oil began the long 'coal crisis' of European mining in 1958 right in the midst of the postwar economic boom. A few statistics capture the extent of the structural crisis: from 1957 to 1969 the share of anthracite coal in total West German energy consumption fell from 70% to 32%.[79] In France, after being hard hit in the 1960s, the number of French coal miners fell in half between 1971 and 1978.[80] Tens of thousands marched year after year in Ruhr cities as well as traveling a short distance down the Rhine to make their voices heard in Bonn, the seat of the West German government. The miners' union, IG Bergbau (after 1961 IG Bergbau und Energie) sought not to prevent mine closures that it considered largely inevitable. Rather, it dedicated itself to securing comprehensive social plans for laid-off miners and a unification of the mining companies under a national coal plan in the hope of preventing the social consequences of a complete and sudden collapse of the sector.

A low point came in 1966 when TEXACO announced the closure of all its mines in Gelsenkirchen, mines that were among the most productive and modern of western Germany and that no one had thought destined for closure.[81] When announced, the closures were estimated to result in a loss of 40,000 jobs in Gelsenkirchen, an enormous blow to the city. Closures hit every area of Ruhr mining, the Möller/Rheinhaben mine in Bottrop, the Hansa mine in Dortmund, the Concordia mine in Oberhausen, the Pluto mine in Wanne-Eickel. Lauschke summarises the Ruhr miners' response in the title of his book, *Black Flags on the Ruhr*, the cover of which depicts a sombre procession of protesters marching in 1966. The black flags they carried symbolised not anarchy, in fact the protesters were explicitly demanding government intervention and a structural national economic plan for the coal sector. Rather, they expressed mourning. A witness was recorded as saying:

> The procession set in motion. The black flags rolled out, one after the other. The faces of the people were solemn. Those who began marching were silent.
>
> I could hardly bear to look at this (...) march of hopelessness (...) from the windows hung fabrics of sadness, as we saw everywhere.
>
> Black was also on the speaker's podium. The crowd marched on in silence. It was one of the saddest funerals I have participated in during my life.[82]

Worst hit by the closures were unskilled workers and workers over the age of 40, who experienced the most difficulties finding new jobs. As the SPD won elections to lead the North-Rhine-Westphalian regional government and joined the national coalition government in 1966, trade union and working-class pressures on the social democrats to take drastic actions ratcheted up. The impetus was assisted by internal SPD polls showing support for the communist-leaning DFU and neo-fascist NPD at 8% and 9% respectively in the Ruhr.[83] The response was the development of social assistance programmes that made miners the largest beneficiaries of social welfare targeted at a single category of workers in German history.[84] Especially painful for the coal regions was that they went through two waves of deindustrialisation, the decline of the coal industry in the late 1950s–1960s and then the wave of closures of steel plants and manufacturing in 1970–1980s. Closures continue to this day: An Opel factory opened in 1964 in Bochum after mass layoffs there in coal but recently it closed in 2014. The last Ruhr coal mine closed in 2019. In the Nord/Pas-de-Calais, the last coal mine closed in 1990 in Oignies, a town next to Courrières that is represented by the FN in the National Assembly after the 2017 election.

Schwartz examines the disintegrative effects that a combination of deindustrialisation and the emergence of mass consumer culture had on society in the Nord/Pas-de-Calais in the 1960–1980s. In both the Nord/Pas-de-Calais and the Ruhr, historians argue that consumer society emerged late by national standards and was little in evidence before the 1960s.[85] Despite communities experiencing deprivation, the mining towns and cities enthusiastically entered the era of mass consumption, buying in particular household appliances like washing machines. By the 1970s such communities had the highest rate of television-ownership in France but also the highest levels of household debt.[86] A stratification process set in among what were largely homogenous communities. Some experienced upward mobility or 'de-prolétarisation' while others eked out a marginal existence or 'précarisation'.[87] For those women who did not join the labour force, this came with a turn inwards towards family and a breakdown of previous social patterns. It became less and less proper to stop by friends' houses unannounced as norms turned towards rituals of invitation.[88]

For men, the adjustment to the new economy was especially traumatic. Unemployment was conceived as a male phenomenon evolving over time into permanent unemployment. The mass nature of the phenomenon blunted some of its psychological damage, as it took the form almost of a natural disaster and came to be perceived as normal. Nonetheless, it often led to a sense of displacement and a loss of legitimacy.[89] In regions with cultures that had long revolved around work, unemployed men and fathers needed to find new ways of spending their time, whether it be with their family at the home, traditionally considered a woman's space, or in male-dominated associations for games or leisure, or just in the bar. Unemployment was especially challenging for laid-off miners from North Africa, with a particularly high number of Moroccans affected. They often found themselves in especially marginal positions, both in material terms, in that they had greater difficulties in finding new positions than other unemployed workers and also psychologically, as many were loath to report to their families back home the loss of prestige and wealth that came with unemployment.[90] For many of them, Marie Cegarra concludes that 'emigration was a failure', with fathers losing face before their children and a sentiment of having been 'sacrificed'. In 2003, unemployment in the Nord/Pas-de-Calais, at 12.5%, remained high by national standards. Among Moroccans, unemployment stood at 34%.[91]

Marion Fontaine asks, 'during the middle of the 1970s, did the miners of the Nord still exist politically?' She explains that coal miners 'did not of course disappear but those who remained felt discarded among the mass of Moroccan laborers, subjected to a regime of precarious contracts and an aging minority of qualified workers and technicians'.[92] Their primary goal became, in her and Kourchid's view, to gain as lucrative a pension as possible by claiming compensation for illnesses, especially for silicosis.[93] Meanwhile, in the late 1980s the Ruhr area had the highest unemployment in Germany (15.6% in August 1988) and the city with the highest unemployment, Herne with 19%, was also in the Ruhr.

The closure of the mines had wide-ranging political consequences, the reach and outcome of which are still developing. In interviews with former local SPD factory councillor officials in the early 1980s, Zimmermann concludes that the 'political model of closely entangled institutions based on the traditionally close linkage of mines, miners' housing, life, work and free time (...) This unity has progressively disintegrated following the coal crisis'.[94] These retired officials criticised their younger SPD colleagues for not being adequately anchored in their local communities, for their technocratic and distant attitudes, and for excessive opportunism and careerism that led them to, in the view of their older colleagues, concern themselves with hierarchical welfare-based policies that neglected the culturally integrative structures that had bound together union, party and worker in the previous generation. A similar story has played out in the collapse of the Communist and Socialist parties in northern France.

We have seen in this chapter how general historiographical trends have taken regional mining history of the Nord/Pas-de-Calais and the Ruhr from labour relations and political culture to various forms of cultural history and ethnographic historical sociology, especially of the consequences of deindustrialisation. Although coal mines are largely closed in France and Germany (with some brief re-openings during the energy crisis following Russia's invasion of Ukraine in 2022), new work continues, as can be seen in the recent edited volume, *Boom – Crisis – Heritage: King Coal and the Energy Revolutions after 1945*. Issues of growing contemporary importance – the impact of coal mining on global and local environments, and a new literature on 'heritage studies' of how mining cultures of the past are commemorated and landscapes are transformed as well as maintained – feature prominently in the new literature on coal mining.[95] Efforts to reinvigorate former mining regions, which range from attaining UNESCO status to preserve the Zollverein, a former pit in Essen, or the opening of a major annex of the Louvre art museum in Lens, testify to the political importance of the regions still shaped by their histories of coal mining.

Notes

1 Stefan Wagstyl, 'Germany: The Hidden Divide in Europe's Richest Country', *The Financial Times*, 17 August 2017.
2 Guy Chazan, 'Germany's Working Class Turns away from the SPD', *The Financial Times*, 21 August 2017.

3 Accessed 30 August 2017, http://www.lemonde.fr/election-presidentielle-2017/article/2017/05/07/presidentielle-2017-la-carte-des-resultats-du-second-tour-departement-par-departement_5123906_4854003.html.
4 Accessed 30 August 2017, http://www.la-croix.com/France/Politique/Legislatives-carte-resultats-second-tour-elections-2017-06-18–1200855991.
5 Brian Shaev, 'Workers' Politics, the Communist Challenge, and the Schuman Plan: A Comparative History of the French Socialist and German Social Democratic Parties and the First Treaty for European Integration', *International Review of Social History* 61.2 (August, 2016), pp. 251–281.
6 Klaus Tenfelde, 'Comparative Research in the History of Mining Workers: Some Problems and Perspectives' in Gustav Schmidt (ed.), *Bergbau in Grossbritannien und im Ruhrgebiet: Studien zur vergleichenden Geschichte des Bergbaus 1850–1930* (Bochum, Dr. N. Brockmeyer: 1985), pp. 18–27.
7 Klaus Tenfelde, 'Zur Geschichte der industriellen Beziehungen im Bergbau' in Gerald D. Feldman and Klaus Tenfelde (eds.), *Arbeiter, Unternehmer und Staat im Bergbau: Industrielle Beziehungen im internationalen Vergleich* (Munich, C.H. Beck: 1989), p. 13.
8 Jürgen Reulecke, *Von Kohlenpott zu Deutschlands "starkem Stück": Beiträge zu einer Sozialgeschichte des Ruhrgebiets* (Bonn, Bouvier: 1990), pp. 18–19, 77.
9 Reulecke, *Von Kohlenpott zu Deutschlands "starkem Stück"*, pp. 146–153.
10 Cédric Glineur, 'Les coalitions ouvrières dans le départment du Nord sous le second Empire', *Revue historique de droit français et étranger* 90.1 (January–March, 2012), pp. 85–113.
11 Marcel Gillet, 'Aux origines de la première Convention d'Arras : le bassin houiller du Nord et du Pas-de-Calais de 1880 à 1891', *Revue du Nord* 39.154 (April–June, 1957), pp. 111–123.
12 Raymond Hainsworth, 'Les grèves du Front Populaire de mai et juin 1936: Une nouvelle analyse fondée sur l'étude de ces grèves dans le bassin houiller du Nord et du Pas-de-Calais', *Le Mouvement Social* 96 (July–September, 1976), pp. 3–30.
13 Hainsworth, 'Les grèves du Front Populaire de mai et juin 1936', pp. 3–30.
14 Judith Rainhorn, *Santé et travail à la mine. XIXe-XXe-siècle* (Villeneuve d'Ascq, Presses universitaires de Septentrion: 2014).
15 Lars Bluma, 'L'ankylostomiase dans la Ruhr. Corps, environnement et réseaux sociaux dans l'industrie minière de l'Empire allemande' in Rainhorn (ed.), *Santé et travail à la mine. XIXe-XXe-siècle* (Villeneuve d'Ascq, Presses universitaires de Septentrion: 2014), p. 37.
16 Christoph Klessmann, *Polnische Bergarbeiter im Ruhrgebiet, 1870–1945: Soziale Integration und nationale Subkultur einer Minderheit in der deutschen Industriegesellschaft* (Göttingen, Vandenhoeck & Ruprecht: 1978), p. 52.
17 Dieter Ziegler, 'Kriegswirtschaft, Kreigsfolgenbewältigung, Kriegsvorbereitung: Der deutsche Bergbau im dauernden Ausnahmezustand (1914–1945)' in Dieter Ziegler (ed.), *Geschichte des deutschen Bergbaus. Band 4: Rohstoffgewinnung im Strukturwandel* (Münster, Aschendorff: 2013), pp. 117–118.
18 Darryl Holter, *The Battle for Coal: Miners and the Politics of Nationalization in France, 1940–1950* (Dekalb, Northern Illinois University Press: 1992).
19 Ziegler, 'Kriegswirtschaft, Kreigsfolgenbewältigung, Kriegsvorbereitung', p. 126.
20 Marion Fontaine, 'Silicose et extrême-gauche dans le basin dans le Nord dans les années 70, Les raisons d'une aporie' in Rainhorn (ed.), *Santé et travail à la mine. XIXe-XXe-siècle* (Villeneuve d'Ascq, Presses universitaires de Septentrion: 2014), p. 101.
21 Fontaine, 'Silicose', p. 135.
22 David F. Crew, 'Rapport/Bericht' in Feldman and Tenfelde (eds.), *Arbeiter, Unternehmer und Staat im Bergbau*, p. 53.

23 Olivier Schwartz, *Le monde privé des ouvriers: Hommes et femmes du Nord* (Paris, Quidrige: 2002, 1990), pp. 61–68.
24 Schwartz, *Le monde privé des ouvriers*, pp. 68–70.
25 Olivier Kourchid, 'Mineurs, cheminots, essai d'interrogations comparatives', *Revue d'histoire des chemins de fer* 36–37 (2007), pp. 220–276, 243.
26 Reulecke, *Von Kohlenpott zu Deutschlands "starkem Stück"*, p. 16.
27 Joël Michel, 'Bergarbeiter-Kommunen und Patriarchalismus in Westeuropa vor 1914' in Feldman and Tenfelde (eds.), *Arbeiter, Unternehmer und Staat im Bergbau*, pp. 61–62.
28 Marie-France Conus, 'Une entreprise face à la gestion de "risques majeurs": la compagnie des mines de Courrières (1852–1944)', *Histoire, économie & société* 4 (2006), pp. 61–78, 64–65.
29 Helmuth Trischler, 'Steiger und Bergleute. Betriebliches Sozialverhalten während der Industrialiserung' in Schmidt (ed.), *Bergbau in Grossbritannien und im Ruhrgebiet*, pp. 152–153, 166.
30 Trischler, 'Steiger und Bergleute', pp. 176–178.
31 Hans-Christoph Seidel, 'Arbeitsbeziehungen und Sozialpolitik Bergbau: Vom Nationalsozialismus bis zum Ende der alten Bundesrepublik' in Ziegler (ed.), *Geschichte der deutschen Bergbau. Band 4*, p. 452.
32 Seidel, 'Arbeitsbeziehungen und Sozialpolitik Bergbau', p. 482.
33 Schwartz, *Le monde privé des ouvriers*, p. 65.
34 Karl Lauschke, *Schwarze Fahnen an der Ruhr: Die Politik der IG Bergbau und Energie während der Kohlenkrise, 1958–1968* (Marburg, Arbeiterbewegung und Gesellschaftswissenschaft: 1984), p. 128.
35 Zimmermann, 'Ausbruchsoffnung', p. 125.
36 Ann-Kerin Einfeldt, 'Zwischen alten Werten und neuen Chancen. Häusliche Arbeit von Bergarbeiterfrauen in den fünfziger Jahren' in Lutz Niethammer (ed.),*"Hinterher merkt man, dass es richtig war, dass es schiefgegangen ist": Nachkriegs-Erfahrungen im Ruhrgebiet. Lebensgeschichte und Sozialkultur im Ruhrgebiet 1930 bis 1960. Band 2* (Bonn, J.H.W. Dietz: 1983), pp. 153–154.
37 Quoted in Zimmermann, 'Ausbruchsoffnung', p. 102.
38 Kourchid, 'Mineurs, Cheminots', pp. 245–246; Diana Cooper-Rochet, 'Les mineurs polonais dans l'histoire de la France du XXè siècle: jalons, originalités, figures', *Synergies* (2011), pp. 45–55, 52.
39 Zimmermann, 'Ausbruchsoffnung', p. 120.
40 Zimmermann, 'Ausbruchsoffnung', p. 121.
41 Kourchid, 'Mineurs, Cheminots', pp. 245–246.
42 Ziegler, 'Kriegswirtschaft, Kreigsfolgenbewältigung, Kriegsvorbereitung', pp. 115–116.
43 Lauschke, *Schwarze Fahnen an der Ruhr*, pp. 17–18.
44 Klessmann, *Polnische Bergarbeiter im Ruhrgebiet*, p. 43.
45 Klaus Tenfelde, 'Religion und Religiosität der Arbeiter im Ruhrgebiet' in Klaus Tenfelde (ed.), *Religion in der Gesellschaft: Ende oder Wende* (Essen, Klartext: 2008), p. 17; Janine Ponty, 'Une intégration difficile: Les polonais en France dans le premier vingtième siècle', *Vingtième siècle* 7 (July–September, 1985), p. 51.
46 Klessmann, *Polnische Bergarbeiter im Ruhrgebiet*, p. 12.
47 Klessmann, *Polnische Bergarbeiter im Ruhrgebiet*, p. 83.
48 Klessmann, *Polnische Bergarbeiter im Ruhrgebiet*, pp. 125–127.
49 Klessmann, *Polnische Bergarbeiter im Ruhrgebiet*, p. 165.
50 Gillet, 'Aux origines de la première Convention d'Arras', p. 113.
51 Alain Dantoing, 'Une manifestation de défense ouvrière contre le travail étranger dans les mines du Pas-de-Calais en 1892', *Revue belge d'histoire contemporaine*, 3–4 (1974), pp. 427–445.

52 Xavier Vigna, *Histoire des ouvriers en France au XXe siècle* (Paris, Perrin: 2012), pp. 28–29.
53 Conus, 'Une entreprise face à la gestion', p. 73.
54 Judith Rainhorn, 'Le Nord-Pas-de-Calais, une région frontalière au cœur de l'Europe', *Hommes & Migrations* 1273 (2008), pp. 18–34, 27.
55 Philip H. Slaby, 'Dissimilarity Breeds Contempt: Ethnic Paternalism, Foreigners, and the State in Pas-de-Calais Coalmining, France, 1920s', *International Review of Social History* 60 (2015), p. 235.
56 Slaby, 'Dissimilarity Breeds Contempt', pp. 238–243.
57 Cooper-Rochet, 'Les mineurs polonais', pp. 50–51.
58 Cooper-Rochet, 'Les mineurs polonais', p. 47; Ponty, 'Une intégration difficile', p. 57.
59 Ziegler, 'Kriegswirtschaft, Kreigsfolgenbewältigung, Kriegsvorbereitung', pp. 34–53.
60 Michael Farrenkopf, 'Wiederaufstieg und Niedergang des Bergbaus in der Bundesrepublik' in Ziegler (ed.), *Geschichte der deutschen Bergbau. Band 4*, p. 201.
61 Seidel, 'Arbeitsbeziehungen und Sozialpolitik Bergbau', p. 472.
62 Lauschke, *Schwarze Fahnen an der Ruhr*, pp. 93–97.
63 Lauschke, *Schwarze Fahnen an der Ruhr*, pp. 161–163.
64 Sara-Marie Demiriz, 'Qualifying the Stranger: Educational Policies for Migrant Workers in the West-German Mining Industry' in Lars Bluma, Michael Farrenkopf and Torsten Meyer (eds.), *Boom-Crisis-Heritage: King Coal and the Energy Revolutions after 1945* (Berlin, De Gruyter: 2022), pp. 107–117, 114–116.
65 Jean-René Genty, 'Repères pour l'histoire du nationalisme dans les communautés algériennes du Nord et du Pas-de-Calais', *Revue du Nord* 78.316 (July–September, 1996), pp. 545–580.
66 Marie Cegarra, 'Du bled au terril: les mineurs marocains dans le Nord', *Hommes et Migrations* 1192 (November, 1995), pp. 19–26.
67 Cooper-Rochet, 'Les mineurs polonais', pp. 52–53.
68 Reulecke, *Von Kohlenpott zu Deutschlands "starkem Stück"*, p. 22.
69 Crew, 'Rapport/Bericht', pp. 56–57.
70 Marcel Gillet, 'Pas d'histoire, les femmes du Nord?' *Revue du Nord* 63.250 (July–September, 1981), pp. 559–568.
71 Marnix Dressen, 'La femme, le mineur et la compagnie', *Nouvelles Questions Féministes* 14/15 (Winter 1986), pp. 117–128, 118.
72 Karen Hartewig, 'Wie radikal waren dei Bergarbeiter im Ruhrgebiet 1915/16–1924' in Tenfelde (ed.), *Sozialgeschichte des Bergbaus*, pp. 629–635.
73 Schwartz, *Le monde privé des ouvriers*, pp. 73–75.
74 Schwartz, *Le monde privé des ouvriers*, p. 65.
75 Lutz Niethammer, *"Die Jahre weiss man nicht, wo man die heute hinsetzen soll": Faschismus-Erfahrungen im Ruhrgebiet. Lebengeschichte und Sozialkultur im Ruhrgebiet 1930 bis 1960. Band 1* (Bonn, J. H. W. Dietz: 1983) and Anne-Katrin Einfeldt, 'Auskommen – Durchkommen – Weiterkommen: Weibliche Arbeiterfahrungen in der Bergarbeiterkolonie' in Niethammer (ed.), *"Die Jahre weiss man nicht"*, p. 269.
76 Einfeldt, 'Auskommen – Durchkommen – Weiterkommen', pp. 266–270.
77 Michael Zimmermann, 'Ausbruchsoffnung: Junge Bergleute in den Niethammer, *'Die Jahre weiss man nicht, wo man die heute hinsetzen soll'*. Dreißiger Jahren' in Niethammer (ed.), *"Die Jahre weiss man nicht"*, pp. 97–107.
78 Zimmermann, 'Ausbruchsoffnung', p. 110.
79 Lauschke, *Schwarze Fahnen an der Ruhr*, p. 2.
80 Cegarra, 'Du bled au terril', p. 22.
81 Lauschke, *Schwarze Fahnen an der Ruhr*, pp. 195–200.
82 Quoted in Lauschke, *Schwarze Fahnen an der Ruhr*, pp. 199–200.
83 Quoted in Lauschke, *Schwarze Fahnen an der Ruhr*, pp. 257–260.

84 Christopher Nonn, *Die Ruhrbergbaukrise. Entindustrialisierung und Politik 1958–1969* (Göttingen, Vandenhoeck & Ruprecht: 2000); Lauschke, *Schwarze Fahnen an der Ruhr*, pp. 245–247.
85 Seidel, 'Arbeitsbeziehungen und Sozialpolitik Bergbau', p. 486.
86 Schwartz, *Le monde privé des ouvriers*, p. 95.
87 Schwartz, *Le monde privé des ouvriers*, pp. 61–62.
88 Schwartz, *Le monde privé des ouvriers*, p. 73.
89 Schwartz, *Le monde privé des ouvriers*, pp. 82–84.
90 Kourchid, 'Mineurs, cheminots' p. 265; Marie Cegarra, 'Récession et immigration: Les mineurs marocains dans les mines de charbon du Nord-Pas-de-Calais', *Moving the Social*, 30 (2003), pp. 123–128.
91 Rainhorn, 'Le Nord-Pas-de-Calais', p. 32.
92 Fontaine, 'Silicosis', p. 123.
93 Kourchid, 'Mineurs, Cheminots', p. 262.
94 Zimmermann, '"Geh zu hermann, der macht dat schon": Bergarbeiterinteressenvertretung im nördlichen Ruhrgebiet' in Niethammer (ed.),*"Hinterher merkt man"*, pp. 307–308.
95 Lars Bluma, Michael Farrenkopf and Torsten Meyer, 'Introduction: "King Coal" and Modern Mining History' in Bluma et al. (eds.), *Boom – Crisis – Heritage: King Coal and the Energy Revolutions after 1945'*, (Berlin, De Gruyter: 2022), pp. 1–24.

PART III

Working-class History in Application

18

REPRESENTATIONS OF WORKING-CLASS LIVES AT CRIMINAL JUSTICE HERITAGE SITES

Dan Johnson and Rose Wallis

This chapter is based on the authors' practical, collaborative work with a number of British criminal justice heritage sites, predominantly former Georgian and Victorian courthouses and prisons. The majority of the personal stories interpreted for public audiences in these contexts might be considered as 'working-class' lives. Most people prosecuted in the late seventeenth, eighteenth, nineteenth, and twentieth centuries were from poor working-class backgrounds, often young men (aged 18–35), in precarious economic positions.[1] Their stories, those of defendants and prisoners, are those most frequently displayed at these heritage sites. *How* we tell these stories, matters.

The courts and prisons were, and continue to be, important regulatory mechanisms. Extending beyond the administration of the law, as sites of social – and indeed political –contest, they shape and reinforce acceptable and unacceptable behaviours and activities, and the social relationships and structures that underpin them. They are also a source of continued public interest. However, as public court attendance has dwindled, and the processes of punishment have been removed from the public sphere, for those not directly affected by the criminal justice system, engagement with it is frequently mediated through its representation in popular culture, and museum and heritage sites.[2] Consequently, many scholars of prison museology have argued that those involved in interpreting these sorts of sites have a significant responsibility, as well as an opportunity, to shape public perceptions of crime, justice and punishment.[3] Too often crime and punishment are presented to the public in ways that emphasise the sensational and salacious, or which offer didactic narratives of the law as oppressive or progressive; but these approaches limit critical engagement with the role of criminal justice in society, and the relationship between past and present practices.

DOI: 10.4324/9780429344084-22

Returning to the theme of working-class lives, the connection between social disadvantage, or lower social status, and offending persists. Those prosecuted in British courts often have lower incomes, poor housing, and have been disadvantaged in terms of education, health and employment prospects. In 2021, the rate of imprisonment for the most deprived local authorities in England was ten times greater than the least deprived areas. Imprisonment perpetuates these patterns of social inequality: on release, former prisoners can experience higher unemployment, lower wages and greater job insecurity.[4] Considering these continuities, and the role of museums and heritage sites in informing public understanding, there are significant ethical and social implications in the ways in which we display the lived experience of criminal justice.

This chapter explores some of the issues inherent in representing criminal justice to the public, and considers in particular the utility of incorporating historiographical approaches in its interpretation. These reflections stem from the authors' research and practice. Dan Johnson is a public historian with experience as a professional heritage consultant. His research has concentrated on public understandings of poverty and punishment in British prison museums. Rose Wallis is a social historian specialising in histories of crime, criminal justice and social protest in the eighteenth and nineteenth centuries. Wallis worked as the historical consultant for the redevelopment of Dorchester Shire Hall as a new courthouse museum (2016–2018) and for the redevelopment of Bristol's Victorian magistrates' courts as a creative enterprise centre with Creative Youth Network (2018–2023). In 2020, the authors were privileged to be part of a cross-sector, interdisciplinary group of social and public historians, academics in law, criminology and heritage tourism, museum curators and heritage interpretation consultants, united by their interest in criminal justice histories and the transformative potential museums and heritage sites have in terms of social justice. Together the group produced a set of principles with examples of good practice – some of which will be returned to here. At the core of their recommendations was the importance of collaboration: between those engaged in historical research and its interpretation; and between heritage organisations and their audiences, and stakeholders from professional bodies and communities directly affected by the themes and issues these organisations seek to address.[5] This chapter will use examples of working-class lives on display from the authors' collective experience to consider questions of interpretation and representation, and how both impact understanding of people's lives and their experience of criminal justice in the past and the present.

'Dark Dungeons' and Histories from below: Reducing the Distance between Viewer and Viewed

The study of prison museums has been a topic for considerable discussion amongst dark tourism scholars. Philip Stone and Richard Sharpley describe sites of dark tourism as places that are linked to death, violence, disaster or suffering.[6] Stone has also proposed a model for understanding different types of dark tourism sites, in which the 'darker', or more serious sites lie at one end of the dark tourism spectrum, whilst 'lighter', or more entertainment-focused sites are situated at the other. 'Dark Dungeons', or sites associated with 'bygone penal and justice codes' are situated in the centre of Stone's spectrum as suppliers of a visitor experience that is both educational and entertaining.[7] While Dark Tourism literature has informed discussion on the commodification of penal history, it has been less concerned with how it is interpreted. Taking a lead from Jacqueline Wilson and her influential work on Australian prison sites, Alana Barton and Alyson Brown, and Sarah Hodgkinson and Diane Urquhart have spearheaded the critique of UK criminal justice sites, interrogating in greater depth the narratives presented in these contexts and their interpretation.[8]

Influenced by Stone's dark tourism spectrum, Barton and Brown use the term 'edutainment' to describe how these museums encompass both educational and entertainment-led interpretations of history.[9] Although this is a means of engaging visitors, and offers a safer, more accessible, way to deal with traumatic events, it has serious ethical implications.[10] Common problematic narrative tropes have been identified in a number of British prison museums, including a tendency to focus on 'the exceptional over the mundane', privileging extraordinary crimes and violent punishments.[11] These representations can marginalise the victims of crime and valorise its perpetrators. Light-hearted representations of physical punishment and execution likewise detract from, end even degrade the experience of suffering. At the National Justice Museum, visitors have been encouraged to take selfies in the pillory and tag the museum on social media. This light-hearted interaction with the device of punishment sometimes leads visitors to take selfies in less appropriate areas of the museum, such as on the trapdoor of Wandsworth Prison gallows, which is presented in a space designed for contemplation about the death penalty.[12] While more sensational cases are used to capture public attention, attempts to manage the more traumatic aspects of personal histories, to make them more 'family friendly', as Johnson and Pickin have noted, result in sometimes significant omissions from the historic record.[13] A lack of context, as we shall see, reduces the historic subjects to representations of crime and punishment without scope to consider the wider causes or impact of their encounters with criminal justice. As Wilson and others have highlighted, these sorts of depictions of past lives distance the audience from the historical actors represented, reinforcing the status of prisoners as 'other', as those excluded from society as 'criminals'; and – importantly – prevent visitors from engaging with the 'personal, emotional and psychological aspects' of people's experiences of criminal justice.[14]

This sort of distance is also created in interpretation that emphasises the oppressive nature of criminal justice in the past. Progressive narratives focusing on reform have also been considered characteristic of British prison museums.[15] The significant changes in English law and penal policy made in the eighteenth and nineteenth centuries are simplified as the transition from a barbaric, brutal system, predicated on physical punishment, to a more rational and humane one – a 'better' one as it resembles the system as it functions now. However, this is inaccurate and unhelpful: it smooths out the complexities, and contested processes, of change; it leaves little room to critically reflect on the way these changes were experienced by those subject to the law, or how the law works in the present.

Evident throughout the burgeoning literature on British criminal justice heritage sites, and reflected in our own practical experience, is the possibility for historical nuance to 'contextualise, complicate, and politicise', as Jessica Moody puts it, the 'dark' stories shared with public audiences.[16] As an approach, 'history from below', Wilson argued, provides an 'inclusive ethos' through which we can develop a more ethical interpretation of lived experiences, amplifying the 'historically voiceless' and diversifying the narratives on display. This has the potential to collapse the distance between viewer and viewed and problematise the operation of criminal justice.[17]

From the 1970s, historians seeking to construct 'histories from below' have made extensive use of the records of criminal justice to recover the lived experience of working people in the past, and to understand the nature and operation of social relations. Some of the earliest works in this field produced by Marxist social historians interrogated the perpetration of crime as acts of popular resistance, and its prosecution as acts of government.[18] Douglas Hay and Edward Thompson, in particular, emphasised the significance of the law in the negotiation of power in the eighteenth century. Complicity in the rule of law by a narrow, propertied elite – they argued – was secured by calculated acts of judicial terror, but equally in public displays of mercy, securing notions of English justice in the minds of the populace. Seeking to recover the agency of those lower down the social scale, Thompson argued that the law set the limits of behaviour for both ruler and ruled, and that both could attempt to mobilise this shared understanding of the law to remind one another of their duties and obligations. The law and the courts therefore, played a fundamental role not just in repression, but as a locus for social interaction.[19]

Subsequent work by Peter King, and Gwenda Morgan and Peter Rushton, amongst others, has demonstrated further the agency of working people and the poor in the criminal justice system. Tradesmen, artisans, labourers, both men and women, called on the law to protect their property and settle disputes, accessing the county courts or summary justice 'to create their own social order'.[20] While the criminal justice system was fraught with inequity, the courts were places where all sectors of society interacted: from the gentleman acting as judges on the bench, the middle classes and tradesmen of the jury, to the men, women and children of all classes who appeared as witnesses, prosecutors and defendants, and who came to witness proceedings in the public gallery. This was a public forum built to accommodate an audience who bore witness to justice and to whom local and national policy could be communicated. The courts were sites of social contest.

Many historians have used the records of criminal justice to reconstruct patterns of crime, and consider how environment, occupation, and gender shaped the recourse to crime. Studies in this vein have done much to expose the lived experience of working men and women, and the place of criminal activity as part of a repertoire of survival strategies to negotiate poverty and the precarity of employment.[21] Indeed, subsequent work in this field, as Steve Poole has suggested, has been 'concerned less with attempts to quantify unequal power relations at law than with broader qualities of plebeian social experiences'.[22] The *Old Bailey Proceedings* project, and its expansion into the records of welfare in *London Lives* and penal transportation with the *Digital Panopticon,* exemplifies how the archives of the courts can illuminate working lives beyond crime by exploiting the mass of information revealed about people's work, leisure activities, living conditions and relationships, incidental to the circumstances of an offence, but recorded in the evidence laid before the courts. Importantly, this material is freely accessible and extending the reach of these stories to new audiences beyond the academy.[23]

The work of social historians has also challenged the 'reform perspective' of English criminal justice in the eighteenth and nineteenth centuries, accounts that presented change as a process of rationalisation: the decline of an archaic, irrational and arbitrary system in the wake of new modern institutions of criminal justice, policing, and penal policy. The work of Hay, Thompson and Beattie has done much to unpack the rationale of the eighteenth-century criminal justice system and resistance to reforming the capital code.[24] Michael Ignatieff has reconsidered the development of the English penitentiary system in the nineteenth century in terms of social stratification and the need to control a growing politicised working class.[25] More recently historians have returned to the question of popular agency in these discussions of power and authority, addressing how men and women at the bottom of society shaped the operation of judicial and penal institutions by their interactions with them. As Tim Hitchcock and Bob Shoemaker have argued, by their contravention of the law, 'in playing the system', and even in mounting successful defences, 'it was the poor and the criminal who primarily determined which reforms appeared feasible, and more importantly which initiatives took root and survived'.[26]

From this brief overview, we hope to have demonstrated the potential identified by Wilson in 'history from below' to reduce the distance between the viewer and the viewed – those subject to prosecution and punishment. In privileging their experience, a more nuanced picture of criminal justice emerges. The historical actors are humanised by considering the contexts, choices and possibilities that informed their interactions with the law. Considering the courts as sites of social contest complicates the operation of criminal justice in a way that foregrounds critical reflection on its social and governmental function. In the following sections we consider examples of museum interpretation that have employed this sort of social-historical approach, to evaluate its utility and what else needs to be addressed to produce more inclusive, ethical and effective interpretation.

Sites of Social Contest

In its redevelopment as a courthouse museum, Dorchester Shire Hall adopted an approach explicitly informed by history from below, seeking to capture the sense of social contest inherent in the courts, as a more effective way of engaging their audiences with 'the history of law and order, and past and present efforts to achieve justice for ordinary people'.[27] Indeed, the museum's foundation is inextricably linked with the movement for workers' rights in Britain.

Shire Hall is best known as the site of the trial of the 'Tolpuddle Martyrs' in 1834; six agricultural labourers who were prosecuted for forming a trades union. While the formation of a union was not in itself an illegal act, the local authorities and central government conspired to construct a charge of administering unlawful oaths, using legislation introduced during the Revolutionary Wars with France intended to put down seditious societies. A jury of yeoman farmers found the six men guilty and they were sentenced to seven years' transportation to Australia. The national campaign for their freedom, led by urban unions but supported by many who questioned the extraordinary severity of the conviction, saw their eventual return and pardon for their crimes.[28]

The case is now an integral part of trades union and Labour history in Britain; as Griffiths has suggested, achieving almost the status of 'a foundation myth'. From its centenary commemorations in 1934, the Trades Union Congress (TUC) has used the story of the six labourers to 're-galvanise and inspire its membership'.[29] The annual festival held every July sees thousands of union members and left-wing activists converge on the village of Tolpuddle for discussions, music, and the procession commemorating the martyrs and celebrating the success of the hundreds of thousands of trades unionists who secured their freedom.[30] The importance attached to this case was instrumental in Shire Hall's preservation as a heritage site. After the court was closed in 1955, the TUC took ownership, returning it to the council in 1968 with a covenant ensuring the courtroom would be available to the public.[31] Redeveloped as a permanent museum in 2018, the Martyrs' trial forms a key part of its interpretation, and the historic case that informed Shire Hall's aim to 'inspire people to make a difference to society, politics and justice for all'.[32]

Their trial is one of four case studies that visitors can explore in detail in the courtroom – the focal point of the visitor experience – but contextualised throughout the museum's exhibition and historic spaces. The introductory gallery discusses the nature of Dorset society in the first decades of the nineteenth century, highlighting the interconnected issues of international war, radical political agitation at home, agricultural depression, and popular unrest as key contexts for the breakdown of social relationships and economic strife that underpinned the martyrs' story.[33]

On their route to the courtroom visitors move through the labyrinth of holding cells beneath it, including one of the Georgian communal cells where the martyrs were held. Intentionally light in interpretation, visitors are encouraged to immerse themselves in this space and imagine what it must have been like, listening to ambient audio recordings of martyr George Loveless' own account of their experience: 'The smoke of this place, together with its natural dampness, amounted nearly to suffocation; and in this most dreadful situation, we passed three whole days'.[34] Visitors then pursue the case into the courtroom, entering if they can, via the winding wooden staircase to the dock, sharing in that moment of trepidation as they emerge to face the judge's bench. The hand-held multimedia-guide encourages visitors to explore the court space, introducing each set of actors and their role in proceedings in the area they would have occupied. Every part of the narrative is based on archival evidence which is actively cited in the audio interpretation and available as digital facsimiles on the multimedia-guide.[35]

The story that is constructed in this exploration of the space draws out the social tensions and context that underpinned the trial. The defendants' motives for forming a union are explained in terms of ongoing agricultural depression, continued attempts to counter poor wages and living conditions (most violently expressed in the Swing riots only a few years before in 1830) and failed negotiations with their employers, local clergy and magistrates. The social conflict that stimulated the prosecution is drawn out in the physical arrangement of social groups in the court and reinforced by Loveless' words:

> I thought to myself, there is no danger but we shall be found guilty, as we have a special jury for the purpose, selected from among those who are most unfriendly towards us: the grand jury – landowners; the petty jury – land-renters. Under such a charge, from such a quarter, self-interest alone would induce them to say, 'Guilty'.[36]

The case concludes with reflections on its continuing significance provided by former regional secretary of the TUC, Nigel Costley, and Jeremy Corbyn MP (Labour Party Leader 2015–2020). Their comments connect the trial to contemporary problems of rural poverty and workers' rights, and emphasise the value of this historic account as evidence of injustice and the power of collective action, 'the way working people can improve or protect their lot'.[37]

The detailed exploration of the court proceedings allows visitors to engage with more historical context to consider the inequities working people faced in the past. Visitors are encouraged to immerse themselves in the historic space – and the archive – to connect them with the lived experience of historic actors. The court as a site of social contest, indeed, of class struggle, is made clear; and owing to Loveless' account, we have a rare insight into the defendants' perspective and their agency. The addition of contemporary commentary on the case aims to support visitors' critical reflection on related issues in the present.

Both Roger Ball and Carl Griffin have challenged the exceptional status of the Tolpuddle unionists.[38] Their critique raises some important questions that have implications beyond the interpretation of this particular case: how far is it representative of working-class lives, or their protests, or their interactions with criminal justice? Griffin has highlighted that the prosecution of the martyrs, and the legal basis on which it was made, was not unprecedented. It has been marked out (in part at least) by Loveless' own account of it. Such reflections by working people were rarely recorded, so the value in Loveless' narrative has contributed to the creation of 'the Tolpuddle legend'.[39] Ball's critique tends explicitly to the public uses of the martyrs' story. He argues that they 'ticked all the boxes': these were six peaceful, non-violent, organised men who suffered extraordinary injustice at the hands of the government. This victim-centred narrative provides a more palatable and, Ball contends, 'valid' account of working-people's struggle than something like Swing.[40] Despite the scale of popular involvement in the disturbances in 1830, and the extent of the repression meted out by the government – more than 500 people were transported and 19 were executed – Swing does not occupy the same place in popular memory as Tolpuddle. As Ball suggests, the Swing 'rioters' did not fit the bill: they engaged in machine-breaking, arson, covert and overt threats of violence; acts that were – and are – easily understood as criminal.[41]

The recourse to violent protest by working people is considered at York Castle Museum and the National Justice Museum. The different approaches adopted at each site highlight some of the difficulties and opportunities in interpreting criminal acts. The *York Castle Prison* exhibition recreates prisoner narratives through video projections on to the historic cell walls to illustrate the eighteenth-century prison experience as 'a dark and brutal history – a time of rogues, thieves and murderers'.[42] Amongst those on display is 41-year-old William Hartley, who left his seven children orphaned when he was hanged in

York along with thirteen others for robbing a house of weapons to be used during a Luddite raid of a factory.[43] A special commission was formed in January 1813 and the subsequent execution of the fourteen Luddites on 16 January was the largest mass execution at the York Castle Gaol.

In the projection, Hartley is accused by another prisoner of breaking machines and being afraid of progress. He retorts: 'If you seen machines steal your livelihood, you'd be afraid of progress and all'.[44] The Luddite protests of 1811–1816 have frequently been reduced in this way as a reaction against technological advances; but machine-breaking and armed retaliation formed part of a more complex repertoire of action, including negotiation, to stop the effective deregulation of the textile industry and the devaluing of skilled labour, against a backdrop of high prices, wage cuts and unemployment. The special court under which Hartley was tried was a calculated act by government to violently suppress these protests.[45] Visitors are encouraged to sympathise with Hartley and his impoverished condition as a working-class widower with seven mouths to feed. However, there is no attempt to contextualise his circumstances or Luddism as a movement beyond the comment about machine-breaking. Consequently, the resort to violent protest is over-simplified as reactionary, 'backwards' even. By confining these people and circumstances to the past, visitors are able to keep their sympathy for the prisoners at arms-length without any call for reflection on similar situations today.

Where the York Castle Museum excludes important context about Luddism and side-steps questions concerning crimes of protest, the re-enactment of the trial of Daniel Diggle at the National Justice Museum provides more context about the movement, and through immersion and participation, engages visitors in discussion about the prosecution of protest. Diggle's trial has been included in the National Justice Museum's daily trial re-enactments in the courtroom of Nottingham's historic Shire Hall. The re-enactment actively engages visitors by encouraging them to play the parts of Diggle, his accuser, barristers, witnesses, and the judge in the trial, with scripts developed from original archive material. As with the core case studies at Shire Hall, the court space plays a central role in the interpretation as visitors are placed in the dock, witness stands, or gallery depending on the role they are assigned. The barristers (costumed interpreters) provide a short introduction to Diggle and some context around his crime of shooting Mr. George Kerry in his workshop as part of a Luddite frame breaking raid in December 1816.[46] Following this brief introduction, the judge opens proceedings and calls various witnesses to the stand.

During the trial, the victim, Kerry was summoned to the stand to present his testimony and receive a cross-examination from the barristers. He explained that a group of men including Diggle broke into his workshop late in the evening of 22 December 1816. Kerry threatened them with a pistol, but before he was able to fire, he was rushed by one of them and a struggle broke out over the weapon during which the gun was discharged, grazing Kerry's shoulder. Diggle was identified as the shooter, despite the fact that it was dark, and the group of men were wearing masks; a fact highlighted by the barrister who also questioned how far the shooting was intentional.[47] Following the rest of the witness testimonies, the judge asks the jury (all of the other visitors not directly participating in the re-enactment) to decide the fate of Diggle. There is no requirement for the visitors to find as the historic jury did; on the author's visit, the jury found Diggle not guilty owing to the lack of evidence. Following the verdict, the costumed interpreters explained to all the visitors that although the evidence was only circumstantial, Diggle was found guilty of attempted murder and sentenced to be hanged, drawing out the wider social and political context that underpinned the prosecution of the Luddites.

The re-enactment provides a more holistic account of the trial, presenting different historic perspectives on events, and importantly, those of the victim, Kerry. The active participation in the trial supports visitors to think critically and reflect on the crime and why their judgement might differ from the historic ruling.

Presenting stories of protest are a powerful way for these sites to consider the courts as a site of social contest, the ways in which social relationships informed the experience of criminal justice, and as a means of demonstrating the agency and activism of working people in the past. The use of the court space at Shire Hall and the National Justice Museum support visitors' critical engagement with these interactions. This is particularly topical considering the recent criminalisation of protest by the British media and the government, that, as Wallis has argued elsewhere, detracts from the social inequalities that underpin popular unrest.[48] These examples also draw attention to issues outlined earlier: the difficulty in interpreting acts that would be widely understood as criminal, and questions of representation. Exceptional events like widespread unrest often leave the richest record, but how far can they reflect the lived experience of people in the past? The final sections of this chapter explore these questions further, addressing whose stories are included, and whose are not, and returns to the value of collaboration for inclusive and effective interpretation.

Lived Experience and Representation

Johnson's research across a number of English criminal justice sites has highlighted the frequently gendered interpretations of crime and punishment. Most of the crimes committed by men were against property, whereas women were more often represented committing crimes against the person, notably violent murders of their husbands or children.[49] Much historical research has demonstrated that while women consistently make up a minority brought before the courts, where they were prosecuted, it was proportionally for the same offences as men, and predominantly for larceny.[50]

The gendered approach is inadvertent in many cases, as with many of the lives on display, the most sensational stories leave behind the most robust records, making interpretation much easier for the contemporary curator. More than any other group, violent women on display in the museums closely resemble popular representations in the media rather than representations in crime statistics and the archive. Shani D'Cruze and Louise Jackson argue that violent women acquired increased cultural visibility, partly through their more severe punishments such as burning at the stake. Their offences were also seen as more heinous than male violent crime because in addition to the crime itself, they had betrayed social and gender norms.[51] The vast and sensational media attention to violent women despite their statistically low conviction rates perhaps gives the museums more sources to use for narrative reconstructions. However, the uncharacteristically high proportion of violent women reconstructed for museum audiences may create a public understanding of women and crime that does not accurately represent the historical record. This sort of interpretation proves especially problematic as it feeds into the enduring 'mad or bad' trope of female offending, one that pathologises social constructions of deviance and neglects the wider social and economic contexts that informed the crimes women committed.[52]

The traumatic nature of violent offences poses problems for their interpretation. As highlighted in Hartley's case, a lack of context and attempts to sanitise violence for the sake of accessibility limits scope for engagement with both lived experience in the past and critical reflection on it. An extreme example of this is the representation of Anne Castledine, who was executed and dissected for infanticide (the murder of her infant daughter) in 1784. In a 'Horrible Histories' style video at the National Justice Museum, her offence was presented straightforwardly as murder, and her execution and public post-mortem dissection as an opportunity for her 'five minutes of fame'.[53] While this interpretation was clearly aimed at engaging younger audiences with difficult subjects in a safe way, it degrades lived experience and obviates any discussion on the circumstances of the crime or its punishment, confining it to part of a long-gone, brutal past.

Shire Hall and Lincoln Victorian Prison likewise spotlight cases of 'violent women', but engage more closely with the archival material and wider historical contexts to explore social issues and the gendered experience of criminal justice in particular. In contrast to Castledine, Lucy Buxton's trial for infanticide is discussed in some depth at Lincoln, exploring how a recognition of her precarious economic position, allied with growing support for the abolition of the death penalty in the 1860s, supported her reprieve.[54] Elizabeth Martha Brown, the last woman to be publicly executed in Dorset in 1856 for killing her abusive husband, has been included as a detailed case study at Shire Hall, not least because of local interest in the case and its association with author Thomas Hardy. (Hardy witnessed her execution and it has long been claimed that this inspired his novel *Tess of the D'Urbervilles*.) Shire Hall use Brown's case to interrogate the experience of women in the courts – a male dominated space at this point – their treatment at law, and issues associated with domestic violence. More recently, the museum situated the case in a longer-view of women's experiences of criminal justice, considering the ongoing double-standard applied to women's behaviour as both victims and perpetrators of crime, and in society more broadly.[55] Indeed, recent research conducted with criminal justice practitioners has highlighted how women who appear 'unfeminine' can still be perceived as more deviant and less sympathetic by juries and judges.[56]

There is value, then, in these cases in terms of exploring the contexts which informed these women's extraordinary crimes, and their experience – not least the ways in which transgressions of what were considered correct feminine behaviours underscored their prosecution and punishment. However, in focusing on violent crimes, do we still project a construction of female criminality that emphasises passivity until some crisis provokes them to a violent act in contravention of their perceived femininity? It certainly does not reflect the majority of women brought before the courts in the past.

Like men, women were most frequently prosecuted for species of theft, although differences in the nature of their crimes were informed by the different patterns of work and sociability in men and women's lives.[57] While Johnson notes that poverty and theft are strongly equated in representations of male crime, there is scope to again contextualise, and to develop the more mundane, or 'everyday' accounts of property crime to consider the experience and agency of the poor beyond their time in court, to complicate our understanding of motive in the past and present. Much work has been done by historians to nuance the relationship between poverty and crime. Perhaps most useful has been the exploration of an 'economy of makeshifts', a concept that encompasses the 'patchy, desperate and sometimes failing strategies of the poor for material survival'.[58] This approach acknowledges precarity but also people's agency in making rational choices to pull together an income from disparate sources, legitimate and illegitimate, and somewhere in between.[59] Prostitution, begging, vagrancy, theft and fencing stolen goods, alongside paid work and parish support, all had their place in 'the plebeian lifecycle'. Crime in this context is viewed through a wider lens, in relation to employment, family, community and welfare. As Shore contends, the 'sharp dichotomies drawn by contemporaries' between poverty and crime, 'were not so tangible in reality'.[60] Interrogating crime in this wider social context has the potential to complicate how the intersection of crime and poverty are understood, an approach that might support a more nuanced consideration of contemporary correlations between offending and deprivation, and the possibilities for people, and the choices they make in these contexts.

Hitherto, much of our discussion, and indeed the lives we have encountered on display, has been focused around defendants, often portrayed as victims of the system, or wider social problems. While these contexts are significant, particularly in terms of critically engaging with the role of criminal justice past and present, there is little sense of those labouring people who were the victims of crime and as such sought to prosecute it. Working people, as well as the propertied classes, accessed the courts to seek justice. Peter King's analysis of the Essex quarter sessions in the second half of the eighteenth century confirms that a significant proportion of prosecutors were tradesmen, artisans and labourers, using the courts to protect their property and settle disputes.[61] Summary courts presided over by magistrates without a jury, were even more accessible for speedy and cheap justice. As Gwenda Morgan and Peter Rushton demonstrated, those at the very lowest social levels used summary justice selectively to regulate relationships and protect *their* social and economic position.[62] Later nineteenth-century police, magistrates, and courts likewise provided popular access to the law. At Bristol for example, in 1881, two-thirds of cases at the newly opened courts were brought by civilians, most of whom were working class.[63] If we are seeking more inclusive and representative narratives, this is important to consider, as the contemporary patterns of social disadvantage that underscore offending are shared by those most likely to be the victims of crime.[64]

Despite the persistent over-representation of minoritised ethnic groups throughout the criminal justice system, the experiences of black people and members of other ethnic groups are underrepresented at criminal justice heritage sites.[65] Indeed, it is only relatively recently that social historians have begun to explore the experience of British criminal justice for different ethnic groups.[66] Criminologist and writer in residence at the National Justice Museum, Martin Glynn, has made a powerful call for a reassessment of the historical black presence in crime and punishment in the UK, challenging a 'monocultural' understanding of historical criminology that has marginalised black voices. In addressing the role of history in shaping contemporary perceptions of crime and criminality, *Invisible Voices* positions race as a more significant and persistent variable in addressing historical continuities, incorporating a broader range of perspectives to recover experiences of power and powerlessness, and the ways in which these inform the operation of the law.[67]

Glynn presents wide-ranging evidence of the black presence in the British criminal justice system in the eighteenth and nineteenth centuries, as defendants, victims, prosecutors, witnesses, and police officers. While he advocates for the importance of discussing the most violent manifestations of oppression from the early modern period, through slavery and the development of scientific racism in the nineteenth century, which underpin notions of white superiority and the subjugation of other ethnic groups, to this Glynn adds the voices of black witnesses, social commentators and activists, emphasising their agency. Recognising and exploring the experiences and perceptions of different communities, Glynn contends, is essential to deepening our criminological understanding to affect genuinely transformative change. This requires listening to subjective perspectives and acknowledging dominant historical narratives that have excluded others.[68] The responsibility for redressing the volume of voices, Glynn argues, rests with 'all scholars, historians, curators and custodians of the past'.[69]

Glynn's work resounds with the arguments outlined in this chapter: to include a multiplicity of perspectives; not to sanitise the past; and to consider broader contexts in discussions of crime and punishment. His work demonstrates further the importance of historical understanding, and an inclusive and intersectional approach to broaden and deepen critical engagement with criminal and social justice.[70] Laurajane Smith has also argued for the inclusion of diverse individual stories at criminal justice heritage sites: the capacity for people to connect with these past lives is 'essential for the development of empathy and critical engagement by museum visitors', particularly in relation to 'dissonant' histories.[71] Visitor feedback from Lincoln Victorian Prison and Shire Hall Museum indicates that encountering 'real stories' makes the past more relatable.[72] For some visitors, these stories have stimulated critical reflections on the causes of crime and how judgements were and are formed. At Shire Hall, class and economic circumstance were repeated themes:

> '[Being] very poor…just like these people…doesn't make you a criminal'
> 'I know it's the same today, the rich and powerful have all the power.'[73]

However, a sense of injustice in the past was also frequently evident in visitor responses:

> 'There is an overall theme of justice (or, rather, injustice) looked at historically.'
> 'How lucky we are…'
> 'be happy that we live in better times.'[74]

Whilst the case studies of historic defendants can connect visitors with past lives in a meaningful way, they can also reinforce a progressive narrative of the operation of the law – 'that it was worse back then'. From our collaborative work and discussions with museum partners, there is significant potential in making explicit the links between the past and present by working with and including the voices of people directly affected by criminal justice.

Ripon Museum Trust encompasses three historic sites: a former workhouse, a nineteenth-century prison and police station, and courthouse.

Together they provide an almost unique opportunity for visitors to explore the links between poverty and crime, punishment, justice and welfare. Two of its recent exhibitions demonstrate how Ripon Museum Trust actively engaged visitors with contemporary social questions through historical reflection. *Rogues and Vagabonds* (2019) explored vagrancy in the Victorian period across its three sites, and examined the realities of homelessness today. Historic accounts of the experience of vagrancy were paralleled with *Homeless Not Faceless*: working with the Harrogate Homelessness Project and Ripon YMCA, the exhibition featured a series of portraits of people who gave their own accounts of being homeless. Ripon also worked with the Labour homelessness campaign to draw attention to the continued criminalisation of homelessness under the 1824 Vagrancy Act and more recent public protection orders, providing a pathway for visitors to pursue the issues they encounter.

Prisoners on Prisoners (2020–2021), an art installation produced with Faye Claridge, connected inmates at HMP Askham Grange with individuals from Ripon's historic prison archives. The conversations produced powerful, candid reflections on the experience of incarceration and changes and continuities in the criminal justice system from a personal perspective.[75] The recorded reflections were shared with the public through audio, textiles and photography displayed in a cell at the Prison and Police Museum.

The National Justice Museum also work with external criminal justice organisations for their *Choices and Consequences* workshop programme for schools. In collaboration with the Ben Kinsella Trust, this award-winning scheme has been proven to help change young people's attitudes to knife crime. The workshops represent all sides affected by knife crime: from perpetrators to victims, the police and medical teams, and the victims' families; as well as considering the law and the realities of prison life. This breadth of perspectives is used to support young people to make up their own minds, creating an informed space to reflect on the consequences of carrying a knife and how to make positive choices to stay safe.[76]

These examples highlight the scope for historic sites of criminal justice to explicitly address contemporary social concerns. In the same way that the stories of individual historic actors can help connect audiences with past experiences, making visible the lived experiences and perspectives of people today humanises the issues presented and makes their relevance clear. Incorporating a range of voices of those directly involved, whether historically or in the present, provides a holistic narrative, and greater context in which social issues and their impact are more apparent. This richly contextual and humanised approach is not didactic, but provides a powerful framework for audiences to reflect and make up their own minds, and even space for them to act.

Conclusion

This chapter has taken a different approach to the theme of working-class histories, focusing on the ways in which class, or structural and social inequalities have – and continue to – inform the experience and operation of criminal justice. The persistence of patterns of inequality and deprivation in the present make engaging with working-class lives in the past all the more important. Echoing the calls of Wilson, Barton, Brown, and others, we have endeavoured to demonstrate the value of social-historical approaches to nuance and contextualise the narratives presented to the public at criminal justice heritage sites.

Offering fuller accounts of past lives can help to avoid sensationalising or sanitising the experience of criminal justice and present it in a more respectful, ethical way. This approach also holds possibilities for more effective interpretation; the practical examples shared here highlight the importance of real, humanised accounts in engaging audiences and reducing the distance between viewer and viewed. Placing these accounts in context, and particularly, in considering historic subjects' lives beyond their moment in court, can complicate understandings of motive (for defendants *and* prosecutors) and the ways in which the criminal justice system operated to regulate social relationships. Taking an intersectional and multi-vocal approach is an integral part of this contextualisation. It is evident from the discussions of gendered interpretation and the underrepresentation of black voices, that a failure to acknowledge the ways in which class, gender and ethnicity intersect, limits understanding of the experience of criminal justice. Presenting multiple viewpoints, and considering historic and contemporary perspectives on these accounts, can support audiences to question and critically engage with the operation of criminal justice.

This is not about 'getting it right'. Historians can be quick to criticise museum interpretation for being inaccurate or lacking nuance, without due regard for the processes of interpreting complex pasts to make them accessible for a wide range of audiences with different knowledge and learning styles. What we have tried to emphasise here is the potential in collaborative practice: between historians and curators, but also with our audiences and stakeholders. The examples from the National Justice Museum and Ripon Museums, in particular, show how the incorporation of more voices, particularly of those affected by criminal justice and social injustice now, can create a space for visitors to engage in critical discussion and alter perceptions.

Notes

1 Drew Gray, *Crime, Policing and Punishment in England, 1660–1914* (London, Bloomsbury: 2016), p. 137.

2 Alana Barton and Alyson Brown, 'Show Me the Prison! The Development of Prison Tourism in the UK', *Crime Media Culture* 11.3 (2015), pp. 237–238.

3 Barton and Brown, 'Show Me the Prison!', p. 252. See also J. Z. Wilson, *Prison: Cultural Memory and Dark Tourism* (New York, Peter Lang: 2008); Laurajane Smith, 'Explorations in Banality: Prison Tourism at the Old Melbourne Gaol' in Wilson et al. (eds.), *The Palgrave Handbook of Prison Tourism* (Basingstoke, Palgrave: 2017), pp. 763–786; Dan Johnson and Rhiannon Pickin, 'Suffering on Display: An Argument for Historical Nuance in British Prison Museums', *Crime, History and Societies* 23.1 (2019), pp. 1–26.

4 Tim Newburn, 'Social Disadvantage, Crime and Punishment' in Dean Hartley and Lucinda Platt (eds.), *Social Disadvantage and Disadvantage* (Oxford, Oxford University Press: 2016), pp. 4–6, 9–10; Robert Jones, Emily Hart and David Scott, 'Four New Prisons Programme: Chorley "Super Prison": The Case against', November 2022, accessed 30 October 2023, https://www.cardiff.ac.uk/__data/assets/pdf_file/0007/2685211/Chorley-Super-Prison-The-Case-Against-1.pdf, p. 6.

5 Rose Wallis, ed., 'More Than Horrible Histories? A Manifesto for Effective and Ethical Interpretation of Criminal Justice Histories', Regional History Centre, 2020, accessed 30 October 2023, https://regionalhistorianuwe.org/2020/12/17/more-than-horrible-histories/.

6 Philip Stone and Richard Sharpley, 'Consuming Dark Tourism: A Thanatological Perspective', *Annals of Tourism Research* 35.2 (2008), p. 574.

7 Philip R. Stone, 'A Dark Tourism Spectrum: towards a Typology of Death and Macabre Related Tourist Sites, Attractions and Exhibitions', *Tourism: An Interdisciplinary International Journal* 54.2 (2006), pp. 151, 154.

8 Wilson, *Prison: Cultural Memory and Dark Tourism*; Sarah Hodgkinson and Diane Urquhart, 'Prison Tourism: Exploring the Spectacle of Punishment in the UK' in Glen Hooper and John J. Lennon (eds.), *Dark Tourism: Practice and Interpretation* (London, Routledge: 2017), pp. 51–52; and Barton and Brown, 'Show Me the Prison!', pp. 237–238.

9 Alana Barton and Alyson Brown, 'Dark Tourism and the Modern Prison', *The Prison Service Journal* 199 (2012), p. 44.

10 Barton and Brown, 'Dark Tourism and the Modern Prison', p. 44; Johnson and Pickin, 'Suffering', p. 6.

11 Barton and Brown, 'Show Me the Prison!', p. 248.

12 National Justice Museum, site visits June and August 2018.

13 Barton and Brown, 'Show Me the Prison!', pp. 246–247; Johnson and Pickin, 'Suffering', pp. 13, 23.

14 Wilson, *Prison: Cultural Memory and Dark Tourism*, p. 1; Hodgkinson and Urquhart, 'Prison Tourism', pp. 51–52 and Barton and Brown, 'Show Me the Prison!', p. 246.

15 Hodgkinson and Urquhart cited in Johnson and Pickin, 'Suffering', pp. 7–8.

16 Jessica Moody, 'Where Is "Dark Public History"? A Scholarly Turn to the Dark Side, and What It Means for Public Historians', *The Public Historian* 38.3 (2016), p. 114; Johnson and Pickin, 'Suffering', p. 23.

17 Wilson, *Prison: Cultural Memory and Dark Tourism*: 1, p. 216; Barton and Brown, 'Show Me the Prison!', p. 252.

18 Douglas Hay, Peter Linebaugh, and John Rule, eds. *Albion's Fatal Tree* (London, Pantheon Books: 1975); E. P. Thompson, *Whigs and Hunters: The Origin of the Black Act* (London, Pantheon Books: 1975); Joanna Innes and John Styles, 'The Crime Wave: Recent Writing on Crime and Criminal Justice in Eighteenth-Century England', *The Journal of British Studies* 25.4 (1986), pp. 380–435.

19 E. P. Thompson, 'The Moral Economy of the English Crowd in the Eighteenth-Century', *Past and Present* 50 (1971), pp. 76–136; E. P. Thompson, 'Patrician Society, Plebeian Culture', *Journal of Social History* 7.4 (1974), pp. 382–405;

E. P. Thompson, 'Eighteenth-century English Society: Class Struggle without Class?' *Social History* 3.2 (1978), pp. 133–165 and Douglas Hay, 'Property, Authority and the Criminal Law' in *Albion's Fatal Tree,* pp. 17–63.

20 Peter King, 'Decision Makers and Decision Making in English Criminal Law, 1750–1800', *Historical Journal* 27.1 (1984), pp. 25–58; Gwenda Morgan and Peter Rushton, 'The Magistrate, the Community and the Maintenance of an Orderly Society in Eighteenth-century England', *Historical Research* 76.191 (2003), p. 77.

21 For example, J. M. Beattie, 'The Pattern of Crime in England 1660–1800', *Past and Present* 62 (1974), pp. 47–95; Lynn MacKay, 'Why They Stole: Women in the Old Bailey, 1779–1789', *Journal of Social History* 32.3 (1999), pp. 623–639; Heather Shore, 'Crime, Criminal Networks and the Survival Strategies of the Poor in Eighteenth-century London' in Steven King and Alana Tomkins (eds.), *The Poor in England, 1700–1850* (Manchester, Manchester University Press: 2003), pp. 137–166.

22 Steve Poole, 'Tales from the Old Bailey: Writing a New History from below', *History Workshop Journal* 59.1 (2005), p. 282.

23 'Tales from the Old Bailey', *London Journal* special edition, 30 (2005); 'Old Bailey Proceedings', accessed 30 October 2023, https://www.oldbaileyonline.org; 'London Lives 1690–1800 Crime Poverty and Social Policy in the Metropolis', accessed 30 October 2023, https://www.londonlives.org; 'The Digital Panopticon', accessed 30 October 2023, https://www.digitalpanopticon.org.

24 Hay et al., *Albion's Fatal Tree;* Thompson, 'The Moral Economy of the English Crowd', pp. 76–136; Beattie, 'The Pattern of Crime', pp. 47–95; J. M. Beattie, *Crime and the Courts in England, 1600–1800* (Oxford, Oxford University Press: 1986).

25 Michael Ignatieff, *A Just Measure of Pain: The Penitentiary in the Industrial Revolution, 1750–1850* (London, Macmillan: 1978).

26 Tim Hitchcock and Robert Shoemaker, *London Lives: Poverty, Crime and the Making of a Modern City, 1690–1800* (Cambridge, Cambridge University Press: 2015), p. 18.

27 Dorchester Shire Hall Trust, Shire Hall interpretation strategy, 2016, p. 3.

28 Carl Griffiths, 'From "Dorchester Labourers" to "Tolpuddle Martyrs": Celebrating Radicalism in the English Countryside' in Quentin Outram and Keith Laybourn (eds.), *Secular Martyrdom in Britain and Ireland* (Basingstoke, Palgrave Macmillan: 2018), p. 61; Trades Union Congress, *The Book of the Martyrs of Tolpuddle 1834–1934* (1934).

29 Trades Union Congress, *The Book of the Martyrs of Tolpuddle 1834–1934* (1934) and Griffiths, 'From "Dorchester Labourers" to "Tolpuddle Martyrs"', pp. 72, 78.

30 'Tolpduddle Martyrs' Festival', accessed 30 October 2023, https://www.tolpuddlemartyrs.org.uk/festival/history; Hilda Kean, 'Tolpuddle, Burston and Levellers. The Making of Radical National Heritages at English Labour Movement Festivals' in Laurajane Smith, Paul A. Shackle and Gary Campbell (eds.), *Heritage, Labour and the Working Classes* (London, Routledge: 2011), p. 266.

31 Shire Hall Museum, 'Shire Hall and the TUC', accessed 30 October 2023, www.shirehalldorset.org/connect/about.

32 Shire Hall Museum, 'Our Purpose', accessed 30 October 2023, www.shirehalldorset.org/connect/about/.

33 Shire Hall Museum, site visits 2018, 2019.

34 Shire Hall site visit, May 2018; George Loveless, The Victims of Whiggery: A Statement of the Persecutions Experienced by the Dorchester Labourers (1838), p. 7.

35 Shire Hall Museum, visitor multi-media guide. Site visit May 2018.

36 Shire Hall Museum, Loveless, *Victims of Whiggery*, p. 8, reproduced on Shire Hall visitor multi-media guide.
37 Shire Hall Museum, Nigel Costley, visitor multi media guide.
38 Carl J. Griffin, 'The Culture of Combination: Solidarities and Collective Action before Tolpuddle', *The Historical Journal* 58.2 (2015), pp. 443–480; Roger Ball, 'Tolpuddle and Swing: The Flea and the Elephant', Bristol Radical History Group, 2009, accessed 30 October 2023, https://www.brh.org.uk/site/articles/tolpuddle-and-swing-the-flea-and-the-elephant/.
39 Ball, 'Tolpuddle and Swing: The Flea and the Elephant', and Griffin, 'The Culture of Combination', pp. 472, 480.
40 Roger Ball, 'Tolpuddle, Hutt and the Meerut "conspiracy"', Bristol Radical History Group, 2014, accessed 30 October 2023, https://www.brh.org.uk/site/articles/tolpuddle-hutt-meerut-conspiracy/.
41 Ball, 'Tolpuddle and Swing'; Eric Hobsbawm and George Rudé, *Captain Swing* (Sale, Phoenix Press: [1969] 2001), p. 262.
42 York Castle Museum, 'York Castle Museum Main Leaflet March to June 2019', accessed 23 March 2019, https://www.yorkcastlemuseum.org.uk/wp-content/uploads/sites/2/2019/02/York-Castle-Museum-Main-Leaflet-Mar-Jun-2019.pdf.
43 Edward Baines, Proceedings under the Special Commission at York, before Baron Thompson and Mr. Justice Le Blanc, Which Commenced on Saturday the Second of January 1813, and Closed on Tuesday the Twelfth of the Same Month for the Trial of Offences Connected with the Late Disturbances in the West-Riding of this County, (1813), p. 58.
44 York Castle Museum, 'William Hartley Video', date visited, 2018.
45 John E. Archer, *Social Unrest and Popular Protest in England, 1780–1840* (Cambridge, Cambridge University Press: 2000), pp. 48–55; The National Archives (TNA), HO42/132, Henry Hobhouse to Home Office, 12 January 1813.
46 National Justice Museum, 'Mock Trial of Daniel Diggle Script', site visit 4 September 2017.
47 National Justice Museum, 'Daniel Diggle Trial: Mr. George Kerry Script', site visit 4 September 2017.
48 Rose Wallis, 'The Spectre of Swing' in Ra Page (ed.), *The Cuckoo Cage* (Manchester, Comma Press: 2022), pp. 133–134.
49 Dan Johnson, 'Incarcerating the Poor: Interpreting Poverty and Punishment in British Prison Museums', *Law, Crime and History* 1 (2018), p. 99; Johnson and Pickin, 'Suffering on Display', p. 10.
50 Shani D'Cruze and Louise Jackson, *Women, Crime and Justice in England since 1660* (Basingstoke, Palgrave Macmillan: 2009), pp. 47–49 and Lucia Zedner, 'Women, Crime and Penal Responses: A Historical Account', *Crime and Justice* 14 (1991), pp. 317–318.
51 D'Cruze and Jackson, *Women, Crime and Justice*, pp. 47–49.
52 Paula Ruth Gilbert, 'Discourses of Female Violence and Societal Gender Stereotypes', *Violence against Women* 8.11 (2002), p. 1282.
53 Site visit, August 2018; Johnson and Pickin, 'Suffering on Display', pp. 12–13.
54 Johnson, 'Incarcerating the Poor', pp. 102–103.
55 Shire Hall Museum, site visit March 2022.
56 Centre for Women's Justice, Women who kill: how the state criminalises women they might otherwise be burying (2021), p. 79.
57 MacKay, 'Why They Stole', pp. 623–639.
58 King and Tomkins, eds, *The Poor in England*, p. 1.
59 King and Tomkins, eds, *The Poor in England*, p. 7.

60 Shore, 'Crime, Criminal Networks and the Survival Strategies of the Poor', pp. 154–156.
61 Peter King, 'Decision-makers and Decision making in the English Criminal Law, 1750–1800', *Historical Journal* 27.1 (1984), p. 28.
62 Morgan and Rushton, 'The Magistrate, the Community and the Maintenance of an Orderly Society', pp. 54–77.
63 David Large, 'The Municipal Government of Bristol 1851–1901', *Bristol Records Society* 50 (1999), p. 95.
64 Tim Newburn, 'Social Disadvantage, Crime and Punishment' in Hartley Dean and Lucinda Platt (eds.), *Social Advantage and Disadvantage* (Oxford, Oxford University Press: 2016), pp. 6, 10.
65 Ministry of Justice. Ethnicity and the Criminal Justice System, 2020, published December 2021, accessed 30 October 2023, https://www.gov.uk/government/statistics/ethnicity-and-the-criminal-justice-system-statistics-2020/ethnicity-and-the-criminal-justice-system-2020#fnref:1.
66 See for example, Peter King and John Carter Wood, 'Black People and the Criminal Justice System: Prejudice and Practice in Later Eighteenth and Early Nineteenth-century London', *Historical Research* 83.239 (2015), pp. 100–124.
67 Martin Glynn, *Invisible Voices: The Black Presence in Crime and Punishment in the UK, 1750–1900* (London, Routledge: 2023).
68 Glynn, *Invisible Voices*, pp. 206–209.
69 Glynn, *Invisible Voices*, p. 12.
70 Glynn, *Invisible Voices*, pp. 7–8.
71 Smith, 'Explorations in Banality', p. 767.
72 Shire Hall Museum, visitor interviews July 2019, visitor survey August–September 2020; Johnson, 'Incarcerating the Poor', p. 97.
73 Shire Hall Museum, visitor interviews, 26 July 2019.
74 Shire Hall Museum, tripadvisor reviews June and December 2018; visitor interview 26 July 2019.
75 Ripon Museum Trust, 'Prisoners on Prisoners', 8 February 2020–28 March 2021, accessed 30 October 2023, https://riponmuseums.co.uk/explore/past-exhibitions/prisoners-on-prisoners/.
76 National Justice Museum, 'Choices and Consequences', accessed 30 October 2023, https://www.nationaljusticemuseum.org.uk/museum/learning/choices-and-consequences.

19

HOW BROADSIDE BALLADS FOLLOWED US INTO THIS CENTURY

Jennifer Reid

Manchester has a substantial collection of broadside ballads – cheap songsheets sang and sold by street hawkers – across a few institutions, yet they have not been utilised much outside of folk singers' research and by a handful of academics. This is a great shame as, although many of the songs are not worth the very thin paper they are printed on, broadside ballads carry a cultural and historical weight that can add dimensions to almost any humanities research. Manchester's collections are interesting because they can be used to show links between businessmen (printers, booksellers, publishers) in the new city, and their lyrics consist of themes of Lancashire, developing industry, city-scale poverty and how the working classes enjoyed themselves amidst all this. Although they may not be fully genuine or representative, the lyrics to these songs were sung by people in Victorian Manchester, and so by default must have resonated with them. Even if they just got stuck in your head, much how I find myself singing Take That on occasion, they had staying power.

Charles Hindley, defines a 'cock' in his *Curiosities of Street Literature* from *Hotten's Slang Dictionary* of 1859:

> COCKS – fictitious narratives, in verse or prose, of murders, fires, and terrible accidents, sold in the streets as true accounts. The man who hawks them, a patterer, often changes the scene of the awful event to suit the taste of the neighbourhood he is trying to delude. Possibly a corruption of COOK, a cooked statement, or, as a correspondent suggests, the COCK LANE ghost may have given rise to the term.[1]

As Leslie Shepard writes, 'the broadside ballad, then, was a kind of musical journalism, the forerunner of the popular prose newspapers, and a

DOI: 10.4324/9780429344084-23

continuation of the folk traditional of minstrelry'.[2] Although the broadsides were incredibly popular – as was most street literature – there has been relatively little research into them and dialect/regional poetry, which both Leslie Shepard and Brian Hollingworth highlight in their works.[3] The broadsides would be pasted up on pub walls and inside the cabins of ships for easy dissemination and learning. Popular tunes were used so that the new songs could be picked up quickly and shared. Their form changed over time, being more succinct and building on cultural memory to build a cultural ecology all of their own.

> In the wider sphere of street literature, pamphlets and chapbooks had a role to play. Whilst the former were mainly bought by the middle classes, being more detailed and expensive, the latter were the literature of the poor. Shepard explains:
>
> A chapbook was a sheet folded in four, eight, twelve, or sixteen, making a small uncut booklet of eight, sixteen, twenty-four, or thirty-two pages… But chapbooks were sold uncut and unstitched at a halfpenny or a penny each. The purchaser would slit the pages and lovingly stitch or pin them – a kind of do-it-yourself paperback. The word 'chapbook' seems to have derived from the Anglo-Saxon term *ceap*, in the sense of 'trade', for these pamphlets were sold by pedlars together with pins, ribbons and other knick-knacks.[4]

Chapbooks were in the same vein as broadsides, but as they consisted of more pages they contained also folklore, longer stories and folk-tales, religious stories and humorous dialogues. The chapbooks and broadsides together influenced the common people and allowed them to express themselves.

The early ballads started life off in the oral tradition, eventually being written down to be sold and, accidentally, preserved. Later ballads were written for the sheets, by capable scribes and musicians who sought to use the form to generate income, reflecting the ballad tradition's infancy in the sixteenth century. The minstrels who performed for kings and travelled the country over, to their audiences' great delight, 'were ancestors to the rogues and vagabonds of the broadside ballad periods'.[5]

Chapbooks and ballads were most popular during the seventeenth and eighteenth centuries, with chapbooks becoming more popular during the latter. Following events such as the French Revolution and the Peterloo Massacre, seditious literature began to billow out of the printers only for the majority to be quelled by the Six Acts in 1819 and the extended enforcement of stamp duty onto all news-opinion publications costing under sixpence. The Six Acts were brought in to limit political literature being printed and disseminated and they also prevented people from gathering and meeting, lest it turn seditious and violent.

As ballads and songs began to address the political and cultural deficits experienced by workers and the poor, their tones changed and the authorities acted accordingly. When people began to sing out against the authorities; the monarchy; the masters and the mill-owners they were forcibly quietened. When the nineteenth-century ballads began to report injustices much like a newspaper, the actual newspapers caught up with them and outsold them.

Manchester Ballads

So, to Manchester then. The collections that are of note are from Chetham's Library, the Manchester Central Library, and the Working Class Movement Library, which have various ephemera and some modern songs, mostly about twentieth-century strikes.[6] A quick enquiry to a librarian will point you in the right direction.

Most of the ballads in the Manchester collections were printed, sold or published by:

G. Swindells (c. 1796–1853)

George Swindells is credited as 'the founder of one of the earliest publishing firms of this city'.[7] After his death in 1796, at the age of 36, a 'Mr. A. Swindells' takes charge of the business, along with his eldest son John. It is believed that this is an incorrect assumption and is actually George's wife, Mrs. Alice Swindells. In the 'History, Directory and Gazetteer of the County Palatine…' by Baines and Parson, Alice Swindells is listed as 'letter press printer' at 8 Hanging Bridge in 1825.[8] Even before that she is listed as printer at the same address in 1820.[9] The family held onto the shop until 1846 and after that a younger son, Henry, conducted a printing business in Deansgate 'for many years'.[10]

As George died when he was relatively young, most of the broadside and penny histories, along with many other types of cheap literature, were printed by Alice and probably John. One source states that 'from whose press were issued chapbooks in an almost endless variety'.[11] The Swindells tome in Manchester Central Library contains a range of material, some signed with 'A. Swindells' and some with just 'Swindells', if they mark the printers name at all. The literature produced by Swindells was usually quite simple, but there are certain broadsides that are heavy with woodcuts, which stand out in the catalogue: 'with their poor paper, old type and crude illustrations they take us back to the days when books were scarce and dear'.[12]

Fancy Lad is a typical example of a Swindells ballad. The type setting is not aesthetically pleasing like some of the later ballads and the woodcuts are smaller and more rudimental. I believe Swindells was from the old school of

Fancy Lad.

WHEN first I came to town,
They call'd me lovely Nancy,
But now the've chang'd my name,
And call me the soldier's fancy.

CHORUS.
Go along, go along Bob
Go along Bob's a dying,
Go along, go along Bob,
Your fancy girls's a crying.
I will buy my love a coat,
Silver buttons to it,
I will let them fee
I am the girl can do it.
Now when my love comes home,
I will roll in riches,
And I will buy my love
A pair of buck-skin breeches.
I for beef and pork,
You for peas and pudding,
Put a clean pair of sheets on the bed
For the fancy lads are coming.
When I first came to town,
I had not a gown to wear O,
O once I had a bed,
But now I am forc'd to plank it,
Hang and take the jade,
She stole my bed and blanket.
Then in came merry Peggy,
Hang her ragged fortune,
She pawn'd her best blue brat,
To raise her lad a quartern.
My fancy lad's in Quod,
I am free and willing,
To work by night or day,
And get an honest shilling.

Swindells, Printer.

FIGURE 19.1 Bod22106 (2806 c.17(123) Slip. Originally a sheet with 2806 c.17 (266)) Roud Number: V7586.

ballad printing, where beauty was not always necessary and fitting as many verses on the slip as possible took precedence. Almost all of Swindells ballads we have are cut into slips, which I believe makes them well used and sold. They also make use of the long 's', which many nineteenth-century ballads do not. When flicking through a collection of ballads these are the things that stand out to me that say it is a Swindells ballad. Nine times out of ten they are right. Now to the subject matter, which is fitting to a city which is swelling with economic migrants. The female voice talking is saying how she has changed her life to being the 'soldier's fancy'. This happened to lots of women coming into the city from rural villages, often found in Victorian literature as 'fallen women', much like Esther in Mary Barton. Something else to note is the use of 'Quod' to describe prison, which came to be used around the end of the seventeenth century.

J. O. Bebbington (Printer, Various Addresses on Goulden-street, Oldham Road, Manchester), c. 1850–1861

I can't find much information on Bebbington, although he seems to have made a good trade. Being based near Ancoats in the mid-1800s meant that he would have most certainly catered for the Irish migrants of the Angel Meadow slums close by. A quick search in the Bodleian Library ballads catalogue shows that he printed 19 ballads on the theme of 'Ireland' that have been digitised. Other themes are various monarchy and noblemen as well as the ballad 'Jone O'Grinfield' which would later become 'The Four Loom Weaver' performed by every folk group imaginable.

Jone O'Grinfield is believed to be a pseudonym of Joseph Lees of Glodwick, who may have written other similar ballads in dialect as the character Johnny Green. 'Johnny Green's Wedding' and 'Johnny Green's Trip fro' Owdham to see the Manchester Railway' are titles that also appear in the series. This ballad is a solemn tale of a weaver's descent into poverty, explaining varied aspects of a weaver's life such as piece-work, diet and disputes with bailiffs. The experience given in this ballad is that of the hand-loom weaver who is on the cusp of industrialisation. The work is slowly becoming uneconomical and the factory or the workhouse is calling. The 'putting out' system meant that weavers had to take cuts to their pay to accommodate middle men selling their pieces at the market, meaning that what they could earn was dwindling. Tragically, in the final stanza, Margit states that if she had clothes to put on she would visit the queen and ask for reform. The ballad makes use of some key Lancashire dialect.

Clem: To starve to death

Picked o'er: To weave

Waterloo porridge: Porridge made with water ('Waterloo' was used as a negative adjective and also helps us to date the lyrics)

Hoo: She

J. Wrigley Jnr. (Printer, 3, Rochdale Road, Manchester [and] J. Bebbington, Printer, 31, Oldham Road, Manchester)

J. Wrigley, Jr. bought Bebbington's plates and together they sold a lot of ballads through J. Beaumont, 176, York Street, Leeds.

JONE O'GRINFIELD.

I'm a poor cotton weaver as many one know,
I've nowt to eat i'th house an I've worn out my cloas,
You'd hardly give sixpence for all I have on,
My clugs they are brassen and stockings I've none,
You'd think it war hard to be sent into th' world,
To clem and do th'best ot you con.

Our church parson kept telling us long,
We should have better times if we'd hold our tongues,
I've houden me tongue till I can hardly draw breath,
I think i' my heart he means to clem me to death;
I know he lives weel by backbiting the de'il,
But he he never pickced o'er in his life.

I tarried six week an thought every day wur t'last,
I tarried and shifted till now I'm quite fast;
I lived on nettles while nettles were good,
An Waterloo porridge were best of my food;
I'm telling you true I can find folks enew,
That are living no better than me.

Old Bill o' Dan's sent bailiffs one day,
For a shop score I owed him that I could not pay,
But he wur too late for d Bill o' Bent,
Had sent tit and cart and taen goods for rent,
We had nou bur a stoo, that wur a seat for two,
And on it cowered Margit and me.

The bailiffs looked round assly as a mouse,
When they saw aw things were taen out ot house,
Says one to the other all's gone thou may see,
Aw sed lads never fret you're welcome to me;
They made no more ado, but nipp'd up th' owd stoo,
And we both went wack upoth flags.

I geer howd of Margit for hoo wur stricken sick,
Hoo sed hoo ne'er had such a bang sin hoo wur wick
The bailiffs scoured off with owd stoo on their backs,
They would not have cared had they brook our necks,
They're mad at owt Brent cos he's taen goeds for rent,
And wur ready to flee us alive.

I sed to our Margit as we lay upoth floor,
We shall never be lower in this world I'm sure,
But if we alter I'm sure we mun mend,
For I think in my heart we are both at far end,
Fer meat we have none nor looms to weae on,
Egad they're as weel lost as found.

Then I geet up my piece and I took it em back,
I scarcely dare speak mester looked so black,
He said you wur o'erpaid last time you coom,
I said if I wur 'twas for weaving bout loom;
In a mind as I'm in I'll ne'er pick o'er again,
For I've woven myself toth' fur end.

Then aw coom out and left him to chew that,
When aw thought again aw wur vext till aw sweat,
To think that we mun work to keep them and awth set,
All the day o' my life and still be in their debt;
So I'll give o'er my trade an work with a spade,
Or go and break stones upoth road,

Our Margit declared if hoo'd closs to put on,
Hoo'd go up to Lundun an see the big mon
An if things didn't sites when hoo had been,
Hoo swears hoo'd feight blook up toth e'en,
Hoo's nought again th' Queen but likes a fair thing,
An hoo say hoo can tell when hoo's hurt.

SALLY SLY.

Printed and Sold Wholesale and Retail,
by John O. Pebbington, 22 Goulden-
street, Oldham Road, Manchester.

At six in the morning awaking,
Coals taking,
Love making,
With barrow, I cry;
I knock and sing at the areas,
My care is
The fairies,
With coals to supply.

I'm in love! I'm in love! Oh my eye!
I'm going for to meet her to-morrow-
Sally Sly! Sally Sly! Sally Sly!
I'm going for to meet her to-morrow-
Sally Sly! Sally Sly! Sally Sly!

We meet where the walls they've bear
While walking (chalking,
And talking;
We're both tall and straight,
With apples and cherries I treat her
Sweet creature,
I meet her
To-morrow, at eight.
I'm in love, &c.

One day, Jemmy Raspell, the baker.
To take her
And make her
His tool, he did try;
He told her to kick Jemmy Snivel
To the devil-
How civil;
Then she blacken'd his eye
I'm in love, &c.

FIGURE 19.2 'Jone O' Grinfield' and 'Sally Sly'. Edition - Bod4190; Firth c.26(2); Roud Number: 937.

Below we have an old favourite of mine, which has stuck with me ever since I heard Harry Boardman sing it. It stuck with me so well that I now sing it in Harry's style to applauding and bewildered audiences. Victoria Bridge is located at the northern end of Deansgate and provides a quick thoroughfare into Salford. It was completed and opened in the summer of 1839 and Queen Victoria visited in 1851. Joseph Aston, in his 'Manchester Guide' of 1804,

Printed an Sold Wholesale & Retail by
J. Wrigley, 3, Rochdale-road.

TOBACCO.

Bebbington, Printer. 26, Goulden-street,
Oldham-road, Manchester, and sold by
J. Beaumont, 176, York-street, and
H. Andres, 27, St. Peter's-street, Leeds.

Tobacco is an Indian weed,
Grows green in the morn and cut down at eve,
It shows our decay, we come from the clay,
Think of this when you're smoking tobacco.

The pipe that is so lilly white,
In which most men take great delight.
Its broke with a touch men's lives are such
Think on this when you're smoking tobacco
The smoke from the pipe doth fly,
It shows we are nothing but dust at all,
For we come from the dust & return we must
Think of this when you're smoking tobacco.

VICTORIA BRIDGE ON A. Saturday Night

Whoever may travel o'er Manchester gravel,
Will see many thing to astonish his sight,
But sure he must notice, wherever his coat is,
Victoria Bridge on a Saturday night,
Such running and rushing, such jolting and pushing,
It looks as though Babel had settled through spite,
Or, Old Nick, to goad one, had took his abode on,
Victoria Bridge on a Saturday Night.

CHORUS.
Hurrooh, what a bother, this, that, and the other,
All jumbled together, - a comical sight!
My oath, I declare on 'tis just like a fair on,
Victoria Bridge on a Saturday Night.

If troubled with pthisic, there are doctors with physic
With l9ozenges, boluses, poppy's and pills,
With ointment for drawing, with baccy for chawing,
Would blister your chops, till you're red in the gills,
There's snuff for your noses. And salve for your toses,
With poultry and pigs, pickled pork, and Police,
With pokers, and fenders, and Newspaper venders,
And Stretford black puddings a penny a piece.

There's cab drivers calling, and fish woman bawling,
Their cod-fish, and haddock, fresh flounder, and fluke
With dory, and dab-fish, and cockles, and crab-fish,
And beautiful salmon, just caught – with a hook,
Their's lots of disparity, folks craving fo charity,
Howling away, you would drop with surprise
And some you will find are so desperate blind,
Sure, they can't see at all till they open their eyes.

There's walking-stick makers, and handkerchief takers,
There are geese by the dozen, and turkeys in flocks,
There's glass-men and potters, and cow-heels& trotters
And lucifer matches a halfpenny a box,
There's oranges and apples, and paper made chapels
There's old weather prophets, and new Almanacks,
With hare skins and rabbits, and lots of bad habits,
And roasted potatoes as mealy as wax.

If you are fond of indicing, there's paper for writing,
And fine patent pencil – without any lead,
And plenty of fellows with good umbrellas
That wont keep the rain or aught else from your head
So busy the trade is, that pretty young ladies,
Will rush in the crowd, aye, and some you will find
So rough in their tussles, they drop off their bustles,
And come out as flat as a flounder behind.

There's prime treacle toffy, and new patent coffee,
And clappers that go at the devil's own rate,
There's sweet sugar candy, with spanish-juice brandy,
And fine pickled muscles a penny a plate,
In season there's cherries, black currants, and berries,
Plenty of balderdash, prunes and plumbs,
With brick-dust, and bristles, and children's whistles,
And rods, when they're naughty, to tickle their bums.

Then some in their panics, pop into the Mechanics,
Far famed institution, and up stairs they trot,
Where those fond of trifles, may pick up their rifles,
And kill the bull's eye at a penny a shot,
Now the truth I have told what are here to be sold,
Such bawling and squeezing as bothers me quite;
Both of good things and bad, there are a lot to be had,
At Victoria Bridge on a Saturday Night.

FIGURE 19.3 'Tobacco' and 'Victoria Bridge on a Saturday Night'. Bod18406; Johnson Ballads 1881. Bod18406; Johnson Ballads 1881

states that, 'until that period [1778]... it was often a work of labour for persons not very active, to get over the bridge on a market day', which shows that the bridge had been used for a market definitely in the eighteenth century if not earlier. The ballad itself is – for once! – a great poem which would have taken a while to devise. I can imagine it would be a great seller as it is not only a quality work but also describes a humorous and chaotic scene.

T. Pearson (T. Pearson, Printer, 6, Chadderton-street, off Oldham Road, Manchester) (c. 1850–1899)

Pearson advertised that he had bought Bebbington's and Wrigley's stock. This is good news for historians as the older ballads and woodcuts were kept by printers and sellers so we can make use of them today. The same logic can be applied to the ballads themselves. They were never meant to last so we should count ourselves lucky that even a few survived. The main reason so many are available to us today in archives, museums and libraries is that there were collectors who chose to keep ballads. We are often at the mercy of their curatorial process but thanks to men like John Harland we can see a broad spread that we otherwise would not.

A Lament for the Manchester Convicts is found on a very busy ballad sheet. It is unusual to see them filled up in this way, with a large woodcut at the top that would probably have been expensive when it was bought. A lot of the woodcuts used on nineteenth-century ballads in Manchester were passed down and around between printers and this serves as a tool for us to link them. It may have been that Pearson was looking to show off his connection to the recently deceased well-known printer who passed on this large woodcut to him or it may have been that he had space to fill. We will never know for sure, but it is always amusing to speculate. The ballad itself is concerned with the story of the ill-fated Allen, Gould and Larkin, also known as 'the Manchester Martyrs', who along with two other men fatally injured policeman Charles Brett in 1867. It may not have been chance that this ballad was placed next to *My Native Land So Green,* as the three offenders were involved with the Irish Republican Brotherhood.

Lancashire Offerings

Dialect poets are incredibly interesting to me because they are afforded class mobility by writing about nothing else but their homely ways and origins. By poetry, someone can be lifted above their one up-one down and be heard by the business folk uptown. If a Baroness had not been enchanted by Edwin Waugh's verses then they may never have reached outside of Rochdale and he certainly would not have been giving speeches at well-respected society dinners. I should state that I am a 'Woffer'. This means I pronounce Edwin Waugh as 'Ned Woff'.

MY NATIVE LAND IS Green.

T. Pearson, Printer ad Stationer 6, Chadderton St., Oldham Road, Manchester.

I am a true born Irishman I came from Paddy's land,
Where the stranger finds a welcome with the grasp of friendships hand,
Where the wit it flows spontaneously and pleasure does bound,
And good nature mixed together in abundance can be found
Where the boys are all so jolly at a pattern race, or fair,
For prudence none with them can compare,
They're the bravest set of boys that ever yet were seen,
The boys of dear old Ireland my native land so green.

You will surely find that Paddy his aid will always lend,
And be ready to assist you if e're you want a friend,
If his cabin you should enter you know as well as me,
He'll treat you with the very best quite welcome you will be.
He'll share his pipe and whiskey, your spirits he will cheer,
O ould Ireland you're my darling the spot I love so dear,
For true hospitality – no matter where I've been,
There's no place like ould Ieland, my nativeland so green

If o'er you're best on pleasure abroad you need no roam,
There's no such sights in foreign lands like those we have at home,
Killerney's lakes are beautiful as every one must own,
And if you're fond of nonsense just kiss the blarney stone
We have scenery in Wicklow there's the Giant's Causeway too,
The bay ar d sights round Dublin are splendid to the view,
I have travelled many a thousand mile, strange countries I have seen,
But none to equal Erin's Isle my native land so green.

Then here's anccess to Erin my own dear native Isle,
May discontent soon vanish, and pleuty on her smile,
May discord and ill-feeling be banished from thy shore,
And prosperity shine on thee as it did in days of yore,
I only wish for happiness that our troubles soon would cease.

So we might live like brothers in unity and peace,
May trade increase and flourish, and shortly will be seen,
The people gay and happy in my native land so green.

A LAMENT FOR THE MANCHESTER CONVICTS.

In the County Gaol at Salford,
Those poor unhappy men,
Upon the fatal gallows tree,
Their precious lives did end,
The jury them Guilty,
And they are doomed you see,
For the murder of Sergeant Brett,
To suffer on the fatal tree.

Allen, larkin, and Gould you see
Have suffered on the fatal tree.

On the 18th of September,
Some persons formed a plan,
To assemble on the Hyde Road,
To attack the prison van;
To rescue Kelly and Deasey,
To the railway arch they went,
But to take the life of any one,
Was never their intent.

But oh, alas! they were condemned
And sentenced for to be
Publicly executed,
On the fatal gallows tree;
Let's hope the Lord has forgiven them,
And Christians far and near,
Sympathise with weeping friends.
Their wives and children dear.

When those poor men they were condemned
And asked what they'd to say,
Allen, he got up and spoke,
In a bold and fearless way;
He said that he was innocent,
But made this bold reply,
For poor oppressed Ireland,
On the gallows he would die.

Then Larkin he got up and spoke,
And said he'd not deny,
That he was at Belle Vue that day,
He went there for to try,
To rescue Kelly and Deasey,
He did did his best that day,
But he ne never fired a shot,
Or took a human life away.

Gould and Shore they spoke in turn,
And made a bold reply,
They said they'd done no murder,
But were willing for to die;
To the hangman they would yield,
But would rather fight for Ireland,
And die on the battle field.

Now to conclude and finish,
These lines that I do pen,
May the Lord above receive the soul
Of those poor, poor unhappy men,
It was a shocking sight to see,
Them stand to meet their doom,
And suffer on the fatal tree,
In vigiour health and bloom.

FIGURE 19.4 'My Native Land is Green' and 'A Lament for the Manchester Convicts'. Bod3518; 2806 b.10(125); Roud Number: V6502.

It has been a bone of contention for many years in the Lancashire dialect community but I have been suitably convinced and this may be my hill to die on. I'm told it comes from a North Easternly name pronounced 'Woff' from which Edwin descended and if that hasn't convinced you then I'll tell you that Harvey Kershaw OBE was a 'Woffer'. He earned that OBE with services to the Rochdale dialect so you're in good company should you wish to join us. The dialect writers of Lancashire often came from the hand-loom weaving industry and had great standing in the community. They were positioned as an eloquent mouthpiece for the community to the wider world. Dialect writing has seen a steady decline but it has had pockets of resurgence which give us all hope.

It is not possible to talk about Lancashire dialect without mentioning Tim Bobbin (John Collier) whose *A View of the Lancashire Dialect; containing the Adventures and Misfortunes of a Lancashire Clown by Tim Bobbin*, set the foundations for the rich Lancashire dialect tradition.[13] Born in 1708, he was a real character, selling his work in Rochdale pubs and painting portraits of willing customers. He became known as the 'Lancashire Hogarth' – high praise indeed. He was brilliant up until the last, writing his own epitaph 20 minutes before dying. It was Collier's witty and mirthful take on the Lancashire dialect that would influence the very best of Lancashire dialect poets to come. The humorous dialogue between Tummus and Meary in *A View of the Lancashire Dialect* was especially important as an influence because it was a self-styled scientific take on the Lancashire dialect, with a glossary of words and phrases. This allowed those not so familiar with the writing of dialect to be privy to this odd yet entertaining style of writing.

Samuel Bamford, 1788–1872

He warbled when Waugh wur a fledglin' i'th' nest,
An' had ne'er had a thowt abeawt meauntin';
An' young 'Lijah Rydin's had hardly begun
To give us his "Streams fro' th' owd Fountain."
Th' owd loom heawse i' Middleton rang wi' his notes,
An' his shuttle kept toime to his songs,
Ere he led up his neighbours to famed Peterloo,
To deneaunce what they felt to be wrongs.[14]

Samuel Bamford is a well-known radical, coming of age in the nineteenth century. He is noted for his involvement in and presence at the Peterloo Massacre, as well as his verses – the most famous of which is *God Help the Poor* which was used by Mrs. Gaskell in Mary Barton. Another of his poems, *Lines to a Plotting Parson*, is focussed on Parson Hay of Rochdale, who Harvey Kershaw describes as 'this here Rochdale vicar made wi' richest living in t'land', in his poem (now put to music) Peterloo.[15] The verse that opens this part about Bamford was written by Lancashire dialect poet Samuel Laycock of Marsden, who later came to live in Stalybridge. The verse references important names in the dialect scene of the time – Edwin Waugh of Rochdale and Elijah Ridings of Failsworth – as well as the place of Bamford's birth and his involvement in Peterloo. It was long thought that Bamford was Tim Bobbin. The fact that the verse speaks about Bamford as being part of a wider scene is important for readers of Lancashire dialect and those who follow working-class traditions, as these are the clues that bring you into contact with rarer and lesser-known poets and their activities.

Edwin Waugh, 1817–1890

> We're silent now, since thou hast left, and gone
> To join the crowd of songsters gone before;
> Prince, Bamford, Swain have winged it, one by one,
> And songs of homely life are heard no more.[16]

Waugh is best known in his homely seat of Rochdale. He was apprenticed to a printer when a boy, which furnished him with a love of books and print. His *Come Whoam to thi' Childer an' Me* impressed Baroness Burdett-Coutts – heir to the Coutts banking fortune – so much that she ordered it to be printed on postcards and disseminated far and wide. This earned Waugh a place in both working-class and middle-class hearts and homes. The verse opening this part was written by Ben Brierley of Failsworth to commemorate Waugh's life. He mentions John Critchley Prince of Wigan, a dialect writer often seen at the Poet's Corner in Blackburn in the nineteenth century. A Rochdale lad being compared to a Blackburn poet shows how large the Lancashire dialect scene was; it covered great distances across Lancashire. Waugh's rhymes embody the Lancashire spirit, from longing and courting to fervent belief in justice and attaining it. In *Tickle Times*, Waugh speaks to those operatives affected by the Cotton Famine (1861–1864):

> One feels, neaw 'at times are so nippin',
> A mon's at a troublesome schoo',
> That slaves like a horse for a livin',
> An, flings it away like a foo;
> But, as pleasur's sometimes a misfortin,
> An' trouble sometimes a good thing, —
> Though we liv'n o'th floor, same as layrocks,
> We'n go up, like layrocks, to sing.[17]

The final two lines of the second verse can be found on the front cover of *Folk Songs and Ballads of Lancashire* by Harry and Leslie Boardman. Similar to woodcuts in ballads showing business links, newer writers and collectors want to show connections to older poets. It is natural to want to belong to a particular, successful, relevant trajectory.

William Billington, 1825–1884

'The Blackburn Poet' began the Poet's Corner from his beer-house in Blackburn, but he is best remembered for his lines on the Cotton Famine. 'Aw Wod This War Were Ended' of 1863 is, in my opinion, an incredibly fine offering. Here are the first, middle and final verses:

> There's nobuddy knows wod we'n gooan
> through
> Sin' th' factories stopt at fost,
> An' heaw mitch life's bin wasted too,
> An heaw mitch brass we'n lost;
> Aw trys sometimes to reckon up,
> Bud keawntin connud mend id;
> When aw sit deawn wi nowt to sup—
> Aw wod this war wur ended.
> As times hes bin, aw owt some "tin"
> For shop stuff ut Lung Nailey's,
> An' case aw cuddent pay 't, yo sin,
> He's gooan an' sent th' bum bailies;
> They'n sowd us up, booath pot an' pooak,
> An' paid th' owd scoor off splendid;
> They just dun wod they will wi fooak.—
> Aw wod this war wur ended!
> Some factory maisters tokes for t' Seawth
> Wi' a smooth an' oily tongue,
> Bud iv they'd sense they'd shut their
> meawth,
> Or sing another song;
> Let liberty nod slavery
> Be fostered an' extended—
> Four million slaves mun yet be free,
> An' *then* t' war *will* be ended.

It is difficult to speak of one of the most significant tragedies that affected weavers and cotton operatives without mentioning Billington, which makes him incredibly important to the discourse on the working classes. The Cotton Famine itself was exacerbated by the refusal of cotton picked by the enslaved in Manchester, which although noble and ultimately won out, was a death sentence for many.

An interesting similarity to ballads here is the term 'bum bailies', which is dialect that features in the ballads of the city (notably Jone O'Grinfield) There is no refined definition I can provide you with, other than the Lancashire people didn't much care for bailiffs so they prefaced their title with 'bum'.

Sam Laycock, 1826–1893

Bard of the loom, the workshop, and the mill,
Whose lowly songs for lowly folks were sung,
Thy death a thousand hearts with grief doth fill;
For thou didst speak to men in their own tongue,
And teach them how to see with clearer light
And hopeful vision through their ills and strife;
So that with patience they might view aright
The comedy and tragedy of life.
Adieu, sweet singer, gone to sing elsewhere,
Thy voice has ceased within our earthly choir,
To join the swelling chorus sung up there;
And we shall miss the music of thy lyre;
But in our memories we shall cherish long
The sweet remembrance of thy life and song.[18]

Sam Laycock was a Yorkshireman, probably the cleverest one that ever lived, in that he decided to write Lancashire dialect. Laycock's 'Shurat Weaver's Song' is a righteous and distinctive contribution to the verses on the Cotton Famine. I have included the most pertinent verses here:

Confound it! aw ne'er wur so woven afore,
Mi back's welly brocken, mi fingers are sore;
Aw've bin starin' an' rootin' among this Shurat,
Till aw'm very near getten as bloint as a bat.
Neaw aw haven't mi family under mi hat,
Aw've a woife an' six childer to keep eawt o' that;
So aw'm rayther among it at present yo see,
Iv ever a fellow wur puzzled, it's me!
Iv one turns eawt to steal, folk'll co me a thief,
An' aw conno' put th' cheek on to ax for relief;
As aw said i' eawr heawse t' other neet to mi woife,
Aw never did nowt o' this sort i' mi loife.
One doesn't like everyone t' know heaw they are,
But we'n suffered so long thro' this 'Merica war,
'At there's lot's o' poor factory folk getten t' fur end,
An' they'll soon be knock'd o'er iv th' toimes don't

mend.
Oh, dear! iv yon Yankees could only just see
Heaw they're clemmin' an' starvin' poor weavers loike
me,
Aw think they'd soon settle their bother, an' strive
To send us some cotton to keep us alive.
Come give us a lift, yo' 'at han owt to give,
An' help yo're poor brothers an' sisters to live;
Be kind, an' be tender to th' needy an' poor,
An' we'll promise when th' times mend well ax yo no
moor.[19]

The encapsulation of the 1860s weaver's situation is hard-hitting. Much how Tommy Armstrong of Tyneside (The Pitman's Poet) came to speak for the community through his eloquent verse, the cotton folk relied on the dialect writers to fight their corner in print, literary and oral tradition. The 'shurat' mentioned here is Indian surat which was used instead of cotton for a brief time during the Cotton Famine (or Distress as it was known.) The shortness of fibres in Surat compared to the long fibres of cotton meant that the goods woven were marred (lower quality and prone to holes) and this brought about the word 'shoddy'. Shoddy goods were those that were of less value and quality which still features in our lexicon.

John Trafford Clegg, 1857–1895

Moving on from the Cotton Famine, we can glean a lot from John Trafford Clegg's output. 'Th' Owd Weighver' had a relatively short life but it was full. Like Waugh he worked in printing and then went into weaving, which is to be expected. His 'A Weighver's Song' gives the reader an insight into a working weaving shed:

Deawn i' th' shed on a summer's day,
Th' owd sun shinin' through th' white-weshed top;
Brids on th' slate are chirpin' away,
An' aw whistle a tune to every cop;
Clatterin' loom an' whirlin' wheel,
Flyin' shuttle an' steady reed –
This is wark to make a mon feel
There's wur jobs nor weighvin' i' time o' need.

Straight-drawn alley an' clen white wo's,
Picking-pegs noddin' their yeads o reaund,
Warps bendin' deawn like waything-fo's,

Cog-wheels rattlin' a merry seaund,
Tidy skips runnin' o'er wi' weft,
Snowy cloth windin' on to th' byem –
Tak' a good sniff o' th' flyin' drift,
It's clay an' dust, an' we're nobbut th' same.

Lads an' lasses stonnin' i' rows,
Wortchin' away fro' morn to neet;
Tenters – Bobs, Sals, Bettys, an' Joes –
Runnin' abeaut o' their nimble feet,
Keepin' time to a steady tune,
Played bi th' engine fro' leet to dark
(Feed him wi' wayther an' coal, beaut spoon,
An' he's olez reet for another day's wark);

Weighvin' cotton o sizes an' mak's,
Tablecloths, hanketchers, owts an' nowts,
Shirts for Africans an' 'Merica blacks,
Towels for Chinamen, India clouts,
Dhooties, jacconets, sheetin's, twills,
Yard-wide, narrow-widths, heavy an' leet,
Brats and petticwots, fancies, drills –
We con weighve owt, an weighve it reet!

Deawn i' th' shed on a winther's day,
Th' sun asleep in his cleaudy bed,
Scores o' gasleets blazin' away
On shinin' pulley an snowy thread;
Clattherin' loom an' whirlin' wheel,
Flyin' shuttle an' steady reed –
This is wark to make a mon feel
There's wur jobs nor weighvin' i' time o' need.

The use of specific work dialect in this poem makes it all the more precious. This is the sound of the nineteenth-century weaver of Lancashire: how they would talk and which words they would use. The dialect chosen for this poem is onomatopoeic and takes you into the factory and the shed. A very powerful line is 'Tak' a good sniff o' th' flyin' drift, It's clay an' dust, an' we're nobbut th' same', meaning that our lives are nothing but dust in the wind, blown away by the winds of time. Very elegant and prosaic for those who think dialect is clunky.

There are a lot of names to be mentioned in nineteenth-century Lancashire dialect poetry, mostly those of men. There were a number of women also writing in the dialect during that time as well as further along. In the middle of the twentieth century, female dialect writers shone a little brighter, aided by performers such as Hydla Baker and Gracie Fields. One of those women was Edith M. Ralphs, whose verses covered the rigs of Oldham's Tommyfield market in its heyday – the 1970s and 80s. In 'Queuing Up', she writes about a recent bread strike where she ended up bumping into an old acquaintance in the queue for bread.[20]

The other is Louisa Bearman, who has a fine vinyl record out on Big Ben records called *Poems in the Lancashire Dialect.* There are 22 poems on there that are asking to be turned into songs.

A discussion of contemporary Lancashire dialect poetry would not be complete without **Harvey Kershaw (1908–1986)** who was interested in working-class events both ancient and modern. His range stretched from ridiculing King Canute, commenting on the injustices of Peterloo, and reminiscing about his own childhood in 'Clogs' of 1958.[21]

These men and women brought to life the working-class experience by mentioning it, not mentioning it, enjoying the other parts of life outside of work and having a crack at authority. We owe to them the rich tradition of Lancashire dialect, a tradition which has no match anywhere else. These are the voices of men and women who experienced first-hand the development of the factory system, were pushed out of their villages in favour of turning their time and lives into capital for somebody else to profit from. These are the people who we should listen to and learn from.

Folk Revival and Contemporary Renditions

In 1957, Ewan McColl and Peggy Seeger released their *Shuttle and Cage* LP on Topic records. The songs McColl sang were related to industry, favouring the North. There is something special about listening to a record and hearing 'Newton Heath' or 'Castleton' being mentioned. The folk revival had begun. I think it took off so well because it brought back songs that were heavily localised but also could be relevant to a number of small communities. People were ready to sympathise with the workers who had toiled and died for our world as it is now. Commemorations came pouring in for the working-class writers, poets and researchers who scrabbled to unearth obscure work songs from small local libraries and archives. Even academics were writing books on specific parts of working-class culture that before then had seemed low brow. E.P. Thompson vowed to honour those workers from the 'enormous condescension of posterity', and now scholars such as Leslie Shepard and Victor E. Neuburg were writing about street literature. Once the poems and songs were found, they were put to music by professional musicians and bought by people like my dad and yours.

The folk revival in twentieth-century England was more focused on contemporary interpretations of folk songs, but towards the latter stages, notably the 1960s, there was a shift to work songs from each pocket of industry. For Greater Manchester and Lancashire this meant the Industrial Revolution, as many towns had been satellites to Cottonopolis. Performers such as Harry and Leslie Boardman, Bernard Wrigley, Mike Harding, Mark Dowding, Gary and Vera Aspey, Mike Canavan, and Sid Calderbank developed their own style using the older songs of the areas they were interested in. There also came collectors and preservers, such as Emma Vickers and Paul Graney, who were instrumental in the dissemination of the older songs from libraries and people's memories into the folk clubs and further still.

I will take some time to introduce these popular local performers, who have both reacquainted the public with traditional songs and put their own stamp on them in the process. Bernard Wrigley, known as the Bolton Bullfrog, began at the Octagon Theatre in Bolton, when Dave and Bernard were asked to perform in and write the songs for 'Crompton's Mule' and 'The Bolton Massacre', both documentaries with local flavour. After going solo he appeared in 'Ballads Of The North West' for BBC North, which included Harry Boardman as the narrator in every episode. Harry was the man who inspired those younger singers at the time. Mark Dowding has since issued albums both of Harry's songs and broadside ballads, alongside his own work with Roy Palmer and Boardman for the *Manchester Ballads*. Wrigley prefers to be known as a singer from Lancashire as he covers a lot of territory, branching out into humorous monologues in recent years. Husband and wife Gary and Vera Aspey are a rare coupling, in that they play and sing well together, being known for their harmonies and their well-researched songs. Songs about picking bass on the Wigan slag heaps come all too easily, as this formed part of Gary's childhood. Contrasted with this is the album cover for *A Taste of Hotpot*, a classic Lancashire tongue-in-cheek image. Sid Calderbank is known for being a living exponent of the Lancashire dialect tradition, first learning Stanley Holloway's 'Sam's Medal' while still at school, similar to how John Collier inspired the nineteenth-century contingent. On discovering folk music in the 1960s and 70s when every town had at least one folk night on every night of the week, he started collecting LPs by The Oldham Tinkers, Harry Boardman, Mike Harding, Gary and Vera Aspey, and other Lancashire singers then fell in with the Roebuck traditional singers club in Leyland. He then began searching the local history sections in libraries during the day for Victorian songs and poems, learning them at night whilst working in Leyland Motors' Comet Shop, and singing them at weekends. He got more and more interested in nineteenth-century dialect writings and found that no other county in England has such a store of songs, stories, and poems as Lancashire. He then realised that these thousands of books by hundreds of authors were actually our social history, written, in the main, by ordinary working men and women. They are an untapped resource as many people find dialect writing inaccessible.

Whilst these singers were collecting in their own right, there are two collectors that aided these performers by supplementing them with songs from the back of archives and libraries. Emma Vickers of Burscough was well known in the area for collecting and more importantly, remembering, the folk traditions that she grew up and was involved with. She played accordion, revived the pace egging tradition, kept the songs of the boat people alive and entertained you whilst doing it. The other collector was Paul Graney, originally of Nelson, but he was very much a Manchester man. Graney made an impression wherever he went, whether he was on tramp in England during the Means Test and General Strike or sitting in the corner of folk clubs with his tape recorder. He delved into the collections at Manchester Central Library and unearthed songs that would later be sang by Mike Harding and Gary and Vera Aspey, among many others. The Cardboard Harry Boardman and Mill Owners Mansions are two that are especially interesting from his notebooks, one ridiculous and one sublime.[22]

Conclusion

To conclude, this whistle-stop tour of Greater Manchester and Lancashire's traditional songs has been brief, but important names have been given their due. I would like to think that my work fits in with these notable people. There is not a lot of interest in street literature solely, with scholars choosing to visit it for interesting anecdotes and occurrences as part of larger, wider research projects. This interest in street literature may have waned because we are moving further away from this singing to printing culture that now may not be recognisable to children and young people. Printed newspapers seem to be a thing of the past and music is so often intangible, being fed to us through earphones, that someone singing on the street from a sheet of paper seems so alien. I sing the ballads and dialect songs as well as use them to teach a range of people, from primary school children to those in care homes. It is important for me to give people a range of options of how to engage with these songs and ballads, as everyone will have different reasons for being interested. I like to think I offer a new approach.

I have sung Lancashire dialect and danced clog steps at the Venice Biennale and taught children mining dialect. I have walked the Leeds and Liverpool canal with nothing but a rucksack and a tent, to bring me closer to those who suffered the Means Test and had to go on tramp. I have put together a group of strangers with the intent that they explore their local industrial heritage through poetry and possibly song. Sixteen months later they have just recorded their first CD and have steady performances planned. This majority female group are based in the National Forest and are fittingly called 'The Coal Tits'. I played the singing landlady 'Barb' in Shane Meadows' adaptation of 'The Gallows Pole', a critically acclaimed period drama about the

Cragg Vale coiners of Calderdale. Not only did I sing, but I researched and musically directed the wake scene in episode one. The material collected and stored in our archives can provide us with wonderful opportunities to share, grow and awaken our heritage. The contemporary and traditional versions of these songs can still be used to describe the situations in Bangladesh and China today. My work now takes me to Dhaka, to explore the links between work songs. Now the mills of Manchester and the surrounding area are derelict, artist's spaces or luxury apartments. This is true of the mills of Kushtia. As the poor moved out of the mills, the rich moved in. Bangladesh must find her own Industrial Revolution in a much shorter space of time, in a world that benefits from mass media, cutting edge technology and a global marketplace. It is the relentless nature of capital that forces humans to abide by certain unlivable laws and out of this, comes music.

Notes

1 Charles Hindley, *Curiosities of Street Literature* (Welwyn Garden City, Seven Dials Press: 1969).
2 Leslie Shepard, *History of Street Literature: The Story of Broadside Ballads, Chapbooks, Proclamations, News-Sheets, Election Bills, Tracts, Pamphlets, Cocks, Catchpennies and Other Ephemera* (Newton Abbott, David & Charles: 1973), p. 21.
3 Shepard, *History of Street Literature,* p. 13; Brian Hollingworth, *Songs of the People: Lancashire Dialect Poetry of the Industrial Revolution* (Manchester, Manchester University Press: 1982), p. vii.
4 Shepard, *History of Street Literature,* p. 26.
5 Shepard, *History of Street Literature*, p. 40.
6 Chetham's Library: Halliwell Phillips, Axon, Holt, Swindells; Manchester Central Library, Pearson 4 vols. (c. 1850–1873), Q398.8 S9, Bebbington, Wrigley, and the Working Class Movement Library.
7 Anon, *Manchester City News*, No. 49, 15 December 1883, p. 179.
8 E. Baines and W. Parson, *History, Directory, and Gazetteer, of the County Palatine of Lancaster* (Liverpool, Wm. Wales & Co.: 1825), p. 269.
9 J. Pigot & Co, *The Commercial Directory for 1818–19–20* (Manchester, James Pigot: 1818), p. 324.
10 T. Swindells, *Manchester Streets and Manchester Men* (Manchester, J. E. Cornish Ltd: 1906), p. 55.
11 Swindells, *Manchester Streets*, p. 55.
12 Swindells, *Manchester Streets*, p. 56.
13 Tim Bobbins, *A View of the Lancashire Dialect: By the Way of Dialogue, between Tummus o' William's, o' Margit o' Roaph's, and Meary o' Dick's, o' Tummy o' Peggy's: Containing the Adventures and Misfortunes of a Lancashire Clown: With the Poem of the Flying Dragon and the Man of Heaton: And a Glossary of the Lancashire Words and Phrases* (1789).
14 Laycock, 'Sam Bamford'.
15 Kershaw, 'Peterloo'.
16 Brierley, 'Edwin Waugh'.
17 Waugh, 'Tickle Times'.
18 Lawton, 'Webs from Fancy's Loom'.
19 Laycock, 'Lancashire Lyrics!'

20 Edith M Ralphs, 'Queuin' Up' in Pennine Hotpot.
21 Kershaw, 'Canute'.
22 Graney 3/2.

Some Suggested Further Reading on Broadside Ballads

John Holloway and Joan Black, eds., *Later English Broadside Ballads* (London, Routledge: 2005).

Roy Palmer and Harry Boardman, eds., *Manchester Ballads: Thirty-Five Facsimile Street Ballads* (Manchester, City of Manchester Education Committee: 1983).

Roy Palmer, *The Sound of History: Songs and Social Comment* (Oxford, Oxford University Press: 1988).

Roy Palmer, *Working Songs: Industrial Ballads and Poems from Britain and Ireland, 1780s–1980s* (Todmorden, David Herron Publishing: 2010).

V. De Sola Pinto and A. E. Rodway, eds., *The Common Muse: An Anthology of Popular British Ballad Poetry, 15th–20th century* (London: Penguin, 1965).

J. E. Reid, *A Selection of Nineteenth Century Broadside Ballads from Collections in Manchester* (Manchester, Pariah Press: 2015).

Paul Bernard Rose, *The Manchester Martyrs: A Fenian Tragedy* (London, Lawrence & Wishart: 1970).

Leslie Shepard, *History of Street Literature: The Story of Broadside Ballads, Chapbooks, Proclamations, News-Sheets, Election Bills, Tracts, Pamphlets, Cocks, Catchpennies and Other Ephemera* (Newton Abbott, David & Charles: 1973).

Martha Vicinus, *Broadsides of the Industrial North* (Newcastle, Frank Graham: 1975).

G. M. Young, *Victorian England: Portrait of an Age* (Oxford, Oxford Paperbacks: 1992).

20

'WE TELL OUR OWN STORIES'

Bussing Out, a Creative Installation about Working-class Children in Bradford

Shabina Aslam

Bussing out is the common name of a policy introduced in Circular 7/65: The Education of Immigrants, 1965.[1] This policy said that no school should have more than 30% immigrants on roll; if they did, immigrant children would have to be dispersed to other schools locally, which would often be outside the child's community. The circular was written by Sir Edward Boyle, Secretary of Education for the Conservative Party in 1963, and published by the Labour Party in 1965.

This chapter outlines how I created an installation about the history of working-class immigrant children in West Yorkshire in the second half of the twentieth century as part of my arts-based PhD research. I started with a vague memory of my own past and built a collection of oral histories from which I wanted to tell the story of bussing out. I used theatre-based improvisation, journalling, and collage to unpick the memories and mine them for stories.

The bussing of immigrant children can be seen against the backdrop of, and as a continuation and development of, colonial racism through the institutionalisation of racism in Britain following the Second World War. This manifested because post-war migration led to a new form of state racism, based on cultural differences, from which black and brown people formed resistance strategies which in turn led to the development of the race relations industry which was created to build bridges between the new black British subjectivities and to develop mutual understanding between host and 'strangers'.[2] This paradigm defines people of colour from the Commonwealth as a societal problem, an economic necessity, and ultimately a threat. This narrative throughline has its roots in colonialism, imperialism, postcolonialism and neoliberalism, organisational modalities that arose alongside capitalism

DOI: 10.4324/9780429344084-24

that establish white privilege and its cultural hegemony. The changing face of race and racism is one overarching narrative through which to tell the bussing story.[3]

Sir Edward Boyle believed that the contemporary secondary-school model was failing working-class children, so he instigated the Plowden Report in 1963 and championed its recommendations when it was delivered to his successor Anthony Crosland in 1967.[4] Boyle's compromise for the immigrant child in 1963 was outlined in Circular 7/65:

> About one third of immigrant children is the maximum that is normally acceptable in a school if social strains are to be avoided and educational standards to be maintained. Local education authorities are advised to arrange for the dispersal of immigrant children over a greater number of schools in order to avoid undue concentration in any particular school.[5]

In *The Making of the Black Working Class in Britain*, Ron Ramdin writes that black people are a faction of the white working class, suggesting that they are not equals as working-class people but rather they can be seen as a sub-section of the white working class in Britain.[6] This is because 'race' further marks them out as different; socioeconomic status suggests commonalities, but 'race' will always make the person of colour different again. Therefore, the bussing out policy can be seen as part of the racialising process experienced by the migrant child and the vehicle through which the sub-class was created. Black and white children received the same education, but bussing immigrant children out of their own area marked them out as 'racially' different because of where they lived, the language they spoke at home and the colour of their skin. My PhD research project was an attempt to understand what it felt like to be the bussed child and to create an archive based on that lived experience, which grew from my own experience of having been bussed out for my schooling.

Creating an Installation on Bussing Out

The Bussing Out installation opened to the public on 13 August 2022 during a 'Weekender' event called 'Wish You Were Here' to mark the reopening of Theatre in the Mill (TiM) after being closed during the Covid-19 pandemic. TiM is a venue as well as an artist development organisation based on the University of Bradford. The installation continues to be housed in Gallery II, Chesham Building on campus at the University of Bradford. It is the result of the work I completed for my PhD, which included producing podcasts, curating an exhibition and creating a verbatim play.

The installation is comprised of several elements: an eighteen-minute binaural audio recording appears to the visitor through the windows of the bus, surrounding them. The percipients sit inside the bus, which is a wooden set, mocked up to look like the front end and upstairs of a double decker bus from the 1970s. Two audience members can experience the installation at one time by wearing headphones and sitting on the second row of seats of the bus.

On entering Gallery II, the installation is not obvious, as it is hidden behind a black wall of theatre flats. Audiences are invited to read a poster giving background information about bussing out, telling them that the installation explores migrant children's experiences of being bussed under Circular 7/65 from 1965 to 1976 (although bussing continued in Bradford until 1980) and how it finally came to an end. The poster ends with a list of the credits, naming all the artists involved in making the installation.

The audience read the blurb on the wall, enter the bus, put on their headphones, and are asked to press the bell which will then start their journey. Pressing the bell triggers an Arduino (a micro-computer) to press play on the computers operating the bus, as the installation is entirely self-contained and runs from two Macs hidden behind the set. On pressing play, the bus driver appears as a miniature in the overhead mirror that would usually connect the driver's cabin to the upstairs seating. The bus driver talks about his understanding of bussing and informs us that the children will be boarding soon. Then through the headphones we hear the children arrive: we hear them run up the stairs and sit down. The engines are heard to start, and the bus feels like it is moving.

At the beginning of the bus journey, we find out that this is the last day of school and that this group of young people have come prepared for a battle, with chilli powder in their pockets. 'Paki bashing' is a term used to describe violence towards Asian people. Although this is something that happened around West Yorkshire in the later twentieth century, it was also an annual event at Tong High School. The passengers on the bus have elected to be here: they are going to fight young white people because they feel they belong in Bradford, know they have the right to be in Britain and know they have the right to be treated equally. Their preparation for violence signals that they intend to claim that right. However, one passenger, Marcia, does not want to go; the others spend the rest of the journey trying to persuade her to stay. Just as the bus pulls up to Tong she jumps out, as this is not her fight. Marcia is black rather than Asian, and feels the planned violence is not intended to include her.

Each character on the bus has a public and private facing persona. For most of the journey, they enjoy light banter and camaraderie with each other. I used monologues to tell some of the back stories of migration for each character; many had fathers who had been in the British Army.

The actors who recorded the script for the installation were recruited by myself using contacts within the South Asian community. They were not professional actors, and I felt able to do this because of my background in creating art for social justice. I have developed a robust practice working with community co-creators within performance. The script was recorded by Helen Skiera, a sound designer, using binaural recording techniques, at Keighley Bus Museum. We did the audio recording upstairs on an actual double decker bus for authenticity. The aim of the installation is for visitors to feel as if they are on the bus with the children themselves, giving them a greater understanding of an aspect of life for working-class children in Bradford.

In addition to the installation, I also developed a creative engagement opportunity. At the opposite end of Gallery II to where the bus is, I built a 1970s replica classroom. It has several old-style school desks in it, plus a chalk board. I worked with four Muslim families who home educate their children to create installations inside each desk. They researched migration stories within their own families and then they created a range of remarkable installations themselves, with support from TiM team.

We Tell Our Own Stories: My Experience of Bussing Out

Although I was bussed myself, I never discussed the experience with anyone. I always knew it was odd, waiting for a bus on the other side of the park, early in the morning and often in the dark; then, at school, getting into fights at the bus stop with some of the boys and being all alone at school where no one would talk to me, except to make comments about my hair.

Years later, I read a footnote about bussing in a collection of testimonies recounting black people's experience of British education. There was a mention of being driven around the countryside and left at an all-white school for the day and brought back in the evening. Apparently, some black intellectuals in London had fought against this discrimination, taking the government to court, and winning, because this was racist. I thought how exciting, what a brilliant story. Of course, it turned out to be much more complicated than that and quite difficult to examine.

There was very little in the archives, and many people did not really want to discuss it either: one woman I met said she had enjoyed the experience and her best white friend had taught her to draw an elephant. She had felt looked after, nurtured. I also had some difficulty persuading institutions to take this research project seriously. One funder asked if it wouldn't be better to forget about such painful histories. An opportunity arose to frame this project as an exploration of heritage and examine the impact it had on identity. Community heritage projects seem to have become part of the race relations industry, a way of building bridges between cultures constituted as different, but now framed as being in danger of being lost. Perhaps this is nostalgia for the days when the difference in cultures threatened the idea of what it meant to be English, but we have been hyphenated since then – Black-British, British-Asian – and our cultural differences might disappear. Yasmin Alibhai-Brown suggests that this type of multiculturalism is a form of divide and conquer: we are ghettoised, fight each other for resources and turn on the new migrants, the refugees.[7] Framing the black and brown experience through a lost heritage is an acceptable outcome for hegemonic institutions, but it is limiting because it does not go far enough – it does not do enough work. We need to probe deeper, into the nature of society as a whole.

We have had many visitors to the installation and plan to tour it to the other cities that experienced bussing. One visitor to the installation wrote in the visitor book:

> I love love the experience. I feel like I was really in a moving bus and the story, so meaningful. Being an immigrant myself, the story is so relatable, and I'll definitely recommend my friends to come see the installation.[8]

It is through processes like the ones I have described that the black and brown working-class subjective experience finds its own expressive utilities. We tell our own stories.

Notes

1 Circular 7/65: *The Education of Immigrants* (London, Her Majesty's Stationery Office: 1965).

2 Chris Waters, '"Dark Strangers" in Our Midst: Discourses of Race and Nation in Britain, 1947–1963', *Journal of British Studies* 36.2 (1997), p. 217.

3 Akala, *Natives: Race and Class in the Ruins of Empire* (London, Two Roads: 2018); Paul Gilroy, *There Ain't No Black in the Union Jack: the Cultural Politics of Race and Nation* (London, Unwin Hyman: 1987); David Olusoga, *Black and British: A Forgotten History* (London, Pan: 2017).

4 David Crook, 'Edward Boyle: Conservative Champion of Comprehensives?', *History of Education* 22.1 (1993), p. 49.

5 Circular 7/65: *The Education of Immigrants* (London, Her Majesty's Stationery Office: 1965), p. 4.

6 Ron Ramdin, *The Making of the Black Working Class in Britain* (Aldershot, Gower: 1987), p. 234.

7 Yasmin Alibhai-Brown, *Who Do We Think We Are? Imagining the New Britain* (London, Penguin: 2000), p. 411.

8 Visitor book at Bussing Out, Theatre in the Mill.

21

'THE PAST WE INHERIT, THE FUTURE WE BUILD'

The Praxis of Working-class History

Rhian E. Jones

When are 'the working class' spoken or written of as 'we', and when are we 'they'? While the former framing can be found in social, cultural, and political rhetoric, the latter is far more common when reading and practising academic history. Although exceptions to this pattern exist, it can be alienating as a working-class student and as a historian from a working-class background to encounter history which seems like your own story, but which is told about you rather than by you.

This chapter is primarily a personal view of how the study, practice, and public perception of working-class history has developed and changed, particularly over the past 30 years. My own practice of public history has been more accident than design, although there is a certain pattern to it. From growing up in a particular context which made me intensely aware of my local, community, and class history, I encountered various challenges and questions in the course of finding a way to study it with any legitimacy within academia. I then realised that there were a variety of ways to do so outside academia, and that doing so was itself part of a long tradition.

Working-class history has always had a home outside academia as well as within it. This statement should be unsurprising – there has never been sufficient room in academia, whether through limits of opportunity, access, or ability, for everyone who has a passion for learning, studying and communicating history. In fact, prior to its professionalisation in the twentieth century, history tended to be seen as the preserve of amateurs and enthusiasts, including antiquarians, and often focusing on local nostalgia, biography, or memoir rather than theory or scholarship. Today, grassroots or civic projects at local libraries, schools, and museums, often looking at the role and experience of individual places and people within larger narratives

DOI: 10.4324/9780429344084-25

and themes, still do much to bring history alive through direct personal connection.

These debates and tensions are not new. As academic history developed, bringing in a tenured career track for historians and creating national associations and scholarly journals, it tended to be shaped by political conservatism or 'Whig' teleologies which focused on the impact of 'Great Men' – or occasionally women – and which framed history as a continual upwards march towards inevitable political, scientific, and social progress. It was not until the 1960s popularisation of 'history from below', led by Marxist historians like E. P. Thompson, George Rudé, and Christopher Hill among others, that mainstream history made room for the stories of disadvantaged and disenfranchised groups, including those considered to be on history's losing side. Initiatives like *History Workshop Journal* were founded in deliberate opposition to what had gone before, with *HWJ* founder Raphael Samuel defining the group's view of history as 'a collaborative enterprise, one in which the researcher, the archivist, the curator, and the teacher, the "do-it-yourself" enthusiast and the local historian, the family history societies, and the individual archaeologist, should all be regarded as equally engaged'.[1]

The development of Marxist and labour histories looking specifically at organisation, political struggle, and conflict 'from below' has done much to disrupt and equalise the mainstream view of those considered to be valid, interesting or important as historical subjects. But it's also useful to make a distinction between 'labour history' – the history of an organised subset of working people – and the history of the working class more generally. While the former has been enormously valuable and influential, it can be prescriptive in its idea of what constitutes working-class identity, often obscuring those members of the class who are not male, white and industrially (occasionally agriculturally) organised. In 1970, a women's liberation conference at Ruskin College Oxford organised by female historians noted that the histories of ordinary women had barely ever been given the same attention and credibility as those of men. Subsequent work by feminist historians developed an understanding of links between gender and class oppression. The accompanying rise of postcolonial and queer history has further broadened and deepened mainstream history's understanding of its subject.

A further distinction is often made between 'history' and 'heritage', with the latter being criticised as unprofessionally simplistic and untheorised. While this attitude can be seen as informed by a certain degree of scholarly snobbery or territorialism, some more valid criticisms of 'heritage' as a wider industry in the UK rest on its development of a 'national story' which complacently accepts the status quo as it has developed, focusing on the ruling classes and relegating the working classes and their stories, particularly those which centre political struggle, to the sidelines. These same narratives can neglect or ignore entirely those aspects of British history that involve imperial exploitation or colonial atrocity – aspects which can implicate the working class as much as our rulers.

In addition to direct local history, it's also possible to become aware of and to develop an interest in history through wider social and cultural experiences, which was certainly the case with my own experience and knowledge of both Welsh and working-class history. I will outline the foundations of this discovery, before exploring how my experience of studying history at university introduced me to differences between theory and practice and also the influence of that milieu on someone from a working-class background. I'll then look at my own attempts to join up these threads in the practice of studying and communicating popular history.

Part One

When I was growing up in South Wales in the 1980s and 90s, history was something that seemed very shallowly buried. This was particularly true of the area's industrial heritage, which could be seen in both the defunct pit machinery that dotted the landscape – occasionally in the form of mining museums – and the memories that people carried of both the coalfield's past as a functioning economic powerhouse and of its destruction in the 1984–1985 Miners' Strike. I came to learn both recent and remote aspects of this local history, and the part it played in larger historical developments, through several intertwined factors. Most of these drew more on civic, community, and personal cultural commemoration than specifically on formal education, although both were important.

When studying nineteenth-century British history at school, we focused in depth on the sweeping economic, political and social changes wrought by the Industrial Revolution. My interest was caught less by the statistics of iron and coal production and more by its generation of the roots of a recognisably modern class structure and culture: a decaying landed gentry, a growing bourgeoisie including both the already wealthy and new, hugely enriched industrialists, and a mass industrialised and urbanised proletariat who created the bulk of industrial wealth but whose wages and conditions meant that they saw little of its benefits. In particular, the response of ordinary people to unequal, exploitative, and oppressive conditions, through forms of direct and organised action from food riots to clandestine trade union forming to formal political campaigns like Chartism, captured my imagination and have still not let go. The drama, romance and tragedy of stories like Peterloo, the Tolpuddle Martyrs, Luddism, or the 1831 Merthyr Rising – their sensational high stakes, and their struggles and losses for real, ordinary people lending themselves well to the actorly brio of the best of my History teachers – seemed far more alive and empathetic than previous lessons on the lives of kings and queens or the defensive advantages of motte-and-bailey castles.

It was also possible to see these same high stakes in recent history, and in continuing political struggles for democracy and equality all over the world, which gave me a sense of historical continuum. This history had echoes outside school, in both local civic institutions and in certain bits of the culture I encountered. The latter included seeing a local theatre company's production of a play called *Treason!* which told the story of the Newport radical John Frost and his part in the ill-fated uprising by Welsh Chartists in 1839. Years later, I took part myself in a community theatre play about the life of Aneurin Bevan, who had been born in my town, worked as a coalminer before becoming an MP and Minister for Health, and used his experience of Tredegar Medical Aid Society's socialised model of healthcare as a blueprint for founding the NHS. Developed as a commemoration and celebration of local and community history, both of these productions had obvious resonances in contemporary life, as we observed the NHS's continual struggle for funding and political credibility under a Conservative government, and thought about the Chartists' struggle to win the vote for ordinary people in a context where popular democracy could often seem taken for granted.

My involvement in these stories inspired me to go from the stage to the page, and find out more about the development of my area and community through reading history, politics, and biography. I learnt how mining towns like my own, built out of economic necessity and initially established more like work-camps surrounding a particular mine or foundry, rapidly developed their own flourishing society, culture, and leisure. Some of this, like my town's Bedwellty Park, gifted to the local community in 1901 by the Morgan family dynasty, was the result of ruling-class philanthropy, but much of it was built by workers themselves, who responded to harsh and inadequate living and working conditions by creating networks of not only mutual aid and welfare but also social and cultural enterprise. Their welfare function was particularly important because at this time there was little or no state provision for financial support or healthcare, so communities developed their own, with individuals paying a small amount of money into a central fund, which then entitled them to help or support or the use of a service when they needed it. In the years before the NHS, this system allowed unions to organise and pay for the building of, for example, retirement homes and convalescent homes for the use of members during illness, injury, or retirement.

A fundamental part of this infrastructure was the buildings, sometimes known as working-men's institutes, or workmen's halls, which sprang up in industrial communities as a multipurpose social and cultural space. Again, these were built on collectivist principles, with workers paying a proportion of their wage into a communal fund, usually something like a penny per week, to pay for the construction and running of the building – sometimes even carrying out the construction work themselves. Created in order to be part of the community's social fabric, they could be used for community meetings or to hear political speakers, and usually included a bar or space for dancing, a pool or snooker room or even a cinema.

Crucially, these buildings also usually housed a library and reading room, where members could freely access books and newspapers. This highlights the tradition of self-education that also became important in these communities. The opening line of the Manic Street Preachers' working-class eulogy 'Design for Life' weighs in by quoting the inscription outside Newport's Central Library, built around the turn of the twentieth century through the instigation of the local labour movement: 'Libraries Gave Us Power'. The importance of free access to books and newspapers, and the education, analysis, and broadened horizons they enabled, underlines the autodidactic tradition which defined so much of this early industrial working-class culture and its politics. The library in my town also housed a mini-museum, in which the broad sweep of the industrial past was more strikingly presented in microcosm. Its displays of household artefacts, from davy-lamps to sugar-tongs, allowed you to imagine how individuals, families, and communities had lived and worked.

These particular politics, and forms of cultural and social life, had been built on an equally particular economic base, and the erosion of this base in the late twentieth century destabilised a whole way of life. Deindustrialisation meant the loss not only of economic identity, but also of the social and cultural pillars of support that had previously defined these working-class communities. Across post-industrial Britain, things like the miners' institutes were occasionally repurposed but in many cases left to decline, as without wages coming in it was no longer possible to financially support the kinds of previous initiatives that had existed. Awareness of this historical perspective answered question I had about buildings in my town and others, like Tredegar Workmens' Hall, its huge meeting-room, red velvet curtains, and dusty bar still used in my childhood by the post-mining community for drama rehearsals, drink, and dancing, but in the following decades falling to disuse and eventual demolition. This melancholy backdrop, with a history that seemed not buried but sedimentary, made it easy to be aware of history, but also positioned it as an oppressive force with you always on the losing side. I began to see the post-industrial landscape around me like wandering backstage in a disused theatre – what story had these redundant and discarded props been used to tell? Where were the actors now? What had the script been?

Part Two

In terms of how the working class were perceived in a post-industrial world, it was evident in the 1990s that the loss of the figure of the working-class scholar, along with post-industrialisation, had left the way open for the presentation of working-class culture and identity, by outsiders, as one devoid of intellectual ambition, skill, or curiosity. Despite the disappearance of this tradition in late-twentieth-century culture, reading cultural histories like Richard Hoggart's *The Uses of Literacy* and Jonathan Rose's *The Intellectual Life of the British Working Classes* had reinforced my certainty of self-education as fundamental to working-class life and history, as well as the subsequent significance of the expansion of higher education from the 1960s, and the class mobility, creativity, and cultural collaboration – and the rise of social history – that it allowed.[2] As I followed a classic trajectory of working-class mobility from the Valleys to London as a student, I classed myself as part of this hidden, buried history that didn't feel quite dead. Was I a zombie or an exhibit out of its glass case?

As a history and politics student, I was predictably drawn to the history of working-class formation. E. P. Thompson's 1963 classic *The Making of the English Working Class* is based on a 'heroic' idea of working-class development, framing the worker as the protagonist and agent of a grand and dramatic story, with the Marxist view of class as the agent of revolutionary change applied to a particular historical narrative.[3] My own ideas for research tended to follow Thompson's fascinating identification of the adaptation of older rural popular culture to newer industrial contexts. He explored this not in *The Making* but in a collection of essays published in 1993 as *Customs in Common*.[4] These essays introduced me to spectacular instances of struggle to regulate aspects of working-class life, messier and less familiar than union organising and constitutional protests. These included eighteenth- and nineteenth-century food riots – which were often led by women as proprietors of community wellbeing – and charivari, preindustrial rituals of community discipline. The idea of ordinary people making sense of the cataclysm that was industrial capitalism through their own existing systems of belief appealed to me because it showed that they (that 'we') had nuanced ways of understanding and responding, even if previous historians had dismissed these as incomprehensible or less sophisticated than later, more recognisably 'political' responses like the Chartist movement. Eric Hobsbawm's book *Primitive Rebels* also explored less organised instances of popular rebellion, and cautioned against modernist bias from both left and right-wing perspectives that dismissed as valueless the seemingly irrational aspects of pre-modern social agitation, with their pre-industrial and pre-literate frames of reference.[5]

My undergraduate reading of Thompson and Hobsbawm rang true with my developing interest in general social and protest history, and specifically my interest in the Rebecca riots, a series of disturbances in 1840s Wales which were characterised by their prominent use of costume and ritual. This use was frequently noted by historians as bizarre but never, to me, satisfactorily explored or explained. Similarly, the conventional account of these events as a successful example of direct action against charging to travel on privatised roads, although valid and inspiring, tended to obscure how broad, eclectic, and simply messy a protest movement it was – looking at times like a Victorian version of the anti-austerity and Occupy movements of the early twenty-first century. We have almost no written personal records from participants in the Rebecca riots, beyond the accounts produced in court reports or trial records, which emphasises both the importance of memory, oral history and storytelling in how the events are handed down to future generations and the need to 'read' this history through other means, looking at oral-visual frames of reference and their meanings rather than – or at least as well as – at written testimony.

Imaginative empathy is important, then, in illuminating how the seemingly irrational may have looked from the inside. Students of history who take this approach to their material can tell stories which leaven the flat accounts of economic historians who, looking only at dry data and broad statistics in debates over standards of living, can present developments like the Industrial Revolution as accounts of general overall progress for Britain, while overlooking the often catastrophic disruption of individual peasant and artisan lives it occasioned. Similarly, positivist or revisionist overviews of the 1930s which focus on generalities can ignore the extent to which industrial districts and their populations were, many times over, dislocated by the vagaries of capitalism. Although the 1930s in Britain did see general rises in standards of living and the growth of new forms of industry, this overview ignores the point that, for individuals affected by it, unemployment is always absolute, not relative.[6] This fact of material experience was expressed by the actions and testimony of the thousands of men and women who took part in Hunger Marches and other actions throughout the decade against means-tested welfare payments and high rents. Attention to this kind of working-class history can also uncover hidden or neglected aspects of the present, as precarious work and zero-hours contracts continue to contradict rosy assumptions about general working life.

As an undergraduate, I was disconcerted by the fact that the kind of history practised by Marxists like Thompson, while making complete sense to me, was falling out of academic fashion and favour. In academia as a whole, the 90s saw a marked turn away from class as both a subject of study and an aspect of identity. While from one side the idea of class's political importance became a casualty of the post-Cold War assertion of the 'end of history' and the left's consequent political exhaustion and retreat, from the other it suffered from the rise in postmodernist theories and the attendant rise in historical revisionism which saw class as a reductionist and limiting framework. Sociologists like Imogen Tyler and Bev Skeggs, both from working-class backgrounds and drawing on this in their work, noted that discussion and exploration of class identity in cultural and media studies during the 90s and 2000s was ebbing away due to its perception as 'paranoid' and an embarrassment – even where it clearly overlapped with questions of gender or race.[7] Even within the field of radical history, from the 1980s the 'linguistic turn' focused on historical events and movements, particularly the popular politics of the late eighteenth and early nineteenth centuries, through the agency more or less exclusively of words and text. Gareth Stedman Jones' influential 1982 essay 'Rethinking Chartism' challenged central assumptions of previous historical accounts by questioning whether the term 'working class' developed as an accurate reflection of social and economic changes, with consciousness determined by conditions, or merely as a rhetorical device used for political organisation.[8]

There are, of course, valid reasons to critique and attempt to deconstruct the 'heroic' narrative of working-class development. While spotlighting important but neglected parts of history, it often consigns political nuance and less explicit political aspects to the shadows. Conservative or reactionary tendencies, for instance, have also always been present in working-class history, from the reactionary eruptions of Church and King mobs to Thatcherism's inroads into twentieth-century working-class voters. There is also the question of how many radical and reform movements were cross-class in membership and leadership, with internal tensions over goals and levels of militancy often causing these alliances of middle and working class to splinter.

On a different but related level, working-class history need not be a 'worthy' tale of political struggle and defeat in order to justify its existence and its interest as an area of study. There is a huge range of nineteenth- and twentieth-century working-class autobiography and writing through which the fabric of ordinary lives can be recovered, from John Burnett's 1994 collection *Useful Toil* to Emma Griffin's study *Liberty's Dawn* or Richard Benson's memoir *The Valley*, which traces the lives of four generations in a Yorkshire mining community.[9] This writing is testimony to the love and pride felt and taken in work as well as its hardness and oppressive nature, and the intergenerational tensions and complexities on which working-class individuals, families and communities are built. A story like that of Yorkshire housewife-turned millionaire Viv Nicholson, immortalised in the book, play, and musical *Spend, Spend, Spend*, reveals as much about working-class lives, and their ambitions and limits, as more conventional academic studies.

In his preface to the tellingly titled *Labouring Men*, Eric Hobsbawm acknowledged that there had previously been 'little work about the working classes as such (as distinct from labour organisations and movements)'. In this collection, and in the later *Worlds of Labour*, he attempted to correct this, looking at the soil in which these movements grew and which caused them to flourish or to wither.[10] Growing up in a post-industrial mining community had already made me aware of often unknown aspects of the 1984–1985 Miners' Strike, including the crucial part played by women's support groups and the solidarity offered by other left activist organisations like Lesbians and Gay Men Support the Miners. This history, often submerged in the stories of industrial struggle, is now receiving its due in more recent histories of the strike and in popular cultural representations like the 2014 film *Pride*. When I went on to study eighteenth- and nineteenth-century radicalism, I was surprised and pleased to learn about the involvement of women in leading roles in food riots and rent campaigns. I also learnt of the historical presence of black British radicals, including prominent figures like the anti-slavery activist Robert Wedderburn and the Chartist leader William Cuffay, and the interaction of anti-colonial and domestic working-class struggle expressed in things like late-stage Chartism's support for Indian rebels during the Sepoy Mutiny. These stories disrupted reactionary ideas of working-class identity, as well as disproving the claim that class struggle past and present was only a concern of, and only concerned with, white male industrial workers.

Critical engagement with orthodox Marxist history, then, need not lose sight of what is compelling and valuable about such narratives. What accounts like *The Making of the English Working Class* often ignore or marginalise, namely attention to race and gender, also played a vital part in the radical and progressive developments they identify. Recognising this fact broadens and deepens the history of working-class radicalism through intersectional perspectives, allowing us to go beyond stereotypes, and to admit what are often uncomfortable aspects of working-class life such as sexism and racism, rather than jettisoning the idea and importance of class entirely in favour of studying it through more abstract aspects like the use of language.

Language itself is both a point of contention and a problem when considering working-class history. The working class and their historical development and achievements are often described by academics from other backgrounds in alienating and othering language, even when the descriptions are positive. Meanwhile, individuals from working-class backgrounds, if they wish to reference or draw on their lived experience, must learn an often alien language in order to make their work credibly understood. So we find ourselves explaining ourselves to others, rather than talking amongst ourselves. There are alternatives to this process, focusing on grassroots rather than top-down analysis and communication, and they can be found both in aspects of community and local history, and in methods of creative engagement with history such as Comma Press's series of anthologies which present dramatic and significant moments of historical protest as accessible and relevant to contemporary life.[11]

Part Three

After the denial and erasure of the idea of class in the 1990s and 2000s, the 2010s witnessed a certain remaking of the English working class in both politics and academia. The UK's turn from a manufacturing economy based on mines, factories and shipyards, to a post-Fordist society characterised by the outsourcing of industrial labour and the spread of a service economy, had inevitably altered both the subjective experience of the working class, and consequently the conceptual frameworks and analytical approaches to it, inherited from the nineteenth and twentieth centuries. As the early twenty-first century progressed, however, 'class' returned as a plausible marker of identity, though by no means a confident one, in working-class histories like Selina Todd's *The People*, and in studies of politicised popular culture like Owen Jones' *Chavs: The Demonization of the Working Class.*[12] These studies, while accepting the decline of a certain political and cultural idea of the 'traditional' working class, also recognised the persistence of class as a material reality.

This was not the working class's first remaking. As industrial capitalism entrenched itself throughout the nineteenth century, the popular resistance to it that had peaked with Chartism evolved into a more constitutional accommodation with what now seemed like a more permanent economic system. From the 1880s, workers' organisation in trade unions – and, eventually, the foundation of the Labour Party – grew in importance as workers sought and won political and industrial representation within capitalism, rather than seeking to prevent or overturn its imposition. This evolution, as we have seen, meant the sidelining of less 'serious' or recognisably respectable forms of protest, like carnivalesque riots against enclosure or high food prices, within the annals of working-class history. It also saw the development of a recognisably modern working-class culture with signifiers – football, chip shop suppers, flat caps – that would persist for decades. This 'traditional' idea of the working class, however, was the product of a historical moment and not something either fixed or monolithic.

After the volatile 1920s and 1930s, in which the British working class was active in opposing fascism abroad and at home, and in economic struggle through rent campaigns and hunger marches, the founding of the welfare state lessened the urgency for struggle through addressing material needs through ameliorated capitalism. The expansion in class mobility, rising living standards and gradual integration into consumer capitalism which followed was seen by some historians as involving a decline in class consciousness and identity. Hobsbawm himself in 1978 produced *The Forward March of Labour Halted*, a lecture on recent working-class history which argued that these economic and social changes, plus the tendency of established trade unions to focus on 'economist' gains for their own members rather than broader class questions, heralded a crisis in the idea of a single working-class identity and, consequently, for the Labour party in its reliance on the support of working-class voters. This analysis, though partly valid, tended to overlook both the historical divisions and nuances in 'working-class' identity and the efforts by some trade unions throughout the 60s and 70s to involve themselves in struggles beyond sectional wages and to ally with new social movements, like the builders union UCATT's support for community campaigns around antiracism and gentrification.[13]

Hobsbawm's analysis, significantly, also failed to anticipate the impact of Thatcherism and the ferocity with which its market-led ideology would impact on both the working class itself and its representation through trade unions. Bastions of industrial working-class identity like coalmining saw a final, climactic defeat in the 1980s, but this was the end of a long process of economic shifts towards finance and services rather than manufacturing as the country's industrial base. The disappearance of political recognition or considerations of the working class in the 1990s – the decade of New Labour's proclamation that the country was 'all middle-class now' – was a response to the triumph of these ideas as well as to the economic and social changes they had effected. In the 2000s, however, it became obvious that those employed in retail, cleaning and care work, warehouses, call centres and customer service, and in the burgeoning 'gig economy', still formed a distinct class, if a disorganised, alienated, and powerless one. The persistence of socioeconomic inequality grew increasingly glaring after the 2008 banking crisis and the imposition of austerity which followed, and led to the belated recognition that the working class's composition may have shifted but it still existed – particularly with the growth of zero-hours contracts and precarious workers, neglected by traditional unions, mirroring to an extent the nineteenth-century workers who waited at factory gates or on the dockside to be hired short-term at the whims of employers.

In the 2010s, if the past was finding echoes in the present, the present was also becoming history. It was impossible to study the Welsh past in particular, with the coalfield's strong economic base and the vivid cultural and social world that it supported, without comparing its present state of structural impoverishment and ensuing social and psychological damage. However, top-down studies of post-industrial malaise in areas like the Valleys – often from commentators who had failed to offer these communities attention or support during deindustrialisation – can ignore the work done to recuperate this recent history in former mining communities, through local workshops, archives, and community projects. Both individuals and groups of activists and historians have made efforts to reclaim the experience and historical meaning of events like the Miners' Strike, through cultural and heritage-based discourse, as a story of working-class agency rather than passivity, defeat or victimhood.

This practice of history can involve thinking beyond nostalgic ideas of the industrial era as a lost 'golden age', a paralysing form of historical memory that uncritically eulogises the past. Mining communities, for all their benefits, could be stifling, claustrophobic, and reactionary, and historically we know that working-class individuals found this way of life could generate alienation, dissatisfaction, boredom, and resentment as much as it provided economic and social security. Instead, projects like those of Castleford Heritage Trust in Yorkshire do not seek a return to mining's working conditions or patriarchal gender relations, but 'ways to navigate these changes', focusing more on reconstructing and commemorating a particular sense of place and community. Exhibitions that simulate the conditions of mining work, acknowledging their harshness and difficulty, offer tactile and direct contact with the past that has proved more engaging for visitors than the more remote, passive display of untouchable artefacts or artworks.[14]

History developed organically in consultation with working-class communities is also more successfully engaging, and more valuable, than official detached representations of events. Participants in the BBC's Open Archive project, composed of miners and police veterans of 1984–1985, criticised the available broadcast material as providing a 'simplified and stereotyped' view of the strike's complex nature. Given collective ownership of the project, those involved in the strike produced their own films, poetry, written testimony, and curated photographs to lend personal as well as political perspectives. Besides adding depth and nuance to the BBC's archive, work of this nature illustrates the continually under-acknowledged creative and artistic capacity of working-class people.[15] Inspiring examples of post-industrial recuperation can be found across the country, from the use of miners' institutes as centres for art, music, and drama, continuing their former social and cultural function, to the touring dance-theatre production *Coal*, developed by Gary Clarke from the Yorkshire mining village of Grimethorpe and based on testimony from veterans of the Miners' Strike including Women Against Pit Closures. Broader and more established archives which explore the lives of ordinary people, like Manchester's People's History Museum and *Llafur*: The Welsh People's History Society, have been joined by collaborative community ventures like the Kennington Chartist Project, a remembrance of the 1848 Chartist rally on Kennington Common developed by a group of local residents as well as historians. Online, projects like Working-Class History use podcasts and social media to highlight archival material, bringing to the surface often forgotten or suppressed aspects of working-class lives, identity and struggle.

Laurajane Smith suggests that 'heritage' has taken on an organising role in many communities, including deindustrialised areas, with local understanding of their own heritage operating counter to the 'authorised heritage discourse' through which national elites attempt to represent their particular heritage as nationally legitimate and significant.[16] The above examples of public history demonstrate that nostalgia can also be a critical and dissonant engagement with contemporary conditions. It also reminds us that 'working-class' heritage should not be understood to mean 'white'. Race is embedded in radical history both through the work of individual figures and through wider structural issues around the place of the British working class and of industrialisation in imperial expansion, the impacts of colonial history and their continuing effects today. Recognition of this in working-class history can help counter political tendencies which depict the history and the interests of a contemporary 'traditional' working class in opposition to migrant populations or to second- and third-generation BAME British people.

Part Four

My second book, and only 'proper' historical monograph so far, began as my MPhil thesis. My postgraduate study took me through the politically fallow mid-2000s, when history itself appeared to have ended but which in retrospect was merely a period of calm before the storm. History is always ongoing, and was decisively shaping the world into which I emerged in 2008. I began writing over the next few years alongside day-jobs in retail and office admin, relying on my own books and access to local and academic libraries as well as online resources. My first book, published in 2013, looked at the 90s erasure of class identity in politics and popular culture, particularly within popular music and particularly in relation to working-class women. While not strictly historical, it used cultural analysis to explore the changing nature of working-class representation in recent history.[17] In the years surrounding its writing, history's failure to end was spectacularly shown in pro-democracy uprisings across the Middle East, riots that spread across London in the wake of police violence and austerity, and autonomous anti-establishment movements like Occupy in the USA, UK, and mainland Europe. Immersion in past radical thought and action allowed me to draw comparisons and contrasts with present actions and events, and there were striking similarities between the actions of eighteenth- and nineteenth-century populations and those of current protest movements: their semi-spontaneous, often anonymous and 'opt-in' nature, their use of symbolism and costume like stylised Guy Fawkes masks, and their emergence in response to deep financial burdens, sweeping socioeconomic dislocation, and the remote, neglectful, or actively corrupt nature of authorities. All this fed into the view of protest and working-class history that informed 2015's *Petticoat Heroes*, which integrated history with previous insights from anthropology, sociology, and cultural studies in the hope of broadening a study of the particular towards the general and of illuminating both past and present conditions.[18]

The book's reception, like its writing had been, was balanced between the popular and the academic. Looking at the Rebecca Riots from a cultural and social perspective, and at their place in past and present political and cultural discourse, enabled them to be seen as a social movement with engaging and enlightening evidence to offer on past ideas of gender, or on the porous quality of borders between agrarian and industrial for early nineteenth-century workers. This offered me eclectic and often unexpected opportunities to practise public history, from contributing to Newport's local Chartism commemorations to collaborating with writers Eley Williams and Luan Goldie for Comma Press's series on fictionalised moments of protest history. I have been surprised, and gratified, at the interest taken in the book by historians and educators outside my immediate field. The US academic Ardel Haefele-Thomas included the Rebecca Riots' political use of costume in the wide-ranging 2019 reader *Introduction to Transgender Studies*.[19] In 2018 I worked on a youth theatre project that brought together groups from Hackney and Powys to develop their own production which drew links between the Rebecca Riots and the 2011 London riots – another way of recovering history as stories, as drama, and as personal and collective memory. Although the events seemed vastly different on the surface, the students were able to identify some common themes – grassroots communities against authority, state power and its agents, the parallels between the New Poor Law and contemporary debates on welfare reform – and to draw comparisons across geography and time, as were the audience. All these interactions are ways of making working-class history accessible and vital both in theory and in practice and of linking it to broader and more intersectional histories and debates.

In the summer of 2019 I gave a talk at The World Transformed's festival in Brighton, alongside other talks and workshops which looked at current and past instances of working-class struggle across the world. In the talk, I aimed to bring together the past of my own community, its relation to the present, and ways to remember the working-class past without romanticising it, acknowledging that its lessons could not be straightforwardly applied to the future but must take account of changed circumstances – recovering the scenery, the script, the props, but using them to stage a more relevant story. The World Transformed is not specifically a history project, but was founded as part of the revival of interest in political, economic, and social alternatives to capitalism following the resurgence of socialist politics within the Labour Party under Jeremy Corbyn's leadership and the visible collapse of many assumptions underlying the capitalist status quo. This political search, currently happening on an international, local, and individual scale, entails discovering or studying alternatives. The history of political and economic ideas in this area, expressed by working-class people themselves, stretches from *The Miners' Next Step*, a 1912 pamphlet encouraging workers to take control of economic resources rather than passively accept their management from above, to the 1976 Lucas Plan, developed by workers facing redundancy, to save jobs by converting their company from arms manufacture to socially useful products. Several emerging projects on the left, including TWT, also aim to recover traditions of political education and the previous institutional, cultural, and social links between Labour, trade unions, and groups outside these institutions, and to explore where particular roads, not previously taken, might now lead.

Earlier in 2019, I took part in an episode of the BBC's pop-history programme *Who Do You Think You Are?*, in which Jack Whitehall traced his four-times-great grandfather's involvement in the 1839 Chartist uprising at Newport – on the side not of the demonstrators but of the authorities, whose actions saw the death of 22 Chartists during their siege of the town's Westgate Hotel. It felt somewhat surreal to have travelled from my childhood captivation by a local drama production on the Newport Rising to now being in a position to present current scions of the ruling classes with the actions of their ancestors, if only within the necessarily streamlined and simplified context of broadcast media. The programme's reception, more than the sheepish 'guilty as charged' response of the Whitehalls, surprised me by how unknown this history was, how much of a shock it often seemed to others to hear the narratives I had absorbed like the air when growing up – not simply in school, but as local historical memory.

2019 was also the bicentennial of the massacre of pro-democracy demonstrators at Peterloo, another neglected but iconic story of working-class struggle. Mike Leigh's cinematic retelling of the events of August 1819 occasioned debate on its release about the place of ordinary people in history, and emphasised that even in an era culturally obsessed with the past in the form of costume and period dramas, 'we' remained comic relief or squalid backdrop, or at most faceless tragic victims, and never the heroes or agents of history. If *Downton Abbey* is an intrinsic part of how we view the national story, so too is something like the Durham Miners Gala. The latter, its form relatively unchanged since 1871 but its content keeping pace with contemporary politics, is a particularly inspiring example of bringing together past and present, functioning as much as a social occasion for the local community and wider labour movement as a forum to reflect on and respond to present questions of domestic and international working-class concerns. The gathering exemplifies one of the best-known mottos on a miners' union banner: 'The past we inherit, the future we build'.

The future of working-class history, from my own perspective, is being built through a coalition of interest, pulling together threads of academia, social media and established media, extraparliamentary politics, popular culture, and local and community organisation and activism. I operate outside academia, frequently with others who, like me, make time for historical research, writing and public engagement alongside other work and family commitments, and who utilise the platforms, networks, and resources available through connections made – often by chance and serendipity – on social media and in person as well as professionally. Working outside any fixed institution or organisation, while leaving one free of institutional constraints and obligations, also means working without the official 'authenticity' which that confers. This tension can produce uncertainty and insecurity, but I see myself within the tradition of extra-academic history and study particularly among the working class in order to understand their own past and present – a tradition which itself remains a hidden history. When practising public history, past and present often clash as ideas, representations, and realities of working-class history and life continue to change. Rather than denying or excluding these conflicts and counter-narratives, a more useful and constructive approach – and one that leads to a more genuinely nuanced and complex historical representation of the working class – is to engage with and include it. This can produce a history that moves beyond 'we' and 'they' to 'us'.

Notes

1 Raphael Samuel, ed., *History Workshop: A Collecteana, 1967–1991, Documents, Memoirs, Critique and Cumulative Index to History Workshop Journal* (Oxford, Ruskin College: 1991), p. 1V.
2 Richard Hoggart, *The Uses of Literacy: Aspects of Working-class Life* (London, Chatto & Windus: 1957). Jonathan Rose, *The Intellectual Life of the British Working Classes* (New Haven, CT, Yale University Press: 2001).
3 E. P. Thompson, *The Making of the English Working Class* (Harmondsworth, Penguin: 1963).
4 E. P. Thompson, *Customs in Common: Studies in Traditional Popular Culture* (New York, The New Press: 1993).
5 Eric Hobsbawm, *Primitive Rebels: Studies in Archaic Forms of Social Movement in the 19th and 20th Centuries* (New York, W.W. Norton: 1959).
6 See John Stevenson and Chris Cook, *The Slump: Britain in the Great Depression* (London, Jonathan Cape: 1977).
7 See Imogen Tyler, 'Chav Mum, Chav Scum: Class Disgust in Contemporary Britain', *Feminist Media Studies* 8.2 (June, 2008), pp. 17–34 and Beverley Skeggs, 'Classifying Practices: Representations, Capitals and Recognitions' in Pat Mahoney and Christine Zmroczek (eds.), *Class Matters: 'Working-Class' Women's Perspectives on Social Class* (London, Taylor & Francis: 1997), pp. 123–140.
8 Gareth Stedman Jones, 'Rethinking Chartism' in *Languages of Class: Studies in English Working Class History 1832–1982* (Cambridge, Cambridge University Press: 1983).
9 John Burnett, *Useful Toil: Autobiographies of Working People from the 1820s to the 1920s* (Abingdon, Routledge: 1994). Emma Griffin, *Liberty's Dawn: A Peoples History of the Industrial Revolution* (New Haven, CT, Yale University Press: 2014). Richard Benson, *The Valley: A Hundred Years in the Life of a Family* (London, Bloomsbury: 2014).
10 Eric Hobsbawm, *Labouring Men: Studies in the History of Labour* (London, Weidenfeld & Nicolson: 1964). Eric Hobsbawm, *Worlds of Labour: Further Studies in the History of Labour* (London, Weidenfeld & Nicolson: 1984).
11 See Ra Page, ed., *Resist: Stories of Uprising* (Bungay, Comma Press: 2019).
12 Selina Todd's *The People: The Rise and Fall of the Working Class 1910–2010* (London, John Murray: 2014). Owen Jones, *Chavs: The Demonization of the Working Class* (London, Verso: 2011).
13 Hobsbawm's original lecture, and several responses and discussion by figures in the trade union and Labour movement, can be found in Martin Jacques and

Francis Mulhern, eds., *The Forward March of Labour Halted?* (London, Verso: 1981).

14 See Laurajane Smith and Gary Campbell, 'Don't Mourn, Organize: Heritage, Recognition and Memory in Castleford, West Yorkshire' in Laurajane Smith, Paul Shackel and Gary Campbell (eds.), *Heritage, Labour and the Working Classes* (Abingdon and New York, Routledge: 2011), pp. 85–105.

15 See Michael Bailey and Simon Popple, 'The 1984/85 Miners' Strike: Re-claiming Cultural Heritage' in Laurajane Smith, Paul Shackel and Gary Campbell (eds.), *Heritage, Labour and the Working Classes*, (Abingdon and New York, Routledge: 2011), pp. 19–33, see McCloud (2008).

16 Laurajane Smith, *Uses of Heritage* (Abingdon and New York, Routledge: 2006). See also Robert Hewison, *The Heritage Industry: Britain in a Climate of Decline* (London, Methuen: 1987).

17 Rhian E. Jones, *Clampdown: Pop-Cultural Wars on Class and Gender* (Alresford, zer0 Books: 2013).

18 Rhian E. Jones, *Petticoat Heroes: Gender, Culture and Popular Protest in the Rebecca Riots* (Chippenham, University of Wales Press: 2015).

19 Ardel Hafael-Thomas, ed., *Introduction to Transgender Studies* (New York, Harrington Park Press: 2019).

INDEX

Note: Page numbers followed by "n" denote endnotes.

www.ingramcontent.com/pod-product-compliance
Lightning Source LLC
LaVergne TN
LVHW021118300926
849160LV00010B/774
* 9 7 8 1 0 3 2 8 8 2 9 6 3 *